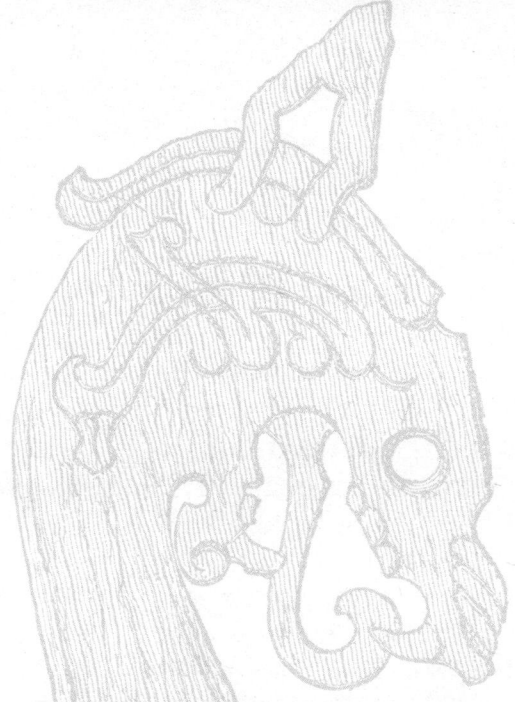

HAMMER OF THE GODS

DEDICATION

For King Olaf.
As for "The Last Viking,"
Harald Hardrada,
may I be his last and greatest skald.

Don
Hollway

King Olaf's
Viking
Conquest

HAMMER
OF
THE GODS

OSPREY PUBLISHING
Bloomsbury Publishing Plc
Kemp House, Chawley Park, Cumnor Hill, Oxford OX2 9PH, UK
Bloomsbury Publishing Ireland Limited,
29 Earlsfort Terrace, Dublin 2, D02 AY28, Ireland
Bloomsbury Publishing Inc.
1359 Broadway, 12th Floor, New York, NY 10018, USA
E-mail: info@ospreypublishing.com
www.ospreypublishing.com

OSPREY is a trademark of Osprey Publishing Ltd

First published in Great Britain in 2026

© Don Hollway, 2026

Don Hollway has asserted his right under the Copyright,
Designs and Patents Act, 1988, to be identified as Author of this work.

For legal purposes the Acknowledgments on p. 382 constitute
an extension of this copyright page.

All rights reserved. No part of this publication may be: i) reproduced or transmitted
in any form, electronic or mechanical, including photocopying, recording or by means of any
information storage or retrieval system without prior permission in writing from
the publishers; or ii) used or reproduced in any way for the training, development
or operation of artificial intelligence (AI) technologies, including generative AI technologies.
The rights holders expressly reserve this publication from the text and data mining exception
as per Article 4(3) of the Digital Single Market Directive (EU) 2019/790

A catalog record for this book is available from the British Library.

ISBN: HB 9781472871589; eBook 9781472871602; ePDF 9781472871619;
XML 9781472871633; Audio 9781472871626

26 27 28 29 30 10 9 8 7 6 5 4 3 2 1

Plate section image credits and captions are given in full in the
List of Illustrations and Maps (pp. 7–9).

Artwork in the plate section previously published in the following Osprey titles: CBT 27:
Viking Warrior vs Anglo-Saxon Warrior (p. 5) and ELI 3: *The Vikings* (pp. 6–7).

Maps by www.bounford.com
Index by Mark Swift
Typeset by Lumina Datamatics Ltd
Printed and bound in Great Britain by Clays Ltd, Elcograf S.P.A.

Osprey Publishing supports the Woodland Trust, the UK's
leading woodland conservation charity.

To find out more about our authors and books visit www.ospreypublishing.com.
Here you will find extracts, author interviews, details of forthcoming events and the
option to sign up for our newsletter.

For product safety related questions contact productsafety@bloomsbury.com

CONTENTS

	List of Illustrations and Maps	7
	Author's Note	11
	Dramatis Personae	14
	Prologue: The Return of the Vikings	19

PART ONE

I	Murder	31
II	Hunted	40
III	Nowhere to Hide	51
IV	Pirates	58
V	Slave	63
VI	Varangians	71
VII	First Blood	81
VIII	The Battle of the Danevirke	89
IX	Warrior	100
X	Conquest of the Rus	113
XI	Prima Signatio	120

PART TWO

XII	Jomsborg	135
XIII	The Slavic Revolt	148

XIV	King of the Wends	163
XV	Of God and Gods	169
XVI	The Jomsvikings	176
XVII	The Prophecy	193
XVIII	A New Beginning	203
XIX	To the Death	215
XX	Ireland	219
XXI	Maldon	227
XXII	The Prince of England	241
XXIII	Crusade	256

PART THREE

XXIV	King Olaf I	275
XXV	Hammer of God	286
XXVI	God's Viking	299
XXVII	Kings and Queens	313
XXVIII	The Trap	326
XXIX	The Battle of Svolder	335
	Epilogue: The Saga of King Olaf	353
	Sources	366
	Bibliography	373
	Acknowledgments	382
	Index	383
	About the Author	392

LIST OF ILLUSTRATIONS AND MAPS

PLATE SECTION ILLUSTRATIONS

In the 1920s Kung Tryggves Grav on the Swedish coast was rebuilt to resemble the Viking Age tomb, which originally dates from the Bronze Age. (Lise Ivanoff, Wikimedia Commons, CC BY-SA 3.0, https://creativecommons.org/licenses/by-sa/3.0)

Some Vikings were both pagan and Christian. Viking smiths cast amulets of Thor's hammer Mjolnir in the shape of a cross. (Photo by Werner Forman/Universal Images Group/Getty Images)

Constantinople's Hagia Sophia is today Istanbul's Aya Sofya, an Islamic mosque. Except for the Arabic symbols, the interior is much as Olaf experienced it. (muharremz/iStock)

The hermitage of St. Elidius on St. Helens, Scilly Islands, where Olaf is said to have heard the prophesy of his life, and was also nearly killed. (Des Blenkinsopp, Wikimedia Commons, CC BY-SA 2.0, https://creativecommons.org/licenses/by-sa/2.0)

The beach on Tresco, Scilly Islands. St. Helens in the distance. The Old Blockhouse at left was built circa 1550 to defend against French attack. (David Chapman/Alamy Stock Photo)

Ruins of the old abbey on Tresco. Olaf very likely walked under this arch as he underwent Christian baptism. (Stephen McKay, Wikimedia Commons, CC BY-SA 2.0, https://creativecommons.org/licenses/by-sa/2.0)

The Viking fleet led by Olaf Tryggvason to ravage the English coast in AD 991 was the largest seen in decades. (Classic Image/Alamy Stock Photo)

Statue of Byrhtnoth, the Anglo-Saxon ealdorman who died fighting Olaf's Vikings at the Battle of Maldon, AD 991. (Oxyman, Wikimedia Commons, CC BY-SA 3.0, https://creativecommons.org/licenses/by-sa/3.0)

Today the battlefield at Maldon is a tidal bog, but a thousand years ago was solid ground, ideal for Viking Age warfare. (Mick Sharp/Alamy Stock Photo)

At low tide the causeway to Northey Island lies exposed, but at high tide is underwater. (Trevor Harris, Wikimedia Commons, CC BY-SA 2.0, https://creativecommons.org/licenses/by-sa/2.0)

The Battle of Maldon, AD 991. Viking raiders cross the causeway from Northey Island as their front ranks engage the Anglo-Saxon shield wall. (Artwork by Peter Dennis © Osprey Publishing)

Leif Erikson Discovers America by Hans Dahl. Sent by King Olaf to Christianize Greenland, Leif was blown off course and discovered the New World by accident. (IanDagnall Computing/Alamy Stock Photo)

Olaf Tryggvason's Last Stand at Svolder by Angus McBride. Whether Olaf survived the battle is still disputed and will probably never be resolved. (Artwork by Angus McBride © Osprey Publishing)

The Icelandic Thing by W. G. Collingwood. Icelanders decided to accept Christianity at their thing, which is still survives as the world's oldest parliament. (© The Trustees of the British Museum. All rights reserved)

England's King Aethelred II, reviled for paying Vikings *danegeld* to stop raiding, named Olaf his foster son to defend against other Vikings. (CBW/Alamy Stock Photo)

LIST OF ILLUSTRATIONS AND MAPS

Statue of Olaf Tryggvason in Trondheim, Norway, where he is revered for bringing Christianity to the Vikings. (Artem Bolshakov/ iStock)

MAPS

Northern Europe, 10th Century   10

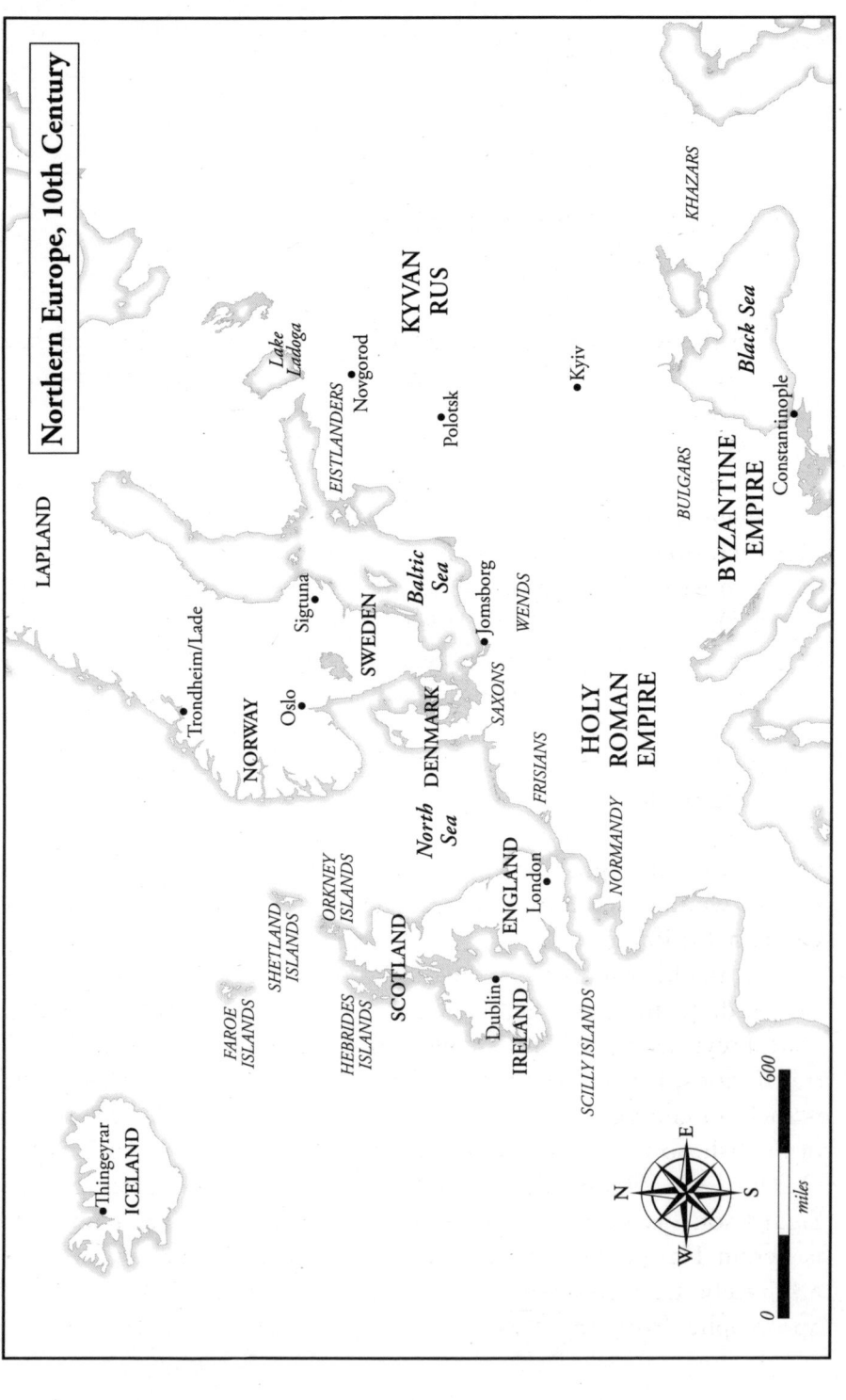

AUTHOR'S NOTE

As with the first two-thirds of what has become my Viking trilogy, *The Last Viking* and *Battle for the Island Kingdom*, I have taken some liberties in translation and spelling. Icelandic, Old Norse and Old English use letters that don't exist in modern English, such as *eth* (uppercase Ð, lowercase ð), *thorn* (uppercase Þ, lowercase þ) and *wynn* (uppercase Ƿ, lowercase ƿ). I've substituted the standard transliterations of *d*, *th* and *w* respectively. I have likewise simplified the extra letters in the modern Scandinavian alphabets – the ogonek O (Ǫ, ǫ), slashed O (Ø, ø), ringed A (Å, å), A-umlaut (Ä, ä) and ligatured AE (Æ, æ) – to their English counterparts. Then there is the Tironian *et* (⁊), an Old English shorthand used profusely throughout the *Anglo-Saxon Chronicle* as a medieval ampersand, &, as in *et cetera*. It meant "and," and was pronounced *ond* except when following the letter *s*, when – because otherwise it would be just too simple – it was pronounced *sond* and meant "water" in the sense of the modern English "sound," as in Long Island Sound. All this is so that we may read, for example, Gudrod and Aelfwine instead of Guðrøð ⁊ Ælfƿine.

Also, in old Scandinavian languages many names had a nominative case ending (for example, Sveinn instead of Svein, Olafr instead of Olaf, Freyr instead of Frey), which, as is the usual practice in English translations, I have dropped. Technically the second 'l' of 'Thorkell' is such an ending, but hardly anybody ever spells it "Thorkel" even in English, so I left that one as is, at my own discretion. And readers of *The Last Viking* might note that book's title character, Harald Sigurdsson (as he is commonly but incorrectly known in English) is herein Harald Sigurdarson, a minor character but with a more accurately transliterated surname. I've also dropped the "silent" apostrophe from the Russian/Ukrainian *Rus'*, which signifies the

Cyrillic soft sign (Ь, ь) as in Русь, which in English pronunciation is the difference between *Roos* and *Rooss,* i.e., none.

Additionally, I have updated some of the Victorian-era translations of the sagas, which relied more on rhythm and rhyme than did the original scribes, and some of the Victorian spellings, punctuation and wording as well – i.e., *scald* becomes *skald* – as I saw fit. Rather than a word-for-word translation of Latin, Old Norse or Old English, which in many instances makes little sense in modern English, I have opted for what I interpret as the original writers' intended meaning. Any transcription errors are therefore mine.

Readers who wish to dive further into Olaf Tryggvason's original sagas will note that they often disagree on the sequence and even the existence of certain events. Concrete dates were anathema to Icelandic monks. To be charitable, the scribes' chronological confusion stems from their limited access to accurate historical records, their reliance on mutable oral traditions, the century or so elapsed between Olaf's life and its first documentation, the difficulty of going back and rewriting chapters based on later information and, undeniably, editorial license – the authors' focus on storytelling and political and religious agendas rather than strict historical accuracy. All this makes it virtually impossible to reconcile the timelines. Even Olaf's birth year is debatable. Working backward from the known date of his accession in AD 995, his earliest biographer, the Icelandic chronicler Ari Thorgilsson (AD 1067/8–1148), set it at 973, and the anonymous author of the 12th-century *Agrip af Noregskonungasogum*, the "Summary of the Norwegian Kings' Sagas," in 968, but they were obviously mistaken; we now know that certain crucial events in Olaf's life could have happened only prior to that. In compiling Olaf's first saga, the 12th-century monk Odd Snorrason went to some effort doing the same backward calculation, arriving at a birth date of 963. Though later historians have set it as early as AD 958, to tell one story rather than accounting for all the different versions, I have followed Odd's reasoning, started from his beginning, and thereafter ordered events in what I see as the most logical sequence, which will necessarily disagree with Odd and some of the other old accounts. Every date herein might best be considered to have a question mark after it.

AUTHOR'S NOTE

Finally, when I wrote *The Last Viking*, back before the 2021 Russian invasion of Ukraine, the *#KyivNotKiev* social media campaign had not yet caught fire, and "Kiev" was still the common Romanized English spelling. I'm now following the United States Board on Geographic Names in using Kyiv.

Don Hollway
April 2024

DRAMATIS PERSONAE

THE NORWEGIANS

Astrid Eiriksdottir: Queen of Viken, AD 946–963, mother of Olaf Tryggvason
Astrid Tryggvadottir: Daughter of Olaf Tryggvason, wife of Erling Skjalgsson
Eirik Hakonarson: Son of Hakon Sigurdarson, Jarl of Lade 1000–1012; Governor of Norway and Earl of Northumbria 1017–c. 1023
Erlend Hakonarson: Son of Hakon Sigurdarson
Erling Skjalgsson: Baron of Sola, Rogaland, 996–1028
Eirik Haraldsson, "Bloodaxe": King of Norway, 931–933; King of Northumbria, 947–948, 952–954
Gunnhild Gormsdottir (or Ozursdottir), "Mother of Kings": Wife of Bloodaxe, Queen Consort of Norway, 931–933
Gudrod Bjornsson: King of Vestfold, 946–963
Hakon Haraldsson, "the Good": King of Norway, 934–961
Hakon Sigurdarson, "the Bad": Jarl of Lade, 961–971; Jarl of Norway, 975–995
Harald Eiriksson, "Greycloak": King of Norway, 961–c. 970
Harald Sigurdarson, "Hardrada": King of Norway, 1046–1066
Olaf II Haraldsson: King of Norway, 1015–1028
Olaf I Tryggvason: King of Norway, 995–1000
Sigurd Eiriksson: Uncle of Olaf Tryggvason, *druzhinnik* of Grand Prince Vladimir
Sigurd Hlodvirsson, "the Stout": Jarl of Orkney, the Shetlands, Hebrides and Man, 991–1014
Svein Hakonarson: Son of Hakon Sigurdarson, Jarl of Lade 1000–1016
Thora Skagadottir: Wife of Jarl Hakon Sigurdarson
Thorir "Klakka": Viking trader, raider, traitor
Tryggvi Olafsson: King of Viken, 946–963, father of Olaf Tryggvason

DRAMATIS PERSONAE

THE SWEDES

Eirik Bjornsson, "the Victorious": King of Sweden, AD c. 970–c. 995
Olaf Eiriksson, "Tax King": Son of Eirik the Victorious and Sigrid the Haughty; King of Sweden, c. 995–1022
Sigrid Tostisdottir, "the Haughty": Queen consort of Sweden, Denmark, Norway and England
Styrbjorn Olafsson, "the Strong": Nephew of King Eirik, attempted usurper; died c. 986

THE DANES

Harald Gormsson, "Bluetooth": King of Denmark, AD c. 958–c. 986; King of Norway, c. 970–c. 985/986
Harald Knutsson, "Gold-Harald": Nephew of Harald Bluetooth
Palnatoki: Chieftain of the Jomsvikings, early 980s
Sigvaldi Strut-Haraldsson: Chieftain of the Jomsvikings, c. 980s–1000
Svein Haraldsson, "Forkbeard": Son of Bluetooth; King of Denmark, 986–1014; King of Norway, c. 999/1000–1013/14; King of England, 1013–1014
Thyri Haraldsdottir: Wife of Olaf Tryggvason, Queen of Norway 999–1000

THE RUS

Dobrynya: Uncle of Prince Vladimir
Olava: Consort of Prince Vladimir
Olga: Grandmother of Prince Vladimir, wife of Svyatoslav I
Svyatoslav I: Prince of Kyiv, AD 945–972, father of Prince Vladimir
Vladimir I, "the Great": Prince of Novgorod 970–1015; Grand Prince of Kyiv, 978–1015
Yaropolk I: Prince of Kyiv, 970–978; Prince of Kyivan Rus 976–978

THE WENDS AND POLES

Astrid: Daughter of Burislav, wife of Sigvaldi, Queen of Jomsborg, early 980s
Burislav: Wendish king, possibly identical with Polish Duke Mieszko I

Gunnhild: Daughter of Burislav, Queen of Denmark, c. 995 (?)
Mieszko I: Duke of Poland, 960–992
Mstislav: Son of Mstivoj, Wendish king to c. 1018
Mstivoj: Father of Mstislav, Wendish king to c. 995
Geira: Daughter of Burislav, Queen of Jomsborg to c. 984

THE SAXONS

Bernard I: Duke of Saxony, AD 973–1011
Dietrich of Haldensleben: Margrave of the Nordmark, Saxony, 965–983
Otto I, "the Great": Duke of Saxony, King of East Francia, 936–973; King of Italy, 961–973; Holy Roman Emperor, 962–973
Otto II, "the Red": King of Germany, 961–983; Holy Roman Emperor, 973–983; King of Italy, 980–983
Otto III: King of Germany, 983–1002; King of Italy, 996–1002; Holy Roman Emperor 996–1002

THE JOMSVIKINGS

Bjorn "the Welsh": early 980s–986
Bui Visetisson: early 980s–986
Palnatoki: Jomsviking chieftain, early 980s
Sigurd Visetisson: early 980s–986
Sigvaldi Strut-Haraldsson: Jomsviking chieftain, early 980s–early 1000s
Thorkell, "the Tall": Brother of Sigvaldi, Jomsviking chieftain, early 1000s–early 1020s
Vagn Akesson: Grandson of Palnatoki, early 980s–986

THE IRISH

Amlaib mac Sitric (Olaf Sigtryggsson), "Cuaran": King of Northumbria, AD 941–944; King of Dublin 945–947
Sitric mac Amlaib (Sigtrygg II Olafsson), "Silkbeard": Son of Amlaib mac Sitric; King of Dublin, 989–1036

DRAMATIS PERSONAE

THE ENGLISH

Aelfwine: Possibly son of Aelfric Cild, Ealdorman of Mercia, c. AD 983–985
Aethelred II, "the Unready": King of England, 978–1013
Byrhtnoth: Ealdorman of Essex, c. 931–991
Gytha: Wife of Olaf Tryggvason, 989–1000, mother of Tryggvi Olafsson

And then the blue-eyed Norseman told
A Saga of the days of old.
"There is," said he, "a wondrous book
Of Legends in the old Norse tongue,
Of the dead kings of Norroway, –
Legends that once were told or sung
In many a smoky fireside nook
Of Iceland, in the ancient day,
By wandering Saga-man or Skald..."

Longfellow, *Tales of a Wayside Inn*

PROLOGUE

THE RETURN OF THE VIKINGS

*In those days raids were often made by the Danes on the English,
and they inflicted serious devastation,
landing as they did in so many places by ship.*

The *Liber Eliensis*

AUGUST, AD 991

It was not supposed to ever happen again: English people dying at the hands of Vikings. It had been almost forty years since the Anglo-Saxons had slain Eirik Bloodaxe, the last Viking ruler of York, and driven his warriors from England. Across the North Sea the Norsemen were said to be divided, quarreling, the Danes laying even stronger claim to Norway than to England. Yes, in the past decade or so there had been some sporadic raids along the coast – Southampton, Thanet and Chester in 980, Cornwall, Devon and Wales in 981, Dorset and the isle of Portland in 982, Watchet in Somerset in 988 – leading one monk to depict the raiders as a biblical scourge, minions of the devil. Still, compared to the old days a century past, when the Great Heathen Army had conquered half of England – the Danelaw – these were small-scale affairs, the attack on Dorset and Portland comprising just three ships. Petty theft, not conquest.

This latest raid was something more. Something bigger.

The first reports came from *Folcanstan*, modern Folkestone, where the English Channel worries away at the chalk cliffs of the Kentish coast. In Victorian times it would be a seaside resort for rich aristocrats, but at the end of the 10th century it was still just a small fishing village of a few hundred people, with the ruins of an old Roman villa on the clifftop to the north, and a 7th-century Benedictine nunnery on the one to the south. The former was abandoned and empty, but the latter suitably defenseless and rich: religious artifacts and reliquaries, gold crosses, silver goblets and the like, not to mention virgin nuns to make prized slaves. Furthermore, a main road led inland, offering easy access to nearby towns and minsters. All in all, a good place to blood new men – give them a taste of battle – but tarrying too long to plunder invited counterattack. Facing an enemy army was not to the Vikings' taste. They preferred to hit and run, and by the time the typical English militia of farmers and villagers, the *fyrd*, could be summoned, assembled, organized and led to the defense, they were long gone.

But they did not go far. The next raid came just twenty-odd miles to the north, up around the convex Kentish coast at *Sandwic*, modern Sandwich. In those days before the river Stour silted up, the village was not two miles inland as today, but a major port right on the water. (*Sandwic* means "market town on the sand.") Vikings had sacked the place in 851, and would do so again in 1006, but in the interim Sandwich had grown fat on trade, a middleman with partners both inland and across the Channel. It boasted a mint and a town wall, though of wood, the stone walls of the Roman-era fortress having long since been abandoned and fallen into ruin. The Vikings could loot the mint of silver, fill their longships with food and supplies and be gone, still ahead of any English reprisal.

Then north again, across the Thames estuary to East Anglia, and the richest target yet: *Gippeswyc*, modern Ipswich, where the river Gipping runs into the tidal, brackish river Orwell. It was one of England's premier port towns, with a population probably exceeding 4,000, trading in pottery and wool, again with its own mint but with better defenses than Folkestone or Sandwich. The Vikings knew those defenses well, because their forefathers had built them, around a little Anglo-Saxon village at the high tide mark, back when East Anglia was part of the Danelaw. Around the year 900 they had circled it with an earthen bulwark topped with a wooden palisade. Ipswich still had a large Danish population with little love for their Anglo-Saxon overlords, who may even have provided the raiders with a safe harbor, but the copy of the *Anglo-Saxon Chronicle* written at the Old Minster in Winchester, around the time of the attack, says the Vikings *eall ofereode*, "overran all." This was no minor sortie, but a full-fledged *strandhogg*, a marauding for plunder and slaves, just like the bad old days.

Whatever business the Vikings had in Ipswich, they did not long tarry there. The fleet doubled back down to the next estuary to the south: the river Blackwater, then called the Panta, which drains the bogs of Essex – *Eastseaxe*, the former "kingdom of the East Saxons" – into the North Sea.

On arrival the raiders had a choice. They could take the Blackwater's northern tributary, the river Colne, to attack the county's largest town, Colchester, or its southern tributary, the river Chelmer, to attack the second-largest, Maldon. For its part, Colchester was defended by a stone wall almost twenty feet high, left over from when the town was Roman Camulodunum. Maldon (Old English *Maeldon*, "Monument Hill"), atop a bluff above a bend in the Chelmer, was a *burh*, a town of perhaps a thousand souls, fortified in the later Anglo-Saxon fashion, with an earthen bank and wood palisade. It had proven strong enough to stand off Danish attacks in 917 and again in 924, as a result of which the town was granted a mint. That only made it, like the others, a more enticing target.

The Vikings decided it was time to test Maldon's defenses again, but probably only because of Northey Island, about a mile south of Maldon in the tidal estuary where the Blackwater lets out into the North Sea. As sea rovers, Northmen preferred islands for anchorages, which gave them maximum shorefront on which to beach their dragon ships, plus a natural moat for defense. The very first recorded Viking raid in England, in AD 793, had been at Lindisfarne, a tidal island off the Northumbrian coast. Easy pickings there had led to more and more Viking raids, and eventually to their conquest of England. The locals had to be fearing that these Vikings were in search of a base of operations from which to launch a new Danelaw, for by all accounts this, too, was a sizable Viking fleet.

Returning south, however, may have been a mistake on the raiders' part. It gave English reprisal a chance to catch up.

The defense of Essex fell to one Byrhtnoth, its *ealdorman*, elder man, a kind of prototypical earl, second only to the king and serving as his viceroy or governor.* The *Liber Eliensis*, the "Book of Ely," a history compiled in the 12th century by the monks of Ely Abbey in eastern Cambridgeshire, reports, "He was articulate, big and strong, dependable in war against enemies of the kingdom, and very brave, unafraid of death." In 991 Byrhtnoth was some sixty years old, old enough to remember the English triumph over Eirik Bloodaxe and the Danelaw, old enough even to have taken part in it, but not too old to do it again.

He issued summons to the chieftains of every village in eastern Essex. Each sent his best warriors, his contribution to his lord's *fyrd*. Villagers, farmers, yes, armed at best with spears, and mostly with hay forks and wood hatchets. How many there were, the old accounts do not reveal. Estimates range from a mere 500 to three or four thousand, which in medieval times was a considerable army, certainly enough to run off a bunch of Viking raiders. On top of that the ealdorman could add another hundred or so men of his own: his *hird*, his personal troops, well-armed and armored, trained and fed at his expense and sworn to fight for him. "And all the shire chieftains swore loyalty to Byrhtnoth, as to a great commander," records the *Book of Ely*, "because of his great integrity and faith, so that under his leadership they could best defend against the enemy."

Colchester, Byrhtnoth's capital in Essex, is actually closer to Ipswich than to Maldon, which was a solid twenty-mile march away. A rider on a good horse might cover that in a few hours or less. Word of the Viking landing could have reached the ealdorman while the invaders were still disembarking and preparing to attack the town. Call it a day at least, though, for his summons to go out to the villages and for the fyrd to respond, then another for the English to march down through the dense forests of inland Essex, accumulating troops as they went. Byrhtnoth could only hope Maldon's walls held off the Vikings until he came to the rescue.

Imagine his shock when, arriving on the south bank of the Blackwater, he could look across the channel to Northey Island.

---

* In the Old English poem "The Battle of Maldon," Byrhtnoth is referred to as *eorl*, a variant of the Old Norse *jarl*, a generic term for nobleman left over from the old Danelaw days. It was not until 1016 that Cnut the Great conquered England and made "earl" an official title, replacing ealdorman – evidence that that poem was written well after the battle.

It's shaped roughly like a triangle pointed north, less than half a square mile in area and not quite a mile on each side. And its banks were packed with a fleet of almost a hundred beached dragon ships, and Viking warriors – three, four, five thousand or more. Far exceeding the little Viking raiding parties of the past few decades, they were on a par with the Great Heathen Army of 865, and all ready to battle Byrhtnoth and his Anglo-Saxons. He could be glad they had arrived at high tide. "Neither army could attack the other because of the high water flooding in after the ebbtide," recorded the anonymous, contemporary English poet who would immortalize the encounter in verse. "The river separated them."

Then and now, however, Northey is only an island twelve hours a day. Recent geological studies of the site suggest that over the centuries the river has carved out the southern channel, today 300 yards wide and at high tide ten feet underwater, but in 991 a little less than half that width and a little over half as deep, though with a current strong enough to sweep away any army afoot. At low tide, though, Northey is a peninsula, connected by its southwest point to the south bank of the Blackwater by a narrow, Roman-era causeway that still stretches across the channel, though now of modern construction, still submerged at high tide – in effect, a bridge over the river. In a few hours the tide would go out, the water level would drop, and nothing would stop the Vikings from storming over to the mainland to kill Byrhtnoth and all his men.

Meanwhile the channel, though flooded, was not so broad that one side could not taunt the other. The poet recorded that a single Viking, versed in Old English, came to the riverbank to where Byrhtnoth could see him, to shout across the water: "In the name of these bold seamen, I command you to send us treasure, and quickly, for it would be better if you paid tribute to avoid this spear-duel rather than fight hard battle with us."

That was a polite offer from the commander of such an army. The *Anglo-Saxon Chronicle* – one of its many versions, anyway – records his name: Anlaf, the Old English version of the Norwegian Olaf.

It was a common Scandinavian name, but in the year 991 there was only one such Olaf capable of putting together so large a fleet, and his name was already well known in England: Olaf, son of Tryggvi. A great warrior, it was said, well traveled, experienced in warfare, but at the same time with the manner of a king, and even claimed by some to be Christian. This Olaf was supposedly an exile, an outlaw in his own homeland of Norway, yet somehow he had assembled the largest Viking invasion fleet England had seen in decades. Perhaps large enough even to conquer the kingdom. Again.

What exile, what outlaw could draw so many Viking warriors to his banner?

Who was this Olaf Tryggvason?

His exploits were first recorded in verse by his skald, his court scribe, Hallfred Ottarsson, called *Vandraedaskald*, "Troublesome Poet." In the late 11th or early 12th century the Icelandic priest-historians Saemund Sigfusson and Ari Thorgilsson set these oral traditions down in writing. (Both men were nicknamed *frodi*, "the Wise" or "the Learned," because they were literate, a relative rarity in those days. Saemund wrote in Latin, and Ari in Old Norse.) Much of their work has been lost, but it served as source material for the Norwegian synoptics, the oldest preserved kings' sagas: The *Historia Norwegiae*, "History of Norway," by an anonymous monk probably around AD 1220, but possibly as early as 1150; the *Historia de Antiquitate Regum Norwagiensium*, "History of the Antiquity of the Norwegian Kings," by Theodoricus Monachus, Theodoric the Monk, probably in the 1180s; and the *Agrip af Noregskonungasogum*, "Summary of the Norwegian Kings' Sagas," written in Old Norse by an anonymous Norwegian around 1190.

That was about the time – 200 years after Olaf Tryggvason's death – that Odd Snorrason, a monk in the Benedictine monastery at Thingeyrar in far northwest Iceland, set down his life story. Though originally written in Latin, Odd's *Olafs saga Tryggvasonar* is considered the earliest extant full-length king's saga. Odd's original text is lost as well, but it was expanded and translated into Old Norse by his brother monk Gunnlaug Leifsson. The 13th-century Icelandic historian and politician Snorri Sturluson incorporated their work in his *Heimskringla*, "Circle of the World," a collection of sagas of Swedish and Norwegian kings. And in the 14th century Olaf's story was embellished and enlarged again as *Olafs saga Tryggvasonar en mesta*, "The Greatest Saga of Olaf Tryggvason," generally believed to have been written, or at least translated from the Latin, by the monk, abbot and scholar Berg Sokkason, with added apocryphal scenes of religious visions and miracles until his version of the story verged on medieval fantasy.

There are plenty of Scandinavian chronicles that mention Olaf: among others, the *Fagrskinna*, "Fair Parchment"; the *Orkneyinga Saga* of the Orkney Islands; the *Islendingabok*, "Book of Icelanders," and many more. Olaf even receives passing mention in the *Anglo-Saxon Chronicle*, the annals of English history. And this says nothing of the myriad praise poems and sagas sung of him by numerous Norwegian skalds. (A complete listing of the major sources may be found in the back of this book; the minor ones are too numerous to list. Olaf was that famous.) As the present volume incorporates all the versions of the sagas, it might be taken as an update to *Olafs saga Tryggvasonar en mesta*, but it also includes background and analysis not to be found in any of the medieval versions of the tale.

It must be said that these many versions disagree with each other to varying extent. Most – Odd, Snorri and Berg; Theodoricus Monachus; the *Fagrskinna*, *Agrip* and *Historia* – are Icelandic or Norwegian, which in those days was the same thing, and they generally take a flattering, not to say propagandistic, view of King Olaf. On the other hand, Saxo Grammaticus was Danish, and Adam of Bremen was German but learned Viking history at the Danish royal court, so we might consider theirs as opposing opinions. Then again, theirs are more general histories, not so focused on Olaf. The lack of detail, confusion of facts, and conflicts in the various accounts renders them impossible to reconcile. To wring a story out of it all requires a certain amount of supposition and speculation, a willingness to surmise (but always based in scholarship) in order to straighten out the timelines and fill in the blanks. On top of that, subjects the ancient writers skipped over, trusting in their audiences' familiarity with them – the Northern European slave trade; Christianity vs. paganism; how to fight with a battleaxe – are entirely alien to modern readers, and must be enlarged upon.

Finally, this story comes to us out of the mists of prehistory, when gods were said to walk the earth and magic was taken for granted.

Certain scenes will strike modern readers as medieval fantasy, as well they should. We are recounting sagas here, legends, the mingling of myth and tradition, and even in the old days imagination often overtook fact. Olaf's earliest biographers were aware of the problem. Theodoric disclaimed, "The amount of absolute truth in my present account depends entirely on those whose stories I have written down, because I have written of things not seen but heard." And Odd Snorrason urged, "I ask readers not to scoff at this story or be more skeptical or doubtful than necessary, for wise men have told us about his great deeds, if explaining little of his wondrous achievements. It often happens that lies and truth mix, and we have little to say about that, but we believe our sources will prove truthful."

On the other hand, later writers edited down Olaf's saga. Incorporating it in his *Heimskringla*, Snorri Sturluson, who was not a man of religion but a politician and historian, cut a full twenty-five chapters containing the more fantastic scenes of magic and prophecy. And in the 1860s the American poet Henry Wadsworth Longfellow, in his retelling of the tale in verse, edited Snorri's 123 chapters down to twenty-two, about 7,900 lines. It may be seen that King Olaf's saga has lost something over the centuries.

Those centuries give us moderns the advantage of cross-referencing, research and knowledge unavailable to the ancient scribes, secluded as they were in their remote monasteries and scriptoriums. We may also flatter ourselves that we're above primitive superstition. It's true that we don't have to believe in magic or gods or miracles, but we should acknowledge that people once believed in all those things, and were motivated by them and acted on them. To ignore that ignores an important part of the past. What was "true" then is part of the story today. Let us recognize when fact becomes fiction, and when legend becomes history, but remember that preserving one is just as important as the other.

This work, then, is more than a retelling of Longfellow's poem, or Snorri's collection, Odd's original saga or Berg's embellishment. It is part compilation, part critique, part adventure, and yes, a little bit fantasy...yet all history.

"But now," wrote Odd a millennium ago, "we should hear of the great deeds of King Olaf Tryggvason." Best just to leave the thinking until later and for now simply enjoy, as did Odd and Berg, Snorri and

Longfellow, and all the scribes who have come before us, the story of King Olaf, son of Tryggvi, in the same spirit Longfellow intended when he wrote "To An Old Danish Songbook" in 1845:

> Once some ancient Skald,
> In his bleak, ancestral Iceland,
> Chanted staves of these old ballads
> To the Vikings.

PART ONE

And King Olaf heard the cry,
Saw the red light in the sky,
Laid his hand upon his sword,
As he leaned upon the railing,
And his ships went sailing, sailing
Northward into Trondheim fjord.

There he stood as one who dreamed;
And the red light glanced and gleamed
On the armor that he wore;
And he shouted, as the rifted
Streamers o'er him shook and shifted,
"I accept thy challenge, Thor!"

Longfellow, "The Saga of King Olaf"

I

Murder

The saga begins in the days when the Norwegian realm was ruled by King Harald Greycloak and Gudrod, the sons of King Eirik Bloodaxe. In those days almost everyone in Norway was pagan.

Odd Snorrason

AD 963

It is a lonely place for a grave. Even today there is not enough soil on the rocky hilltop for digging; if a man is to spend eternity there, he must lie above ground. Only shrubs and a few scrubby trees cling to the rocks and struggle against the bitter wind where, on the highest point of a barren, flat-topped island in Sweden's bleak, cold Skagerrak archipelago, stands a cairn, a pile of stones some sixty feet across and eight or ten feet high. It is only about 150 feet above sea level, but that's enough to give the dead a clear view of the ocean to the west and the mainland to the east. The monument is thought to date from the Bronze Age, thirty centuries ago, raised over a man whose name, lost before the arrival of writing in Scandinavia, is long forgotten. No road, no path, no signs lead to it. The only way to get there is the same way men have done since the dawn of time: by foot or on horseback, across a knee-deep channel from the mainland, or in winter by crossing the ice, and climbing the steep slope to the crest.

But a thousand years ago – back before these Swedish islands were part of Denmark, back when they were part of southern Norway, called Viken, or the Vik – the cairn, even then twenty centuries old, was a local landmark, known and visible to seafarers and wayfarers alike, a place where far-flung travelers could agree to come together.

On a spring day that millennium ago, twenty men in woolen tunics with cloaks pulled tight against the ocean gusts – for if it was not a cold grey day in terms of weather, it was in spirit – made their way from the mainland, across the shallow channel to the island and climbed the hill to the cairn. Hard men these were, faces carved by wind and wave, bearing old scars, long beards and hair streaked with grey from having fought their way to the top of a brutal age. They wore armor and bore shields and weapons, too – swords, axes, spears – from bitter habit, for they were *huscarls*, housecarls, household troops, the personal guard of a king.

The king's name was Tryggvi Olafsson. He ruled Viken. According to Snorri Sturluson's *Heimskringla*, "Tryggvi was bigger and stronger than anyone," but then Snorri never met him, and the sagas tend to describe every hero as bigger, stronger and more handsome than every other. That said, Tryggvi was a veteran of Viking raids as far across the western sea as England, Scotland and Ireland, and his purpose atop the barren island this day was to lay plans for a fresh raid that summer, this time to the east, into the Baltic Sea. According to some of the sagas Tryggvi's cousin and fellow royal, Gudrod Eiriksson, had sent heralds – messengers, envoys – with an invitation: "Gudrod told them to inform Tryggvi that he wished to become friends and partners. If Tryggvi provided ten ships he would command a third of the fleet, yet keep half of all the riches they reaped."

This would be more than the usual business of Scandinavian farmers setting down their hoes and scythes and taking up swords to spend the summer, as the verb goes, a-viking. It was a chance to heal a family rift among the cousins, the grandsons of the legendary King Harald *Harfagri*, Fairhair.

Traditionally the "first king of Norway" – *Nordveg*, the 1,600-mile "Northern Way" from Denmark to the whaling and fishing grounds of the Barents Sea – Fairhair in actuality had only conquered and ruled over the *Vestlandet*, the Western Land, the rich southwestern curve of Scandinavia, making him merely the greatest king among many.

As king, his primary fault had been too many wives and consorts, and by them too many sons. "Many kings descended from him," recorded the 14th-century Icelandic chronicler Berg Sokkason. "They ruled various regions, large realms, or islands."

Fairhair's eldest son, Eirik, had been bequeathed overall rule but became reviled, in no small part due to the machinations of his wife, Gunnhild. According to some sources raised by wizards in Norway's far north, in others a Danish princess, according to the anonymous, almost certainly biased *Agrip af Noregskonungasogum*, "Summary of the Norwegian Kings' Sagas," it was she behind Eirik's evil ways: "Of all women, Gunnhild was the most beautiful, not tall but extremely crafty. She became so evil in her advice, and he so easily led to cruelty and oppression of the people, that it was difficult to bear...He came to be called Bloodaxe, because he was so cruel and ruthless, mostly at her direction."

As he thinned the ranks of possible rivals, Eirik earned another nickname: Brother-Slayer. By murder, battle or suspicious circumstances his brothers all died except the youngest, his half-brother Hakon, who for his own safety Fairhair had sent to be raised in England. Grown to manhood, Hakon had returned to drive Bloodaxe and his sons out of Norway. Later known as "the Good," Hakon was only about twenty and had no sons, but named his various dead brothers' sons as kings – petty kings, chieftains really; Norwegians awarded the title of king to any man who could lead others. As Berg put it, "We speak of those who ruled on the coast and as supreme kings of the land, but in the highlands and hinterlands there were lesser kings descended from Harald who ruled. These realms were often beyond mountains and forests. Among these kings the most distinguished and famous descended from King Harald was King Tryggvi."

Tryggvi's father Olaf, a son of Fairhair, had been a king himself, one of those brothers slain in battle by Bloodaxe. King Hakon had entrusted Tryggvi to fight off the Danes and raiders plaguing southern Norway.

These raiders were the *Eirikssonnene*, the sons of Bloodaxe. He had died in England, and the English had expelled them much the way Hakon had expelled them from Norway. They might now be more rightfully called the *Gunnhildssonnene*, for they had found safe haven with their mother Gunnhild in Denmark. The *Heimskringla*, the "Circle of the World" history of Scandinavian kings written by

12th-century Icelandic historian, poet and politician Snorri Sturluson, tells us, "Eirik's sons then turned with their army north to Viken and raided there, but King Tryggvi sailed with his army to meet them. They fought many battles with the victory going first one way, then the other. Eirik's sons sometimes raided Viken, and Tryggvi sometimes around Halland and Zealand."

One might have thought Hakon and the sons of Bloodaxe would get along strictly on the basis of common religion, for during their time in England all had become believers in the *Hvitakrist*, the "White Christ." "King Hakon was a faithful Christian when he arrived in Norway," confirms his saga, "but because the land was heathen, with many pagan worshippers among the chieftains, he felt he lacked support and approval among the commoners, and chose to practice his faith in secret, on Sundays and Friday fasts."

The Norwegians were happy in their paganism. Hakon's most powerful jarl, Sigurd Hakonarson of Hlade, modern Lade near Trondheim, was practically his co-king, but knew better than to go against the old gods. In fact, he threw a great feast in their honor, footing the entire bill himself. According to the *Heimskringla*,

> Everyone brought ale to this festival, and many cattle and horses were slaughtered, with the blood taken from them called *hlaut*, and the jars in which it was saved called hlaut-jars. Hlaut-pieces were made, like sprinkling brushes, with which all the altars and temple walls, both outside and inside, were sprinkled, and the people too were sprinkled with the blood, but the meat was boiled into savory stew.

Hakon would have done best to keep his Christianity to himself. Things began to sour the moment he tried to impose it upon his subjects. In 950 he attended a *thing*, a proto-democratic convention, atop *Tinghaugen*, "Assembly Hill," across the fjord from modern Trondheim.* Hakon

---

* In those days Trondheim was not yet a town, but merely an island in the fjord, the "home of the Tronders," the "people who thrive." The 12th-century monk Theodoricus Monachus wrote, "At that time there were only a few huts belonging to various traders there, though now it is the capital of the entire realm." And the *Fagrskinna* concurs: "Lade was the chief domain in Trondheim then."

announced his intention that all the people should abandon the pagan gods, undergo baptism and put their faith in Christ. After a murmur from the crowd, one among them rose as spokesman: "If you insist on this business to the point of forcing it on us like a tyrant, then we farmers have all decided to break with you and raise up another king who will allow us freedom of religion."

Hakon the Good was too good to force his faith on Norway. He backed down, and even attended sacrificial feasts, though he refused to drink to Odin, instead making the sign of the cross over his cup. (Jarl Sigurd told his confused men, "He is blessing the goblet in the name of Thor, making the sign of his hammer over it before he drinks.")

Still, Hakon's unrepentant Christianity alienated his pagan subjects and weakened his overall power. He managed to fight off repeated incursions by the sons of Gunnhild, but in 961 they mortally wounded him in battle. His poet, Eyvind Finnson, called *Skaldaspillir*, "Skald-player," wrote a dirge in which, regardless of Hakon's submission to Christ, Odin nevertheless welcomed the blood-drenched king to Valhalla to drink ale with the old gods and sit reunited among his dead brothers: "The wolf Fenrir [the monster that would devour Odin at Ragnarok], unbound, will walk the earth before so good a king again treads the empty path."

If the Norwegians resented Hakon's Christianity, they feared it in his successors, the sons of Bloodaxe. "Gunnhild's sons became Christian in England, as told before," admits the *Heimskringla*, "but when they took over Norway they made no attempt to spread Christianity, merely pulling down the temples and idols and casting away the sacrifices where they could, and in doing so raising great acrimony."

The eldest, Harald, called *Grafeld*, Greyhide or Greycloak – but perhaps not to his face, for once setting a fashion trend by wearing faux fur made from cheap Icelandic wool – took over as King of Norway. His Norway, however, was only his grandfather's same small slice of the western coast; even with his brothers behind him he did not have the manpower to conquer it all. "There were then many chiefs in the land," reported Snorri. "There was Tryggvi Olafsson in the east, [his cousin] Gudrod Bjornsson in the west, and Sigurd Jarl of Lade in Trondheim, but that first winter Gunnhild's sons held the middle of the country."

Greycloak agreed to allow them all to retain their stations as his vassals, if not necessarily happy ones. "They believed they had just as strong a claim to the crown as the sons of Gunnhild," confided Berg Sokkason. "King Tryggvi Olafsson was a great man and honorable, whom the men of Viken regarded as most deserving to rule the entire country."

The real ruler of Norway, however, was Gunnhild, whose hand guided her sons' reign as much as it had their father's. The *Heimskringla* declares, "She was now called *Konungamodir* [Mother of Kings]."

She was furthermore said to dabble in *seidr*, Viking sorcery, using trances and visions to divine the future and manipulate fate. By such means she concluded that her nephews Tryggvi and Gudrod, Jarl Sigurd and his son Hakon were all conspiring against her sons.* The 12th-century Icelandic monk and historian Odd Snorrason had her chiding them, "You bear the titles of kings as your forefathers did, but you have piddling armies and territories and there are many claiming a piece of it."† She professed to not understand how sons of Bloodaxe could tolerate anyone else ruling over their rightful lands.

Greycloak replied that conquering Norway would not be as easy as slaughtering a calf. He and his brothers did not have the power, nor enough of the people's love, to conquer it all.

---

* It may already be seen that 10th-century Norwegians chose male names from a confusingly short list. Our story already features two Gudrods, King Gudrod Eiriksson (son of Bloodaxe, brother of Greycloak) and his cousin King Gudrod Bjornsson of Vestfold. There are also two Hakons, King Hakon the Good (brother of Bloodaxe) and Hakon son of Sigurd, Jarl of Lade. Rest assured our story will soon simplify – half of those named will shortly die violent deaths – but as the tale unfolds their descendants will play prominent roles, and their origins are worth mention.

† The conversation here, and those elsewhere in the book, are combined from the many versions of Olaf's saga, which differ in detail but not in general. Odd Snorrason, Snorri Sturluson and Berg Sokkason could only have surmised these exchanges, and we, all these hundreds of years after them, can but report what they wrote.

Gunnhild, whom the *Historia* refers to as "a vicious and most evil woman," told them, "Then we shall devise a very different plan."

In late 962 they caught Jarl Sigurd at a feast and burned down his hall with him in it. It might be expected that to forestall blood vengeance Greycloak and his brother Gudrod would set upon Sigurd's son Hakon and their cousins in turn, and indeed they laid plans to set out together. According to Snorri, though, before they even set sail, the brothers, drunk, fell out over who was to lead. Greycloak and Gudrod almost came to blows before their men parted them, and they went their separate ways.

Rumor of the split between the brothers reached Viken, probably on the tongues of Gudrod's heralds along with his invitation to Tryggvi to go a-viking.* It behooved Tryggvi to mend fences with his cousins and break the cycle of violence or, failing that, to exploit this breach in their ranks. Tryggvi's name meant trusty, reliable; evidently he placed that same trust in Gudrod's heralds and his proposal. According to Odd, he told them, "This venture seems to me to bear promise, and it may be a good idea if there are no tricks. The sons of Gunnhild are known for it, but you appear to be good honest men."

His queen, Astrid, bore no such trust. "My lord," she told him, "I have a bad feeling about this business. I dreamed I wore a great golden armlet, but I saw it broken in two, with blood dripping from both pieces. I believe this is an ill omen and that you face treachery."

Astrid Eiriksdottir was the daughter of a *stormann*, a "big man," a wealthy landowner of Oprekstad, thought to be modern Obrestad, up across the Skagerrak on Norway's southwest coast. That she and her father were not of royal blood speaks well of the love between her and her husband, her king. Perhaps still a teen – Norse girls being considered marriageable at the onset of menstruation – she had already borne him two daughters, Astrid and Ingebjorg (probably about one and two at this point), and she was pregnant with their third child. A man of that time and place, especially a king, would have desired a son.

---

* Where exactly in Viken Tryggvi and Astrid lived is an open question. The *Agrip* and *Fagrskinna* claim Ranrike, on the south coast; the *Historia Norwegiae* says Romerike, up near modern Oslo. It's not unlikely that a Viking chieftain would have multiple residences.

But a good king would long more for peace. As for his wife's dream, Tryggvi told her, "It is of no importance."

After Tryggvi's and Gudrod's ships put in at the anchorage, arrangements were made for the kings to meet on suitably neutral ground and work out the details of their little enterprise. According to Odd, "Gudrod sent word to King Tryggvi, bidding him to go up onto the headland with twenty men. He said he would come with an equal number to have a friendly discussion about their battle preparations."

And so Tryggvi and his housecarls waited, atop the high ground by the cairn. Meanwhile, down below, Gudrod told his men, "I think it foolish to go to such effort, risking life and property for power, rather than seize what is free for the taking without risk. We shall now go up onto the headland with forty men in order to cut up King Tryggvi's realm among us."

His heralds, having delivered his proposition to Tryggvi in good faith, told him, "You sons of Gunnhild are shameless, treacherously confiscating the realms of your vassals and kinsmen. No honorable men will serve you, and we will depart and never aid you in this."

Gudrod replied that he would carry out his plan with or without them. (It is to his dubious credit that he let them sail away with their lives, rather than murdering them on the spot.) He took his forty housecarls up the hill to meet Tryggvi's twenty. The sagas record no conversation, but then no words needed to be said. Sixty men in that little island-top arena drew blades and set to their bloody work. Odd admitted, "Even though King Tryggvi was a great fighter, he was taken by surprise, and he could not resist."

Whether he died fighting, or was held fast while his cousin murdered him outright, as he was a pagan we might hope that King Tryggvi Olafsson died with sword in hand, and that Odin welcomed him into Valhalla. Down in the ships, the rest of his men were likewise outnumbered two-to-one, and the outcome was the same. "After that," wrote Odd, "Gudrod took over his realm." And as for Tryggvi, "He rests in a cairn there on the headland, with monument stones to mark his head and feet. It is called *Tryggvareyr*, Tryggvi's Cairn."

By the dawn of the 20th century the mound of stones atop the island had been almost completely demolished by medieval grave robbers and later souvenir hunters. Excavations in the 1920s revealed a tomb in its heart, though so badly damaged that almost nothing remained of a body, Bronze Age or otherwise, but a few shards of bone. In memoriam, the cairn was rebuilt to what's thought to be some semblance of the original. Today the Swedes call the island Tryggo, and the cairn *Kung Tryggves Grav*, King Tryggvi's Grave.

But King Tryggvi Olafsson left much more to the world than a pile of stones.

II

Hunted

*Gunnhild and her sons thus carried out their plan
and went in search of Astrid.*

Odd Snorrason

AD 963

Word of King Tryggvi's murder reached his queen Astrid before his killers could. Gudrod's heralds, themselves betrayed, on leaving his service must have gone straight to Tryggvi's farm to warn her: The supposed split between the sons of Bloodaxe had been a ruse. As Berg put it, "The quarrel was only a trick by the brothers, which their mother Gunnhild had planned, so that, appearing to be at odds with one another, they would not be suspected of the treachery which they had planned together, and afterwards carried out."[*]

Greycloak and Gudrod met up, combined their forces, and took on Tryggvi's surviving men. With the King of Viken out of the way, and adding his ten shiploads of men – or, at least, those who submitted – to theirs, the Eirikssons might well conquer all of Norway, but only if they eliminated all rivals, including those as yet unborn.

Among Vikings, killing women or children was considered shameful, the act of a weakling – unless, perhaps, commanded to do the deed by one's overlord, or goaded by a royal mother. In those days, however, one murder often led to another, blood justice. A common plot in medieval

---

[*] Theodoricus Monachus' *Historia de Antiquitate Regum Norwagiensium* and the *Agrip af Noregskonungasogum* claim it was Harald Greycloak who killed Tryggvi, and the *Historia Norwegiae* that he was slain in the course of a local rebellion, but it seems safe enough to put the blame on the Eirikssons.

Norse ballads is that of he who carries out the ancient law of an eye for an eye, slaying his kin's killer. (In some songs it's the daughters who exact retribution; wives and lovers are equally justified.) Gunnhild and her sons clearly had no qualms about murder, but not even kings were safe from blood vengeance. As the brothers saw it – as Gunnhild saw it – the job would not be finished until Astrid and her entire family had joined her husband in the grave.

Tryggvi had taken his housecarls, the family fighting men, along to go on Gudrod's supposed raid. Any who refused to serve the Eirikssons would have been put to death. The rest were Gudrod's men now – Greycloak's men, Gunnhild's men – and they were all coming for Astrid. She could not trust that the survivors would remain as loyal to her commoner's blood, or her daughters, as to their late king. She could not stand against them. She could only run.

Pregnant as she was, she could not make the trip alone, but was accompanied by a few servants, her girls Ingebjorg and Astrid and her *fostri*, her foster father, Thorolf.* Thorolf bore a rather unflattering nickname, *Lusarskegg*, "Lice-Beard" (but give the man a chance, that could have been the result of a single unfortunate incident he never lived down). In the sagas he is devoted to his foster daughter, despite having a six-year-old son of his own, Thorgils, whom he did not leave behind on the journey.

With the family goods loaded up, the procession set off, bound for her father Eirik's farm on the west coast, some 250 miles away. As queen, and with her time near, Astrid would have been put on any available cart or horse. By this time Christianity had been known in Scandinavia for the better part of a century and a half, and she must surely have heard tell of the Mother Mary, who had ridden a donkey from her home carrying her unborn child to flee royal persecution.

---

* In contrast to blood justice, the fostering of children, even with natural parents still living, was also common practice among Vikings, even across social classes, in order to reconcile rivalries, cement bonds of patronage or simply to provide childless couples with children. In some situations the child might amount to a hostage against good behavior, but in the sagas a child's bond to a foster parent is often deeper than to a natural parent. Hakon the Good had been a foster son of English King Aethelstan, which is how he became Christian; King Tryggvi's cousin Gudrod Bjornsson, King of Vestfold, was also his foster brother.

Astrid was not long gone when Greycloak and Gudrod arrived at her farm. They could learn nothing of her whereabouts, but confirmed she bore Tryggvi's child. They could not pursue. For Bloodaxe's sons the conquest of Norway was a higher priority than a woman bearing a dead man's unborn whelp. Probably the Norns – the three otherworldly sisters representing Past, Present and Future, who lived beside the Well of Fate at the foot of the World Tree and wove men's destinies – would solve the problem for them. In those days of disease and malnutrition almost a fifth of all infants were stillborn, and only half the rest lived beyond the age of seven.

Contrary to depictions in modern media, which tend to follow aristocrats living in relative luxury off the hard work of the mundane, uninteresting lower classes, life in Viking Scandinavia wasn't all raiding and revelry. In those days not even ten percent of Norwegian land was arable, or really even habitable. There were few towns, nor even what we would call villages, just scatterings of small, outlying farms around big landowners' halls. By far most people lived in what today would be considered unimaginable poverty: several families, along with their servants, farmhands and thralls (servants, slaves) – perhaps ten to twenty people in all – plus their farm animals, all jammed under one roof, in a smoke-filled longhouse, a firetrap of wood and thatch with a floor of packed dirt.

It was just such hardship, however, that had forged them into the toughest people in Europe. The 11th-century German historian and chronicler Adam of Bremen got no farther north than Denmark but heard:

> Because of its rough terrain and extreme cold, Norway is the most barren of all nations, suited only for livestock. They graze their cattle like the Arabs, in distant solitude. The people live off their animals by using the milk of the flocks or herds for food and the wool for clothing. This makes them very valiant fighters, unsoftened by too much fruit, who attack others more often than they are attacked... Poverty has forced them to leave home, and from pirate raids they

bring home in great quantity the wealth of other lands. In this way they overcome the emptiness of their own land.

To survive required hard work of men and women alike, yet it was not without reward. This was the era of the Medieval Warm Period, of favorable climate across Iceland and Northern Europe. (On the far side of the North Atlantic there were 5,000 or more people thriving in Greenland.) As spring turned to summer the sunny fields would have been growing thick and high with barley, rye, wheat and buckwheat, and garden plots with beans and peas, onions and angelica, hops, parsnips and wild carrots, cabbage and garlic. That said, these were Vikings; with the field work done until harvest time, many menfolk went away for the raiding season, and this summer many would be fighting either for or against the sons of Gunnhild.

It was through this world that Astrid and her party made their secretive way westward, passing as commoners, mingling as little as possible with any locals who might betray them. Thorolf and the children stayed at their queen's side, but she ordered the rest to spread out to learn whatever they could of Gunnhild and her sons.

As expected, those were conducting something of a pogrom, a purge against anyone who had stood against them or was likely to. Greycloak surprised Tryggvi's cousin, King Gudrod of Vestfold, at a banquet in his capital of Tunsberg, modern Tonsberg on the banks of the Oslofjord, and slew him along with many of his men. They would doubtless have murdered Gudrod's son Harald as well, but he had already escaped to Sweden and would ultimately go as far as Greenland to escape their reach.[*] Gunnhild was determined to not let Astrid likewise slip through her fingers, but her sons found nothing but rumors. As a skilled *volur*, sorceress, the queen would certainly have consulted Freyja, goddess of fertility, who had taught the Vikings' tribal ancestors, the semi-mythical Aesir, the ways of magic, and would surely have revealed any knowledge of a pregnant woman on the run.

---

[*] Again, Harald Gudrodarson and the descendants of Gudrod Bjornsson bear mention by name, as they will figure later in our story.

"The rumor is likely true," Gunnhild announced of Astrid, "and she will raise a son of Tryggvi's if nothing is done to stop her."

"Astrid, now in hiding and in mourning," wrote Odd, "realized that she was soon going to give birth, when they came to a lake called Rond."

That's the medieval name for today's Randsfjord, not a saltwater fjord but a landlocked, freshwater finger lake, Norway's fourth largest.* A flooded valley running roughly north-south some forty miles between mountain ridges, it lay astride the fugitives' path to safety in the west, but at its widest is less than two miles across, an easy boat trip on a summer's day.

Astrid, however, could go no further. According to the sagas, she and her party took shelter in a *naverstad*, a boatshed, on an island in the lake. (Vikings valued their ships so highly that to house them over Scandinavian winters they built special shelters, themselves looking somewhat like overturned boats, some so large that in summer they could double as feasting halls.) There are still a few islands just off Randsfjord's southeastern shore, secluded enough that from within the walls of a *naverstad* the cries of a woman giving birth might not be heard from land.

Astrid's foster father Thorolf Lice-Beard could not help her in this. Childbirth was women's business. The sagas, written primarily by men (and celibate monks at that), give us few portrayals of delivery, fewer still of hard labor, and almost none in which the mother dies. Norse ballads, on the other hand, better represent the feminine experience: that of anxiety, pain and frequently the death of mother, child or both.

Presumably Astrid retained a qualified *bjargrygr*, a "helping woman," a midwife, among her servants. Perhaps a local *seidkonur*, a priestess, was brought in, for in those days midwifery and witchery were almost the same thing. Spells and incantations, *galdrar*, were sung, and mystic runes drawn to invoke Freyja and Frigg, goddess of

---

* Randsfjorden was well known to the family of Tryggvi as the place where his great-grandfather, Halfdan the Black, father of Harald Fairhair, died a most un-Viking death while crossing the frozen lake in a horse-drawn sleigh, falling through the ice to drown.

motherhood. It was thought the three Norns attended births as well, to begin spinning the newborn's thread of fate.

Astrid brought forth a boy. As was the custom, he would have been laid on the floor, untouched until the father, or in this case nearest male relative Thorolf, examined him for any abnormalities, to determine if he was worthy of life or should be taken outside and left to the whim of the gods, death by exposure. On acceptance, though by some accounts nine days after the birth, came the ritual of *ausa vatni*, the sprinkling of water.* Afterward, the infant counted as a person, and death by exposure as murder.

Astrid's son survived. She named him Olaf, after his father's father, Olaf *Digrleggr*, "Fat Leg," son of King Harald Fairhair.†

The remote lakeside boathouse was a good place for a new mother and child to recover in seclusion. They would not lack for food. In summertime Astrid's daughters could go ashore to pick raspberries, blueberries, lingonberries and cloudberries, and Thorolf take his son hunting with bow and spear after willow grouse and ptarmigan, red and roe deer, even reindeer and moose. The Randsfjord is still famed for its trout, salmon and pike. Well fed in their island refuge, Astrid and her family could believe themselves safe. Snorri confided, "There she hid herself all summer."

With Tryggvi Olaffson and Gudrod Bjornsson dead, the sole remaining opposition to the sons of Gunnhild that summer was Hakon Sigurdarson. News of Jarl Sigurd's murder had shaken all Norway. Not everyone was ready to accept Harald Greycloak in his place. The Tronders (people of Trondheim) came by land and sea to the assembly, and proclaimed Sigurd's son Hakon to be their new jarl. Hakon had everything required of a ruler: ancestry, wisdom and

---

* This ritual cleansing predated Christianity. The ancient Babylonians, Egyptians, Greeks, Persians, Hebrews, Romans and Hindus all practiced variations of it, which might indicate it derived from some common, primordial Proto-Indo-European purification rite.
† That he was not named after his late father, as was the usual custom, leads some historians to believe the account in the *Agrip*, which claims Olaf was already three years old at the time of Tryggvi's murder, but then a father might well have named a prospective son prior to birth, and had his wish carried out by his widow.

shrewdness, bravery and luck. Odd admitted, "He was very handsome and wise, and in many ways the most distinguished of the nobility. He was also a great warrior."

Jarl Hakon's struggle with the sons of Bloodaxe would suffice to comprise its own Viking saga. They would not let him stay in power, but he would accept nothing less. He summoned his forces and moved to intercept the brother kings, down on the central Norwegian seaboard, and Greycloak advanced to meet him on the peninsula called Stad. A mountainous, wave-carved plateau that drops steeply from as high as 2,100 feet straight into the ocean, it divides the North and Norwegian Seas, a place of strong winds, hard rains and rough water. Its name derives from the Old Norse word for city, but also from stop or wait, as in for better weather before sailing. This Greycloak and his brothers did, sheltering in the fjords below. Hakon promptly sailed around them, out of sight over the horizon, down through the Skagerrak and into the Baltic. With him gone, the sons of Bloodaxe moved into Lade unopposed and made it their de facto capital, extorted taxes and dues from the helpless farmers and villagers Hakon had left behind, and generally acted as though they owned the place, because they did. Norway was theirs, and gained with hardly a fight, only a little treachery and murder.

Now Gunnhild could turn her attention to lesser concerns. Odd wrote, "She felt sure that Astrid was with child, and believed that spelled danger for herself and her sons."

"When nights grew longer and days shorter, and the weather cooler," wrote Snorri, "then Astrid and Thorolf set out with a few others, only moving through settlements at night when they could go hidden, meeting no one."

We can assume they resumed their trek as soon as possible. The most direct route from Randsfjord to her father's estate at Obrestad was up over the highest part of the Scandes, the Scandinavian mountains, what the Norwegians call the *Kjolen*, the "keel" of Norway. In that southern part of the country the mountains split into separate ranges riven by deep valleys, with much of the highlands above the tree line and several peaks over a mile above sea level. Part of the reason Norwegians clustered along the coasts and became so adept at sea travel was so they could sail around, rather than having to hike over, that rugged, barren, largely uninhabited *Opplond*, the "upper land." Astrid's party most likely went down to Oslofjord and hired a boat to take them around the coast of *Sorlandet*, the "Southland," to her father's farm on the southwest coast.

As a *stormann*, a man of means, Astrid's father Eirik (called *Bjodaskalle*, "Bald Head") led a life not unlike his queenly daughter's, with more authority, responsibility, privilege and comfort than the average Viking Age peasant, less manual labor but more overseeing that of the farmhands and thralls living on and around his property, looking after his crops and animals. Adam of Bremen testified, "In much of Norway and Sweden cattle herders are men of the highest rank, living like patriarchs by their own hard work."

In addition to his longhouse or hall, Eirik's estate would have included a separate barn and stables, a cookhouse, brewery, workshop, smithy and more – plenty of room for Astrid, Thorolf and their children, even considering the necessary discretion. According to the sagas he lodged them in an outbuilding and saw to their provisions himself. Few of his workers even knew they were there.

In those days of such high death rates that a third of all people never reached adulthood, and half of all men and a third of all women never made it past thirty, folk counted themselves lucky if they lived to see grandchildren. No mention of Eirik's wife, Astrid's mother, is made in the sagas, but Astrid had several elder brothers, Sigurd, Jostein and Thorkell *Dyrdill* ("Short Tail" or "Hanger-On," as little brothers are apt to be known). Snorri attested, "They were all men of rank and wealth, living in the lands to the east." Of them we know Sigurd, the eldest, had left home to fight as a mercenary across the Baltic, a lifestyle not exactly conducive to a stable family life, nor to keeping in touch with home. Eirik had probably given up hope of knowing the fate of his progeny. Now here was his old friend Thorolf, having raised his daughter and brought him three grandchildren besides. Safe at last, Astrid released her retainers to go their own way. Thorolf Lusarskegg, his son Thorgils, Astrid's daughters and of course little Olaf remained. Snorri wrote, "And they stayed there all winter."

Between bickering with Jarl Hakon and trying to control their new kingdom, Gunnhild's sons were too busy to hunt for Astrid that winter. They split up. Greycloak returned south to rule there, leaving Gudrod and Gunnhild up in Lade. News of this divide soon spread over the mountains to the Swedish side, where Jarl Hakon had landed his fleet on the Baltic coast. Although he could not hope to defeat both brothers and their combined armies, he might well defeat one of them. That autumn he left his ships and marched his force over the Kjolen, farther north than Astrid would have crossed, where the going was a little smoother. On his arrival back in Lade his former subjects, wearied of the Eirikssons' domineering ways, welcomed him home and flocked to his banner.

Taken by surprise, Gudrod hastily abandoned his throne, took to his ships and retreated down the coast to More. Hakon did not pursue, contenting himself to have regained his jarldom. The two sides proceeded to annoy each other all winter, making sporadic attacks and killing each other's men as the opportunities arose.

While her sons were busy with Hakon, Gunnhild was still obsessed with finding Astrid and her newborn son. The next spring, AD 964, she sent spies south to find them. They returned with no news except that Astrid had to be at her father's estate.

The Mother of Kings had two problems – Jarl Hakon and Queen Astrid – and it occurred to her to solve them both at once. "She summoned Hakon Sigurdarson and spoke harshly to him," reported Odd.* "She said he deserved death for his treachery against her sons, the same as King Tryggvi. She said he was guilty of disloyalty in their business and that his only chance was to bring her the boy Olaf, who had wintered with Eirik at Obrestad."

---

* For his part Snorri (and some modern historians) opined that Jarl Hakon would not stoop to do his rival's dirty work, and so this must be some other Hakon, but again we go with the majority of our sources.

Though Hakon had no personal axe to grind against Tryggvi's widow or his children, their deaths would be a small price for peace with Gunnhild and her sons. Gunnhild supplied him and thirty men with horses and weapons and bade them on their way. She would have done better, though, to send a smaller, more discreet team of nameless assassins, for news of the approach of the mighty jarl and his retinue preceded them.

Eirik awoke Astrid and Thorolf: "Gunnhild's sorcery has revealed that you are hidden here, and I wish to avoid your capture. Hakon Sigurdarson's henchmen are nearby, and will be here today." He gave them beggars' clothing as disguises, and guides with instructions to take them east to Sweden, to see one Hakon *Gamli*, "the Old": "We are old friends and raided together. Since those days we have concealed and protected men with each other. You will be safe there."

Father and daughter had to know they would never see each other again. According to the sagas, they embraced before he bade her go, and quickly, for little Olaf's life was on the line: "I think Gunnhild and her sons wish the boy to suffer the same fate as his father."

The *Historiae* claims Astrid and her party departed aboard three ships bound for the Orkney Isles, which might have been a cover story. (It also claims she was still pregnant and gave birth to Olaf there.) On the other hand, Odd and Snorri agree that Astrid, Thorolf and Thorgils made a day's march overland, headed east. Astrid's "serving girls," little Astrid and Ingebjorg, must have stayed behind, as for the time being they vanish from the saga. Girls being not so important in royal successions, they may not have been on Hakon's hit list.

Meanwhile, early in the morning the jarl and his men came searching for Astrid. Odd would have it that Hakon got downright belligerent with Eirik, accusing him of hiding her and her son over the winter. As a stormann, Eirik had the right to carry weapons and retain his own household guard, but knew better than to draw sword on a jarl. He admitted they had been there, but – truthfully – said they were gone. Hakon and his men spent the day going over the house and grounds, finding nothing, but toward evening they received word of her.

At their first stop, a rich man's hall, Astrid and her party had been driven away as beggars, but a local villager had given them shelter for the night. Stopping at the same hall, Hakon and his men learned they could probably still find her in the village in the morning. Again, however, word of their arrival went ahead of them. (There was evidently little sympathy among southerners for Gunnhild and her sons.) Astrid's host woke her in the middle of the night and sent her and her people to hide on an island in a nearby lake, and when Hakon and his men arrived in the morning, led them on a wild goose chase. Jarl Hakon was forced to go home empty-handed to face Gunnhild. That night the villager provided Astrid and the fugitives with provisions and a guide to take them the rest of the way east to Sweden, and safety...but not for long.

III

Nowhere to Hide

Astrid did not rest on her journey until she, her son, and her companions came to Hakon the Old, with whom they happily dwelt a long time.

Berg Sokkason

AD 964–966

At just over a thousand miles, the border between modern Norway and Sweden is Europe's longest. A millennium ago, however, there was no such line over which one could step and go from one country to the other. There was only a gradual mix of speech among the locals, a change of dialect, of accent really, like that between American and British English, between those who spoke Old West Norse and those who spoke Old East Norse. A speaker of one would have had no trouble understanding, or being understood, in the other. Astrid's former home, Tryggvi's realm of Viken, lay between Norway and Sweden, where the dialects likewise overlapped, and its landscape is less like rugged Norway than lush south-central Sweden. Even today nearly three-quarters of the country is forested in broadleaf and conifer, and dotted with almost 100,000 ponds and lakes. Not quite a century after this, Adam of Bremen, visiting the royal court in Denmark, learned, "The Swedish lands are very fertile, rich in fruits and honey, exceeding all others in cattle, streams and woods aplenty, and the whole region is wealthy with merchandise from foreign lands."

According to him, sailing round southern Sweden and up the coast took only days, but in those days the Baltic was a dangerous sea. (In the year 829 the Frankish priest Ansgar, the "Apostle of the North," had risked a crossing from Denmark to convert the Swedes to Christianity, been captured by pirates, stripped of his belongings, had to finish the trip overland, and could count himself lucky to have survived it.) Odd would have it that Astrid's party crossed by land, which might have required a month-long hike. The sagas do not specify where in Sweden Astrid's father Eirik's friend Hakon the Old lived, whether the mountainous boreal north, the fertile central lowland or the southern highlands. The fact that Eirik claimed he and Hakon the Old had "been freebooters together for a long time" might indicate the Swede lived near the coast, from where they would have more easily launched Viking raids, and there are passages of the sagas that suggest that he lived in the south.

Though not titled in the sagas as a jarl, old Hakon must have been the next best thing: a *lendermann*, "landed man," holding his fief by grace of the king, though it might be more accurate to say the king did not have the power to take it. The political structure of Sweden in those days, as in Norway, consisted of such petty, largely independent chieftains, but the Swedes had never been united as had the Danes under Harald Bluetooth or the Norwegians under Harald Fairhair. Hakon the Old was for all practical purposes king of his land, powerful and wealthy, and he received Astrid and her party with open arms. They resided with him for two years before, as the *Heimskringla* puts it, "Gunnhild Mother of Kings learned that Astrid and her son Olaf were in Sweden."

Despite his previous service in her attempt to capture Astrid, or perhaps because of his failure, Gunnhild and her sons had been pressing their contest with Jarl Hakon. The *Heimskringla* attests, "Jarl Hakon and his warriors defended the Trondheim area for three years [AD 963–965], during which time Gunnhild's sons took no tribute from it. Hakon had many battles with Gunnhild's sons, and many men lost their lives on both sides."

The queen and the jarl were two of a kind. What Gunnhild lacked in stature she made up in beauty, guile and (as written by male monks, at least) sexual promiscuity. The *Heimskringla* calls her "the most beautiful of women, clever, wise, and lively, but a very false person, and of very cruel character." Hakon was her male counterpart.

The *Agrip* tells us, "Jarl Hakon was the most handsome of men, not tall, but impressive," and the *Fagrskinna* concurs, "Hakon was extremely good looking, very refined, medium tall with thick hair and beard, a man of many abilities, articulate, inscrutable, patient, generous but cruel to his rivals, both in open action and in secret plots, a holder of grudges."

At last, with their underlings urging peace, these two agreed: Jarl Hakon could rule over Lade in place of his father Jarl Sigurd, and Gunnhild's sons over the lands of the late King Hakon. Part of the deal, however, was that the jarl would still do the queen's dirty work, just as she had demanded before.

The idea of going a long way to murder a child must have had little appeal for Hakon. By this time he was a father himself. His son Eirik was about Olaf's age, born a bastard out of some unknown Opplond woman when Hakon was just fifteen. He had at least one daughter, too: Aud, whose mother could have been the same woman, or another. (The *Heimskringla* admits, "Jarl Hakon was very obsessed with women, and had numerous children.") He may have been doing a little plotting of his own. According to Odd, "Hakon departed Norway, going east to Sweden, accompanied by his daughter Aud, who was the fairest of women. King Eirik gave him a warm welcome."

The sagas name an "Eirik" as King of Sweden around this time, and the earliest historically attested King of Sweden is Eirik Bjornsson, eventually to be called "the Victorious," notably not because he was a great conqueror but because he managed not to be conquered. Though his reign is generally thought to have begun around 970, Eirik may have claimed the title these few years before then, or the sagas' dates may simply be off by that much. He ruled from the Uppland (in this case meaning "up the coast," rather than the Norwegian Opplond, "up in the mountains") near modern Stockholm. Snorri's *Ynglinga Saga* tells how the gods founded the line of Swedish kings at Uppsala, after which their descendants became the ancestors of the Norwegian kings, including Harald Fairhair (and so of King Tryggvi and his son Olaf). King Eirik's welcome, as Hakon had surely anticipated, was as much for young Aud as for her father, for the old king was in the market for a new queen, and a child bride was not off-limits. As Adam of Bremen heard of the Swedes, "In their sexual relations with women they know no limits. A man of means has two or three or more wives at once, rich men and princes as many as they like."

However, Eirik was not looking to add to his harem. His marriage had recently dissolved. Some said this was because when a husband died his widow was to be interred with him. (There is not a lot of evidence of widow sacrifice in Viking funerals, though as double interments have been found in some gravesites it cannot be ruled out.) As shall be seen, his queen Sigrid, who will have a role to play in our story, was much younger than her king – she is thought to have been a Slavic princess, originally named Swietoslawa – and had no intention of spending the afterlife with him. Actually, Eirik was not much insistent that they spend even the rest of their earthly lives together. As described in the *Heimskringla*, Sigrid was "both young and beautiful, but also proud and arrogant." A separate saga, thought also to have been written by Odd Snorrason, claims that Eirik loved her but "parted with her because of her unpredictable moods, for she was the most quick-tempered woman ever."

Unusually for European societies in this period – probably because the Christian church had as yet made few inroads among them; Father Ansgar's 9th-century mission had been largely in vain, despite which he became a saint – divorce among Vikings was easily accomplished by either spouse, on grounds of infidelity, infertility, failure to provide, absence, physical abuse or simple incompatibility, by nothing more than one or both parties declaring it before witnesses. Furthermore, the ex-wife could come out of it retaining or even gaining property. According to Odd, both Sigrid and Eirik did well in ridding themselves of each other: "He gave her Gotland."

Because Gotland, modern Gotaland in southern Sweden (and the home of Beowulf's Geats), very likely included the lands of Hakon the Old, it might also have bearing on our story, for in bringing his daughter Aud to the newly single king Jarl Hakon was playing a long game. King Eirik courted his daughter, Hakon gave her away, and thus gained himself a powerful ally who might not object to, and might even help with, his meddling in the southlands. He confided to the king that Gunnhild had dispatched him on his errand, requesting that Eirik assist him in gaining custody of Olaf Tryggvason and taking him back to Norway where the queen would raise him as her own.

According to Odd, Eirik warned his new father-in-law that Hakon the Old was not to be trifled with. "He is in many ways more powerful than we, and not long ago he got the better of it when it came to fighting between us." Nevertheless, he agreed to supply the jarl with a hundred fighting men.*

Luckily for Astrid and Olaf, Old Hakon's son was at court and overheard the plan. A hundred warriors did not sound like a friendly visit. He hurried ahead to his father's estate. When Jarl Hakon arrived, Old Hakon had 300 warriors on hand to welcome him and his men. Odd claimed the jarl refused his host's offer of food and drink:

> Queen Gunnhild sends me to say that she invites the son of King Tryggvi, whom she believes to be here under your protection, and wishes to foster him and honor him to console his mother Astrid and other kin. She bade me come here and raise this matter because she regrets his father's death, and wishes to make amends first to the gods and then to men, and to make up to the son the wrong that was done to his father. She believes that the greatest honor she can bestow is to foster his son with love and raise him as her own foster son.

Old Hakon was well aware of the Konungamodir's reputation for trickery and treachery, but left the answer up to Olaf's mother. The *Heimskringla* says, "Astrid refused to hear of it."

"Astrid chooses her own path, for herself and her son. She believes if Gunnhild has her way she will do to him what she did to his father," Old Hakon informed the jarl. "I can tell you, Hakon, that this boy will never get into your hands or Gunnhild's if I can prevent it, so you will have to come through me."

Three-to-one odds did not appeal to Jarl Hakon. He returned to Uppsala empty-handed. King Eirik was not surprised, but agreed to give him another hundred warriors. With more manpower and more surprise on his side, on his next visit the jarl did not mince words, declaring the boy would go with him whether Old Hakon liked it or not.

---

* In those days Scandinavians numbered by the so-called "long hundred" of 120.

Old Hakon practically laughed in his face. "Your big talk is wasted, for I do as I will, and defend my rights, against more formidable men than you, however many warriors you brought with you."

It was not necessarily up to Old Hakon, however. One of his brawny fieldhands, a thrall, had taken a break from forking dung to listen in, and decided he had nothing to lose by taking his master's side. According to Odd he faced down Jarl Hakon with a pitchfork full of manure: "Who are you, foreigner, to talk so to our lord? Shut your mouth and begone, ere I give you a thrashing with this dung fork that people will laugh about forever."

The jarl realized his Norwegian title carried little weight in Sweden. He would be shamed forever if word got around that he had been humiliated by a slave. He backed down. But to deliver bad news to the Mother of Kings, twice, was to invite her lethal wrath, unless one had powerful backing. Having just made an ally of the King of Sweden, rather than return directly to Norway, Hakon took a circuitous route home to make another. As Snorri put it, "He went to Denmark and resided for some time with King Harald Gormsson, and there is much to be said about that."

This King Harald, son of Gorm, is better known to history as Harald *Blatonn*. Bluetooth.

Now that Gunnhild had found Astrid and her son, however, it was only a matter of time before she tried again, more subtly this time, to have Olaf kidnapped or killed. Theodoricus Monachus related, "Olaf could hardly find a safe hiding place for all of Gunnhild's traps, she fearing that he would succeed to the kingdom rather than her sons."

Sweden, like Norway, was no longer safe for them. Unlike Jarl Hakon, Astrid knew no one in Denmark.

But she knew someone across the sea. Her brother Sigurd still served as a mercenary on the other side of the Baltic in what is modern Russia, and by all accounts was well regarded. Astrid and Olaf could lose themselves in what the Vikings called *Gardariki*, the "land of cities," sheltering under his protection. Not even Gunnhild could reach them there.

Old Hakon arranged for Astrid, Thorolf and the children to travel with some merchants bound for Russia, providing whatever they needed for the trip, and kept watch over them until they were safely aboard ship.

Both Odd and Snorri mentioned that the trip was made via merchant vessel. The Viking *langskip*, "longship," was ideal for exploration, raiding and war, but too sleek and shallow for hauling much in the way of people or goods. For trade the Scandinavians employed the wider, deeper *knarr*, with an open hold and extra cargo decks fore and aft. Some of these were quite large. *Skuldelev 1*, the knarr excavated from Denmark's Roskilde harbor in 1962, was about fifty feet long, sixteen across the beam, and would have displaced about twenty tons, but *Hedeby 3*, discovered in 1980 in what is now northern Germany, was seventy-five feet long and twenty across, and sixty tons. Such ships were capable of crossing even the North Atlantic but – with fewer oars to maximize cargo space, relying mostly on sail power – slowly, at about five to seven knots. According to Adam of Bremen, from Sweden to Russia by sea was a voyage of five days.

Most of Astrid's party would not survive the trip. Snorri reported: "On that journey they had nothing but hard luck and grief."

IV

Pirates

These islands are infested with pirates and very bloodthirsty robbers who spare no one passing that way.

Adam of Bremen

AD 966

As Odin's pet ravens Huginn and Muninn might fly it, setting out from Asgard in the morning to circle the world and return to the god's shoulders at nightfall with the news, from Uppsala in Sweden to Novgorod in Russia was a straight line of about 480 miles. That the standard, roundabout trade route was almost twice as long – 750 miles east to Lake Ladoga, then 120 miles south to Novgorod – was necessary for travelers to circumvent *Eistland*, "East Land," modern Estonia. It was every bit as notorious as the Bahamas in the 17th century, Madagascar in the 18th, the Barbary Coast in the 19th, or today's Malacca Strait and South China Sea, and for the same reason: It had myriad secret anchorages, all within easy striking distance of a main trade route. The *Heimskringla* calls its denizens "Vikings out of the East," but they were not Vikings. In Baltic waters the only thing more terrifying than Viking marauders were the Estonian pirates who preyed upon them.

"Olaf was now aged three," related Snorri. This Baltic crossing was probably the first time he had ever been out of sight of land. What an adventure for him and his foster brother Thorgils too, to stand at the rail and see nothing but water all the way to the horizon! And what a relief for their parents Astrid and Thorolf, to finally be beyond the reach of Gunnhild and Greycloak. At last, they were all safe…

…until a sail appeared in the distance.

At his age Olaf could scarcely have understood the apprehension overtaking the ship's crew and passengers, but he would certainly have sensed it. They couldn't even run for home; the wind over the Baltic is primarily out of the west, and square-rigged knarrs were even slower when tacking into the breeze. The Swedes could only flee to the east. Running before the wind, a knarr could do thirteen knots, but like Vikings the Eistland pirates utilized fast, sleek longships. The 12th-century Danish historian, theologian and author Saxo Grammaticus, writing in Latin, called them *liburnae*, from the Roman for galleys, oar-driven warships, and they could hit seventeen knots. However little good it did, what few oars the knarr bore were run out and put to work. Olaf and his mother could only have kept out of the way as the rest of the crew broke out bows and arrows, spears and swords and shields, and made ready for a fight.

Considering that the Vikings were sea raiders, there are surprisingly few tales of ship-to-ship action in medieval Scandinavian literature. One of the best is the account in the *Orkneyinga Saga*, of Rognvald Kali Kolsson, Jarl of Orkney, during his pilgrimage through the Straits of Gibraltar to visit the Holy Land, c. AD 1151. (Ship design did not evolve much in the centuries between his story and Olaf's. The knarr was not superseded by the more advanced cog, with a rudder instead of a steerboard, until the century after that, and naval tactics didn't vary much either.) Rognvald's tale is told from the opposite point of view from ours – that of the attacker rather than the defenders – but still illustrates how such an action might have taken place.

Off the coast of *Serkland* – Saracen Land, North Africa – at the head of a fleet of nine longships, Rognvald takes time off from his pilgrimage to attack a lone *dromund*, a merchant vessel. (The name was a corruption of *dromon*, the typical Byzantine war galley, but by the time the saga was written meant any large medieval ship. In those Mediterranean waters it probably differed from Olaf's knarr in flying a triangular lateen sail rather than northern-style square, and in being carvel-built of planks joined edge-to-edge rather than clinker-built of overlapping planks in the northern manner, but those differences matter little to our story.) Rognvald orders his ships to close in around the target. "But when they came aside the dromund, her sides were so high that the Northmen [or in Olaf's case, the Eistlanders] were unable to attack," tells the saga. "The others poured molten brimstone [sulfur] and blazing pitch over them [Greek fire, medieval napalm], but most of it fell in the water...and they did not need protection from it."

Still, their initial assault repulsed, some of the longships draw off and begin showering the defenders with arrows. "This was the most effective attack," reveals the saga. "The crew of the dromund took shelter under their shields, and little heeded what those in the ships close aside were doing."

Easy to believe, what with a murderous rain of arrows bristling the deck and the defenders' shields, that few on Astrid's ship dared move from cover, much less raise a head over the gunwales. In their day Thorolf and probably even Thorgils would have done what they could in the defense, while Astrid and her children sheltered below decks. Anyone down there might have been first to see a renewed assault: "Jarl Rognvald ordered his men to use their axes to smash the dromund's siding where the iron fastenings [rivets] were fewest, and when the men aboard the other ships saw what his men were doing, they did likewise."

The murderous two-handed Dane axe would have been of no use for this work; its razor-thin blade was ideal for shearing through mail armor, limbs and spines, but too light for chopping wood. No Viking Age ship, however, would have lacked woodworking tools necessary for emergency repairs if stranded far from home, and in those days, before they needed to withstand cannon fire, ships were built as light as possible and no sturdier than they had to be. With the incoming flights of arrows keeping the defenders' heads down, a few heavy splitting axes or mauls in the hands of brawny men would have made short work of bashing through a hull. "Standing as close as they dared, they chopped away at the planks with all their strength," goes the saga. "When they had opened a hole wide enough to get through, they prepared to board. The jarl and his men went in on the lower deck...there commenced severe fighting."

Toward the merchantman's bow its anchor lay hooked by a fluke over the gunwale, with its shank dangling down toward the attackers.*

---

* By Olaf's time Vikings were using iron anchors of near-modern T-shaped design. One found in a ship burial at Ladby, Denmark in 1934 dated from the year 925 and was forged of Norwegian iron, with a chain of Swedish metal welded with Danish iron and a wooden stock.

One of them grabbed hold, hauled himself up, and pulled the others after him until there were more attackers than defenders aboard. The decks of a knarr, no matter how large, were a crowded place for a sword fight. In their short lives little Olaf and young Thorgils had survived some narrow escapes, but they had not witnessed men killing each other with sharp steel, screaming as they died, limbs and heads rolling away, guts spilled and bodies littering a deck slippery with blood. Outnumbered defenders could have only put their backs to bow or stern with their passengers cowering behind them, all hoping to make victory costly enough to be granted quarter. With pirate ships full of bowmen all around them, though, such a fight could go only one way. Olaf's voyage ended much as had that of St. Ansgar, some 130 years earlier – "The merchants traveling with them defended themselves forcefully and with success for a while, but eventually they were overwhelmed and defeated by the pirates, who claimed their ships and everything they had" – and, for that matter, that of the Muslim victims of Jarl Rognvald and his Vikings almost 190 years later, who burned their captured *dromund* and sold the captives into slavery before proceeding on their Christian pilgrimage. According to the *Heimskringla*, the Eistlanders "took both goods and captives, and killed some, but the rest they divided among themselves as slaves."

The captives could only mutely await their fates. There was no point in pleading. Eistlanders looked like Vikings, dressed like Vikings, and certainly fought like Vikings, but did not sound like Vikings. Their language was nothing like Old Norse, East or West. (Modern Estonian, divided into North and South dialects, is more like Finnish, both Uralic languages originally out of Asia, possibly as far away as Siberia, and unrelated to Germanic tongues.) There was no telling what the Eistlander captains were nattering at each other, but anybody could guess the verdict, as Adam of Bremen remarked of them: "They kill captives whom others would usually sell."

The Swedish knarr itself, if not too badly damaged, was a valuable prize; otherwise it would be abandoned, left to sink. Its cargo could be sold in port, and its crewmen, skilled in the ways of the sea, might prove useful as slave rowers on Eistlander liburnae, or at the least as strong backs in the fields. Rich merchants, besides being robbed of everything they had, could be ransomed for further profit. And in

Estonian slave markets a beautiful woman like Astrid might bring three times the price of a man.

As for old Thorolf and the boys...

"Olaf was taken from his mother," reported Berg. "A man named Klerkon claimed Olaf, his foster-father Thorolf, and Thorolf's son Thorgils. Klerkon, seeing Thorolf as too old for servitude, and unfit for hard labor, killed him."

There would have been no point in drawing things out. The Eistlanders were businessmen. They had places to go, things to do, and no time for niceties; for them it was no different than slaughtering a chicken for lunch. A quick stroke with knife, sword or axe, and that was that. Astrid and the boys would have seen their foster father's body stripped of any valuables and dumped over the side, and possibly his head after it, along with the rest of the Swedish dead and too-grievously wounded. Astrid was put aboard her new master's ship.

Then, wrote Berg, Klerkon "took the boys with him to Eistland."

V

SLAVE

Yngvar, called "the White," was slain on campaign on a Baltic Sea island which the natives called Eysysla.

Historia Norwegiae

AD 966–972

In his *Ynglinga Saga*, Snorri tells of the 7th-century King Yngvar Harra of Sweden, who crossed the Baltic to plunder a place called Stein in Eistland. According to him, the locals countered with a great army, slew the king and ran off the invaders. Snorri claimed that Yngvar was buried on the shores of *Adalsysla*, "the heart of the sea," where the Baltic still sings him to sleep.

In 2008 work crews removing earth for the construction of a cycling track outside the village of Salme, on the island of Saaremaa off the Estonian coast, unexpectedly discovered the remains of a ship. Its wooden hull had long since rotted away, but its outline could be discerned by the stains left in the earth and 275 iron rivets that once held it together. Almost forty feet long and seven wide, it contained seven bodies aged eighteen to forty-five, initially thought to date from the Second World War. Two years later, however, another ship was discovered just a hundred feet down the road, over fifty feet long and almost ten across the beam, with the remains of 1,200 nails and rivets and no less than three dozen men, these with grave goods including swords, shields and spearheads indisputably identifying them as Vikings. Forensic examination of the ship remains indicated that they were built between AD 600 and 650, and buried between 700 and 750, with many repairs and patches in between, and furthermore that the largest one had carried a sail – the earliest known use of such technology in the Baltic.

DNA analysis revealed the dead were Swedes. Judging by the numerous arrowheads found embedded among the wreckage – including three-pointed fire arrows – and wounds indicating they had raised their arms to ward off blows, they died fighting. Whoever buried them, however, did so with great respect, neatly arranging them four layers deep, men with cheap single-edged swords on the bottom, those above better equipped, five with double-edged, decorative swords, and on top a man with a jewel-hilted blade. The weapons were all bent or deformed, to discourage grave robbers or perhaps so the dead couldn't use them in Valhalla; that the jeweled sword went untouched might be a further sign of respect, or of a curse. All were covered under a dome of shields, over which the ship's sail was draped like a burial shroud. The men in the smaller boat, on the other hand, were buried carelessly, dumped there alone or in pairs, some lying up against the inside of the hull, all more poorly equipped than the men in the bigger boat – possibly servants or slaves not worthy of fine burial. The site is over 800 feet from, and almost fifteen feet above, the nearest shore, but thirteen centuries ago it was right at the high tide mark, and eventually covered by sand.

Nobody knows if this is the grave of King Yngvar of legend. It does prove that the age of Viking expansion did not start, as has been widely assumed, with the raid on Lindisfarne Abbey in English Northumbria in AD 793, but fifty to a hundred years earlier, and in the Baltic, what the Vikings called the *Austrveg*, the "East Way."

And that, by the time Olaf Tryggvason arrived there, the Estonians had been hating and killing his kind for perhaps as long as two and a half centuries.

Then, as now, the eastern Baltic was dotted with some 2,300 islands. It's hard to say where little Olaf got off the boat, and probably makes little difference. Today *Eysysla*, as mentioned in the *Historia*, is generally thought to refer to Saaremaa (until the mid-20th century known as Osel), and Snorri's *Adalsysla* to mean the Estonian mainland, across the Gulf of Riga. Both shores had been inhabited since the Bronze Age, but the sandy lowlands and islands, cut into sections by swamps, streams and lakes, had the effect of isolating populations – Oselians, Kurs, Semgallians, Selonians, Letts, more – perpetually at war with each other and everybody else, too. In the 880s, having ventured around the eastern Baltic, the traveler and trader Wulfstan of Hedeby wrote, "This country called Eistland is vast, with many towns, and each has its king...There is a great deal of war and strife between the different tribes of this land."

The Estonian cities that would become bustling commercial centers of the Hanseatic League – Parnu, Tallinn, Tartu, Viljandi – were still 300 years in the future. The Eistlanders of Olaf's day lived in scattered farmsteads of a few huts or longhouses clustered around hillforts, numbering no more than 100 to 200 people at most. They required no more governance than town councils, like Viking things, each overseen by a *vanem*, which translates today as parent, but back then as senior, elder, or at a stretch, chieftain, something like a jarl. Even less than Scandinavians, who farmed most of the year and went raiding on occasion, the Eistlanders had little use for agriculture, craftsmanship or trade, but simply took whatever they wanted from their neighbors. They were not poor, as Adam of Bremen admitted: "There is plenty of gold, the horses are among the best." Their main trade goods, to the extent that they traded with anyone, were Baltic amber, bog iron, slaves and furs. "They have a surplus of rare pelts, the [mustelid] scent of which has intoxicated our world with the sin of pride," Adam continued. "But they regard these furs as worthless – to our shame, say I, for right or wrong we desire a marten-skin robe as we do supreme happiness. So they trade their valuable marten furs for woolen clothes."

Or fresh young slaves.

As soon as the Eistlander pirate ship ground to a stop down on the beach, Olaf and Thorgils would have been tossed down into the surf and herded uphill to learn their fate. The going rate for an adult male slave in Eistland at this time was about one mark, seven ounces or so of silver, meaning only noblemen could afford one. Though Saaremaa has yielded more Viking coin hoards than anywhere else except for the Swedish island of Gotland, to judge by the sagas the common folk maintained a barter economy, as evidenced by Olaf and Thorgils meeting their new master. According to the *Heimskringla*, Klerkon sold the boys to a man named Klerk for a fine billy goat.*

That a human life was worth one goat – not even that, half a goat – is a sad comment on that place and time. In retrospect, however, the boys were lucky to survive. The Eistlanders would be even later than the Swedes in coming to Christianity. They are said to have been animists, worshipping spirits and fairies at sacred rocks and sacrificial springs, and their thunder god Therapita was worshipped in forest groves. Adam of Bremen maintained that they practiced human sacrifice during that period:

> The people, exceptionally bloodthirsty due to their stubborn devotion to idols, are shunned by everyone...the houses are full of pagan soothsayers, diviners, and necromancers, who even wear monastic habit [but are] utterly ignorant of the Christian God. They worship dragons and birds and sacrifice to them live men whom they buy from the slavers. They carefully inspect these men all over to make sure they have no blemishes for which, they say, the dragons would refuse them.†

On the other hand, just what value two small boys had as slaves in those days can only be conjectured. Thorgils, now aged nine, could pitch in on farm work – herding cattle, pigs and sheep; caring for horses; mucking out stables; manuring fields, plowing, planting and harvesting; cutting turf for insulation and digging peat for fuel; helping to build houses and repair the hillfort's walls and ramparts; and general drudge work. Little Olaf, at his age barely able to speak Old Norse, let alone Old Baltic, would for the time being have been confined to lighter, simpler jobs – gathering eggs, grinding grain, churning butter and the like – learning such skills

---

* The similarities in the names Klerkon and Klerk might indicate a family relationship, father and son or brothers. The meaning of the names is lost, as the western Baltic languages then spoken in the area are all extinct.

† It must be said that Adam's comments on Eistlanders should be taken with a grain of salt. He was better informed about the Viking colonies in Greenland than he was about the alien, Finno-Ugric lands just up the Baltic coast from Bremen. He also thought the Eistlanders lived next door to the legendary tribe of warrior women, the Amazons.

at the end of a switch. Thralls bought at such a young age must have been seen by their owner as an investment, to be matured into full-grown slaves and resold at a profit...unless a better offer came along.

"Not long afterward Klerk sold Olaf to a third man for a good cloak or cape," documented Berg. "His new master was a native of heathen lands, named Reas, with a wife Rekon, and their son Rekoni.* Along with him Reas bought his foster brother, Thorgils."

Their lives each worth half a goat – half a fur cloak – Odd wrote of Olaf and Thorgils, "They spent six years in servitude."

As though the gods looked dimly on the reign of Gunnhild's sons, in Norway the weather turned so foul that winter ran into summer, there were poor harvests, and starvation stalked the land. "All across the country people found themselves having almost no grain and fish," reports the *Heimskringla*. "In Halogaland [northern Norway] hardly any grain grew, and there was famine and starvation." And according to the *Fagrskinna*, "There was so much snow in midsummer that all farm animals were kept inside for feeding."

"The longer they ruled over the land, the worse things got," continues the *Heimskringla* of Greycloak and his brothers, "and the farmers blamed everything on the kings."

When the renegade Norwegian jarl Hakon Sigurdarson, hiding in Denmark for having failed in his mission to capture Astrid and Olaf, heard murmurs of discontent in Norway, he did what he could to fan the flames. The Eirikssons had left one of their younger brothers, Erling, to rule Hakon's former jarldom of Lade; Hakon sent word encouraging his former subjects to pave the way for a homecoming by murdering him, which they did. With the rest of the *Gunnhildssonnene*

---

* These names are better attested than Klerk and Klerkon, but instead of personal names may denote occupations or social status. Reas, also given as Heres, might be related to the Lithuanian (in which a *v* between vowels is often unspoken) name Revas, "a man of open space" or "free man." Rekon and Rekoni relate more to the Baltic, Lithuanian and Prussian words for master/mistress or household manager. Put together, they might suggest Reas, the "native of heathen lands," was not Estonian.

still in power, Hakon did not yet dare to return, but that was not the end of his trickery. The *Agrip* confides, "He was very intelligent, and more cunning than Gunnhild in his schemes."

He cozied up to his host Bluetooth's nephew, Harald Knutsson. This Harald was such a successful Viking that he was called Gold-Harald, but he had tired of freebooting and wished to settle down in land of his own, namely half of his uncle's Denmark. Hakon advised him to demand it from the king, knowing full well how that would turn out. Once the two Haralds, Gold and Bluetooth, were suitably angered with each other – to the extent that Gold confided to Hakon he wished to murder his uncle and take Denmark by force – Hakon advised Bluetooth to furnish Gold-Harald with another kingdom, Norway: "All the people there hate the kings, everyone wishes them misfortune, and they deserve it. It has long been known that you greatly helped Gunnhild's sons, and they have returned you nothing but evil."

"Norway is large, its people are tough, and difficult for a foreign force to attack," Bluetooth said. "Harald Greycloak, my foster-son, has sat on my knee."

Hakon said, "Send him a message. Tell him to come visit. Offer him a fief in Denmark, that which he and his brothers once held. Then Gold-Harald may quickly win a Norwegian kingdom from Harald Greycloak."

"I will be thought evil for betraying my foster-son."

"The Danes will think it better to slay a Norwegian Viking than a Danish nephew."

Bluetooth agreed. Hakon then convinced Gold-Harald to accept Norway instead of Denmark, and with that all three men plotted together, and two against the third.

In the spring of 970 Bluetooth sent word to Harald Greycloak in Norway that he was welcome to come reclaim his former Danish lands. Greycloak raised the matter to his mother and brothers, whose opinions were divided. Some thought it was a trick. Others thought he had nothing to lose, since the famine in Norway was becoming so severe that they could barely feed their own men.

Greycloak sailed for Denmark with six ships. Gold-Harald sailed to meet him with nine. And Jarl Hakon readied twelve, but before he sailed, according to Berg, he went to Harald Bluetooth to play the other side:

> Gold-Harald will kill Harald Greycloak and seize his kingdom in Norway. Do you think, O King, that he will remain loyal to you, who are giving him such power? He told me last year that he would kill you if he got the chance. Better you should win Norway as I suggest. I will slay Gold-Harald if you promise to forgo reprisal afterward. Then I will be your jarl, and swear to bring Norway under your rule, with your help, and hold the land in your name, paying you tribute. You will then be a more powerful king than your father, as you will rule two empires.

Bluetooth had already agreed to the death of one kinsman; another was no great leap. Greycloak and Gold-Harald met at Hals, in the Limfjord, the inland sea which cuts the Jutland peninsula in half. There Greycloak died as he had lived – as had Tryggvi Olafsson – by treachery, outnumbered and slain in battle. But before he died, the *Agrip* claims, he laughed at Gold-Harald, "Your victory will be short-lived, because I know that it is Jarl Hakon's doing. As soon as I am dead he will come after you and kill you, and I will be avenged."

True to his prediction, Jarl Hakon and Gold-Harald met soon after Harald Greycloak fell. They fought, Hakon won, Gold-Harald was captured and Hakon hanged him. Bluetooth named Hakon Sigurdarson a Danish jarl now, ruler of Norway in the name of Denmark. Hakon took his new Danish/Norwegian army north and met Gudrod and his brothers in battle. "So many men were killed," the *Fagrskinna* records, "that the jarl walked away from the battle treading on men's heads." Gudrod, his mother Gunnhild and surviving brothers fled to the Orkneys.

Hakon married Thora Skagadottir, possibly Danish, who soon bore him another son, Svein. Secure on his throne, with a wife and a couple of little princes, the jarl now ruled Norway as a king. Hakon's skald, his court poet, Einar Helgason, called "Einar of the Shieldmaiden," wrote a *drapa*, a praise poem, about him: "The Eirikssons, who dared to destroy sanctuaries [i.e., were Christian], once occupied the land,

and were the talk of all men. Now the god of shields of the spear-ford [Jarl Hakon], bold in battle, the greatest of rulers, is established where those powerful princes once reigned."

These momentous events shook the Viking world, all while little Olaf was in Eistland, growing up as a slave. Yet the gods had not forgotten him. Because in 972, after he had spent six years there, the village of Reas received visitors.

VI

Varangians

I have never seen such perfect examples of manhood.
They are tall as palm trees, blond and ruddy...
Each carries an axe, a sword and a knife,
and never let themselves get far from them.

Ahmad ibn Fadlan

AD 972

No Eistlanders, these visitors to the village of Reas, no Slavs, but by their noble bearing and Scandinavian features, *Vaeringjar* – Varangians, "sworn companions" in the tongue of their Viking ancestors. (The Slavs called them *Rus*, from the Finnish word for Sweden.)

"He traveled in wealth and style," wrote Snorri of their leader, "with great magnificence and many well-equipped men in his retinue." Nor was he an ordinary Varangian. By his fine horse, his embroidered, fur-trimmed tunic and cape, his gilded and silvered helmet and trappings, his western-style arms and armor and eastern-style horse harness, he was a member of the *druzhina*, the retinue of bodyguards, advisors and companions – the housecarls – of the Prince of Novgorod. He and his men had come to collect the tribute and taxes owed by the Eistlanders to their Rus overlords.

Reas, the master of the house, had gone to work in the fields for the day, and apparently Olaf's foster-brother Thorgils, now fifteen, with him. Olaf, nine, was left behind, for as Odd declared, "Reas, out of love for him, would not put him to work, but treated him as a foster son, training him in manly exercises and bearing, clothing him and seeing that he lacked for nothing." At that age Olaf was no more able to do heavy labor than Thorgils had been on their arrival six years earlier, but here we see the hero's myth begin. According to Odd, "Olaf, seeing the strangers ride into the courtyard, greeted their chieftain warmly and with great courtesy, and all the others with him."

The Varangian said, "I see, young man, that you are a foreigner here, for you differ in speech and looks from everybody else. Tell me your name and of your land and family."

"My name is Olaf. I am from Norway, where my family was of royal blood."

The Varangian had probably never met a slave who did not claim to be a prince, but he humored the lad. "What are the names of your father and mother?"

"My father's name was Tryggvi and my mother was Astrid. She was the daughter of Eirik Bjodaskalle, stormann of Oprekstad."

At this, reported Odd, the Varangian jumped down from his horse and gave Olaf a kiss – "This is surely a happy day, for we have found each other!" – and revealed that Eirik the Bald was his father as well, for he was none other than Olaf's uncle, Astrid's brother Sigurd. "How did you come here? How fare you?"

Olaf told him the story of his capture and enslavement, the beginnings of which he probably didn't even remember, but had been told by Thorgils.

Sigurd asked, "Do you wish, kinsman, that I should purchase you from your master so that you will no longer be his slave?"

"I am well off, compared to before," Olaf replied, "for Reas, my foster-father, grants me everything I wish. Yet I would gladly go from here if Thorgils, my foster-brother, is also freed, and comes with us."

Sigurd promised to spare no expense. He was made welcome in the home of Reas, though perhaps not in the manner to which a Varangian was accustomed. "There is an abundance of honey and fish," Wulfstan of Hedeby reported of the Eistlander menu. "Even the king and the nobles drink mare's milk [fermented, called *kumis*, still popular in Russia], though the poor and slaves drink mead [honey wine]...The Eistlanders brew no ale, but they have mead in plenty."

With matters of tribute and payment concluded, and sufficient mead and kumis to smooth the way, Sigurd got down to business with his host. The sagas recount the dealmaking. "You own two foreign boys whom I wish to purchase."

Reas replied, "I will sell you the older boy at a set price, but the younger one is not for sale, for he is both clever and handsome." In Odd's telling it's possible to hear the seller working his buyer like a true salesman. "I love him greatly and it would pain me that much more to lose him. I will not sell him except for a very high price."

So he was for sale after all. "Name it, and I will pay it."

A customer who has not balked at a price is a customer willing to pay more. "In fact, I love him so much that I would never sell him into slavery. But since you are perceptive in seeing his true value, I will agree to let you buy him and take him with you, though it will cost you. You must, however, give me your word that you will never sell him, and will treat him as well as I have."

"Put on him what price you will," replied Sigurd. "I will purchase him even with all the conditions you have set. I have no intention of selling him when he comes with me, for he is my kinsman."

Need, as opposed to want, from a buyer is music to a seller's ears, but Reas had to be careful not to overdo it, for a Varangian *druzhinnik* might well simply take whatever he wished from an Eistlander and be done with it. In Old Norse Sigurd was called *Karlshofud*, "Carls' Chief," leader of housecarls.* "His word was law everywhere in the prince's realm," declared Odd. "Sigurd pressed the issue all the more, and the result of all this haggling was that the older boy went for a gold mark, but the younger for nine."

That was a dear price indeed. In those days a gold mark was worth ten to twelve times a mark of silver, meaning Sigurd paid at least ten times the going rate for Thorgils, and ninety to over a hundred times for Olaf.

---

* In some modern translations of the *Heimskringla* Astrid's brothers are listed as "Sigurðr, Karlshǫfuð, Jósteinn and Þorkell *dyrðill*," as though the second is a given name and separate brother. In older translations there is no comma (which wasn't invented until the 15th century), making *karlshofud* a title or nickname like Thorkell's *dyrdill*. Punctuation is important.

Odd allowed, "Their master was, however, more sorry to lose the latter."

From coastal Eistland to Novgorod, the city of the *Knyaz* (Prince) Vladimir in Rus, is 250 miles or so east along the dividing line where the deciduous woodlands of southern Russia merge with the coniferous forests of the northern taiga, a ride of a week to ten days. Time, in the saddle and around night-lit campfires, for Olaf to become acquainted with his uncle Sigurd and his *druzhinniki* companions, to listen to their jokes and boasts, to thrill to their stories, to learn of their history and heritage, and his. To become Viking again.

Much of what we know of the Varangians in the East – the Rus – comes to us as Olaf might have learned it, from personal experience, as did the 9th- and 10th-century Arab and Persian explorers of that land: emissaries, merchants and travelers who chronicled their adventures. The Arab Muslim geographer and writer Muhammad ibn Hawqal traveled there right around this time, and recorded, "Some Rus shave their beard and others twist it, like animal manes, and plait it. They wear little tunics."

About six decades earlier the Persian explorer and geographer Ahmad ibn Rustah had also enountered the Rus, and noted, "Their clothing is clean. Their men wear gold bracelets, and treat their slaves well. They dress well because they are merchants. They have many cities."

Not all such accounts were flattering. The anonymous Persian author of the *Hudud al-Alam*, the "Boundaries of the World," written around AD 980, claimed the Rus were "ill-tempered, obstinate, arrogant, quarrelsome, and warlike. They fight with all the infidels living around them, and always win." And ibn Fadlan may have admired the Varangians' physiques, but famously also wrote, "They are the filthiest of God's creatures. They have no shame about defecating and urinating, nor do they wash after sex, nor wash their hands after eating. They are like asses who have gone astray…"

> Every day, unfailingly, they wash their faces and heads with the dirtiest, filthiest water you can imagine. A young serving girl [or in this case, probably the ex-slave boys Olaf and Thorgils] brings

breakfast every morning, along with a great washbowl of water. She offers it to her master, who cleans his hands and face in it, and his hair as well. He washes and combs his hair in the basin, and then he blows his nose and spits and does every dirty thing imaginable in the water. When he is done, the servant carries the bowl to the next man. She continues passing the bowl from one to another until she has taken it to everyone in turn, and each blows his nose and spits and washes his face and hair in this bowl.

Perhaps the Varangians' personal hygiene left something to be desired, but not their fighting ability. A hundred years earlier, their forefathers had followed the rivers down out of the north to impose their will on the locals. As ibn Rustah recorded in those days, "They raid the Slavs, sailing in ships to hunt them and capture them, then they go to the Khazars and Bulgars to sell them. They have no farms, but they eat whatever they take from the Slavic lands."

Ultimately, however, no handful of Vikings could conquer that vast land. "The Varangians' subjects drove them back beyond the sea and refused them further tribute, aiming to govern themselves," claims the 12th-century *Russian Primary Chronicle*, also called *The Tale of Bygone Years*. "There was no law. Tribe fought tribe. Anarchy reigned, and they warred against one another until they said, 'Let us seek a prince to rule over us and judge us according to law.'" And they went back to the Varangians: "Our land is great and rich, but there is no law. Come rule and reign over us."*

So, if the chronicle is to be believed (and many historians regard it as fable), the Varangian chieftains, the brothers Rurik, Truvor and Sineus – in Old Norse, Hrorek, Thorvard and Signjot, or Svein – agreed to rule the Slavs, Truvor in the north, Sineus in the west, and Rurik where the account says, "They built a city called Novgorod [New Town]." When Truvor and Sineus soon died of unknown causes, Rurik claimed the entire land as his own. The *Tale of Bygone Years* declares, "Because of these Varangians, the region of Novgorod became known as the land of Rus."

---

* An analysis of the many theories of the actual foundation of Kyivan Rus – whether Varangian, Slavic or Finno-Ugric – particularly in these contentious times, would be enough to fill a book in itself, and has.

The blood of Rurik had run in the veins of his son Ingvar, called Igor by the Rus. He had gone so far as to lay siege to Constantinople not once, but twice, with (the Varangians claimed) 10,000 ships. He might even have succeeded if not for the Byzantines' diabolical Greek fire, but in the end exacted a treaty and gifts confirming his stature as Prince of Kyiv. Little good it did him when he was caught by a subject people, the Drevlians. They had bound his feet to two bent trees and released them, ripping him in two. When Igor's widow Olga (in Norse, Helga) assumed the throne as regent for their three-year-old son Svyatoslav – and first queen of Kyivan Rus – the Drevlians demanded she marry their prince. She had their envoys buried alive in their boat, their best soldiers burned alive in a bath house, and their city of Iskorosten (modern Korosten, Ukraine) burned down upon its citizens.

And Svyatoslav, grown to manhood as the Grand Prince, took after his mother. Around AD 965 he conquered the centuries-old Khazar Khaganate, the trade empire of the Turkic Khazars, thereby gaining a stranglehold on the Silk Road and Volga trade routes feeding the Byzantine Empire. In their capital of Constantinople the Byzantines recognized the threat. Heirs to both ancient Rome and classical Greece, they were past masters at managing foreigners, as the 10th-century Saxon monk and chronicler Widukind of Corvey noted: "Whoever they could not defeat, they subdued by guile."

Instead of fighting Svyatoslav, they hired him to fight their mutual enemies. In the following years he destroyed his second empire, the Bulgarian, laying waste some eighty of its fortresses. Rather than hand the territory over to the Byzantines, however, he made his new capital at Pereyaslavets on the Danube River. That was too close for his paymasters' comfort. Not wishing to become his third conquered empire, they hired new proxies: the semi-nomadic steppe horsemen of the Pecheneg Khanate. The Pechenegs laid siege to Kyiv, home of Svyatoslav's mother Olga and his sons. Svyatoslav was distracted long enough to drive the Pechenegs back to their steppes, but it was obvious he must eventually tackle Byzantium head-on.

In the spring of 970 Svyatoslav finally attacked Constantinople directly, at the head of (it was said) 30,000 men, including Bulgarian and Pecheneg mercenaries, only to be ambushed and routed by just ten or twelve thousand Byzantines. Chastened, he withdrew to lick his wounds and, in view of his increasingly high-risk ambitions, arranged for the disposition of his empire among his sons, Yaropolk, Oleg and Vladimir. The *Primary Chronicle* reports:

> Svyatoslav gave Yaropolk Kyiv and Oleg Dereva [former domain of the Drevlians, in what is now northwest Ukraine]. Then the people of Novgorod asked for a prince of their own. "If you will not come to us," said they, "then we will choose a prince ourselves." Svyatoslav agreed that they needed a prince, but Yaropolk and Oleg both refused, so [Vladimir's maternal uncle and tutor] Dobrynya suggested that the city should be offered to Vladimir…So the people of Novgorod requested Svyatoslav to give them Vladimir as their prince, and he went to Novgorod with Dobrynya, his uncle. But Svyatoslav went back to Pereyaslavets.

The Grand Prince secured his legacy just in time. In 971 an army of thirty to forty thousand Byzantines laid siege to him in the Bulgarian fortress of Dorostolon, modern Silistra on the Danube. To curry the favor of their deities – Perun, god of the sky and war, and Veles, god of the earth, waters, cattle and underworld – the Rus sacrificed children by drowning them in the river. It did them no good, so Svyatoslav instead swore by Perun and Veles that he would make peace with Byzantium.

The Greeks knew better than to trust him. On his return home the following spring Svyatoslav was attempting to scale the Dnieper rapids by boat when he was attacked by the Pechenegs, again at the behest of Constantinople. The *Primary Chronicle* attests, "The nomads took his head, made a cup out of his skull and, overlaying it with gold, they drank from it."

It was perhaps not the worst way for a follower of Perun and Veles to spend the afterlife. It's thought the Pechenegs worshipped Tengri, a sky god, the universe personified. The Khazars were Jewish, the Arab and Persian merchants Muslim, the Byzantines Christian. It was said that in later years, despite her murderous deeds – or perhaps because of them – Svyatoslav's mother Olga had journeyed to Constantinople and been baptized, and had often urged Svyatoslav to convert.*

---

* In 1547 she was officially named a saint in the Russian Orthodox Church.

He had been resolute, though, in his worship of Perun and Veles. In 959 Olga had even dispatched emissaries to Otto I, requesting priests and a bishop for Kyiv. Soon after the clerics arrived, Svyatoslav chased them out of town, telling his mother, "How can I accept another faith? My men will laugh at me."

One can almost hear the Varangians chuckling around their campfire as they regaled Olaf with their tales. Some of them would have been about his age when all this happened, old enough to have taken part. Certainly Olaf's uncle Sigurd and these druzhinniki had ridden with Prince Svyatoslav in the old days when he conquered the Khazars and Bulgars, living on horseback like Pechenegs, surviving on strips of roasted horseflesh, sleeping on horse blankets with saddles for pillows. Probably they had been at Dorostolon, too, possibly even drowning children on the prince's orders, in the name of Perun and Veles. Theirs was a merciless world from the day they came into it. Ibn Rustah wrote of the Rus, "If a son is born to a man he presents the infant with a drawn sword, placing it in his arms and saying: 'I shall give you no fortune. You will have nothing but what you win for yourself with this sword.'"

"The Rus live on an island, surrounded by a lake that takes three days to walk around," wrote ibn Rustah of what is believed to have been Novgorod. (He almost certainly heard about it secondhand, as he is not thought to have traveled that far north.) The Varangian name for it, *Holmgard*, meant "Island Town." The modern city is not on an island, but just down the Volkhov River – on the map, up – from the shore of Lake Ilmen, "Weather Lake." Even today, however, the lake's surface area varies widely with the rainy season, from some 200 to over 800 square miles, and was perhaps a quarter larger 1,100 years ago, when the water level was much higher. Today, as then, when the lake is low the input from the Volkhov's tributaries actually overcomes its drainage and the river flows backward into the lake. The surrounding country is low-lying, waterlogged, swampy and flood prone. "It is unhealthy and dank," sniffed ibn Rustah. "If a man sets foot on the ground it squelches, it is so sodden."

Little land suitable for fields or cattle, frequent floods and resultant crop failures, lake-effect storms, hordes of mosquitos and biting flies in summer, ice floes and blizzard winds across the frozen waters in winter; one might wonder why anybody ever chose Novgorod to settle down. The answer is that Lake Ilmen was a fork in two great riverine trade routes. Both involved much rowing and poling upstream and portaging overland around rapids and between rivers, but the branch to the east eventually led to the Volga, the Caspian Sea and the Persian Empire, and the other south to Kyiv, the Dnieper, the Black Sea and the Byzantine Empire. Novgorod was a trade hub, where supply came to fill demand, and merchants from north and south met to buy and sell.

Olaf must have heard tales along the way of the greatness of this city, and perhaps, as the caravan emerged out of the endless forest into the swamps and meadows surrounding it, he was impressed. Novgorod was not built in stone, for any in that marshland soon sank from sight, but there was more than enough wood in the surrounding forests – oak, spruce, maple, birch – for any purpose. The houses, walled with tree trunks cut, split, stacked and joined with tongues and grooves, notches, mortises and tenons and sealed with moss and river clay, were raised completely by eye, without expensive nails and only with axes; chisels and saws were used only for decorative trim. Furniture was of carved wood, floors of hewn planks, roofs perhaps shingled with aspen, cedar or pine, with steep pitches to shed snow. Along the riverfront and among the cabins ran streets, not dirt tracks but actual paved streets – probably the first Olaf had ever seen – parallel rows of split logs running lengthwise down the track, and shorter ones laid over them widthwise with their flat inner sides up as paving.* It's thought Novgorod's original settlements grew up around its streets, which were laid down first as boat ramps to stabilize the riverbanks where the constant loading and unloading of cargo cut up the mud.

The truth is that Novgorod was as yet nowhere near the grandeur of 14th-century *Veliky Novgorod*, Great Newtown, capital of the Novgorod Republic and one of Europe's largest cities. Today its

---

* As the logs sank under traffic, new layers were laid over them, and would be, according to archaeological evidence, up to twenty-eight times from the 900s to the 1400s.

population of almost a quarter million spreads over thirty square miles, but in Olaf's time it wasn't yet a city, just a few separate hamlets clustered atop hillocks on either side of the Volkhov, which functioned as the main thoroughfare. The contemporary Arab geographer Muhammad ibn Ahmad al-Muqaddasi put the population at 10,000, but like ibn Rustah never actually visited it. If we combine the villages and compare them with the similar Estonian hillfort settlements with which Olaf was familiar, Novgorod was a couple of neighboring villages altogether numbering a few thousand people at most, with traveling merchants and caravans filling out the numbers.

But to Olaf, Novgorod, the New Town, would have been a great city indeed. The original town was a mile and a quarter to the south, on the shore of Lake Ilmen: *Rurikovo Gorodische*, "Rurik's Settlement," now solely the residence of his great-grandson, the Knyaz Vladimir. On arrival Sigurd would necessarily need to go pay homage, deliver his share of taxes and tribute, and make his report. But he did not intend to report everything.

"It was the law of the land that no foreign or outlander royalty could be brought there without the prince's knowledge," confided Odd. "Sigurd said nothing of Olaf's ancestry, but took him into his home in secrecy, known only to a few people, yet in good style." Olaf might have lived in Novgorod in relative luxury for the rest of his life.

The Norns had different plans.

VII

First Blood

[The Rus] spend extravagantly on themselves, and are generous to their guests and to strangers who reside with them, and to their kin, and they allow no one to wrong them or transgress against them, but aid and defend them against any who try to wrong them or transgress against them.

Ahmad ibn Rustah

AD 972

Uncle Sigurd would have found it impossible to keep a country boy like Olaf home in the big city, much less in the three (later five) separate hilltop villages, *kontsy*, that made up 10th-century Novgorod. The high ground today, on the east side of the Volkhov, is the *Slavno konets*, Slavic neighborhood, but in the 900s the high ground was on the west side, where stood two other *kontsy*, the *Nerev* (Finnish) and *Lyudi* (People, presumably everybody else). Each fronted on the town's main street, the river.

Everything in Novgorod moved by boat, even just to cross from one riverbank to the other. (The earliest reference to the city's Great Bridge over the Volkhov is in the year 1133.) Dugout boats the Slavs hewed from single trees and sold to the Rus for negotiating the downriver rapids, some equipped with masts and outriggers, could bear up to forty people or tons of cargo. From the riverside piers and quays it all made its way to or from the *Torg*, the marketplace on the east bank, where the three riverine trade routes converged and all the goods of the medieval world came to be bought and sold.

What nine-year-old boy could resist the exotic, hectic, chaotic Torg? It was the very heart of the city. There was the smell of fresh-baked breads, vegetable stews and meats cooked over open-air fires: not just beef and mutton and chicken, but also duck and goose, venison and moose, European bison, bear and wild boar. Fish, straight out of Lake Ilmen and all the rivers – sturgeon, pike, perch, bream and smelt – fresh, salted, smoked, dried. Roe and caviar. Mushrooms on strings, dried figs and lemons, salted nuts. Mead and cider, kumis and *kvass* (beer made from fermented rye bread), even for children, for to drink raw water was to invite bellyache, possibly fatal.

Meanwhile raw materials came down the Volkhov from the north: ingots of iron, copper and lead; beeswax and honey; walrus ivory and Baltic amber. Arctic pelts: sable, marten, ermine and miniver (white winter coat of the red squirrel), beaver and rabbit and black fox. Finished products arrived from the south via the Volga and Dnieper: wine and olive oil, perfumes and spices (cinnamon, nutmeg, cloves and pepper in those days being worth their weight in gold); jewelry, glass and ceramics; bolts of canvas, silk and linen, brocade and cloth-of-gold. Craftsmen worked in silver and gold, leather, copper, wood, bone. Mercenaries sought the highest bidder, or shopped the weapons marts for everything from man-high Dane axes to curved Persian scimitars, shirts of mail both chain and scale, Eastern-style recurve bows, plumed helmets, breastplates and shields all damascened, gilded, inlaid.

There were horses from all across the world – cold-blooded, big-boned Scandinavians for bearing armored men; hot-blooded Arabians, fleet and agile; ambling ponies from Shetland and Iceland, smooth-gaited, prized for long-distance travel. Cattle, sheep, goats, two-humped Bactrian camels. And slave markets – the lands of the Rus were such a rich source that the word *slave* comes from the innumerable Slavs sold into servitude – captives, war prisoners; those convicted of arson, horse theft or loan defaults, born in slavery or married into it. *Kholopy*, males, suitable for field work and heavy lifting, and *roby*, females good for household duties, child-minding, wet-nursing, nurse-maiding, or simply for the bed, all were bought and sold.

The air reverberated to the strum and pluck of *guslis*, lap-sized box harps, and *gudoks*, big three-stringed violins; the trill of birch pipes and reed flutes, the beat of tambourines. Animals braying and neighing, bleating and lowing. The clang of hammers on anvils, the crack of whips, the clink and tinkle of gold and silver changing hands, the shrill laughter of women, the carnival-barking of vendors and auctioneers. A jabber of Scandinavian, Mediterranean and Middle Eastern tongues, the haggling and wrangling and bartering and bargaining of bare-chested Varangians, robed and turbaned Persians, Greeks in long silk tunics. Merchants and mercenaries, ship captains and slave traders...

...and *there*. Klerkon, the Eistlander pirate who had murdered Olaf's foster father, Thorolf.

Among the multiple editions of Olaf's saga, there are two versions of what happened next. As it's a turning point in his life, let us hear and judge the crime and the punishment alike, perhaps by what we shall come to know of him in later life.

Both stories start the same. In Odd's words, "One day Olaf was in the marketplace, which was very crowded. There he recognized his foe, the man who six years earlier had slain his foster father in front of him and sold him into slavery."

Where they diverge is Olaf's reaction. The simpler version is, "Olaf had a small axe in his hand, and going up to Klerkon, struck him in the head with it, so hard that he cleaved Klerkon's skull down to the brain. Then he ran home and told Sigurd, his kinsman, of what he had done."

The longer version has Olaf no less vengeful, but a bit more cold-blooded. Though incensed at the sight of Klerkon, he does not kill him on the spot. Instead, displaying respect for the law – or possibly just not having an axe handy – he returns home. When Sigurd arrives, he sees his nephew is upset and inquires why. Olaf replies, "Considering the grief and deep shame that man has caused me, I wish to avenge my foster father."

Sigurd agrees to help. As ibn Rustah noted of the Varangians, "If some are provoked they all go out as one, becoming as one hand against the enemy until they are victorious." He and his men follow Olaf back to the market. What follows is perhaps even more chilling for not being an impulsive, but a premeditated, killing.

When Olaf points out Klerkon, Sigurd's men seize him and hold him down. They give Olaf a long-handled Dane axe. The boy raises it up and brings it down, taking off the Eistlander's head. "At this time Olaf was nine years old," wrote Odd. "This was considered a great deed for such a young man."*

In Novgorod, however, murder was a capital crime. Enraged citizens soon gathered to capture the killer and carry out the sentence. Sigurd, realizing Olaf could expect no mercy from the mob, resolved to seek it from his patrons. He hustled the boy down the *Slavnaia* street that ran from the Torg over a mile along the east bank of the Volkhov to Rurikovo Gorodische.

It stood on high ground, such as there was in that vast marshland, a small island – undoubtedly the one to which ibn Rustah had referred some seventy years earlier, before the New Town even existed. The lakefront and surrounding rivulets and tributaries formed a natural moat, as al-Muqaddasi described the island: "It is their fortress against whoever attacks them." Over the intervening centuries the site has been partially washed away by flooding, and nothing remains of any hillfort.† The surest indication that the Gorodische was once fortified is its name; an unfortified village was a *selo* or *ves*; *gorod* or *grad* refers to walls and fortifications. A drawbridge, probably, led inside a wooden stockade, certainly, which protected the usual stables, workshops, troop barracks and the great hall where flew the *tryzub*, the trident flag of the Rurikid Dynasty, the residence of Prince Vladimir and his *Knyaginya* (Princess) Olava.

The prince was not in residence, but Berg wrote, "Right away Sigurd took him to the princess's quarters, told her what had happened, and begged her to help him."

---

* Again, the *Agrip* has him three years older, but no matter which version is to be believed, they all involve a boy, an axe and murder.
† The ruins of brick and stone on the modern island are of the Cathedral of the Annunciation, built in 1103 and reconstructed in the 14th century.

FIRST BLOOD

By her name Olava – the female version of Olaf, though in Greek rendered as Allogia – was even more purely Scandinavian than her Rus husband.* Vladimir was, after all, half-Slav, the result of a tryst between his father Svyatoslav and his grandmother Olga's housemaid, Malusha. The old woman was still alive, and furthermore said to have the gift of prophesy. Vladimir had a custom at Yuletide (as shall be seen, a pagan festival before it became a Christian one) of having her brought to his throne room and asking her whether she foresaw any threats to his rule. A few years earlier Malusha had answered that she saw no ill fortune in store for him or his realm but – at least, according to Olaf's sagas – at the same time had beheld a wondrous vision:

> In the north, in Norway, a king's son was recently born who will be raised in this land, and become a distinguished man and a glorious leader. He will do no harm to your realm, indeed he will restore to it peace and freedom, increasing your glory many times. When at last he is grown to manhood he will return to his native land and gain the kingdom which is his by birth. As king he will shine with bright glory and become a savior to many men of the northern regions.

Olava had long expected this unknown Norwegian's arrival. Hearing Sigurd's story, she gave Olaf a second look. He wore a hooded cloak, but she was not fooled. Odd wrote, "She looked him in the eyes and knew right away that he was the one in the prophesy."

She told Sigurd, "It will not do to put such a fine boy to death."

But the crowd had discovered Olaf was at the Gorodische, and that the knyaginya was sheltering him. With the mob approaching, she ordered her personal guard to don their armor and take up arms. The matter looked certain to come to bloodshed when her husband, the Prince of Novgorod, arrived.

---

* Based on scant references in old chronicles, some historians suggest she was a daughter of the Swedish king Eirik the Victorious, others that her name is a corruption of Olga, the prince's grandmother, though she, as stated, is thought to have died by this time.

No physical description of Vladimir survives, but we might assume he resembled his father, who was described by a Byzantine Greek a few years earlier: broad-shouldered, bull-necked, medium tall, with bushy brows, blue eyes and a snub nose; head and beard shaved, but with a long moustache and lock of hair on one side in the Turkic manner, signifying the nobility of his clan. An earring in one ear, a clean white tunic.

To read the sagas one envisions Vladimir as a middle-aged king, bearded and imperious, because writing centuries later and knowing no better, that's how the chroniclers had him in mind. Vladimir, however, as yet probably lacked much of a moustache; he was in fact only about five years older than Olaf, still in his early teens, and Olava was probably even younger. (Some historians even assert Vladimir was two years younger than Olaf, but this is another of those occasions we need to look at events rather than dates.) Yet for all his youth, Vladimir's was the blood of Rurik. His authority did not come from age and experience, but by the decree of his late father Svyatoslav, grandmother Olga, his uncle Dobrynya and, of course, his karlshofud Sigurd and his *druzhina*, armed, armored and ready to shed whatever blood their prince felt needed shedding.

His very presence put an end to the disturbance. All waited while he heard both sides before passing judgment.

For her part, Olava spoke firmly on behalf of Olaf. Odd wrote, "She led him before the king and revealed to everyone that the one she had long sought had been found."

The Slavs had their own system of popular assembly, like a Viking thing, that predated the Rus, called the *veche* and headed up by their *posadnik*, the mayor. Ibn Rustah recorded, "They have elders who rule over their kings like gods...If the elders pass judgment they cannot oppose it. Then the elder takes the guilty man or beast and ties a rope around his neck and hangs him on a wooden post until death, saying, 'This is a sacrifice for the gods.'"

The fact that the current posadnik was Vladimir's uncle, Dobrynya, probably made the veche more likely to accept the prince's verdict, but it was not certain. Even as prince, Vladimir was obliged to respect their wishes. Nobody could forget they had expelled the Varangians once already. Novgorodian justice was little different than that of the Vikings: an eye for an eye. Even though he was only nine years old, Olaf had murdered; therefore, he deserved a sentence of death.

Yet there was another way.

The *Russkaya Pravda*, Rus Justice, was a legal code not set down in writing until the 12th century, but is thought to document unwritten laws dating at least from the beginning of the 11th, in fact to settle a dispute between Dobrynya's son Konstantin, then posadnik, and the Varangians in the city. It abolished blood vengeance in favor of what the Scandinavians called *weregild*, and the Rus *virevnaya*: bloodwite, blood money. It dictated the worth of a man's life in terms of *grivny*, about equal to a mark: seven or eight ounces of silver, or the equivalent value in *kuny*, marten pelts, of about a hundred, or up to 600 *vekshi*, squirrel pelts. Not all lives were considered of equal value. Compensation for the murder of a male slave was five grivny; for a female, six. Craftsmen rated twelve, but an *ognishchanin*, a servant of the prince, up to eighty.

Odd wrote, "[Vladimir] ordered a truce, settling the terms of resolution, fixing the price to be paid for the death of Klerkon."

The blood price for a *liudin*, an ordinary free man, was forty grivny: seventeen and a half pounds of silver, or 4,000 marten furs, or 24,000 squirrel pelts. (One wonders if there were enough martens and squirrels in all the Torg to make such a payment.) Olaf didn't have that kind of money, and not even Sigurd had such a payment at hand.

Princess Olava did.

Thus was the matter settled. Klerkon's friends or relatives received compensation for their loss, and were obliged to be happy with it. If they resorted to blood vengeance thereafter, the guilt would be theirs. Olaf was free to go.

His secret, though, was out. Sigurd decided he owed it to Olava to reveal the truth. He told her the secret of Olaf's ancestry, and that he had come to Rus to escape his enemies, and asked her to intercede for him with the prince. This Olava did, gladly. With Sigurd backing up his nephew's story and Olava on his side, Vladimir had little choice but to relax his rule about visiting royalty. (Sigurd was, after all, the Karlshofud, the chief of carls. His opinion must have carried weight.) He took Olaf in as a welcome visitor, treating him as a fellow royal.

The citizens of Novgorod had thought they had been dealing with a vagabond street rat, not a lad of royal blood. Such personages were due more leeway than commoners. All was forgiven. Berg wrote, "After this Olaf remained with the Queen, beloved by her, and favored by all the people."

VIII

The Battle of the Danevirke

That spring the generous king of Denmark desired to test the warrior from the north, as the king required him to defend the rampart against the enemy.

Einar Helgason

AD 972–974

Again, to know Olaf Tryggvason the man, it is necessary to keep up with faraway events while he was still a boy, and the villains of his saga.

Having more than doubled the size of his kingdom with the addition of Norway, King Harald Bluetooth of Denmark that year aspired to expand it a little more, this time to the south. Back in 934 the King of East Francia, Henry "the Fowler," had pushed his borders north of the Eider River into the isthmus of Schleswig, traditional Danish territory. "Henry attacked and defeated the Danes because they had raided the Frisians [modern Netherlanders]," explained Widukind. "After forcing the Danes to pay tribute, Henry had their king, Knuba, baptized."

This weakling Knuba (given in various sources as Chnuba or Gnupa), had soon been overthrown by Bluetooth's father Gorm and grandfather Harthacnut – the founders of Bluetooth's line – but, as Adam of Bremen wrote of Henry, "Then he invaded Denmark with an army and so thoroughly defeated King Gorm that the latter pledged his fealty and sought peace as a vassal. The victorious Henry then set the border at Schleswig, which is now called Hedeby, appointed a margrave [*mark graf*, count of the marches], and ordered a colony of Saxons settled there."*

Henry may have accomplished both victories in one campaign. Forty years later it still rankled Bluetooth that the southern Christ-worshippers laid claim to land and title that rightfully belonged to sons of Odin.† The longer he delayed his vengeance, however, the stronger the Christians became.

Meanwhile Bluetooth's vassal, Jarl Hakon of Norway, ruled despite the efforts of his archfoe Gunnhild Mother of Kings. She, with her surviving sons, now plagued Norway from their new base in the Orkneys. The *Agrip* tells us, "Early in his reign Hakon was opposed by Gunnhild Konungamodir, and they often traded vicious ruses, for neither was lacking in trickery."

Hakon had realized the best way to stop Gunnhild's sons was to stop their mother from goading them on, and the best way to do that was to enlist her former host Bluetooth. He was still on good terms with the Dane, and asked him to send her an offer of marriage (rather overturning the theory that she was Bluetooth's sister; foster-sister, perhaps), an old queen with an old king, and she agreed.

Bluetooth had sent a wagon and an escort to meet the queen on landing and transport her in luxury to his hall, an all-day trip. In the evening the procession passed a bog. According to one account, what happened next is perhaps all the more horrific for the fact that the original manuscript is partially illegible and garbled. One can almost hear the struggle: "They grabbed Gunnhild, dragged her out of the wagon and acted rather…large [to the neck]…[to her head, cast] then out into the swamp where they drowned her, and so she died, and that has since been called *Gunnhildarmyr* [Gunnhild's Marsh]."

On news of her death, Bluetooth remarked, "Now she is honored as I intended."‡

---

* These Saxons were not from modern Saxony or Saxony-Anhalt, in southeast Germany, but from Lower Saxony (lower in the sense of being downstream) between the Ems, Eider and Elbe rivers, on the Danish border.

† Widukind had it that Bluetooth himself converted to Christianity sometime in the 950s or 960s but, judging by future events, that was the Dane paying lip service to Otto I to avoid further invasions.

‡ Astute readers may note that the date of Gunnhild's murder is sometimes given as later than this, AD 977, but that is without historical basis. The primary sources do not give a date and, as shall be seen, by that time Bluetooth had no reason to help Jarl Hakon.

When in 973 Holy Roman Emperor Otto I died, the imperial crown passing to his son Otto II, not yet twenty, Bluetooth saw his opportunity. Having twice aided devious Hakon in his ambitions, he now called in his marker, informing the jarl of his plans against the Christians. One saga relates, "Jarl Hakon quickly answered the summons, believing it an outrage for Danes and other northern peoples to be forced into Christianity rather than keep to the rituals and beliefs of their ancestors."

One would think the Danes and other northern peoples would be relieved to give up their pagan ways. The early 11th-century Prince-Bishop Thietmar of Merseburg recorded:

> Because I have heard breathtaking things about their sacrificial rites, I will not leave them unmentioned. In those parts, the capital of the kingdom is called Leire, in the region of Seeland [modern Lejre, on the island of Zealand]. Every nine years, in January, after the day when we celebrate the appearance of the Lord [January 6th], they all gather there and offer their gods an offering of ninety-nine people and an equal number of horses, along with dogs and roosters, the last being used in place of hawks. As I have said, they believed that these would serve them with those who dwell under the earth, and ensure absolution for any sins.

In defense of his gods, Hakon is said to have assembled over a hundred warships packed with fighting men. His skald, Einar Helgason, may have made the trip with him, and composed a drapa in part about it. Stripping away the obscure imagery, allegories and metaphors that make Viking skaldic poetry almost indecipherable to the uninitiated, he wrote, "So it was that the valiant warrior's ships ran south towards Denmark. And the ruler of Hordaland, the lord of the Norwegians, wearing the dragon helmet, to rendezvous with the Danish king."*

---

* Or, to quote Einar a little more exactly, "It so happened that the draft-animals of the sand-plank ran southward under the successful victory-tree toward Denmark. And the lord of the Hordar, the ruler of the Dofrar, wearing the helmet of the island-fetter [i.e., the dragon Fafnir] sought a meeting with the Danish king." It probably loses something in translation.

As late as Easter of 973, Bluetooth's envoys were among those from the far-flung parts of the realm appearing before Otto I to assure him of their loyalty and deliver the customary tribute. Just a month later, though, Otto I was dead. Otto II's attitude toward pagan Denmark was well known. One Christmastide he had sworn to go to Denmark three summers in a row as necessary and, if he could, convert the entire country to Christianity.

On August 13 Otto II was at Memlaben in Saxony when he learned that almost 250 miles away Bluetooth and Jarl Hakon had erupted out of the north. Whether this was a raid for plunder or a serious attempt at conquest is not certain. As Adam of Bremen reported: "Determined on war, they had murdered Otto's legates and the margrave at Hedeby and had utterly exterminated the entire colony of Saxons."

Otto, however, had something the Vikings never had: an imperial army. His father and grandfather had reassembled the shards of the Carolingian Empire on the backs of its soldiery, and the army was the means by which they held it. According to the *Heimskringla*, he ordered Bluetooth to accept baptism and the Christian God, and his subjects with him. Otherwise Otto would bring his army to make him. (Writing from the Scandinavian viewpoint, Snorri cast Otto as the villain, provoking the war, but in doing so also demonstrated that no one really believed Bluetooth's professed Christianity.) By the beginning of September the empire was ready to make good on the threat. The imperial troops included Saxons, Franks, Frisians and even Wends from northern Poland, the cavalry greatly outnumbered by foot soldiers.

Some 325 years earlier – and according to recent archaeology, perhaps 475 years earlier – back before the Scandinavians were the terrors of the North and still feared the Franks, Frisians and Saxons to their south – the Danes had begun work on a defensive line to wall off their peninsula from invasion. (Though the archaeology suggests they may have started by capturing and enlarging works begun by the Frisians to keep them out.) These *Danavirki*, the Danevirke, "Danish Works," ran the length of the vital road from the port town of Hedeby in the east, where the Schlei River cut in from the Baltic Sea, halfway across the isthmus to the Treene River, a tributary of the Eider, which runs to the North Sea in the west. From one river to the other was about nineteen miles, a shortcut compared with sailing up around Jutland to deliver goods, risking pirate attack all the way.

Over the centuries, in four phases (and after this period, two more), the Danes fortified the south side of the road with a layered defense of earthen ramparts comprising millions of stones weighing up to 220 pounds and wood palisades composed of some 30,000 oak trees, ten feet high and fronted by moats ten feet deep and thirteen feet wide. After Henry the Fowler's invasion Bluetooth himself had undertaken the fourth phase. He raised the ramparts from thirty to fifty feet, and the palisade in places to fifteen feet, with bastions every hundred feet, and had the moat carved out to fifty feet deep and sixty wide. Finally, he connected the wall to the semicircular rampart protecting Hedeby. The Danevirke required an estimated 1.4 million man-hours to build, a kind of Viking Hadrian's Wall, a defensive line that made Denmark a walled fortress. The two main supply routes, the *Haervejen* or Army Road coming down from the north and the east-west Danevirke Road running just behind the wall, crossed right behind the only way through: a single gate, referred to in Frankish imperial annals as *Wiglesdor* and by the Danes as *Viglidsdor* or *Karlegat*, the Warrior's Door, Carl's Gate.* Nor were the Vikings totally without military organization. Some sources have it that after Bluetooth's father Gorm's defeat by Otto I, when his mother Queen Thyra had begun building up the Danevirke, she assigned the defense of its western half to the Scanians (from what is now southernmost Sweden), its eastern half to Danes from the islands of Funen and Zealand, and resupply and provisioning to the Danes from mainland Jutland. According to the *Heimskringla*, defense of the Warrior's Gate itself fell to Jarl Hakon and his Norwegians.

Otto's army, both infantry and cavalry, well trained, well supplied and highly motivated by monetary reward in addition to the opportunity for plunder, arrived on battlefields nourished both physically and spiritually, convinced of the justness of their cause.

---

* In 2010, about two and a half miles west of Hedeby where the Army Road crosses the Danevirke, archaeologists uncovered the Warrior's Gate: almost twenty feet wide, complete with wagon tracks, and the remains of a customs station, inn and bordello.

Theirs, after all, was not just the empire of Rome reborn. It was literally the Holy Roman Empire, and theirs was a kind of proto-crusade. It was their practice, prior to battle, to fast and pray, to have their confessions heard and penances assigned, to celebrate the mass and holy communion, to sing psalms and the *Kyrie eleison*.

The pagans behind the Danevirke were apparently unimpressed with such ritual. Thietmar lamented, "During this campaign, shouts of evil mockery were for the first time directed at the clergy."

That, of course, would only have served the imperial leaders in whipping up their troops into even greater religious fervor. Otto's officers were educated, literate, well versed in military handbooks handed down to them from the original Roman Empire, and experienced in war – actually, more experienced than their young emperor. Imperial strategy consisted largely of sieges against fortified cities, including some of the largest of the day: Paris, Prague, even Rome. Their engineers knew well how to employ siege machinery: rams, ballistae (spear launchers, giant crossbows) and trebuchets (catapults, stone throwers), even siege towers. Not that much of that would prove effective against the Danevirke. It was a defensive line, not an enclosed city that could be surrounded, isolated, cut off and starved to death.

Few hard details of the Battle of the Danevirke exist, but then there would have been little in the way of clever tactics or maneuver. The only way to breach such an unflankable river-to-river defense was to go straight at it, but neither cavalry nor siege machinery could cross those ditches, moats and ramparts. Even imperial foot soldiers would be required to approach under a *testudo*, the old Roman "tortoise" formation, a mobile infantry square with a roof of upraised shields overhead, under fire from bowmen and slingers atop the wall and catapults behind it, lugging scaling ladders while their own archers, slingers, ballistae and trebuchet crews did their best to keep the defenders' heads down. Crossing the ditches and moats on improvised rafts or bridges built on site, they would then need to climb the ramparts, raise the ladders and scale the palisades while holding their swords, spears and shields, and being showered with more arrows, rocks, and boiling and flaming oil, and – if they were very, very lucky – survive to reach the top of the palisade, only for defenders to spear them as they clambered over.

Little wonder, then, that little is said of assaults on the walls. The imperials likely did not put much effort into it. The key objective was the Warrior's Gate, where the Army Road itself breached the wall. Here, at least, the imperials could employ an *arietes*, a battering ram.

More than just a tree trunk on wheels, a well-built ram came complete with overhead protection, a wooden framework sheathed in layers of fire-retardant felt, leather and sand to shelter the crew as they rolled the ram back and forth. Now the battle became one of repeated pounding on the gate, while the defenders tossed burning oil in clay pots (unfired, so as to shatter on impact on the ram's housing), and once the layers of cloth and leather burned off, stones to bounce away the inflammable sand, then more oil to light the leatherbound framework itself and hopefully the men laboring below. If that didn't get to them, a layer of oil on the road surface leading to the gate could be ignited to burn them from underneath. And a blazing ram and crew withdrawn back into the attacking ranks would disrupt their formation almost as well as an attack, thereby actually inviting one.

Hakon's skald Einar reported, "It was not easy to go against their army, although the commander of the battle fence made a hard attack...The seafarer called for battle." By some interpretations, this implies Jarl Hakon and his Norwegians opened the Warrior's Gate and came charging out to meet the imperials on open ground.

In defense Vikings employed the *skjaldborg*, a wall of overlapping shields impervious to cavalry, from behind which they could strike with spear and sword and axe, or at the very least literally push opponents off the battlefield. In offense they used the *svynfylking*, the "boar's snout," a wedge formation intended to focus all its momentum on one point in a shield wall. Said to have been devised by Odin, it was more likely handed down via the Germanic *schweinskopf*, "swine's head," from the old Roman flying wedge, the *caput porcinum*, the "boar's head." Imperial infantry, on the other hand, generally employed the phalanx, a square of men bristling with spears, dating back to Alexander the Great. A wedge was effective against a line of defenders, but not so much against a square; even if successful in breaking its front ranks, on driving deeper the wedge would be enveloped, swallowed up. The Battle of the Danevirke, whether assault versus wall or boar's snout meeting phalanx, was a matter of irresistible force meeting immovable object.

"The noise of battle rose where the warriors set their shields together," penned Einar. "The eagle-feeder [Jarl Hakon] grew aggressive. The attacking commander of the ships drove the Saxons to flight, where the king with his men defended the palisade against the troops."

Both sides, however – all sides in medieval warfare – also employed the *ruse de guerre*, the feigned retreat. This tactic, dated at least as far back as Hannibal's destruction of eight Roman legions at Cannae in 216 BC, was well known to attackers and defenders alike, yet surprisingly common, and effective. After a day of fighting and bleeding, of binding cuts and stab wounds, of armor rent and bones broken, of choking on smoke from burning oil, the coppery tang of blood, the stench of opened guts and the roasted-pork aroma of burnt human flesh – of seeing friends die and barely making it through alive oneself – the urge to simply finish it, get it all over with, give chase and destroy a fleeing enemy, was nearly overpowering. The trick was to bait the trap well enough for the enemy to bite, break formation and give chase, at which point the infantry or cavalry on the flanks could sweep around, envelop and annihilate them.

If they employed feigned retreat before the Danevirke, however, the imperials apparently did not do it convincingly enough. Jarl Hakon's Norwegians withdrew once again behind the Warrior's Gate and closed it. Time spent on rebuilding a ram could also be spent on strengthening the gate. All that could ensue was more irresistible force meeting immovable object, coming to nothing. By some accounts the battle lasted three days, at the end of which Otto rode down to the shore with a gilded, bloody spear and stabbed the sea three times, swearing, "When next I come to Denmark I shall either succeed in making Denmark Christian, or else die here."

The Battle of the Danevirke was a tactical draw. For Otto II in his first big combat, however, it was a strategic victory. The invading Danes had been taught a lesson, driven back whence they came. Yet the emperor could not afford the luxury of wars far from home. In the south his cousin, Duke Henry II of Bavaria, was already cooking up a rebellion. Otto was forced to hurry home and deal with it, which took the better part of a year.

THE BATTLE OF THE DANEVIRKE

But he was not yet finished with the Vikings.

In August of 974 the imperial army returned to the Warrior's Gate, this time catching Bluetooth unprepared and all alone. Jarl Hakon, having survived his close call in front of the Warrior's Gate and made good on his feudal service to his liege, was not interested in defeating the entire Holy Roman Empire. If he left Norway undefended too long, somebody (namely, Gunnhild's remaining vengeful sons) might swoop in and take it from him.

And the Warrior's Gate was not impervious – after all, Otto's grandfather Henry the Fowler had defeated it back in 934.* It seems more likely that the emperor once again aimed to go around the wall, this time successfully. The *Heimskringla* claims, "Otto returned with his army to Schleswig, collected warships and transported his army across the fjord there to Jutland."

With the Danevirke outflanked, Bluetooth was forced to withdraw into the Danish heartland. He called once again on his devious jarl, but Hakon drove a hard bargain for his continued service, namely the abrogation of any further tribute from Norway to Denmark.

"It is true," grumbled Bluetooth, "that you outwit everyone with cleverness and schemes, and I now have two difficult choices, neither of which appeals to me."

"Choose wisely," advised Hakon, "but it seems to me that Norwegian tribute will be of little use to you if you die here in Denmark."

In this the king submitted to the jarl, but in open battle not even the combined might of the Vikings could withstand Otto. Crossing what had been the frontier at Schleswig, the emperor put the land to fire and the sword, right up to the Skaggerak, which the imperials afterward called *Ottensond*, "Otto's Sound".

Bluetooth took refuge on the island of Mors in Limfjord, the shallow inlet that cuts upper Jutland in two. Otto sent mediators to arrange a truce and meeting. Thoroughly beaten and forced, like his father and grandfather before him, to bend the knee to the empire, Bluetooth underwent one final humiliation. Otto ordered him to

---

* Some of Olaf Tryggvason's sagas credit him, grown to manhood, with defeating the Danevirke on Otto's behalf by rolling barrels full of blazing tinder up against the gate to burn a way through, but then they also credit him with having come via Ireland, on which he would not set foot for years to come.

undergo baptism, and furthermore to swear to have his wife, son and all Denmark do the same.

The son, Svein, was, like Jarl Hakon's sons, about Olaf Tryggvason's age, but may not have been born of Bluetooth's wife. According to some accounts he too was a bastard son of a Wendish girl, whom Bluetooth did not acknowledge as his and left to be fostered in a Viking colony there. In any case, as Snorri heard it, Emperor Otto became godfather to Svein and gave him his own name, baptizing him as Otto Svein. When Otto went back to Saxony he and Bluetooth were said to have parted as friends. (Though Thietmar pointed out, "The emperor raised a fort on this border [Hedeby] and stocked it with a garrison.")

To alleviate his shame, and since Norway was still part of his domain, Bluetooth sent for Jarl Hakon, ordering him and his men to undergo baptism and providing him with priests to take north to baptize all of Norway as well.

The jarl did not react well to this. He'd had quite enough of Denmark and was longing for home. He returned to his ships and, as soon as there was a favorable wind, had Bluetooth's priests put overboard. He raised sail into the Oresund, the strait that separates Denmark from Sweden, raiding and burning and slaughtering on both banks, then doing the same down the Scanian coast and up the Gautish. His rage somewhat slaked, he finally put ashore and conducted a great pagan sacrifice. Two ravens appeared, screeching loudly, convincing him that Odin had accepted the sacrifice and it would be a good time to fight. He burned all his ships and crossed overland with his troops, ravaging everywhere until he came home to Norway.

Another saga confirms, "Jarl Hakon threw off faith and baptism to become the greatest apostate and heathen worshipper, never performing more sacrifice than he did then."

He was now Norway's sole ruler, and ceased paying tribute to Bluetooth. But Berg wrote, "Afterward he was a worse man in every way, and more of a pagan than before his baptism."

THE BATTLE OF THE DANEVIRKE

The Battle of the Danevirke was to affect Olaf's life even though, despite the sagas' claims, he was far from it and had played no part. He was still a boy, still in Novgorod, when Jarl Hakon took over his father Tryggvi's kingdom in Norway. The Norns, laying out the threads of their lives, would have foretold that their lines would tangle in due time.

Before then, Olaf the boy needed to become Olaf the man.

IX

Warrior

*Prince Vladimir loved Olaf as though he was his own son,
and ordered him instructed in the use of arms and military exercises,
as well as etiquette and princely behavior.
Olaf was quicker than anyone to learn every accomplishment.*

Berg Sokkason

AD 972–978

Olaf had already demonstrated his ability with an axe, but now that his identity was out in the open his uncle Sigurd, and Vladimir's uncle Dobrynya, could instruct him in its proper use: how not only to shear off heads, but limbs, and to use the *oxarhyrnur*, the points of the blade, to stab, or to hook an opponent's shield out of the way, or pull his ankle out and trip him, or to yank his neck down for a killing blow. To parry with the blade, to use the shaft to block, sweep or punch. And that would have been only the beginning. There was the shield – how to hold it at an angle to deflect a blow, rather than stop and absorb it, and how to use its rim as a weapon. How to throw, thrust and fence with the spear, the weapon of Odin. Then the sword, that highest expression of medieval metallurgy, the very symbol of manhood – vertical, diagonal, horizontal cuts; how to parry and riposte. (Swordsmen in the Icelandic sagas overwhelmingly favored the cut; troops of the Holy Roman Empire, fighting in close formations, were taught to stab, to avoid hitting their own men in the swing.) Archery practice, too, with the longer European bow and short Asian recurve; how to fire from horseback and how, when the pull weight was a hundred pounds or more, to draw the string with the thumb (using a ring to protect it) instead of the weaker fingertips.

Days on Lake Ilmen learning mastery of boats, the ways of sail, wind and water; how to read the clouds, how to tack into the breeze, how to use a steering board to guide the ship (the stern-mounted rudder had not yet arrived in the North), how to ride rapids on the Volkhov and portage a boat around them. The marshes and waterways around Novgorod were rife with ducks and geese to be taken by arrow or falcon, and fish to be taken with arrow or trident.

In that age when man was not far distant from his hunter-gatherer forebears, part of becoming a man was taking game with horse, hound and spear, not only for pleasure but to test and prove oneself. The forests of Rus were veritably left over from the Ice Age, abounding with aurochs – giant cattle, now extinct, the bulls standing six feet at the shoulder – European bison, brown bear and wild boar. To kill any of them was an accomplishment for a grown man, let alone an aspiring warrior like Olaf.

Finally, how to command. Strategy, tactics. When and how to deploy the *skjaldborg*, the shield wall, and the *svynfylking*, the boar's snout. How to deal with nomadic, light steppe-rider cavalry and fully mail-clad Byzantine heavy cavalry. How to keep men calm and confident while facing a shower of arrows or a horse-borne charge, or attacking an impervious shield wall. How to capture a city, whether by surprise or by siege. How to live on horseback like a Pecheneg, as had the old prince Svyatoslav (and presumably Sigurd with him) when they conquered the Khazars and Bulgars. How, until one grew to become a fierce Viking warrior, to be the kind of leader such warriors would follow. Odd wrote:

> The king and queen raised Olaf with love and attention, giving him many advantages as though he was their own son. He grew up in Rus, gifted with strength and intelligence. He matured as well as aged, so that very soon he was far ahead of his contemporaries in all ways that befit an exceptional leader...In a short time he had learned everything of nobility and military skill, equal to the boldest and most courageous in those fields.

At his foster father's side Olaf learned how to be a prince. He and Vladimir certainly shared a kind of spiritual kinship, both of royal blood, both having at a young age lost their fathers to violence. The knyaz was probably still learning princely ways himself, as taught by his uncle Dobrynya, with Olaf privy to the lessons. An education befitting a nobleman did not necessarily include math or literacy – reading, writing and calculating were for clerics and scholars – but it required the teaching of command, governance and good judgment, of when to work with Novgorod's veche and posadnik and when to overrule them, of when to employ diplomacy in dealings with the neighboring Pechenegs, Finns and Baltic tribes, and when to make war on them; of negotiating with merchants, ambassadors of the all-powerful Byzantine Empire, and their Christian priests.

The Varangians might still worship their gods, Odin, Thor and the rest, but the Rus had adopted the deities of their Slavic subjects, which if anything were just as savage. As knyaz, Vladimir's duties were more secular than religious, but he took the gods seriously. At Peryn, the island across the river from Gorodische (today a peninsula except during the spring floods), stood the idol of Perun, god of thunder, lightning and war, the chief of the Slavic pantheon: a tree trunk carved in his likeness, like a totem pole, to which the Novgorodians sacrificed oxen and sometimes, it was said, their own children.* Red-bearded and silver-haired was Perun, with a golden moustache, a bow that shot lightning bolts, and an axe. (The Rus wore axe amulets the way the Nordics wore Thor's hammer.) His idol stood in the middle of a circle with four great bonfires at its edges in the four cardinal directions, and four more between them. The easternmost was kept hottest, but each of the eight could serve as an altar to a different aspect of Perun, of which there were no fewer than nine (his idol being the ninth): the sky, thunder, justice, fertility, war, agriculture, mountains and oak trees, the supreme god.

---

* Historians caution that most of what we know of Slavic religion comes to us via the Christian monks who chronicled it. They were biased against pagan faiths and took every opportunity to disparage them. That said, mention of Slavic child sacrifice comes up repeatedly in the *Primary Chronicle*, sometimes in great detail, and there is archaeological evidence – child skulls found among ritual items – supporting the idea that child sacrifice was practiced among pagan Slavs.

Yet it appears that, unlike Vladimir, after all he had been through – or as written by the Christian monk Berg three and a half centuries later – Olaf had little faith in pagan ritual. "There was one thing about him of which the king disapproved, and only one: He would not bow down to pagan gods, and he was firmly against all sacrifice."

He would accompany Vladimir and Olava to Peryn, but not set foot inside the temple. The knyaz feared that this invited the gods' wrath. According to the sagas, Olaf replied:

> I do not fear those gods you worship, for they cannot hear, or see, or speak. They have no will or intelligence. I see what they are because your regal state and appearance, my foster-father, is always pleasant and optimistic, except when you enter the temple to sacrifice to the gods. Then you appear dark and evil to me. By that I know that those gods you serve rule over darkness, and so I will never worship them. Still, I do them no dishonor, because I have no wish to offend you.

Given that they were writing centuries later, they could only have heard of this conversation (if it ever happened) as passed down over the generations, and probably in some part made it up, this passage is one of the monks' best characterizations in all of Olaf's saga. It shows the young warrior not as a mere pagan, but as a nascent religious thinker, a Christian in the making. Yet it also foreshadows good Prince Vladimir's dark side.

Even a good king needs a brutal streak to rule. Good kings do not let brutality rule them.

To the south Vladimir's elder half-brothers, Yaropolk in Kyiv and Oleg in Vruchiy, modern Ovruch in Ukraine, had managed so far to get along.[*]

---

[*] Little is known of their mother, Predslava, who is thought by historians to have been variously the daughter of a Hungarian prince, a Kyivan boyar or Pecheneg khan. After she attempted to have her rival, Vladimir's mother, the Slav serving girl Malusha, murdered, Svyatoslav is said to have banished her. Her sons were raised by her mother-in-law, Olga of Kyiv.

Yet it had been their father Svyatoslav's mistake, when doling out their princedoms, to put the elder brothers so close together. From Novgorod to Kyiv is some 550 miles, even farther if following the winding river route. From Kyiv to Vruchiy was less than a hundred: too little neutral ground between the brothers.

In the year 977 Oleg caught one of Yaropolk's *druzhinniki* poaching on his land, and killed him for it. No Rus knyaz could be seen to brook such an affront. Goaded on by his men, the next year Yaropolk sought retribution, invading Oleg's principality of Dereva. Their armies met outside Vruchiy. Oleg's was defeated. He and his surviving men, in their panicked attempt to get back inside the city, became jammed on the bridge over the surrounding moat. Men and horses went over the side. When Yaropolk took the city, he ordered his brother found, and when the moat was cleared Oleg lay among the dead.

It does not seem that Yaropolk intended his brother's death, and indeed regretted it, but who else was there to rule Vruchiy or the rest of Dereva? Yaropolk claimed Oleg's goods and property and *druzhinniki* and declared his lands to be under new ownership, to be ruled from Kyiv.

All those 500-odd miles to the north, Yaroslav could only look on this news with trepidation. Vladimir had committed no transgressions against Yaropolk, but perhaps no transgression was required. If Yaropolk treated his own brother thus, how would he treat a half-brother, a half-breed son of a Slav serving wench? Three brothers, three realms, could maintain a balance of power; any aggressive one had to face the other two. But now Yaropolk could bring the fighting men of both Kyiv and Dereva against Novgorod.

Perhaps Vladimir feared a religious crusade, for Yaropolk was said to be interested in Christianity. Like their grandmother Olga in 959, at Easter of 973 he had sent emissaries to the court of then-Emperor Otto II (the same assembly Harald Bluetooth's tributaries attended prior to his rebellion). And Yaropolk had a Greek wife, a former nun, awarded him by his father Svyatoslav as the spoils of war after the capture of some Byzantine abbey, and though her name is lost she evidently had some influence over his religion. In 977 his court in Kyiv had been visited by legates of Pope Benedict VII, whom Otto had installed in Rome; both pope and emperor might have wished for the Rus to serve as a counterweight against the Byzantines. The timing of Yaropolk's conquest of Dereva suggests the murder of his *druzhinnik* may have been the excuse he needed to bully his pagan brother Oleg into the faith. But when word came that Yaropolk was indeed on his way north, Vladimir had a choice to make.

His *druzhina* did not have a chance of standing against Yaropolk's combined armies. He and his men might hold out inside the Gorodische, but for how long, and to what point? Yaropolk could simply wait them out, with his army living off the goods of the Torg until the inevitable surrender. Despite its *gorod* name, Novgorod itself was still just a cluster of villages, not yet a walled town.* In the event of attack some of the citizenry would seek protection in the Gorodische, but the majority would flee into the countryside, or simply surrender. Yaropolk would not wish to kill them, nor destroy the town. As a trading center on the Volga route (Kyiv being on the Dnieper route), it was too valuable. His desire was to own it, to claim its tribute and profits for himself. Whether, in his view, that would require killing Vladimir, only Yaropolk knew.

Vladimir could not wait to find out. He had a family to think of, and not just his "foster son" Olaf; in 977 Olava had given birth to a boy, Vysheslav. If Yaropolk killed his last brother, he might well kill his brother's family, too. The only thing that seemed certain was that once he arrived, Novgorod would be his. Vladimir would have to live with that, or die of it.

The rest of the family, Princess Olava, Uncle Dobrynya, Olaf and even Sigurd, could offer their input, but to the knyaz went the final decision. There's no denying that it could have been simple fear that drove it. No man knows how he will react to imminent death until the moment is upon him, and Vladimir was still untested himself. The *Primary Chronicle* admits, "When Vladimir heard that Yaropolk had slain Oleg, he became afraid, and fled abroad.

---

* The modern kremlin, on the west side of the river across from the Torg, was not raised until the 1490s, over the foundation of a castle built in 1116, on the site of a wooden fortress built in 1044, as an enlargement of a bishop's palace dating to circa 990. Before that, nothing.

Yaropolk then sent his emissaries to Novgorod, and so became the sole ruler in Rus."

This chapter in the lives of both young princes, Olaf and Vladimir, is for the most part an undocumented, somewhat confused mystery. The authors of the *Primary Chronicle* had little knowledge of Vladimir's movements while he was out of the country, and for them Olaf the teenaged foreigner was beneath notice. For their part Odd Snorrason and the Icelandic chroniclers who came after him knew only in general of events in faraway Rus, and do not even seem to be aware that Olaf and Vladimir ever left Novgorod. Odd simply admitted of Olaf, "He accomplished many deeds in Rus and all across the East, even though little of it is reported here."

Most historians take the *Chronicle*'s assertion that Vladimir "fled abroad" to mean Scandinavia, and some theorize that he sought refuge and aid in the courts of supposed kinsmen. This kinship can exist only in the general sense, in that Vladimir's ancestry had Viking roots. It's very likely that his great-grandfather Rurik had left some family on the far side of the Baltic before coming to rule Novgorod. However, as Rurik is himself semi-mythical, for Rus tradition to have preserved some ancestral lineage running from Vladimir up the line to his great-grandfather and then back down to Vikings on the far side of the Baltic seems tenuous at best, and there's no solid evidence to establish any direct kinship. Probably the closest we can get is that *if* we accept the premise some historians assert (but can't prove either), that Vladimir's consort Olava was not a Bohemian princess as stated in the *Primary Chronicle*, but actually a daughter of Sweden's king Eirik the Victorious, then everything else follows.

Logically, then, Sweden would have been Vladimir's first stop. By this time, the late 970s, King Eirik would soon, or perhaps already had, moved from Uppsala to his new base of operations at Sigtuna, nearer the mouth of the fjord, with easier access via ship or ice-sledge. Its name is thought to derive from the Old Norse word for "victory," but perhaps simply "swampy place" – in those days the water level was sixteen feet higher than today. The settlement was a cluster of large half-timber halls facing the shore, with a population of some

750 or so, but in those days that was a town of note. DNA analysis of burial remains from gravesites north of town have revealed that most of its menfolk were Swedish, but most of the women were from across the Viking world: England, Iceland, Estonia, Rus, the Balkans and Mediterranean, likely imported as wives, concubines and/or slaves. Yet the manner of their burial suggests that Sigtuna was a Christian town, one of the very first in Sweden, possibly founded as an alternative to ghastly human sacrifices conducted up the fjord at pagan Uppsala. Adam of Bremen recorded:

> It is customary to celebrate in Uppsala, every nine years, a general feast for all the provinces of Sweden. All must attend. Kings and subjects, all bring gifts to Uppsala and, what is more worrying than any kind of chastisement, those who are Christian redeem themselves in these ceremonies. They sacrifice by offering nine heads of every living thing that is male, the blood of which is used to appease their gods. The bodies they hang in the holy grove beside the temple. This grove is so sacred to the heathen that each and every tree in it is believed divine, thanks to the death or rotting of the victims. Even dogs and horses hang there aside men. A Christian told me that he had seen seventy-two bodies hung in dedication. Furthermore, the customary incantations chanted in the sacrificial rituals are many and shocking, so it is better to keep quiet about them.

Nor in Viking-Age Sweden were such sacrifices, called *blot*, limited to Uppsala. In the far south, at Trelleborg, a sacrificial well dating from about this period has been found to contain the bodies of five people, four of which were boys aged four to seven. The Swedes were among the last of the Vikings to turn Christian.

Vladimir, having doubtless overseen or even conducted a few human sacrifices himself, had long since proven his tolerance for other religions – Jewish Khazars, Muslim Persian and Arab tradesmen, Christian Byzantines. He would not have cared whom the Vikings worshipped, as long as they were willing to fight for him. The boat trip of a week or two from Novgorod down the Volkhov to Lake Ladoga and west through the Gulf of Finland and the Baltic (probably accompanied by a small fleet of heavily armed Rus longships, enough to dissuade any Eistlander pirates from molesting them) would have given the knyaz time to regain his nerve and – aided by Sigurd, Dobrynya and Olaf – to lay plans. He had abandoned his throne in Novgorod because he did not have an army big enough to keep it. He intended to go back with one large enough to regain it.

King Eirik of Sweden had to this point not won the nickname "the Victorious," but he would undoubtedly have seen the advantage of aiding Vladimir to regain his realm, in exchange for silver, gold or concessions of territory across the Baltic in Eistland. He would also have been only too happy to contribute surplus fighting men, particularly Christians from Sigtuna objecting to pagan sacrifices, rather than have them start a religious crusade at home. And his young queen Aud, daughter of Jarl Hakon of Norway, would have provided Vladimir with another familial link to further assistance. Whether Hakon was coincidentally visiting his father-in-law's court at the time, or Vladimir and his party sailed around southern Scandinavia to Norway, is immaterial; Hakon's name comes up as one of the Viking "kinsmen" from whom Vladimir sought help.

"Exceedingly cruel," wrote Adam of Bremen, "of the sons of Ivar and descended from a race of giants, this Hakon was the first Norwegian to seize a throne where before chiefs had ruled."* Despite his break with Harald Bluetooth, Hakon had retained control as Jarl of Norway. (As he was not of royal blood, he continued to go by his father's title, even though he ruled as a king; as Berg put it, "Jarl Hakon had sixteen jarls under him.") Cruel he may have been, stupid he was not; he neither attempted to extend his realm against that of his former patron, nor to make amends. At one point newly Christianized Bluetooth had mounted something of a crusade against his pagan, rebel jarl, but despite some initial success against helpless farmers in

---

* The Ivar mentioned is either Ivar *Vidfamne* (the "Wide-Fathoming," wide-traveled; died c. AD 700) or Ivar *hinn Beinlausi* ("the Boneless," died c. AD 873). The Boneless founded an empire in Ireland and England, more of which later; the Wide-Fathoming's daughter, Aud *in Djupudga* ("the Deep-Minded"), married Radbard, a king of Gardariki, which might provide a tenuous basis for Hakon's kinship with Vladimir of Novgorod.

southern Norway, he soon found that Hakon had unified his people much better than Harald Greycloak and the sons of Gunnhild ever had, fielding a larger army than Bluetooth's. Forced to turn back, the Dane gave up his Norwegian ambitions. He and Hakon settled down to an uneasy truce. According to the 13th-century *Jomsviking Saga* (much more of which later), "Hakon now resides quietly in the land and rules all Norway himself and never pays tribute to King Harald Gormsson. Their friendship is much on the wane."

The jarl had thoroughly recanted Christianity. The monk Theodoric accused, "As soon as he secured control of the kingdom, Hakon soon became infamous as a slave of demons, constantly making sacrifices to call upon them for aid," and the *Fagrskinna* agrees: "Powerful Hakon began to conduct sacrifices more brutally than ever."

Whatever he was doing seems to have worked, for his jarldom thrived. Under the reign of the Christian Harald Greycloak and his brothers, the people of Halogaland had starved, but according to the *Fagrskinna*, under Hakon, "The seasons rapidly became more promising, grain and fish became plentiful again, the earth bloomed." And Snorri attested, "While Jarl Hakon ruled Norway, there were good harvests and peace among the farmers of the land. The jarl was popular with the farmers for most of his life."

He was a fervent disciple of Thorgerd Holgabrud, "Holgi's Bride," described variously as a Nordic giantess, troll or ogress, or an incarnation of the old Vanir goddess Freyja; she was said to have a sister, Irpa, an earth goddess who might simply have represented another aspect of her. Thorgerd may, however, have originated as an actual person, a foremother or family matron of the Haleygjar family, up in far-northern Halogaland.* Over generations she had been elevated into a *fylgja*, a guardian spirit, and by the time of the Haleygjars' descendant Jarl Hakon, much more than that. Hakon put all his faith in her, prostrating himself before her idol in a small woodland chapel complete with a picket fence and gilded and silvered carvings lit through glass skylights (which surely reflects more on the author's Christian faith than the jarl's). She was his *fulltrui*, his

---

* Saxo Grammaticus told the story of how Helgi, once king of Halogaland, wooed the Finnish princess Thora. Helgi could well be Holgi, and Thora Thorgerd, even though in another saga he is her father; incest was taboo among Vikings, but not among Viking gods.

"god-friend," but much more than a friend; Hakon was said to have called her Thorgerd Shine-Bride, and to be her *bondi*, her husband. She did not require him to be celibate. Thorgerd was both warrior goddess and a fertility goddess, and in her honor, besides taking lives on the battlefield, Hakon also took virginities. He would have nearly a dozen known children, less than half of them by his long-suffering wife Thora. Berg sniffed, "Jarl Hakon was of such immoral conduct with women that he considered them all equally at his disposal – mothers, daughters, sisters, highborn maidens or wives."

His promiscuity, however, gave rise to yet more problems. As with old Harald Fairhair and his multitude of wives and sons, both Bluetooth and Hakon suffered the kind of fatherhood issues only medieval fathers could suffer. Their eldest sons, Hakon's Eirik and Bluetooth's Svein, both around the same age as Olaf and Vladimir, were both said to have been born of low women, rejected by their fathers, and fostered by other men, each retaliating in their own way.

Of Hakon's Eirik Odd wrote, "Eirik was a bastard, both like and unlike his father, alike in his wit and warlike qualities but not in appearance or character. He was kind and generous with advice and very determined to keep peace between the nobles and the commoners. He was even-tempered except with his enemies, toward whom he was fierce and resolute." At the age of ten or eleven, feeling himself belittled by his sister's husband, his father's best friend, Eirik had acquired a ship, gathered a crew of housecarls, caught and killed his foe in battle – an act that would be lauded by his skalds – then fled to Denmark and the court of Bluetooth, who awarded him a jarldom in what is now southern Norway for his trouble. The *Fagrskinna* records, "Afterwards Jarl Hakon and Jarl Eirik detested each other."

Meanwhile Bluetooth's bastard Svein, likewise raised by a foster father on the neighboring island of Fyn, modern Funen, was even more troublesome. One anonymous chronicler of the family later admitted, "Even as a boy everyone loved him except his own father. It was not the boy's fault, but because of envy. As he grew to manhood, the people loved him all the more, and so his father's envy grew as well, so that he openly desired to banish him, swearing that he would not rule after him."

Svein went so far as to go to his father's court and demand recognition, only to be bluntly rebuffed. Bluetooth told him, "You are unequalled in boldness, daring to come see me. You are both a Viking and a marauder, one of the worst men in everything you do. Do not expect me to acknowledge you as my son, for I know for certain that you are no kin of mine." Svein handled rejection about as well as Eirik, and in the same way: by gathering ships and men to harry his father's Danish domain.

Grown to manhood, both Eirik Hakonarson and Svein Haraldsson would bedevil Olaf Tryggvason much the way they did their fathers. There is even a chance that he met them, fellow princes in exile, at the Swedish court as he and Vladimir shopped for troops, but if so, judging by the sagas, rather than support a prince of the Rus both Eirik and Svein preferred to pursue their own thrones at home.

And if Jarl Hakon met with Vladimir in the course of his recruiting, he probably met with Olaf too, but if he connected the teenaged boy to the three-year-old Gunnhild had sent him to murder in Sweden all those years earlier, he would have considered it of little consequence. Gunnhild was herself murdered, and even as the son of a petty Norwegian king Olaf presented no threat to the jarl, particularly if he was off fighting for a foreign prince in Rus – all the more reason for Hakon to see both him and Vladimir on their way.

By most accounts Vladimir lived in Scandinavian exile for a year, possibly two. Hard years, for one accustomed to rule rather than begging for scraps from foreigners and hearing their whispering behind his back that he had fled his home rather than face his brother in battle. Yet time enough, too, for his own Varangian heritage to come to the fore, to remember that his grandmother Olga had burned and buried her enemies alive, that his father Svyatoslav had conquered the Khazars and Bulgars and very nearly the Greeks of Byzantium, and that no man born of the Rus earned his fortune except by the sword. And for Olaf, too, it was a reminder that he was not just a Viking, but a prince.

As more and more Vikings were lured by Vladimir's promises of women, loot and glory in *Gardariki*, the Land of Cities – in Novgorod, Kyiv and perhaps even fabled *Miklagard*, Constantinople – Olaf made good on his years of training. According to Odd, he told Vladimir,

"Give me command of troops and ships so that I can try to retake your lost territory. I am eager to make war and do battle against those who have disgraced you. With luck, it may turn out that I will either kill them or drive them into retreat."

Odd attested, "Vladimir soon promoted him to command of his retinue and to lead the warriors who were charged to regain his honor."

We should no more scoff at the idea of a youth leading medieval warriors into war than at the pre-teen boy who slew his first man with an axe. Viking crews, Rus crews, would have had no problem serving under a young prince. In those days men simply assumed that, unless proven otherwise, even children of nobility were worthy of obeisance, or at least symbolic of their cause. Such sons were born and raised to command, and sons of lesser men to follow. Berg attested, "It was customary among the Vikings to regard kings' sons who commanded an expedition as king, even if they ruled no lands. Thus Olaf's company titled him King."

X

Conquest of the Rus

Vladimir and his Varangian allies returned to Novgorod, and instructed Yaropolk's emissaries to return and tell him that Vladimir was coming, prepared to fight.

Russian Primary Chronicle

AD 978

From the Gulf of Finland, up the Neva River to Lake Ladoga in Russia, then south up the Volkhov River to Novgorod was close to 800 miles. And those last legs were all upstream, either by sail, by poling or horse-drawn towing, or by portage – beaching and unloading the boat, then carrying the goods and dragging the hull around the obstacles. Slow, laborious work. In 1996, as an attempt at archaeology by experiment, the Swedish "Holmgard Expedition" launched a reconstructed Viking ship, the *Aifur*, from Sigtuna on Lake Malar in Sweden, bound for Novgorod. The trip required almost two weeks.

A later Russian chronicle credits Vladimir with raising 70,000 troops. An exaggeration, surely; a tenth of that would have been a respectable medieval army. One source alludes to 200 ships, and a few thousand men is possible, but hundreds is more likely. Even that many men, coming that slowly, would surely have alerted the Novgorod garrison of their approach, but as it happened that did not matter. Yaropolk did not personally rule his New City, but had left it in the hands of some druzhinniki, who were no more inclined to fight and die for it than Vladimir had been. The former prince landed his fleet on the banks of the Volkhov and the shores of Lake Ilmen and marched into the Gorodische unopposed. Yaropolk's men were doubtless relieved when the prince did not kill them but sent them on ahead to warn his brother, as was honorable – as their father Svyatoslav had notified his enemies – that he intended to make war on him.

So Vladimir's banner flew once again over Novgorod. Whether his Viking mercenaries were happy to see it is debatable, as they reaped none of the promised glory or loot, and probably few of the women. They would not have long to wait, though. It's perhaps indicative of Vladimir's lingering self-doubt that however many men he had, he wanted more. He needed allies. And if fresh blood was spilled at the feet of the idol of Perun, or a few small children drowned in the Volkhov in thanks to the Slavic gods, that was just a taste of things to come.

About halfway down the river route from Novgorod to Kyiv and perhaps a hundred miles off to the west, in what is now northern Belarus, was the land of the *Krivichi*, the "Blood Relatives" of the Rus. Nearly two dozen rivers ran through their domain. Their capital, Polotesku, modern Polotsk, rose where the Polota River (thought to derive from the Slavic word *polot*, swamp or marsh) flowed into the Daugava (Western Dvina) River. As the Daugava flows not east toward the Novgorod–Kyiv route, but westward into the Gulf of Riga, it made Polotsk something of a strategic crossroads for boat traffic. It is said in the *Bygone Days* to have been founded in AD 862, around the same time as Novgorod, but archaeologists have uncovered Arab dirham coins there dating from no later than 818.

In the 970s the knyaz of Polotsk was Rogvolod. As the *Bygone Days* claims he was from "overseas," and his name bears semblance to the Scandinavian Rognvald, we can be certain he was Varangian, perhaps a son of a minor branch – a *krivich* – of the ever-prolific Rurikids. As has been shown, though, kinship mattered less to the sons of Rurik than matters of lust and blood vengeance. Rogvolod had two sons and a daughter, Rogneda – Ragnheld – whose beauty, as with so many such women in medieval times, would cause her misery.

"At this time," confides the *Bygone Days*, "it was intended that Rogneda would marry Yaropolk." Vladimir had other plans.

An alliance, fighting men, a new trophy wife, and spite for his brother made Polotsk irresistible to him. He proceeded diplomatically, however, sending his uncle Dobrynya as an envoy to propose marriage. As a knyaz and a father, Rognvald was equally diplomatic, passing the question on to his daughter: "Do you wish to marry Vladimir?"

Rogneda, alas, had not learned diplomacy: "I will not pull the boots off a son of a slave.* I desire Yaropolk."

Not unreasonable, considering that Yaropolk had already driven off his brother once and remained the Grand Prince of Kyivan Rus. Still, the *Chronicle of Vladimir-Suzdal*, a continuation of the *Primary Chronicle* written in the early 13th century, claims, "Dobrynya grew angered and filled with fury." He swallowed his pride, however, and dutifully reported back to Novgorod with this insult to the prince, his mother and their entire family. If Vladimir's standing among his warriors was already dubious, then such a slight, unanswered, would be his downfall; no self-respecting warrior would follow him. An example would need to be made of Polotsk.

As Novgorod was divided by the Volkhov River, so was Polotsk by the Daugava. The outer suburb or *Sloboda* – the modern Slobodskoy *posad* (neighborhood) of Polotsk – lay on the south bank of the river. On the north bank, where the Polota joined the main stream, stood the craftsmen's district, the *Zapolotye*, modern Zapolotsky posad, and on the headland above that the *Verkhny Zamok*, the "Upper Castle," the residence of Rogvolod and his insolent daughter.

Unlike Vladimir, Rogvolod had no intention of abandoning his home, nor even of trying to hold out against a siege. He assembled his army and led them out onto the surrounding plain to wager all on one battle. Of course, Olaf gets no notice in the Russian chronicles, but according to Odd, "It was confirmed, as already written, that he was bold in all courtly and military matters. He deployed his troops as sensibly as though it had always been his calling."

Against Vladimir's alliance, apparently including even some of Rogvolod's own people, he was outnumbered and defeated. The continuation of the *Primary Chronicle* says simply, "Rogvolod fled into the fortress."

---

* To do so for her husband was part of a bride's role in medieval Russian weddings.

The *Verkhny Zamok* was a typical hillfort of the age: moat, rampart and timber palisade, accessible only over a bridge. Whether the easy way (by surprise, before the gates could be shut), or the hard way (over the walls against a shower of arrows, spears and rocks), Vladimir's forces fought their way inside. Whatever his talents, Olaf would have found combat very different from sparring with his uncle in the courtyard of the Gorodische, or even axe-murdering Klerkon in the Torg. This was war. Kill or be killed, sending men to their deaths and personally cutting a few to pieces. Friends dying amid screams of pain and rage, innards spilling, red flesh gaping and blades dripping hot blood. Olaf did not shy from it. Berg wrote, "Though he was a youth, his skill as a commander of troops showed right away, for he slew some chiefs and drove others away, who through injustice and violence had aspired to King Vladimir's tributary lands."

Both of Rogvolod's sons were slain. The knyaz, his wife and daughter were captured. The *Primary Chronicle* reduces all this to a line or two, but the *Chronicle of Vladimir-Suzdal* goes into more, perhaps fervid, detail over Rogvolod: "Dobrynya insulted him and his daughter, calling her a slave's daughter, and ordered Vladimir to be with her in front of her father and mother."

"Be with her" means, of course, to have sex with – in this case, rape – Rogneda, in front of her parents. Which, according to the tale, Vladimir did. But that's not all. "Then he slew her father and took her as his wife, calling her by the name Gorislava."*

Brutal, yes, and modern readers are right to be appalled. But our tale has already had child brides and child murder, and even assuming the story is the warped fantasy of some celibate monk centuries later, readers of that age would have found it readily believable, even justifiable. If Olaf, as a high-ranking soldier in Vladimir's army, stood as witness, he would not have been shocked or even surprised. The parental audience was an imaginative touch, and the idea of marrying the girl afterward probably struck him as foolish, but otherwise she was simply a trophy, her virtue a victor's right. Rogneda – Gorislava – surely wasn't the only daughter raped in Polotsk that night, nor her

---

* That new name was rubbing salt in the wound. In Slavic *Gorislava* means "mountain glory." Vladimir was commemorating the taking of her father's hillfort. Every time she was called by that name Gorislava would remember how she got it. She was literally a trophy wife.

father and brothers the only men to die. What happened to them had been the way of war – the way of the world – for thousands of years, and has changed little in the centuries since.* After what he did, Vladimir could just as easily have murdered Rogneda as well, out of sheer spite. He did not, nor did he kill her mother.

And that, in their cruel medieval world, was mercy.

Rapine and looting in Polotsk perhaps filled the coin purses of Vladimir's Viking followers, slaked their lust, and convinced them they were following a worthwhile leader, but it would have not much impressed Yaropolk. He was 350 miles away, in Kyiv.

Like Novgorod, the "City of Kyi" (its semi-mythical 6th-century founder) was as yet nowhere near its Golden Age of the following century, let alone later glory as today's capital of Ukraine, the seventh-most populous city in Europe. There was as yet no mosaic- and fresco-filled cathedral of St. Sophia, no golden-domed monastery of St. Michael, no Golden Gate modeled on that of Constantinople. Archaeological analysis of the Podol, the original town where the Lybid and Pochaina rivers enter the Dnieper, indicates there was a cluster of thatch-roofed log cabins on the floodplain, none built before the 880s. That was right around the time the first Varangians arrived, took what had probably been no more than a Khazar ferry crossing and seasonal trading post, and began building it into the "mother of the towns of Kyivan Rus." By the late 10th century its population was climbing toward 15,000 or more, by far the biggest city Olaf had ever seen. Yet, like Novgorod, the Podol was a collection of hamlets and neighborhoods with no all-encompassing city wall, wide open to attack. Fishermen, farmers and craftsmen would have mounted no real defense, and unlike Polotsk – but as with Novgorod, and much to his Varangians' annoyance – Vladimir's goal here was not to destroy Kyiv but preserve it intact, for his own use.

---

* Lest we consider ourselves above all this, we should remember that in the course of the Second World War almost one in every two people in Polotsk, over 30,000, were killed, and that was just a fraction of the 500,000 to 800,000 murdered in Belarus – not in combat, not gassed in concentration camps, but simply lined up and shot, part of the "Holocaust by Bullets."

Similarly, when the prince, Olaf and their army arrived, the stronghold atop the pine-shrouded, 300-foot bluff above the Podol was not yet the *Verkhny Gorod* (Upper Town), the imposing fortress of a half-century later, with earthen ramparts two miles around, fifty feet high and twice as thick, and a palisade of whitewashed oak enclosing a 250-acre palace complex. No, despite all their accomplishments Svyatoslav and his mother Princess Olga had ruled their Kyiv from a modest 250-acre hillfort on the northwest corner of the plateau, overlooking the Podol below. The surrounding ditch and palisade are thought to have protected a central wooden tower raised on a bed of unworked stones.

Those defenses, however, were imposing enough to give Vladimir pause. By his attack on Polotsk he had given Yaropolk plenty of indication that his threat was serious, and plenty of time to secure his fort against a siege. The steep bluff above the Podol was unscalable, the ditch and rampart impregnable.

There was another way, however. Vladimir halted his army just to the west of the fortress where a ravine cut through the plateau, to await developments.*

Yaropolk had a general who went by the moniker Blud, which sounds rather straight out of sword-and-sorcery fantasy fiction, but in Russian translates as debauchery, lechery or, perhaps in his case, treachery. Vladimir contrived to send this Blud a message: "Be my friend. If I kill my brother, I will consider you my father, and honor you greatly. I did not begin this fight with my brother, he did, and I was overcome by fear, but now have returned to the fight."

To this Blud agreed. He managed to convince Yaropolk that there was indeed treachery afoot, but by his own subjects, who were conspiring to surrender, overthrow him and deliver him to Vladimir. Yaropolk found this believable. Perhaps he had not been a benevolent ruler, or his flirtation with Christianity really had turned his subjects against him. At any rate, he lost his nerve, abandoned Kyiv and his

---

* As further proof that modern man is every bit as cruel and violent as his medieval forebears, this ravine, later known as Babyn Yar ("Old Woman's Gully"), was also the site of a World War II massacre. In one 24-hour period on September 29–30, 1941, some 33,700 Jews were shot and buried in a mass grave there, and during the Nazi occupation some 100,000–150,000 Ukrainians, Russians, Gypsies, criminals and other "undesirables" exterminated there on top of them.

army, and fled. As they had at Novgorod, his men threw open the fortress gate and welcomed their new knyaz.

Vladimir pursued Yaropolk some seventy miles down the Dnieper to Rodnya, where the Ros River entered the main flow. The town was no better prepared than Novgorod or Kyiv for attack.* Vladimir, however, simply camped his army outside and waited. Rodnya's provisions soon ran low. Famine set in. Though Yaropolk's other commanders pleaded with him to escape again to the Pechenegs and raise an army, Blud now convinced him that he could not defeat Vladimir. Yaropolk agreed to surrender. He was brought to meet his brother in their father's hall atop the hill in Kyiv. According to the *Bygone Days*, "So Yaropolk appeared before Vladimir, and when he came through the door, two Varangians stabbed him in the chest with their swords. Meanwhile Blud bolted the doors and would not allow his men to enter. Thus was Yaropolk slain."

If we accept that he had achieved high posting in Vladimir's druzhina, there's a good chance that Olaf was one of the Varangian assassins – the other being Sigurd? – who put Yaropolk to death. Again, the *Bygone Days* never mentions him by name, but Berg gave him practically all the credit for Vladimir's return: "He fought numerous battles, and was ever victorious, during his first summer winning back all the kingdoms and tributary lands which King Vladimir had lost."

---

* Rodnya no longer exists, having been destroyed by the invading Mongols in the 1240s and never rebuilt.

XI

Prima Signatio

*Olaf spent his summer leading raids, defending by his skill and toughness
the realm of Garda from the attacks of the raiders,
and bringing many towns and districts on the Baltic coast
under Prince Vladimir's rule.*

Berg Sokkason

AD 978–982

"Olaf fought several battles, and luck was with him," reports the *Heimskringla*. "He retained numerous men-at-arms at his own expense from the money the prince paid him. Olaf was generous to his men, and so very popular."

Here the Icelandic chroniclers, knowing little of Olaf's actual doings in Rus, speak of him in only the most general terms. (As shall be seen, some of them took the opportunity to fill in the blanks.) He was now about twenty, a *voivode*, a commander, one of the closest advisors of the knyaz. Ibn Fadlan, who had met the Volga Rus in the 920s, described the prince's voivode as "a viceroy who leads his armies, attacks his enemies, and represents him before his people."

Olaf's was the right, as had been his uncle Sigurd's, to collect taxes from, and administer justice to, the far-flung portions of the realm that Vladimir delegated to him. (That Berg made reference to Olaf's ventures on the Baltic coast, where Sigurd found him, might indicate that Olaf had inherited his uncle's rank and domains. The sagas have no more to say about Sigurd for some time; perhaps he stayed closer to his prince's side.) "In the autumn he returned victorious with splendid booty," wrote Odd. "He had much treasure, gold and precious fabrics and stones for the prince and princess, winning him renewed honor. All welcomed him with the greatest pleasure."

Not all of Olaf's fellow Varangians were in his service, however, and those who had to depend on Vladimir for their income were not happy. The prince's conquest had been for the most part bloodless. Unlike as at Polotsk, they had not had to fight their way into Kyiv and Rodnya, and the prince had not permitted the destruction of what were now his cities. Plundering hapless steppe riders was not filling their hands with coin. They were feeling cheated. According to the *Bygone Days*, they told Vladimir in Kyiv, "We took this city, and it belongs to us. For that reason we demand tribute from it, two grivny per man."

The prince replied that he would need a month to collect the necessary kuny, marten pelts. (Recall that one *grivna* was equal to about a hundred kuny; the Varangians were demanding 200 pelts per man.) To this they agreed, but when a month passed and payment was not forthcoming, they'd had enough. They'd heard tales of fabled Constantinople – to the Rus, *Tsargrad*, the City of Caesar. To the Varangians it was *Miklagard*, the Big City, and in their imaginations practically *Asgard*, the City of the Gods. Having come this far, they wished to go the rest of the way, and sell their swords to the Greeks.

Vladimir bade them go. He was now the Grand Prince, ruler of all Kyivan Rus from Lake Ladoga in the north to the Black Sea in the south, the Baltic in the west to the eastern steppe. He had no need of grumbling ruffians looking for trouble and, if they could not find it, all too willing to make it. The *Bygone Days* attests, "He then chose the wisest, best and bravest of them, assigning them cities, while the rest left for Tsargrad in Greece."

But he sent word ahead of them to the Byzantine emperor, Basil II: "Varangians are coming to your city. Do not keep many of them within, for they will cause you harm as they have caused here. Scatter them, then, to various places, and do not let any return."[*]

One would think Olaf was among the good, wise and brave men Vladimir retained in his service. Yet this is the most logical point at

---

[*] Although Scandinavians had been serving as mercenaries in the empire's armies for a hundred years, the fabled Varangian Guard would not be instituted until 988.

which to tell one of the more debatable, yet important, chapters in his life.

It begins with Olaf's dream of climbing (depending on which version of the story) a great rock or stone pillar, up through the clouds to find himself in a sweet-smelling, flowery meadow, among men garbed in white. For all he knows he has arrived in Folkvang, the goddess Freyja's "field of the host," where that half of those slain in battle who did not attain Valhalla dwelt after death. A voice from on high praises him for having never worshipped heathen gods, but decrees that he is not yet worthy of heaven. He is ordered to go to Greece, where the truth will be made known to him, "for God has chosen you to convert many people." On his way back down to earth Olaf has a vision of hell. Not the Scandinavian Hel, the frozen underworld where those who failed to die a heroic death spent eternity, but the fiery Christian hell, in which Olaf recognizes the souls of heathen friends, including Vladimir and Queen Olava, writhing in torment.

As evidence of the sagas' monkish authorship, historians point out the similarities of the story to that of Jacob's Ladder in the Book of Genesis, or the Acts of the Apostles in which the spirit of Jesus appears to Saul of Tarsus on the road to Damascus. All three men are sinners, Jacob having deceived his father to gain his brother's birthright, Saul a zealous Roman prosecutor of Christians, and Olaf a murderous pagan Viking. But Jacob goes on to become the father of the Israelites, Saul changes his name to become the apostle Paul and write half the books of the New Testament. And Olaf?

Olaf goes to Greece.

Again, many historians dismiss this supposed visit to Byzantium, but mainly because for his own reasons Odd tells it years later in the saga, inserting an all-too-improbable and redundant loop in the story arc, requiring our hero to double back, all the way from his later adventures in Scandinavia, down through Kyiv again, to visit Constantinople. Even Snorri ignored the tale completely and left it out of the *Heimskringla*.

And yet...

As a critical part of Olaf's saga, the trip is worth examination rather than complete disregard. We have seen already that Odd was susceptible to error, deliberate or otherwise, in his dating, moving the Battle of the Danevirke from AD 973 to 988 in order to have Olaf old enough to attend the fighting. It's generally agreed that Vladimir sent official emissaries to Tsargrad within a few years of this. If we accept that, as stated in the *Bygone Days* (itself notorious when it comes to dates), many Varangians elected at this time to go on ahead to Constantinople, and that this was as close as Olaf ever got to it, then there's no reason he might not have taken the opportunity to join them and see fabled New Rome for himself. Odd most likely mistook, or contrived, his sequence of events to make him one of the later Rus ambassadors, when Olaf was actually part of the earlier, expatriate Varangian fighting force. In either case, Olaf would quite believably have beheld the grandeur of Tsargrad much as they did.

At this time already some 650 years old, Constantinople – where Europe from the west, Asia from the east, the Black Sea from the north and the Mediterranean from the south all came together – was the crossroads of the ancient world, the largest city on earth. Despite recurrent earthquakes, sieges and plagues, which in the 8th century had reduced the population to perhaps just 25,000, by the end of the 10th century it was working its way back up to its peak of some half a million people from all over the medieval world – larger than Kyiv, and Novgorod, and Polotsk, and every other city Olaf had ever known, all put together, several times over and with room to spare: a breathtaking vision of marble palaces, spires and church domes rising atop seven hills (the same as the original Rome), shimmering in the distance like a city of dreams. For a visitor from the cold, barren North it would have been like traveling in time, to the glory of classical Rome or some fantastic realm of the future.

Its defensive walls were not of wood and earth like those of the Rus, but of limestone and brick, double-layered, up to twenty feet thick, forty feet high and thirteen miles around. Within, homes too were built of brick and stone, with courtyards and metal roofs, mosaics and frescos (though often right next to squalid multi-story tenements, another feature unknown in Rus). There were hospitals and pharmacies, inns and taverns, city services – nightwatchmen and firefighters. Firewood and drinking water were available for sale, deliverable right to the front door. (The 600-year-old Aqueduct of Valens fed the city fresh water from springs over 260 miles away.) There were cisterns and wells aplenty, and forty public baths – the people bathed all the time! The city craftsmen did not labor at petty necessities like those of the Rus, but in luxuries: fabrics and glass, perfumes and furniture, goldwork and artwork and books – so many books, there were public libraries full of them. And (a complete novelty to a Viking), actual schools, with boys educated to the age of fourteen, girls to twelve. Up to half the citizens could read and write! Truly the god of the Greeks was all-powerful, in that his children were so blessed.

The city streets were paved, really paved, with stone. Going up the main boulevard, the *Mese*, the Middle Street – twenty-five yards across, colonnaded and lined with icons and statuary, shops and forums – one arrived at the crest of First Hill, on the heights above the glittering seaway, the Bosporus. There stood the *Milion*, the great marble gate from which all distances in the empire were measured, and through it the *Augustaion*, the Great Square, 250 feet across and 200 wide. In its center stood the Column of Justinian, over 435 years old and 225 feet high, top-heavy with a bronze statue of that emperor on horseback, his outstretched hand pointing to the east. That way was the meeting place of the Byzantine *Synkletos*, the Senate (which Olaf would have understood as a Greek version of a Viking thing or Rus veche). Southeast was the Chalke Gate, the Bronze Gate, entryway to the emperor's walled palace complex. Southwest, the Hippodrome, the chariot-racing stadium, with a track 500 yards around and fifty yards wide and seating for 100,000 spectators. Northeast, the Patriarcheion, the palace of the city's church patriarch, the high priest of Byzantium. And to the north, what the Varangians called *Egisif*: the Hagia Sophia, the Church of God's Holy Wisdom.

Almost four and a half centuries old when Olaf would have seen it, the Hagia was the world's largest cathedral, and would remain so for near another five and a half centuries. In those days its exterior was still clad in gleaming stucco and white marble with gilded details, blinding in the sunlight. The 6th-century Byzantine scholar and historian Procopius of Caesarea, writing around the time of its construction, declared: "It soars to such height as to reach the sky, and as though surging up from among the lesser buildings it looks down on the rest of the city, beautifying it because it is part of it, but...at the same time towers above it so high that the whole city is viewed from there as from a watch-tower."

Olaf – who, it was said, had never set foot in a pagan temple – evidently felt compelled to enter within. (Although Odd does not mention the Hagia Sophia by name – in faraway Iceland, he may not have known it – as shall be seen, it's where Rus emissaries were introduced to God.) "Whenever one enters this church to pray," wrote Procopius, "it is immediately understood that it is not by any human power or skill, but by God's hand that this edifice has been raised. Thus the mind is lifted up toward God and exalted, certain he cannot be far, but dwells with love in this place which he has chosen."

When crowds were attending services, all the Hagia's entrances were open to worshippers, but in quieter times visitors entered through an apse flanked with mosaics of the Archangel Michael, commander of the heavenly host, and Gabriel, the guardian of Israel. Gabriel, on the right, has survived the best, holding an orb and the shaft of a spear or crosier. The depiction of Michael, to the left, has been almost totally defiled – only a foot and part of a wing remain – but it still existed a hundred years after Olaf's time, when the Byzantine historian and politician Niketas Choniates described it as a "superb mosaic of the very first and greatest of God's archangels with drawn sword, standing guard over the temple." Such martial imagery would have reassured Viking Olaf that the Christian god was not necessarily a peaceable one.[*]

Inside, all was green and white marble, purple porphyry and creamy alabaster, a forest of columns, the whisper of sandals on mosaiced floors and the echo of soft voices under the Great Dome soaring 180 feet overhead and 100 feet across. In those days it was infused with light through forty arched windows around its base, a number of which have since been closed up. Procopius had enthused, "Indeed one might say that the interior is not lit by the sun outside, but from within, that such brilliant light bathes this shrine...It does not appear to rest upon a solid foundation, but to hover over it as though suspended from heaven by the fabled golden chain."

---

[*] Since the Hagia Sophia's 2020 reconsecration as the Great Holy Mosque of Ayasofya, both images are concealed from public view.

It's hard to say exactly what image Olaf might have beheld at the apex of the dome. It's thought that it originally held a mosaic of the Holy Cross and then of Christ as the *Pantocrator*, the Ruler of the Universe, but that first dome had been pitched too shallow and during an earthquake in AD 588 had almost totally collapsed into the nave. Then, during the Byzantine Iconoclasms of 726–787 and 814–842, most of the Hagia's images were destroyed as idolatrous. Though restored afterward, a Pantocrator at the center of the dome circa 980 would have been damaged or destroyed again in the earthquakes of 986, 989 and 1354. Vladimir's emissaries were said to have visited in 987, when the place must still have been a shambles, but according to the *Bygone Days* they were nonetheless awestruck: "The Emperor accompanied the Russes to the church, and led them to the wide open space, calling their attention to the church's beauty, the chanting, and the pontifical services and the deacons' ministrations, while explaining to them the worship of his God. The Russes were astonished, and wondrously praised the Greek ceremony."

"We didn't know if we were in heaven or on earth," they reported back to Vladimir, "for surely there is no such magnificence or opulence anywhere else in the world. We cannot begin to describe it. We know only that God dwells among the Greeks, and that their service surpasses the worship of any other land, for we cannot forget that beauty."

According to Odd, Olaf was sufficiently moved to want to learn more: "There he met brilliant and pious teachers who taught him the worship of the Lord."

Berg added, "He is said to have become a catechumen [an initiate], for the first time given the sign of the Cross." Prime-signing, *prima signatio*, the sign of the cross made on an initiate's forehead by a Christian priest, was an early church rite considered the first step toward baptism, giving an initiate the right to attend church services and become a kind of apprentice Christian, without being christened. (Odd's version of the saga has Olaf baptized here, and then signed, but that would not have been the normal process. Berg's later rewrite corrects the error, omitting mention of baptism.)*

---

* Not all Varangians in Constantinople took Christianity so seriously. Multiple places in the Hagia's second-story aisles and galleries – notably, called the *catechumena* – are decorated with

The various versions of Olaf's saga then have him return to Kyiv with evangelical passion to convert everyone there to the true faith. Here again we can see the saga evolve in the retellings. In Odd's 12th-century original, he gives Olaf a few lines to preach to Vladimir, who is skeptical, though the (unnamed) queen is less so. A century later, Berg has Olaf actually preach to Vladimir, "Better that you should believe in God rather than false gods, carved images which help no one, and cannot even move from where they stand, unless carried or dragged away by others. Long ago, before I knew God, I told you that it seemed to me altogether senseless to serve them."

Berg gave the prince and the queen (here Allogia, Olava) long speeches as well in reply, though to the same end: She convinces Vladimir to convert, a Greek bishop baptizes them all, and they live happily ever after.

As noted, Snorri, not being a monk, ignored this part of the saga. Indeed Vladimir and his court did convert to Christianity, but years later, in 988, when the prince's emissaries returned from Constantinople (and he negotiated for yet another wife, the Emperor Basil's sister, Anna Porphyrogenita). In this way Odd, and Berg after him, credited Olaf with the pivotal role in converting the entire Rus to their true faith.

However, assuming Olaf did visit Constantinople with his fellow Varangians earlier in the 980s, his return evidently went a little differently.

If Olaf spent time in Constantinople, Vladimir might have looked on it as something of a betrayal. He was not, after all, the prince's sole druzhinnik, and the fact that he was not a native Rus, and was now perhaps even dabbling in a foreign religion that had lured away

---

Viking graffiti scratched into the marble, probably with dagger points: images of longships, including details of sails, oars, masts and even dragon prows, or runic names: Arni, Halftan ("Half-Dane"), "Arinbard cut these runes." Perhaps these were prayers to the Christian god by seamen imploring protection for their ships, or bids for immortality, or simple amusement. Up in the *catechumena* a man could sit behind a pillar or with his back to the rest of the church, out of sight of the priests down in the chancel, and pass the time during interminable services by practicing his drawing or writing, thereby leaving his mark on history.

Vladimir's grandmother and brother from worship of Perun, did him no favors. Odd confided, "We are told that when Olaf was so honored, some people became more jealous than supportive, and slandered him to the king."

Though he omitted the story of Olaf's trip to Constantinople, in his *Heimskringla* Snorri found this slander worthy of inclusion: "They warned the king that he should be careful not to make Olaf too powerful, 'for such a man may be a danger to you, if he were to permit himself to be used in doing you or your kingdom harm.'"

And Berg elaborated on their rumor-mongering: "He greatly exceeds other men in manly achievements, popularity and natural gifts. Also, we do not know what he and the Queen are always whispering about."

This last insinuation, the implication of an intrigue between Olaf and Olava, would have been the final straw. It seems the Grand Prince had grown quite acquisitive and territorial when it came to women. He had not married dead Yaropolk's widow, the unnamed Byzantine Christian nun, but got her pregnant anyway. His Polotskan trophy wife, Gorislava, bore him a son, which is the only reason he spared both their lives when she tried to stab him in his sleep. It was not as if he would ever have to bed her again. He is said to have conquered the Vyatchians in what is now the area of Moscow, the Lyakhs in what is now eastern Poland, and the Yatvingians in what is now Lithuania, but it's debatable whether he took most of the women of conquered regions as trophies or conquered those regions simply to fill out his seraglio. "Vladimir was obsessed with lust for women," accuses the *Bygone Days*, which credits him with no fewer than 800 concubines in various harems across his domain. "He was insatiable in his wantonness. He even seduced married women and violated young girls, for he was as libertine as Solomon."

(In Vladimir's defense, this was in the finest tradition of his grandfather Igor, whom ibn Fadlan heard kept a harem ever ready for use: "Forty slave girls, who are his bedmates, sit by him on his throne. He may copulate with one of them in the presence of his men.")

Now, Olaf would hardly have been a virgin. Berg reported, "He was very handsome, very tall and strong, and more skilled in manly feats than all the Northmen whose deeds are recorded in the sagas." As a druzhinnik, he had his pick of women to use however he wished.

Ibn Fadlan testified, "Each has a slave girl to serve him, wash him, and prepare his food and drink. He has another slave girl with whom he has sex."

So there was no reason for Olaf and Olava to pursue an affair, except that, of course, the heart chooses what it will, but also no reason for Vladimir to suspect them, except out of imagined jealousy. That, apparently, was enough.

"It so happened that the prince listened to those who slandered Olaf," wrote Berg, "and became somewhat cold and ill-tempered with him." When Olaf urged Vladimir to abandon his graven idols, which could not so much as move from where they stood, much less aid their worshippers, the prince was not inclined to listen. Having conquered his kingdom by their power, he found no fault with his gods, no matter how much blood they demanded.

He had sent his uncle Dobrynya to rule Novgorod in his stead. The *Bygone Years* attests, "When Dobrynya came to Novgorod, he raised an idol beside the river Volkhov, and the Novgorodians sacrificed to it as if to God himself."

And Vladimir made Kyiv not only his capital, but the center of pagan worship. "He raised idols on the hills outside the fortress," continues the chronicle. "The people called them gods, and brought their sons and their daughters to be sacrificed to these devils. They defiled the earth with their offerings, and the land of Rus and this hill were stained with blood."

And when the supply of native-born sons and daughters began running low, the Slavs looked to the foreign-born. The *Bygone Years* tells the sad tale of the Varangian Tur (Thor), and his son, who had evidently converted to Christianity in Greece (taking the names Feodor and Ioann, Russian for the Greek Theodore and Ioannes, John). Like Olaf, they made the mistake of returning to Kyiv. His name drawn by lot – in which, the chronicle insinuates, the devil had a hand – Ioann is chosen for sacrifice. Messengers inform Feodor, "Since the lot has fallen on your son, the gods have chosen him as their own. Let us then make of him a sacrifice."

Feodor replies like a Viking, but a Christian one:

> They are not gods, merely wood. Today they exist, tomorrow they will rot. They do not eat, drink, or speak, but are carved by human

hands from wood. The only God is he whom the Greeks serve and worship. He created the heavens and the earth, the stars, the moon, the sun, and man, whom he ordained to live on earth. What did your gods create? They themselves are created. I will not hand over my son to demons.

Incensed, a mob breaks down Feodor's stockade and demands his son in the name of the gods. From his second-floor gallery (evidently standing on pillars against the Volkhov's floods) the Varangian faces them down: "If they be gods, let them send one of their own to take my son."

The Kyivans do not wait for the gods, but cut the pillars out from under the house. Father and son both die, not in sacrifice, but by plain murder.*

Neither Varangians nor druzhinniki were safe from the whim of the Kyivan Rus, nor of their knyaz. As ibn Fadlan heard, "One of the customs of the Russian king is that he has with him in his palace four hundred of his most valiant and trusted men. When he dies, they die, killed for his sake."

There was no future in Kyiv for Olaf. Probably only his past service stood him in good stead thus far; that, and the queen's protection. Vladimir would not have been wise to antagonize Olava, at least not any more than his philandering already had. Snorri asserted, and Berg agreed, that as knyaginya she had her own bodyguard, equal in strength to that of the knyaz. (Part of the food for gossip may have been her attempting to talk Olaf into siding with her.) According to Berg, she reminded Vladimir of their foster son's years of faithful service, and of his mother Malusha's vision: "And this word of mine has more truth than that of evil men who think that my intimacy with him means unfaithfulness towards you."

Vladimir was at least convinced of her fidelity, though not about Olaf's new god. Odd wrote, "Although the king long resisted and would not renounce his religion or his belief in the gods, with God's

---

* Vladimir would eventually raise a church on the site of their deaths. Less than a hundred years later the Russian Orthodox Church venerated Theodore and John as the first Christian martyrs in the land.

mercy he came to understand the great difference between his faith and that which Olaf preached."

For Olaf, that was as good as it would ever get. He informed Olava that he wished to return north, to his homeland: "There my ability would be most likely to fulfill its promise."

There was no standing in the way of the gods, whether they were Scandinavian, Slavic or Christian. Old Malusha's prophecy was bearing itself out: *When at last he is grown to manhood he will return to his native land and gain the kingdom which is his by birth. As king he will shine with bright glory and become a savior to many men of the northern regions.*

"The princess wished him a successful journey," reports the *Heimskringla*, "and said he would be thought a brave man wherever he went. Olaf then made ready, went aboard, and raised sail for the Baltic."

PART TWO

All these thoughts of love and strife
Glimmered through his lurid life,
As the stars' intenser light
Through the red flames o'er him trailing,
As his ships went sailing, sailing,
Northward in the summer night.

…Thus came Olaf to his own,
When upon the night-wind blown
Passed that cry along the shore;
And he answered, while the rifted
Streamers o'er him shook and shifted,
"I accept thy challenge, Thor!"

Longfellow, "The Saga of King Olaf"

XII

JOMSBORG

Then the prince's many ship-stems, marvelously equipped with shields,
sped from Russia all at once, under the generous ruler.
The most admirable son of Tryggvi, Olaf, harried the western coasts
and slashed the sons of men with steel blades.

12th-century Icelandic poet Hallar-Stein

AD 982–983

The Danish island of Bornholm, lying like a bottle cork in the mouth of the Baltic, has always been a literal outlier. Closer to the coasts of Sweden, Germany and Poland than it is to the motherland, it has been fought over and changed hands multiple times in history. In Viking days it was called *Burgundaholm*, "Mountainous Island," and in the same way as the isle of Gotland was the original home of the Roman Age Goths, was said to be the original home of the medieval Burgundians before they migrated south to France.

High, steep, rocky cliffs front the island's northern coasts, where the Baltic currents force their way through a 25-mile-wide channel between it and the Swedish coast. On the south point, though – fifty miles from the Polish shore – Duoedde ("Dove Point") Beach is to this day one of the most popular tourist destinations in Europe: almost twenty miles of sugary white sand, fine enough to run through an hourglass, and several hundred yards wide at its southernmost. A perfect site on which to land a fleet of attacking dragon ships.

"As he came from the east," wrote Snorri of Olaf, "he reached the island of Burgundaholm, where he landed and looted. The country folk hurried down to the shore and gave him battle, but Olaf won the victory, and much booty."

Olaf was by now a veteran fighting man, but this was his first raid as a sole commander. The loot taken was undoubtedly substantial; today Bornholm has yielded by far the largest concentration of buried hoards of Viking Age and early medieval coins and ingots in Denmark, and those are just the caches that the original owners, for whatever (probably tragic) reasons, never came back to retrieve. As for the inhabitants of Burgundaholm whose homes and families were destroyed, those lives taken and those lives lost, the saga writers cared little. To them it was, sadly, all too familiar. Lives in that age were cheap. What mattered was that Olaf profited by their loss; his initial venture paid for itself. But what of his long-term goals?

Bornholm's strategic location, in the choke point between the European and Scandinavian coasts, gave whoever owned it control of sea traffic in and out of the Baltic. The oceanic climate was good – to this day Bornholm is nicknamed *Solskinsoen*, "Sunshine Island" – the inhabitants were demonstrably weak, and whoever set himself up to rule them could establish a sea-roving empire to rival the Eistlander pirates or, for that matter, any petty Scandinavian Viking kingdom. If, as Wulfstan of Hedeby noted (admittedly, a hundred years earlier), Burgundaholm was ruled by one king, then it would have been only natural for Olaf to wonder why that king should not be him. In his time the island was said to be ruled by a King Veseti, who had a pair of formidable sons, Bui *inn Digri*, "the Stout," and Sigurd *Kapa*, "Cape," plus a grandson, Vagn. They will be of some consequence to our story, but a bit later. For now, rather than set Olaf against them, the Norns had another fate in mind. "As Olaf lay at Burgundaholm," wrote Snorri, "bad weather, a storm and a heavy sea blew up, so that his ships could not remain there."

Njord, the Norse god of wind and wave, sent a tempest to wipe Olaf's fleet off the Bornholm shore, or perhaps it was more like the storm God sent to blow the Apostle Paul's ship around the Mediterranean for two weeks, from Crete to be shipwrecked off the Maltese coast, whence he ultimately journeyed to Rome and his destiny, martyrdom. In either case, a wise sailor rides out a storm at sea, rather than risk breakers battering his ship aground, even on a soft sandy beach. Berg wrote of Olaf and his crew, "They sailed south to the shore of Wendland, where they found a good harbor, and spent some time in complete quiet."

Almost seventy miles due south from Bornholm across the Bay of Pomerania, the Wendish coast, what is now northeast Germany and northwest Poland, is likewise almost all smooth shoreline. So the "good harbor" mentioned is most certainly the 260-square-mile Oder Lagoon, shielded from Baltic waves by the islands of Usedom and Wolin in the Oder River estuary. With their sails lowered to negotiate the tight, twisting entry channel by oar, Olaf's ships would have glided out onto the placid waters of what amounted to an inland sea, surrounded by well-watered, fertile lowlands. As ibn Fadlan had visited and documented the Rus, the 10th-century Jewish Arab merchant Ibrahim ibn Yaqub, on his visit to the Holy Roman Empire, heard of the Wends and recorded, "Their land is lavish with pastures and rich with crops. They are hard-working farmers in pursuit of their daily bread, and in that they excel all other peoples in the north. Their traders reach Rus and Constantinople by land and sea."

Fat Scandinavian knarrs laden with Wendish produce – leather, fur, wax, grain, salt and slaves – threaded the seaward straits on their way home, while Slavic dugouts and cargo hulks full of Scandinavian amber, walrus ivory and Swedish iron ore set off upriver, inland, as they had since ancient times. The Oder Lagoon was a terminus on the Amber Road connecting the Baltic to what had once been the Western Roman Empire, just as Lake Ilmen and the Dnieper connected Novgorod and Kyiv to the Eastern. According to an anonymous 9th-century German author, known only as the "Bavarian Geographer," Wendland numbered some seventy *civitates* – villages, strongholds. And the greatest of these was a veritable Constantinople of the North: Jomsborg.

To this day Jomsborg's exact location – for that matter, its very existence – remains a topic of some contention. The ancient accounts are so confused and conflicted that some historians assert the town was nothing more than legend, a figment of the saga writers' imaginations.

Some concede it may have been on the Usedom Island coast, or others of the small islands thereabouts, or even that since Viking times it has sunk like Atlantis beneath the sea. The general consensus, though, is that it stood on the lagoon's eastern shore, where a channel runs out to the Baltic and the modern town of Wolin, Poland, stands on the island of the same name. Ibn Yaqub either visited or at least heard of a major town in the vicinity. Adam of Bremen, writing about a hundred years after Olaf's arrival, placed Jomsborg at the outlet of the Oder, "the largest river in the Slavic country. At its mouth, where it waters the Scythian [i.e., wild, untamed] marshes, the noble city of Jumne [Jomsborg's German name], is a very well-known center of trade for the barbarians and Greeks who live in those parts."

Archaeologists believe a Stone Age habitation there, on a bit of high ground between the Oder channel to the east and low-lying peat bogs to the west, had by the 6th century become the site of a small fishing village named after Jomala, the Finno-Ugric sky god, and around AD 850 was fortified in the typical fashion. Ibn Yaqub wrote:

> The Slavs build most of their fortresses by choosing meadows with plentiful water and woods. They mark out a circle or square outlining the fortress and the size of courtyard that they want. They dig around it, filling the trench and piling up the dug-out soil. Then they strengthen the walls with timbers and wood, as a stronghold, until the walls are the desired height. They install a gate on whichever side they need. One enters it across a wooden bridge.

In his day Adam of Bremen described Jomsborg as a great, though pagan, metropolis:

> It is truly the largest of all European cities, and Slavs and many other peoples, Greeks and barbarians live there. Even foreign Saxons have the right to live there on equal terms with the natives, provided only that while they reside there they do not openly practice Christianity. In fact, the citizens still ignorantly perform pagan rites. Otherwise, so far as morals and generosity are concerned, a more principled or gentler people cannot be found. Rich in the goods of all the northern nations, the city lacks nothing either gratifying or valuable.

That, however, was a hundred years after Olaf's time. To judge by its archaeology, when he and his ships came cruising into its channel in the early 980s, Jomsborg, rather like Novgorod, was a collection of villages clustered for more than a mile along the riverbank. The original stronghold, *Stare Miasto*, Old Town, lay directly across from some mid-stream islands. On high ground to its south, today a public park called Hangman's Hill (said to have been the site of executions and human sacrifices back in the day), excavations in the 1930s, '50s, '70s and 2020s unearthed a suburb with bread ovens, a tannery, shops for workers in leather, wood, glass beads, horn and amber, plus pottery shards, animal bones, weapons and jewelry, and furthermore what are thought to be the remains of 10th-century wooden structures, a cemetery and defensive ramparts. To the north, Silver Hill, archaeologists have uncovered more workshops and a marketplace. Altogether the towns might have numbered ten thousand inhabitants, which in those days and parts did constitute a major city.

Unlike the completely unprotected neighborhoods of Novgorod (and doubtless because they were constantly menaced by Baltic, Danish and Saxon raiders, and even other Wendish tribes), Jomsborg's settlements were each shielded by a C-shaped stockade, opening on the waterfront river ports, lending credence to the idea that the town's primary defense against waterborne attack was block chains or some other barriers across the strait itself. Old Town was protected by a double-wall palisade, the outer approximately man-high and the inner two or three times that, not of vertical posts but of split logs laid horizontally atop each other and reinforced with vertical poles and guy wires. Inside this formidable defense, the town's mixed and mingled citizenry maintained their independence from Vikings, the empire, and evidently even their fellow Slavs: the Polany, the "people of the fields," the Poles. Ibn Yaqub wrote, "Slavs war on Romans, Franks, Lombards other nations, with varying amounts of success."

Part of the reason for the Wendish tribes' dearth of victories was doubtless the fact that their various tribes – Obotrites, Polabs, Lutici, Sorbians, Veleti, others – had never been united under one overall leader. Ibn Yaqub admitted, "They follow no king and bow to no one, but are ruled by elders." This sounds a lot like a Viking thing,

Rus veche or Byzantine senate, and given Jomsborg's mixed citizenry was probably a combination of all three. Though it's generally thought that ibn Yaqub was correct in that the Slavic tribes followed no overall king, in his day Snorri wrote, "The Wendish king was called Burislav."

This Burislav or Burizlief is otherwise unknown, his name appearing only this once in the Icelandic narratives. He is usually taken to be Duke Mieszko I of what is now central Poland, and/or his son Boleslav Chrobry, "the Brave."* In the early 960s Mieszko had established his rule around the Warta River, in what would become the nucleus of modern Poland, with its capital at Stargard, forty miles south of Jomsborg. Ibn Yaqub visited Emperor Otto's court and learned, "The country of Mieszko is the largest one among the [Slavic] countries...He has three thousand warriors wearing coats of mail; a hundred of them is worth a thousand of other warriors in battle. He gives those men clothes, horses, arms, and everything they need."

It would have benefited the Wends to have Mieszko and the Poles as allies, but it benefited Mieszko more to ally with Emperor Otto. He took a devout Christian princess of Bohemia as his queen, converted to Christianity himself, declared all his people to be Christian as well, and paid homage to Otto. By 966, the year Olaf was enslaved (and Mieszko's son Boleslav was born), Mieszko was called *amicus imperatoris*, "Friend of the Emperor." In those years ibn Yaqub wrote of the Wends, "They fight with Mieszko."

So the sagas' King Burislav might have traded a daughter in exchange for peace.† Snorri's *Heimskringla* asserts, "His daughters were Geira, Gunnhild and Astrid. Geira ruled when Olaf and his men

---

* The name Mieszko is of unknown origin and meaning in the Polish tongue, and Burislav or Burizleif is a corruption of Boleslaw, "great glory," the preferred dynastic name of Slavic rulers. They included Mieszko's son, his father-in-law Boleslav I "the Cruel," Duke of Bohemia (r. 935–972), his brother-in-law Duke Boleslav II "the Pious" (r. 972–999) and even the later Duke of Poland, Boleslav Krzywousty "the Wrymouthed," who made himself known to the 12th-century saga writers by conquering Pomerania when many of their accounts were being written. Mieszko's son Boleslav Chrobry was about Olaf's age, at this time too young to have a marriageable daughter. So the sagas' Burislav, the "king of Wendland," was either Boleslav II claiming overlordship from afar, or else some petty and otherwise unknown Slavic chieftain in the vicinity of Jomsborg.

† Queen Sigrid of Sweden is thought originally to have also been his daughter.

came to land." And Berg concurred, "The harbor where Olaf took shelter from the storm was in Geira's lands, and the capital town where she lived lay inland a short distance."*

She was said to be the youngest sister, but fate had made her the most powerful. Berg had it that Geira "had been married, but her husband having died, she ruled over his kingdom as queen."

It should be said that her connection with Jomsborg is almost as tenuous as the town's existence. That she ruled over it gets no more than passing mention by the Icelandic scribes; by their time the town had been destroyed and her exact seat of power mattered little to their stories. Odd narrowed it down no further than, "Queen Geira reigned on the western border with Germania, where both the land and the people are better." And the Norwegian authors of the *Agrip* and *Historia*, writing during and after the 12th/13th-century Northern Crusades against the Slavs, regarded a long-dead Wendish queen as beneath notice, but they named Jomsborg, practically next door to them, as Olaf's headquarters in Wendland. It's left to us to put him and Geira together there.

If Geira owed fealty to her father Burislav, she was a queen only in the sense that Olaf was king: a leader of men, the nearest thing to a ruler at hand. For all that Odd admitted, "She had a large domain and ruled it well…She was powerful and honorable in her widowhood. Her worthy and faithful aide maintained her honor and reputation."

Berg explained, "Her steward's name was Dixin. He was wise and popular, and a powerful chieftain."† According to Olaf's saga, in her hall in Old Town, he informed Queen Geira of the new arrivals. For once Odd gives this Dixin a longer speech than does his usually more loquacious successor Berg, but both write to the greater glory of their subject, Olaf. Dixin tells Geira:

> Many ships have arrived in the harbor. They are very well equipped with all necessary armaments. They are also loaded with precious fabrics and many other treasures, and the crews themselves are

---

* Like her father's and her sisters', Geira's name is not Slavic, but Germanic, Nordic, Scandinavian: the feminine form of *geir*, spear.
† "Dixin" is an even less Slavic name, more like the Celtic, Scottish Dixon.

impressive and well-armed. We do not often see such men here. There is one, however, who well exceeds the others. I am sure he is a king in disguise, for he is distinctive and charismatic. He is tall and strong, with a striking face and a fine build. His look is so arresting and just that I have never before seen his like.

Certainly the scribes are exaggerating Olaf's attributes, but if half of it was true the new arrival would have intrigued a widowed queen. Hardly any women in those patriarchal times ruled their lands except as figureheads – puppets – for powerful male relatives or as regents for underage princes.* Few warriors worthy of the title would deign to take orders from a woman. Geira would have known full well that she held her throne only until she found a suitable king, or at least while she maintained the illusion of searching for one. Dixin seems to have perceived that there might be an eligible suitor among the newcomers:

> If you are willing, my lady, I would suggest you do as required by your rank: greet him with an honor guard and extend to him our hospitality. I think he will respond well if invited politely with good will. I hear his men say that they desire to winter here in our land. I believe we can make the best of his arrival if we handle this correctly. And Majesty, if you are of a mind to share your realm with one who can lead and defend it and save it from your enemies, who can you find nobler and better suited than this? You will never again find such a protector.

"If you deem this fitting to my rank," replied Geira, "then go meet him and speak on my behalf, inviting him to come here with all his men."

According to Berg, Dixin ventured down to the Viking landing with an armed guard, introduced himself and extended his queen's offer to Olaf: "She invites you and all your men to winter in the chief town of her realm, where she herself lives, with her chieftains and

---

* A notable exception was Aethelflaed of Mercia, eldest child of England's King Alfred the Great and widow of Aethelred, Lord of the Mercians. She led Mercia in her late husband's stead, even in war against the Vikings, the only female ruler in all of Anglo-Saxon history.

bodyguard. The summer is now well along, the weather is poor, and the storms are violent."

Having already learned that the hard way, Olaf accepted the invitation. He ordered his men to haul their ships ashore, and to place them and their cargo under their hosts' protection. Odd wrote, "The queen rode out to greet him with great spectacle and hailed Olaf, who was rightfully called a king. She welcomed him with every mark of courtesy and asked his name and rank."

Olaf the worldly traveler may not have regarded Jomsborg and its princess as particularly impressive, but once in her presence he evidently reconsidered. Berg confided that Geira was (of course) "a most beautiful and highborn woman."

For his part Snorri declared that "Olaf was the best looking of men, very well-built and strong, and physically he exceeded every Norseman that ever was."

Berg wrote, "They proceeded into town, where the Queen entertained them with the utmost cheer and thoughtfulness."

In medieval times Wendish villages were not laid out as street grids, but in a circular fashion the Germans called a *rundling*, roundhouse, and the Slavs an *opole*, "about the field," with farmsteads arranged like pie slices around a central marketplace, low-lying and often bisected by running water like the Oder Strait through Jomsborg. Widespread by the 12th century, the layout is thought to date back to the 7th. Excavations in modern Wolin, however, have revealed that Jomsborg was laid out as a grid, indicative of Viking influence: houses stave-built with posts and lintels – timber frames on load-bearing pine posts, a Scandinavian technique not typical among the Wends. Novgorodian-style wood-paved streets led down to the waterfront, where quays built of thirty-foot oaken crates filled with fascines, dirt and rock formed piers extending right out into the river. In the central courtyard, the town square, a small temple, only about fifteen feet on a side, had been raised to the Wendish gods. (Writing around the end of the 11th century, the Dane Saxo Grammaticus described such a temple at Cape Arkona on the island of Rugen, about seventy-five miles northwest of Jomsborg on what is now the German Baltic coast, as highly carved and brightly painted, facing the east.) Geira's residence was likely at the south side of town, where a steep three-sided hillock offered a natural site for a tower fort. Excavations there have revealed no less than a triple palisade circling the crest. Odd wrote of Olaf, "The queen gave him fine quarters, well furnished, along with appropriate servants, both men and women."

Olaf and his men settled in for the winter. Ibn Yaqub, the Arab from temperate southern Spain, remarked, "The Slavic lands are the coldest of all, coldest on moonlit nights when there are no clouds." He described their saunas, in which the Wends poured water on sizzling-hot stones and thrashed their bare skin with whisks of grass to bring their blood to a flush.

That Geira had already been another man's woman did not come between her and Olaf. "When a maid loves a man," wrote ibn Yaqub of the Wends, "she gives herself to him and satiates her lust. When a husband finds his wife is a virgin, he says, 'There is something wrong with you, else men would have coveted you and you would have chosen one from among them to take your virginity.' Then he turns her out and divorces her."

That did not happen here. Quite the opposite. As Snorri confided: "They grew fond of each other. Olaf courted Queen Geira."

The sagas make no mention of Geira's religion, if any, and Olaf the agnostic (though by this time perhaps Christian-curious) would have found the Wendish gods just as nonsensical as those of the Rus. Svetovit, "Holy Lord," the god of wealth and war (thought to be the Baltic version of the Rus thunder god Perun), was humanlike, though larger than human, with four heads, beardless and short-haired, two facing forward and two behind, but each looking to the side.[*] Triglav, the "Three-Headed One," also humanish but short of one face compared with Svetovit, ruled over heaven, earth and the underworld,

---

[*] In 1973 archaeological excavations in the center of Wolin unearthed a hand-sized figurine of yew wood with four faces. Dated to the second half of the 9th century, it's thought to have represented Svetovit in private devotions or magic rituals, possibly in the god's temple.

and may have represented Perun's opponent Veles, the Rus god of the netherworld. Black horses were sacrificed to Triglav, white to Svetovit. Christianity was known to the Wends, but had been rejected, or mutated. The 12th-century Saxon priest and historian Helmold of Bosau, in his *Chronica Slavorum*, a history of the Slavic peoples from about the year 800, took Svetovit to be a corruption of Sveti Vid, the Slavs' name for the semi-legendary early 4th-century Sicilian martyr St. Vitus, whose relics had by the 830s somehow found their way to northern Germany and supposedly inspired a cult among the Slavs. Today the connection of Svetovit and St. Vitus is considered a 12th-century fabrication, possibly to justify the Wendish Crusades, as Helmold wrote of the Slavs: "No barbarians on earth abominate Christians and priests more."

But no matter their beliefs, long before the advent of Christianity and Christmas all the various peoples of Wendland celebrated the midwinter festival. For the Slavs it was *Koleda*, named for the new year's sun personified, and mostly involved singing – the word translates as "carol." The Germanic Yule (from the Old Norse *jol*, "winter feast") called for toasts to Odin, Njord and Freyja, to peace and a good year and in honor of the departed, with cattle and horses sacrificed and their blood sprinkled over the temple and idols. Solemn oaths, *heitstrenging*, were sworn with hands laid on the biggest boar-pig available, the *sonargoltr*, which was also sacrificed to Frey, god of kingship and prosperity.

Odd wrote, "When the feast was ready, the queen went with her company to invite Olaf to join her in the hall where she usually drank with her retinue. He accepted courteously, and the feast was celebrated. Olaf and the queen sat beside each other on thrones, drinking mead and wine from fine goblets."

In such an atmosphere, matters reached their natural conclusion. Berg confided, "King Olaf proposed to marry Queen Geira. She put the proposal before her steward, Dixin, her kinsmen and supporters, and they all agreed it would be an excellent match."

Odd proclaimed, "The chieftain Dixin addressed them each in turn, imparting great wisdom."

> He told her what great power and repute she would gain with such a man overseeing her realm. To him he suggested it would

be desirable to rule a flourishing domain...He said that if they searched the entire world, neither would find greater honor than he would in her as his wife, or she in him as her husband. When he had planted this seed in their hearts, it took root and grew in them, as both desirable and auspicious.

"So," wrote Berg, "according to their wishes, the wedding of King Olaf with Queen Geira was celebrated, and the marriage-feast was magnificent."

Odd wrote, "It went on for many days, with every day's amusements more spectacular than the day before, and nourished with all the best food and drink available, as suits a powerful king."

Neither party being Christian, they would have been wed in a handfasting ceremony (Old Norse *handfesta*, to agree by joining hands), a Germanic *troth plight*, truth pledge. The details of the ritual were little recorded at the time and largely lost today. The *Ruodlieb*, a chivalric romance written in Germany a few decades after this, describes such a wedding, in which the groom offers his bride a gold ring over the hilt of his sword. The wedding vows might be considered...*unusual* today. The warrior promises, "Just as the ring surrounds the whole finger, so I bind you with firm and enduring troth, and this you must give me or lose your head."

The bride, after a little goose-and-gander justification, declares, "It is proper that we both endure the same judgment."

To which the groom agrees: "If I ever wrong you, I shall forfeit the possessions I gave you, and you shall have the power to cut off this head of mine."

So romantic!

But there is another tradition, at least in modern Polish weddings: that if any candle on the altar goes out during the ceremony, either the bride or groom will die young.

Snorri wrote, "So it was that Olaf married her that winter, and was king, beside Queen Geira, over her domains."

But a king has duties as well as pleasures. Olaf rose to the occasion, sharing in the management of royal affairs and the government of the kingdom. Of course, one of those kingly duties was making sure the royal income was sufficient. He is said to have asked Geira, "Are there any towns or lands or domains once yours that have been lost because robbers and raiders captured them from you?"

She said, "Lord, I shall name for you the towns no longer ours. We have long suffered their insults."

Berg wrote, "He soon learned there were many regions of Wendland which had been under Queen Geira's rule, but had ceased to pay tribute and obey her."

It goes back to what has been said about female rulers in those patriarchal times: that they were seen as weak and could be defied. No warrior king of that day and age could afford to let such an affront pass. Not only would the royal income be lessened, so would his authority and prestige.

"After that," wrote Odd, "Olaf readied his army to set out with a great force."

XIII

THE SLAVIC REVOLT

*Then the Slavs, unjustly oppressed by their Christian overlords,
finally threw off the yoke of servitude
and were forced to take up arms to defend their freedom.*

Adam of Bremen

AD 982–984

Blood hatred between Germans and Slavs goes way back before the murderous 20th century. The two peoples have been slaughtering each other since before the dawn of recorded history. In the winding Tollense River valley in northern Germany, about fifty miles west of Jomsborg – back during the Bronze Age, something of a dividing line between the Teutonic cultures to the west and the Slavic tribes to the east – archaeologists have uncovered the remains of 4,000 warriors who slew each other some thirty-two centuries ago. Their differences would not seem to have been religious. As far back as that, perhaps even during the European Stone Age, the Saxons' Germanic forefathers had worshipped "pole gods," carved wooden tree trunks or branches fixed in piles of stone, a tree cult reminiscent of Grand Prince Vladimir's Perun, the Wends' Svetovit and Triglav, and Yggdrasil, the world tree of the Vikings.

In the year 782, however, Emperor Charlemagne's Franks had brought God to Saxony at Verden on the river Aller, casting down the great wooden pillar representing the German god Irmin, raising a Christian church in its place and massacring 4,500 Saxons, though not before baptizing them to save their souls. The hard lesson was well learned. Two hundred years later, considering themselves as having gained the civilization of Rome and the benefits of Christianity, the Saxons looked down on the Slavs to their east as barbarian, pagan savages. Helmold grumbled:

> Their entire race is consumed by idolatry, ever restless and shifting about, launching bandit raids upon its foes, the Danes on one hand and the Saxons on the other. So great emperors and priests have often and by many wise methods tried somehow to bring this arrogant pagan people to acknowledge God's name and the grace of the faith...Of all the peoples of the northern nations, the Slavs alone remain more stubborn and reluctant to believe than the rest.

Charlemagne's first incursion into Wendish lands, seven years after Verden, had been carried on by the Saxon Ottonian emperors, encroaching farther across the Elbe. As Widukind of Corvey put it, "The king customarily led the army personally, attacking them, inflicting great losses on them, and finally driving them to all but total defeat. Still they chose war over peace, accepting all misery in the name of freedom."

In 929 Henry the Fowler had utterly annihilated a Slavic army outside their fortress at Lenzen, after which, according to Widukind, his prisoners were all put to the sword. Henry went on to lay siege to a second fortress at Gana and, taking it after a siege of twenty days, ordered all the defenders put to death and their children enslaved. And Henry's son Otto I was just as brutal. In 955, he defeated another Slav army, decapitated its leader, and planted the head in a field where it could watch as he had 700 prisoners massacred around it. Despite all that, Saxons did not fool themselves into thinking their new neighbors were domesticated. Helmold wrote, "The temperament of the Slavs, naturally deceitful and treacherous, could not be ignored."

The Ottonians studded their newly conquered territory with monasteries and bishoprics – Magdeburg in 937; Havelberg and Brandenburg, 948; Merseburg, 967; Meissen and Zeitz, 968 – and fortresses, *burgs*, around which their villages, *wards*, clustered for protection. "There were very few defenses apart from these bastions," wrote Widukind, "and even these had weak stockades."

The Saxons viewed these churches and burgwards as an effort at civilizing the locals, but as their settlers moved in, the local Slavs were pushed out, enslaved or murdered; the survivors could see it only as occupation. Either way, the empire gained new subjects, and the Church new converts (whether they liked it or not), not to mention their land, workers and especially tribute, of which Helmold wrote, "It indeed took the place of a tithe, consisting of an allotment of grain, forty small bales of flax, and twelve pennies of pure silver from every plow [as much land as could be worked by one horse or a pair of oxen]. Additionally, one penny went to the tax collector."

In their efforts to milk the Slavic cow dry, however, the Saxons were to find that their new subjects paid only lip service to the *Teutonicus Deus*, the German god. Adam of Bremen lamented, "Plainly the efforts of the Christian priests would long ago have borne fruit there if the princes' greed had not impeded the conversion of the people."

Two centuries of contention between German Christians and Slavic pagans were coming to a head. What finally set it off was this: Emperor Otto II, having marched into Apulia, the boot-heel of Italy, intent on taking it from the Byzantine Empire, left his Slavic subjects in the hands of his northern nobles. Helmold attested, "In those days, Margrave Dietrich and Duke Bernhard reigned over the Slavs, the former ruling the eastern lands, and the latter the western."

Dietrich of Haldensleben was margrave of the Nordmark, the Northern Marches on the border with Slavia. Margraves were some of the most powerful nobles on the frontier, exacting their own taxes, conducting their own military campaigns, and generally reigning over their own private little fiefdoms. Regardless of their fealty to the empire, Dietrich ruled his new subjects with nothing but scorn. (That he had recently become father-in-law to the Polish Duke Mieszko, whose Christian Bohemian first wife had died, did not improve his opinion.) On the other hand, Bernhard I, Duke of Saxony, had served Otto II against the Vikings Harald Bluetooth and Jarl Hakon at the Danevirke in 973. Adam called him "a good and noble man, except that he differed from his father in burdening his subjects with taxes." Helmold declared, "Only Duke Benno

[Bernhard] of Saxony seemed to exert some influence, although feeble at best, which the Slavs respected enough to neither renounce the Christian faith nor take up arms."

In 981 or 982 Bernhard proposed to march south to fight alongside Emperor Otto against the Byzantines. For that he had enlisted the aid of a Wendish chieftain, Mstivoj. Now, Mstivoj's Wends had not always been loyal – it was the head of his uncle Stoigniew around which Otto the Great had massacred those 700 Slavic prisoners – but Mstivoj had, in literal good faith, taken as wife the sister of a Saxon bishop and converted to Christianity himself. He took the baptismal name Billung after his godfather, Hermann Billung, margrave of the Saxon Billung March on the Baltic coast. Since Hermann was also Duke Bernhard's father, Bernhard and Mstivoj were brothers in the eyes of God. Their subjects were not. As Helmold pointed out, "Because of this the Slavs, taking advantage of the situation, began bit by bit to exert themselves not only against the heavenly commandments but also against imperial law."

Mstivoj's son, Mstislav, did not have his father's tolerance for Christianity, and chided him for collaborating with the enemy. Mstivoj considered dropping his Saxon wife, recanting his religion and encouraging his subjects to do the same. But he knew, as Helmold wrote, "On repudiation of the bishop's sister and the breaking of religious bonds, war would of course immediately ensue."

So when Bernhard proposed to march south with Otto II, Mstivoj pledged to send along a thousand horsemen – in those days, an army of consequence – in exchange for Bernhard's niece in marriage to his son Mstislav. Bernhard promised.*

Meanwhile the Byzantines had allied with the Muslims of Sicily against Emperor Otto. In July of 982, at the Battle of Stilo down in the sole of Italy's boot, he blundered into a double envelopment, lost almost his entire army and barely escaped himself. Nearly all Mstivoj's horsemen were slain. On his return north, according to Adam, when the Wend requested delivery of the wife promised him,

---

* According to Adam of Bremen, Helmold said the girl was promised to Mstivoj, but father and son are often confused. Demonstrating how intertwined European royalty was already becoming, it was Mstivoj's daughter, Tove, who had supposedly birthed Harald Bluetooth's bastard son Svein.

Margrave Dietrich annulled the plan, saying that a duke's kinswoman was "not to be given to a dog."

"On hearing this," wrote Helmold with some understatement, "the Slav chieftain went away in great resentment."

Trying to repair the damage, Duke Bernhard sent messengers after Mstivoj with a promise that the wedding could proceed. Too late. According to Helmold, the Slav replied, "It is only appropriate that a great prince's well-bred niece should marry a man of high rank and not, after all, be given to a dog. The appreciation given us for our service is to be considered not men, but dogs. Well then, if we Slavs are dogs, you will see how we bite."

As ibn Yaqub knew even in his day, "Slavs are keen for war and bloodshed, and if not for their quarreling due to their many various traditions, divisions and tribes, no nation would be able to resist them."

About 130 miles east of Hamburg, and fifteen miles upstream from the Bronze Age battlefield on the Tollense River, stretches *Tollensesee*, "Low Valley Lake." On its northern shore, in the 13th century, was founded the walled city of Neubrandenburg, today called *Stadt der Vier Tore*, "City of Four Gates," a modern metropolis with a population of some 65,000. About six and a half miles away, however, down at the southwest end of the lake, lies the little rural village of Wustrow, with a population of just 750 or so. To rattle over its brick-cobbled, one-lane streets on a bicycle, you would never guess that, 1,100 years ago, before Christian monks had even founded the monastery around which Neubrandenburg would be built, Wustrow was the religious capital of all Wendland.

"Every part of this land has its temple and idol which is worshipped by these heathen," wrote Thietmar, "but the town mentioned above has priority over all. It is surrounded by a great forest which the denizens hold to be inviolate and holy." He called the town Riedegost (probably a corruption of the Slavic *Radgosc*, "happy guest," a most peaceful moniker), and claimed its wall had three gates: "Two of the doors open to all. The smallest one faces east, opening onto a path toward a lake and a very dreadful sight."

Fifty years later, though, Adam of Bremen called the site Rethra, from the Wendish *Ratara*, war temple: "There a great temple was raised to demons, the chief of which is Redigast. His idol is golden, his altar draped with purple. The temple itself, with nine gates, stands in the middle of a deep lake. Only those who would make sacrifices or seek the oracle within, may cross the wooden bridge to it."

The remains of the bridge were discovered in 1886 when the lake's water level dropped during construction of a canal. The islet is still there too: *Fischerinsel*, "Fisher Island". Just 500 feet long and 130 across, it is shrouded in trees, its only building a dilapidated half-timbered, gable-roofed fisherman's shack, mentioned in local documents dating as far back as 1729, but now deserted, abandoned, forgotten. In 1887, however, excavations in the island's center, just northwest of the shack, revealed remains of a wooden structure and silver coins, knives, axes, spear points and jewelry. Further work in 1969 uncovered a pair of oaken cult figures five and a half feet high, one showing a two-faced male (males?) with prominent eyes, noses, mustaches and helmets, and the second – judging by the breasts – female. Though dated to the 11th or 12th century, they recall the multi-faced gods of Jomsborg and what Thietmar knew of the inner sanctum of Rethra: the temple of Svarozhits, the Slavic god of fire.*

> The temple is empty but for a skillfully fashioned wooden shrine standing on a foundation of horns of different animals. Visitors pass awesome sculpted images of gods and goddesses adorning the outer walls. Inside there are gods made by man, each with its inscribed name and frightful helmets and armor. Among them, Svarozhits occupies the place of honor and all the heathen honor and worship him above the rest. Their banners are never removed except in wartime, and then only by warriors afoot.

---

* Despite the similarity of their names, Svarozhits and Svetovit were distinct deities. Svarozhits was more a pan-Slavic god, while Svetovit was primarily worshipped among the Baltic Slavs.

Thietmar could only have been reporting hearsay. The only Christians to have reached the little temple on the lake met with martyrdom. Adam recorded, "The story goes that in those days two monks came from the forested uplands of Bohemia to the city of Rethra. Because they publicly asserted God's word there, they were tried by the pagans, first by various tortures, as they had anticipated, and finally beheaded for the glory of Christ."

"First he went to Rethra," wrote Helmold of Mstivoj, where he "summoned all the Slavs who lived in the east and informed them of the insult to him, and that in the Saxon tongue the Slavs are called 'dogs.'"

It was not in Mstivoj's power, however, to summon all the Slavic nation to war. "There is no one lord who reigns over all of them," wrote Adam. "When important issues are debated at a gathering, an agreement must be unanimous before any action is taken."

Not just anyone was allowed to enter the temple of Svarozhits, as Thietmar attested: "The people employ special priests to stand guard at this shrine." In light of such a weighty matter as war, the assemblage filed across the footbridge to the island to gather before the idol and seek his wisdom. "When they gather there to make sacrifices to the idols or appease their anger, these priests sit. Everyone else stands."

According to Helmold, they scolded Mstivoj: "You, who spurned your fellow tribesmen and courted the Saxons, a treacherous and greedy race, deserve to suffer. Swear to us now that you will renounce them and we will stand with you."

Mstivoj so swore.

Thietmar told us of the priests' decision-making process:

Whispering together secretly, they shudder and dig in the dirt so that, upon casting lots, they may receive answers in regard to any questions. When this is done, they lay green grass over the lots and place two spears crosswise on the ground, then humbly lead their largest horse, which they venerate as sacred, over them. Whatever the casting of lots has revealed, must be confirmed by this holy beast. If the same omen appears again, it is obeyed. Otherwise, the discontented folk reject it at once. An ancient but equally erroneous tradition also has it that, if the pain of a long internal war threatens, a great boar, its white teeth gleaming with foam, will rise from that same lake and be seen happily rolling in the mud with an excessive shaking.

Whether the decision was for peace or war, unanimity was paramount. According to Adam, Svarozhits, or his priests, brooked no dispute: "If any of them opposes a decision during an assembly, he is beaten. If outside in the open, everything he has is taken from him and burnt, else he must come before the assembly and, according to his rank, make restitution for his sin."

In such a way, and in the name of their god, was the unity of the tribes enforced. Whether or not the boar emerged from the lake to wallow in the mud, by the buried lots, the crossed spears and the prancing of the horse (any one of which might have easily been manipulated by the priests), the decision was rendered. Thietmar concluded, "Margrave Dietrich's arrogance so incensed people who had already accepted both Christ and the payment of tribute to our kings and emperors, that their members as one decided on war."

Practically everything we know of the Slavic Revolt of 983 comes from writers on the Saxon, Christian side – Thietmar of Merseburg, Adam of Bremen, Helmold of Bosau – with all their agendas and biases. None of them concerned themselves with a little-known, newly crowned, Norwegian-born king in Jomsborg, on the far side of their subject lands. Likewise, Olaf's distant, later Icelandic biographers, Odd, Berg and Snorri, knew little of the upheaval on the faraway Saxon-Slavic frontier centuries before their time. They could only cast their story in personal terms, including their hero's motivation, which was to impress his new wife by reclaiming her lost lands and income. Snorri wrote, "He went that winter to those towns in Wendland which had been subject to Queen Geira but had refused all allegiance and payment of tribute to her."

These burgwards were now in Saxony, paying their tribute to the empire instead of their former queen. And the saga writers set the scene in winter, with Olaf's initial attacks in the months leading up to the events at Rethra that summer. In this way his biographers gave him sole credit for the fighting against the Saxons and rebel Wends, when he probably just assaulted the towns nearest Geira's domain. That was enough.

"He gave them two choices," reported Odd of the first town Olaf faced, "whether to pay tribute and serve and obey or that he should attack. 'In that case, you may expect to end up with neither peace nor property.'"

"The townsmen shouted back that they would never yield nor pay tribute," wrote Berg.

Odd would have it that Olaf laid siege to the place, even employing catapults. Well known in the scribes' time, these are not often seen in Viking warfare, but then Vikings preferred surprise attacks and rarely resorted to sieges.* Soldiers of the Holy Roman Empire, however, were vastly experienced with siege engines and siege warfare, and it's very believable the Wends, some of whom had served in the imperial armies, would have learned the construction and use of catapults from them. In any case, Olaf and his men overcame the defenses and burst into the town.

"All who had fought back and spoken so bravely were now conquered and disgraced," proclaimed Odd. "All who did not meekly plead for mercy were slain, and Olaf got whatever terms he wanted."

With this success he proceeded to a second town, where he made the inhabitants the same proposition: siege and defeat, or surrender. "We have heard of your reckless rule and how those who oppose you will suffer," they told him. "We choose more wisely than our neighbors. We will surrender and permit you entry."

Berg recorded, "Pleased, King Olaf promised them great and well-earned reward, and immediately prepared with his army to enter the town. As soon as he and a few of his men had passed inside, however, the huge iron doors were suddenly closed and barred."

---

* They had laid siege to Paris back in AD 885–886, in which they even used ballistae and mangonels in addition to catapults, but for all that the siege failed.

As Odd wrote of the trap, "Then as one, all the chieftains and warriors and common folk rose up with great vehemence. They ordered that no one, great or humble, be allowed to escape."

And Berg added, "From all the huts and lodgings rushed the townsmen, fully armed, urging one another not to let a single one of the king's men escape alive."

Havelberg, where the Havel River enters the Elbe, was, in the 10th century, of strategic importance as the northernmost burgward in the Saxon Marches. Its bishopric had been among the first founded by Emperor (at that point merely King) Otto I, back in 948, to undertake the Christianization of the Wendish people from the middle Elbe up to the Baltic coast, including Usedom Island west of Jomsborg. (That Havelberg was thought immediately worthy of a bishopric suggests that it was already an important Slavic town, built, like so many of their hamlets, on an island in the river.) In reality, however, the empire had less to offer the Wends living in the Baltic watershed than did the Scandinavians – the Vikings – whose trade brought in silver from as far as Araby and Ireland, and who did not insist on dictating their customers' religion. Havelberg, marking the very frontier of the empire, was for the Slavs a constant irritant, and therefore a tempting target. Helmold attested, "They involve themselves in foreign wars for no reason other than treasure, normally safe in holy churches, is there for the pillaging."

"The atrocity began on 29 July," of the year 983, wrote Thietmar, "with the slaughter of the garrison and destruction of the Havelberg cathedral."

Slavic warriors stormed across the bridges over the river into the island town with fire and sword. Unlike Olaf, they were not interested in making threats or waiting out a siege. They had no intention of taking the town intact, nor of sparing any citizens loyal to the empire or to God. Helmold recorded of the Slavs, "They are called into foreign wars so often they prove truly brave in combat, but extremely merciless when it comes to rapine and murder. They do not spare monasteries, nor churches, nor tombs." Havelberg would remain pagan for the next 164 years.

Thietmar continued, "Three days later, at the sounding of prime [the ringing of bells to summon the faithful to dawn prayers], Slavs all attacked the bishopric of Brandenburg, a see founded beyond Magdeburg some thirty years prior."

About sixty miles upriver from Havelberg, Brandenburg-an-der-Havel had in Slavic times been Branibor (from *braniti*, defend, and *bor*, forest). After the Battle of Lenzen in 929, Henry the Fowler had taken it and established its bishopric at the same time as Havelberg's. It may have been a hotbed of Slavic unrest; its bishop Dodilo had been murdered – strangled – by his own congregation in 980. His successors did not linger to experience a similar fate. "Folkmar, the third bishop of that see, had fled already," reported Thietmar of 983, "and his defender, [Margrave] Dietrich, barely got away with his warriors on the day of the attack. Any clergy who stayed behind were taken captive." The attackers dragged Bishop Dodilo's corpse from his tomb. "The greedy dogs plundered it and threw it back without a care. They furthermore stole all the church's treasures and brutally spilled much blood."

That was just the beginning. Slavic mobs rampaged across northern Saxony. Adam recorded, "They fired all the churches and tore them all down. They murdered the priests and the other church ministers with varied tortures and left not a sign of Christianity beyond the Elbe." Thietmar admitted that the Slavs "chased our people like fleeing deer." They reached all the way over to the far side of Bremen to Oldenburg, of which Helmold wrote:

> The old men among the Slavs who remember all the barbarians' deeds tell how Oldenburg had been a city full of Christians. There sixty priests, the rest having been slaughtered like cattle, were kept as objects of mockery. The oldest of these, the provost, was named Oddar. He and the others were martyred in this way. The skin of their heads was cut in the form of a cross, and then each man's brain was laid bare with an iron. With hands bound behind their backs, God's confessors were then dragged through one Slavic village after another until they died. Thus made "a spectacle...to

angels and to men,"* they breathed out their triumphant spirits along the way.

The Slavic tide rolled right up to Hamburg, on the banks of the Elbe. Adam of Bremen wrote, "At Hamburg, immediately and afterward, many clerics and townsfolk were taken off into captivity, and many others were killed out of hatred of Christianity."

Thietmar claimed that Mstivoj "burned and wasted Hamburg, which had been the bishop's residence. Yet all of Christendom should reverently hear of the miracle that Christ in heaven performed there." What follows strikes a modern audience as pure fiction, but an 11th-century readership would have taken it, particularly coming from the Prince-Bishop of Merseburg, as gospel: "A golden hand came down from on high and, with fingers extended, reached into the midst of the fire. This happened in plain view of all. The army saw this with astonishment, and Mstivoj was both terrified and amazed... In this way God raised the relics up to heaven and, simultaneously, frightened away the enemy."

Both Adam, writing about a hundred years after the fact, and Helmold, about a hundred years after that – largely by plagiarizing Adam's text – skipped this scene entirely. Even so, they have been accused of conflating the supposed sack of Hamburg in 983, of which no contemporary records have survived, with that of 1012, which is recorded as having been led by Mstivoj (but since he died in 992, more likely by his son Mstislav).

Thietmar, however, who was living at the time (although still a boy), fixed the attack on Hamburg within his account of the events of 983. And Adam, apparently already defending his lack of documentation, pointed out, "Many such deeds, because they were not written down and are now considered to be fables, are remembered as having happened at this time in several Slavic provinces."

---

* 1 Corinthians 4:9. "For it seems to me that God has put us apostles on display at the end of the procession, like those condemned to die in the arena. We have been made a spectacle to the whole universe, to angels as well as to human beings."

Trapped and surrounded with his men inside the rebel town, King Olaf, still just twenty years old, made the kind of snap decision befitting a leader, and the hero of a saga. Odd credited him with the idea: "I see just one way out. Over the town wall."

Wooden stockades were made to be insurmountable from the outside. On the inside, though, ladders and parapets allowed defenders, or escapees, to quickly reach the top. None of this town's defenders had been manning the walls. They had been hiding down on the ground, and could only chase Olaf and his men as they climbed, the king leading the way. No matter how high the stockade, on the outside they typically crested down-sloping embankments, letting a man hitting the ground roll and slow his fall. Odd wrote of Olaf, "He jumped down, and it happened as he predicted. He called on them to follow, even though they thought it a long way down. They obeyed and jumped down, and with his help everyone survived."

They had escaped the trap, but the town remained untaken. Odd has Olaf resolving to do it the old-fashioned way: "Then they laid siege to the town and mounted such a forceful attack that they made great breaks in the wall and all went through."

Berg admitted, "As the villagers resisted, an awful fight followed, in which everyone in the town was finally slain. Everything valuable was claimed as loot, and the town was burnt to ashes…* King Olaf did not cease warring until he had conquered all the towns and districts that had denied Queen Geira's rule and authority." And Odd added, "Olaf returned in triumph and brought the queen gold, silver and precious objects."

---

* Odd also noted, "People claim that the town that Olaf besieged and where people sought to betray him and where he was trapped with sixty men was Jomsborg," but his sources were in error. Nowhere else in any of the sagas – not even the saga of Jomsborg itself – is Olaf implicated in the town's destruction, which in any case would not happen for another sixty years. "People claim" implies Odd's own doubt in the matter. In his later rewrite, with access to more sources, Berg declined to mention it. For Olaf to "reclaim" Jomsborg on Geira's behalf, though, would at least confirm that she ruled there.

Thietmar recorded, "By the time the Slavs had razed and looted all the burgs and towns as far as the river Tanger, there were more than thirty warrior bands afoot and on horseback. Taking no losses and with their god's help, they went on to ravage the rest of the land, as their blaring war horns announced."

The Saxons were attacked on two fronts. To the north, in Schleswig, the Danes took advantage of the weakened empire. Feigning loyalty, they infiltrated Emperor Otto's stronghold on the Danevirke, retook it and burned it down, and took Hedeby by siege. Sources differ on whether the attack was led by Harald Bluetooth in rebellion against Emperor Otto, or his son Svein on behalf of his father, or Svein in rebellion against his father. Various Scandinavian runestones raised by the victors refer to the siege and to *Suin Kununkr*, Svein the King, which he may have been by the time the runes were carved.

Margrave Dietrich had lost Schleswig, but he had no intention of losing Saxony. He used the time and sacrifice of his cities to unite the bishops and counts of his domain and his fellow Saxon margraves in organizing a counterattack. Thus far the Slavs had been having their way with defenseless townspeople. Now they would meet an army.

It's said the two sides came together near modern Stendal at Tangermunde, the "mouth of the Tanger [River]," where that tributary joins the Elbe. "At dawn on Saturday, they celebrated mass together," wrote Thietmar of the Saxons. "Then, after fortifying body and soul with the heavenly sacrament, they fell confidently upon the advancing enemy and, except for some who took refuge on a hill, completely exterminated them. The victors praised God, wonderful in all his works."

The battle, or slaughter, having lasted until nightfall, the imperials gave pause. The surviving Slavs did not rest. "Unfortunately," wrote Thietmar, "as night fell and our forces encamped some distance off, the Slavs of whom I have spoken above secretly escaped."

The Slavs may have lost the battle, but they won the war. They never had any hope of conquering the Holy Roman Empire, or even just Saxony, but they halted the Germanic – the Christian – advance into their lands. The Northern and Billung Marches were theirs, and would remain theirs, remain pagan, until the middle of the

12th century. Not the Oder but the Elbe would be the eastern limit of imperial control and influence of the *Teutonicus Deus*. As Adam wrote, "And so all the Slavs between the Elbe and the Oder and who had practiced Christianity for seventy years and more, during the reign of the Ottos, separated themselves from the body of Christ and of the Church of which they had been part."

Again, Olaf's role in the Great Slavic Revolt is wide open to interpretation. His biographers merely depict him fighting on the Slavs' behalf in the area at the time; Saxon writers, having no idea who he was, give him no credit and indeed fail to mention him at all. Certainly he did not rank as a leader of the entire Slavic nation. But the revolt was a turning point in European history, and Olaf's role in it, however small, foreshadows his influence on it in years to come.

XIV

KING OF THE WENDS

King Olaf waged more war in Wendland than any other king before him, and won victory in every fight.

Berg Sokkason

AD 984

"Olaf waged war, slew many people, drove out others, looted much property, and subjected them to his authority," declared Snorri, and Berg went on: "Then he returned to his own town, where he resided through the winter."

To merely reconquer Geira's domain, however, was not enough. Olaf was a king now – a real king, not just the chieftain of a pack of sea rovers – and in those days a king needed to keep his fighting men happy (meaning rich and powerful), or he would not remain king for long. Snorri continued, "Early in spring Olaf raised sail and put out to sea. He went to Skane [modern Scania, southernmost Sweden] and landed there. The country folk came and put up a fight, but King Olaf triumphed, and took a great amount of booty."

His fleet proceeded south and east around the coast, past Bornholm Island into the Baltic. Off the island of Gotland – coming full-circle from the pirate raid that had seen him enslaved nigh on twenty years earlier – Olaf attacked a Swedish merchant knarr, slew many of its crew and robbed it of its cargo. On Gotland itself he fought a third battle, won the victory and yet more loot. (To this day Gotland is the richest source of ancient Arab silver dirham coins in Europe, with finds almost as plentiful as in the Muslim world.) The voyage was notable enough for Hallfred the Troublesome Poet to have included a few lines on the subject in his praise poem for Olaf, the *Olafsdrapa*: "In his youth he achieved this. The sword-bold ruler threatened the lives of Gotlanders. I learned that the generous man unleashed a spear-storm on Skane."

Possibly because Hallfred went on, "The relentless seafarer cut down the mail-shirted warriors in Denmark south of Hedeby," without saying exactly when, it is here that Snorri and Berg had Olaf and his father-in-law Burislav join Emperor Otto in his assault on the Danevirke.* As noted, the battle was actually fought a decade or so earlier. In fact, Otto II died in December 983, just a few months after the Slavic Revolt, and the imperial throne passed to his three-year-old son Otto III.† Berg has Olaf return from his Baltic raid to join his father-in-law Burislav and Emperor Otto II and play the same vital, though totally erroneous and fictitious, role at the Danevirke: "In his heart he contemplated most thoroughly the miracles he had seen in Denmark," meaning the conversion to Christianity of the Viking Bluetooth, which Olaf never personally witnessed, though he doubtless knew of it.

Having thus contrived to credit their hero with a hand in the religious conversion of two kings, Vladimir of the Rus and Bluetooth of Denmark, Olaf's biographers return somewhat to reality. Berg picked up the story: "Olaf passed the winter after his [fictitious] meeting with the Emperor Otto in his Wendish realm, and come spring he readied his ships and embarked on a freebooting raid."

By this time, having picked the southern Baltic clean, Olaf and his crews sailed west, up one side of the Danish peninsula and down the other into the North Sea. Oldenburg and Hamburg were still

---

* Berg went so far as to have a victorious, grateful Otto offer Olaf a job by naming him a noble of imperial Saxony, which Olaf graciously declines in favor of his Wendish kingdom. In reality, as shall be seen, Olaf did not exactly maintain friendly relations with the empire.

† Dietrich of Haldensleben, Margrave of the Nordmark, having lost his post, his rank, his power and his inheritance, died in 985 as a lowly prebendary in the church at Magdeburg. Mstivoj would live until 995, according to Helmold, converting back to Christianity and dying of old age, but an anonymous scribe noted in Thietmar's *Chronicon* that Mstivoj went insane, underwent something like an exorcism, and died screaming that the holy water was burning him.

recovering from the Slavic revolt and, given the old chroniclers' mishandling of dates, Olaf's seaborne end-around may have been a part of it, a scheme to attack the Germans from the rear. Hallfred chronicled, "The ruler, Tryggvi's son, had the corpses of Saxons cut down often."

Farther down the coast, what is now northwest Germany and northern Netherlands was then called Frisia. As with other European coasts over the centuries, the high water mark has changed greatly, the sea having eroded the shoreline and forced its way inland. Many of today's offshore islands were then part of the mainland, and what is now the wide-mouthed bay of the Zuiderzee was in medieval times the Almere, a brackish lake connected to the sea only by a narrow channel, much the way the Oder Lagoon was connected to the Baltic. Since its conquest by the Franks in the early 700s, Frisia had been part of the Holy Roman Empire, and Dorestad and Utrecht on the Rhine had established a trade network on a par with Hedeby in Schleswig and Jomsborg in Wendland. For 150 years Vikings had alternately settled, traded and raided in Frisia. Olaf's visit, according to his skald Hallfred, was the latter: "Far and wide the popular prince gave the black wolf the dark blood of many Frisians to drink.'"

Olaf continued down the coast to what is now Flanders, but was then West Francia, the ashes of the old Carolingian Empire. As with the death of Otto I in 973, the death of Otto II had set off a power struggle, this time between Charlemagne's last Frankish descendants – Lothair of France and his son Louis V – and the Saxon Ottonian dynasty. While Lothair looked east, his back was turned on his Flemish shore. Olaf took full advantage. Hallfred attested, "The just king destroyed the bodies of the Valkerar [the inhabitants of Walcheren Island on the Flemish coast]. The war-leader had the Flemings' flesh fed to the ravens."

Walcheren had once been the seat of Danish Vikings, the brothers Harald and Rorik, who had fought as mercenaries in the Carolingian civil wars of the 830s and been granted the island as a buffer against further Danish incursions. Being Vikings, they had ultimately overstayed their welcome and been ousted. Whatever King Lothair's troubles with the empire, he would not have permitted Vikings to regain a foothold there again, and in any case Olaf had not come to stay.

Since Roman times, though, Walcheren had been a traditional stepping-off place for ships bound across the western sea. It was said that various small Viking bands had resumed scattered but successful raiding on that far coast.* To this point Olaf's adventures had all been to the east. However, this Angle-land – England – was well known to the Scandinavians of his day. It was said that half a millennium earlier, not long after the Romans abandoned it, two other brothers from Denmark, Hengist and Horsa, had crossed over with three ships full of warriors to fight as mercenaries for the Britons against their enemies, the Picts. When that fighting was done, however, the brothers and their men – Jutes from the northern Danish peninsula, probably Frisians and perhaps even some Swedes, but predominantly Saxons and Angles from the area of Schleswig – had not only stayed, but turned on their employers and ultimately conquered the island. Those Anglo-Saxons, as they came to be called, were only the first wave of the great Scandinavian diaspora of the 8th and 9th centuries; they had in turn lost half of their Angle-land to invading Danes, and only by the efforts of their king Alfred the Great and his descendants had regained it.

The current king of the Anglo-Saxons, Aethelred II, was a few years younger than Olaf. He had achieved the throne only because his mother had ordered his elder half-brother assassinated. He was not well liked, and had never had to face a foreign invasion. A strong Viking leader might have found England ripe for the retaking, but first he would need to become that strong Viking leader.

And Olaf already had a kingdom.

One likes to think, however, that as his fleet put out from Walcheren and Flanders, bound northward for home, that they swung just far enough west to give Olaf a glimpse of that foreign coast that had rebuffed the Viking tide.

---

* It's thought that this nascent "Second Viking Age" was driven in part by an Islamic silver crisis, a drying up of the supply due to exhaustion of mines, war and political upheaval in the Abbasid Caliphate. Arabic coins, 95 percent silver up to mid-century, were down to 65 percent near the end. German and English silver coins were still reliably 90 percent pure, but the newly discovered (AD 968) silver mine at Rammelsberg in Germany's Harz Mountains was under the Holy Roman Empire's control. The Vikings were looking again to England for their silver.

According to Berg it was in Saxony, during Olaf's return voyage, that he first met a character who was to play a role in his future, and to some small degree the future of Christianity. Thangbrand of Saxony was a clerk, but in the old sense of the Latin *clericus* – a cleric or clergyman, a priest. According to Snorri, Thangbrand was less an adherent of the New Testament, love-your-brother, God the father of Christ, than of the wrathful Old Testament God, "a very unpredictable man and a great man-slayer, but clever and a good cleric." When Olaf came across him in the vicinity of Brima, modern Bremen in West Saxony, Thangbrand was bearing a shield, not exactly everyday wear for Christian Saxon priests, unless in the midst of a Viking raid. Nor was his just any shield, for it bore an image of the Crucifixion. On seeing it, Olaf did not have this warrior priest cut down, but paused in the fighting to ask, "Who is that man on the cross whom you Christians worship?"

Thangbrand told him, "Our Lord Jesus Christ."

"Why was he crucified? What crime did he commit?"

One would think that Olaf might have learned the story of the Passion and Crucifixion during his time in Constantinople, but in the sagas he has not yet made his (at this point ever-more improbable) journey to Greece, and this is his first intimation of Christianity. Berg wrote, "On this Thangbrand explained to him in detail the passion of the Lord, and the miracle of the Cross."

Thangbrand was said to be the son of a Saxon noble in Brima, which makes sense; in those days many sons of nobles who were not the eldest, and therefore not first in line to inherit, found their way into the Church or law. In his role as a clerk Thangbrand had accompanied his bishop on a visit across the western sea to Cantwaraburh, modern Canterbury, "the city of the men of Kent," in the land of the Angles. The bishop there had told Thangbrand, "You conduct yourself like a warrior, so I give you this shield."

Such a splendid shield, simply given away, was proof not only of the wealth of the English church, but also that the Christian god had once again proven superior to those of the Vikings, protecting his children just as he favored his people in Constantinople, just as he now protected Thangbrand from Olaf. The king offered to buy the shield, but the priest simply gave it to him.

"This gift greatly pleases me," Olaf told him, "and if you ever feel that you need help and protection, come to me and I will repay you for it. I would rather, though, that you accept a little money from me." Olaf paid for the shield in silver, Thangbrand accepted, and they parted as friends. Berg wrote, "In the autumn King Olaf sailed home to Wendland, and remained there for the third winter."

His royal lands, income and honor restored, Olaf might have lived out his allotted span in Jomsborg, in comfort and luxury, reigning alongside a queen who loved him. Alas, as in Novgorod, as at Burgundaholm, the gods had other plans for him.

"When King Olaf Tryggvason had spent three years in Wendland, something happened which brought him and many fellow countrymen great anguish and grief," wrote Berg, "for his wife Queen Geira fell ill with a sickness that led to her death."

XV

OF GOD AND GODS

He had ruled the country so well that everyone loved him deeply, despite which he could not be consoled.

Odd Snorrason

AD 985

"They are afflicted by a pair of diseases," wrote ibn Yaqub of the Slavs, "and are rarely free from either. These are two varieties of rash, red rash and carbuncles."

Without putting too much faith in his medieval diagnostic skills, we might assume the Wends suffered much the same poxes and plagues that afflicted most peoples throughout history. Red rash and carbuncles – boils or more likely *buboes*, infected, swollen lymph glands – sound very much like two of history's all-time killers, smallpox and bubonic plague. Admittedly the 10th century presented something of an interim for both. Smallpox had spread along with the 6th-century Muslim expansion into northern Africa, Spain and Portugal, and would again in the 11th century via the Crusades. And this was some 200 years after the end of the first major European plague pandemic, the Plague of Justinian, and still some 350 years before the onset of the Black Death in Europe. Yet both pox and plague always lurked in the background, and local village-sized micro-pandemics must have been so common as to be beneath historians' note, except ibn Yaqub's passing mention.

Neither malady provides an easy death. Smallpox inflames the lungs and kidneys, causing death via subcutaneous bleeding and that of internal organs, on average fatal to three out of every ten victims. Plague ends in bloody vomit, seizures, gangrene, skin literally decomposing and ultimately organ failure, killing up to nine out of ten. And if not those, there was always dysentery and cholera to make every sip of water a possibly fatal gamble, or tuberculosis, polio, diphtheria, rinderpest, anthrax, erysipelas...the list is so long it's a wonder anybody survived to adulthood.

Western civilization, modern medicine, has come a long way. Plague survives, but outbreaks are vanishingly rare, quickly treated and halted. Smallpox and rinderpest are effectively extinct. Death still strikes at random, but only at the end of lives twice as long as our forebears' a millennium ago will most of us see it reap friends and family on its way to claiming us. How would any of us have fared in a similar state of near-constant grief, with so many of our loved ones so quickly lost to us, knowing most of the rest soon would be, and that barely out of childhood our own lives were more than half over? For people of Olaf's day that awareness was a constant weight, and surely why life, so brief and woeful and held so cheap, was yet enjoyed to the fullest, in fervent belief that some higher power must be behind it all.

Prior to Christianity funeral rites among medieval Slavs, as among pagan Vikings, usually involved cremation. (Ibn Fadlan, observing a Rus funeral along the Volga, was told, "You Arabs are fools. You bury those whom you love and honor most in the dirt, where animals and worms may eat them. We, however, burn them at once, so that they immediately enter Paradise.") The singing, wailing funeral procession bore the body to a pyre of birch, considered holy, or oak, sacred to the Rus father-god Perun and presumably to his Baltic incarnation, Svetovit. Along with gifts from the mourners, men were laid to rest with their weapons or tools, women with their jewelry. Favored pets, slaves and sometimes wives were slain and sent along to accompany chieftains in the afterlife. (Ibn Fadlan famously witnessed the ritual murder of a slave girl who volunteered to join her late owner in death.) Afterward the ashes, bones and funerary objects were collected in a ceramic urn to be buried in a raised earthen mound or barrow between the sky, the realm of the gods, and the underworld, the realm of the dead. In this way the soul joined with the heavens and the body with the earth. The life of the departed was celebrated with a *trisna*, a kind of wake, with eating, drinking and games.

For Olaf the agnostic, such ritual was of no meaning and even less consolation. Berg declared, "It is said that Olaf Tryggvason never worshipped carven images, and greatly scorned all belief in them." Geira's death was no cause for celebration. The sparks of a funeral pyre simply mingle with the stars, and are gone. Snorri confided, "Olaf felt this loss so keenly that he could never be happy in Wendland again."

And Odd wrote, "He prepared his army to leave the country, thinking that in this way he could sooner come to terms with the grief he had suffered."

"Many Norwegians, Danes, Gotlanders and Wends joined his fleet," attests the *Historia Norwegiae*, "flocking to his winter quarters in Jomsborg, that great Wendish town." It's now, after the loss of Geira, that Snorri has Olaf set off on his raiding voyage down the Saxon/Frisian/Flemish coast, though without mention of Thangbrand of Saxony. Meanwhile Odd and Berg have Olaf intent on a return to Kyivan Rus, for as Berg put it, "in his grief he would naturally first go where he had spent the happiest time in his life."

The wind is against him, however, so he first stops off westward, on the Danish coast, and naturally disembarks to do a little raiding. Odd admitted, "They supplied themselves with local livestock, as is customary, seizing many animals and herding them to the shore."

By this time, though, the back-and-forth fighting in Denmark between King Harald Bluetooth and his bastard son Svein was heating up. Many Danes still resented the king forcing them into a Christianity which better represented the interests of the Saxons and Holy Roman Empire. (Another reason why many of them had resumed raiding England.) They were inclined to support Svein, who, despite being baptized as a child, was indifferent to religion, caring less to whom men prayed than for whom they fought. As a result, the people had become accustomed to raids by one side or the other, hardening themselves to fend off both, and foreign invaders like Olaf as well. A local militia assembled to chase his Vikings back where they came from.

Olaf and his men were caught by surprise. Odd related, "When they looked back and saw a great many heavily armed men, they ran for their ships. But because they had gone deep inland and it was so far to their ships, their enemies nearly caught them."

Berg wrote, "They found no easy escape, for the forest near them was thick with brush, and was no safe place to hide."

Then, according to the scribes, Olaf, like many men facing imminent death, found inspiration. "I know there is a mighty god who rules in heaven. I have also heard there is a victory token of great power, the sign of the cross upon which he suffered. We should humbly pray to him to aid us, lie down on the ground, and lay two sticks over us in the figure of a cross."

"Their enemies entered the woods with clamor and war cries," continued Odd. "They believed they would capture them, having just seen them clearly. They went past them and walked over them, but did not find them."

The trick works until Olaf and his men jump up to flee, then works again even when they lie down in a barren field. Their pursuers simply do not see them. "They went home with neither honor nor victory," wrote Odd. "And so the holy cross rescued Olaf from danger both in an open field and in a thick wood. Olaf made it back to his ships and thanked God he got away."

Call it a complete fabrication, or simply the Icelandic monks' way of crediting their god for the narrow escape of Vikings clever enough to camouflage themselves with some brush. Soon after this incident, according to them, Olaf dreams of his ascent to heaven, and is inspired to go to Constantinople via the long route, doubling back down through Kyivan Rus to receive his *prima signatio* in the Hagia Sophia. As noted, that episode is disregarded by historians as implausible, and at this stage of the saga it certainly is. Remember, though, that Odd and Berg were often wildly mistaken in their dates, the ten-year 973–983 discrepancy in the Battle of the Danevirke being the prime example. Odd may well have realized how unlikely Olaf's Constantinople visit was at this point, but who among his readership was to know? He shoehorned it into his narrative closer to the time that Grand Prince Vladimir really did convert to Christianity, in order to give Olaf credit for the conversion. In his own day Berg saw no reason to dispute the claim, insisting, "These tales which have now been told of Olaf Tryggvason preaching Christianity in the realm of Garda are not incredible."

As has also been noted, however, Snorri didn't believe any of it, and left it out of the *Heimskringla*. He had Olaf spending those years voyaging in the other direction, west: "Olaf Tryggvason sailed to England and raided far and wide."

According to the *Anglo-Saxon Chronicle*, after decades of peace since the death of Eirik Bloodaxe and the expulsion of his Vikings, the early 980s had seen a gradual resurgence of Viking raids, at least in southern England. (In their raids the Norwegians tended to sail the roundabout route, north of Scotland and down Britain's western coast. It was predominantly the Danes who crossed the North Sea to attack the east.) This middle of the decade was relatively quiet again, but that may be because the raiders switched to targets in the north. The English annalists, most of whom were down in the south of the island, cared little for the doings of the northerners, who had lived under Viking rule for the better part of the past century. Many folk up there were of Danish blood, and considered little better than Vikings themselves.

None of that mattered to Olaf. He had no Danish blood. And he hadn't come to England seeking friends and allies. "The wide-renowned warrior steered his ships westwards towards England," relates the *Olafsdrapa*. "Young, he soon reddened swords."

"He sailed along the coast, northwards to Northumbria, where he fought a battle," concurred Berg, "and from there to Scotland, where he laid many places to waste."

The skald Hallfred wrote, "The young, overwhelming king proceeded to battle against the English. That warrior ordered the killing of the Northumbrians. The prince beat the inhabitants of the British land and cut down the Cumbric peoples; the eagle was sated."

Of this the *Olafsdrapa* says only, "Dwellings burned, and the miserable Scots ran for the forest."

The *Historia Norwegiae* records, "During this misguided looting he performed great feats in Scotland and spared no one in Ireland."

At this time the king of Scotland, or Alba as it was then known, was Coinneach mac Mhaoil Chaluim – Kenneth II – called *An Fionnghalach*, "The Fratricidal" or "Kinslayer."[*] He had his hands full with unifying his land's various Gaelic clans and settlers, Picts, Britons, Anglo-Saxons and Norse. They were all battling each other for supremacy, leaving themselves open to lightning raids from across the sea. The only thing they all had in common was that Scotland was already predominantly Christian – full of fat churches just waiting for a godless Viking to sack. In this way Olaf and his men rounded the northern coast and headed down the far side.

"From there he went to the Hebrides and fought some battles there," continued Snorri. The Hebrides Islands – what the Vikings called the *Sudreyjar*, the Southern Isles, as opposed to the *Nordreyjar*, the Northern Isles, Orkney and Shetland – were if anything a scene of greater anarchy than Scotland. In the 870s Norwegians had fled there to escape Harald Fairhair's subjugation of their homeland and declared their independence. Since then, the Kingdom of the Isles had been fought over by the Irish, the Scots, the Viking jarls of Orkney and kings of Ireland.

At this point Vikings had been on the Emerald Isle for over 200 years. From their coastal footholds in Waterford, Limerick and Dublin, they had interbred with the natives to produce a new race: the *Gall-Goidil*, the Foreign Gaels, the Norse-Irish. The mixed-blood clan of the *Uí Ímair* – the "sons of Ivar" (possibly Ivar the Boneless, son of Ragnar Lodbrok) – had at one point ruled the Irish Sea from Dublin to the Isle of Man, part of Scotland and of northern England. Theirs was a loose empire, though, more an association of kindred lords, lacking a single ruler. Since the loss of Northumbria, and under the constant threat of overthrow by the Gaels, their dynasty was on the wane. In the previous two decades, defeats at the hands of the native Irish had set loose roving packs of unemployed Norse-Irish fighting men upon the Irish Sea. Ringed with trading ports like Dublin, Wexford, Waterford and Cork in Ireland, and Bristol, Gloucester, Worcester and Chester on the English side, it was as much an international thoroughfare as the Baltic or the North Sea, crisscrossed by laden merchant ships just

---

[*] Recall that old Eirik Bloodaxe was also known as "Brother-Slayer"; blood relations, so important among Northern Europeans, often called for alliances, but just as often resulted in murder.

begging to be robbed. As Olaf's skald Hallfred Ottarson would later record in verse, "The generous lord made sword-sport on [the Isle of] Man, the battle-glad feeder of wolves put the Scots to the sword. The bow-string terror slew the army of the Isles and the Irish, the god of precious spears eager for glory."

In such anarchy Vikings, even vagabond homeless Vikings like Olaf and his band, could thrive. Raid here, trade there, find a hidden cove or inlet where dragon ships could be beached and camp set up for as long as necessary, or at least until the ale ran out. Along the way Olaf accumulated something of a fleet, a half-dozen ships, and with them made himself a minor terror to the western coasts. The *Agrip* agrees with Hallfred: "He harried widely, in Wendland and Flanders, in England and Scotland, in Ireland and in many others, generally wintering in Wendland, in the town of Jomsborg."

But Jomsborg was not the same after he left.

XVI

The Jomsvikings

King Harald Gormsson raided in the land of the Wends and had a great stronghold built there at a place called Jom, and since then that stronghold has been called Jomsborg.

Fagrskinna

AD 985–986

While Olaf was in the midst of his pirate cruise around the Irish Sea, back in Jomsborg the people quickly came to regret losing their leader. There seems to have been a period of anarchy, in which different sagas have different men on the throne. Let us again diverge from our central story – as did Olaf's original biographers – to keep up with goings-on in our hero's absence, for it is in Jomsborg that another villain enters our tale.

As usual, the dates are uncertain, but the *Fagrskinna* would have it that Harald Bluetooth, having failed to regain Norway from Jarl Hakon – but having reclaimed Hedeby from the empire and seeking a Danish foothold in Wendish lands – captured Jomsborg. Captured, not destroyed; the town was too valuable, both as a source of tribute from the Slavs and a military outpost against them. "He put a man in command, and went back to Denmark, and for a long time afterward there was contention between the Wends and the Danes, with each side raiding in the other's lands."

By some accounts Bluetooth's man in Jomsborg was a Swedish prince, Styrbjorn the Strong, a nephew of Sweden's King Eirik, married to Bluetooth's daughter Thyri. With Danish backing, however, Styrbjorn, whose name translates as something like "violent bear," soon took it upon himself to attempt a conquest of Sweden. He was defeated and slain by his uncle Eirik at Fyrisvellir near Uppsala, the battle which gained Eirik the epithet "Victorious." According to other accounts, Bluetooth's puppet ruler in Jomsborg was his jarl Palnatoki, "Toki son of Palnir," or perhaps "Arrow Toki"; he was a famed archer who, like William Tell and many other semi-legendary figures in European legend, was said to have shot an apple off his own son's head. Still others claim Palnatoki, "big, clever and popular," was not raised to power by Bluetooth but by King Burislav, the late Geira's Wendish father. In this telling of the tale, Burislav offered Jomsborg to Palnatoki as a means of establishing a buffer between him and Bluetooth, to whom he was paying tribute. It's not too hard to believe that Palnatoki ruled on behalf of both kings, playing them against each other.

In any case, what matters to Olaf's story is that Palnatoki is also said to be the foster father of Bluetooth's rebellious son Svein, and encouraged that rebellion as a means of furthering his own. With this new source of fighting men, the boy pressed his father ever harder. "Svein raided Denmark day and night," records one saga. "He slew men, looted everything and set the land afire. The country folk fled in terror before him and beseeched the king, who could not let things go on."

"Now the king thought something must be done," goes another, "for he had too long endured from Svein what he would not have from others. Now he readied fifty ships, and sailed himself with this force, meaning to kill Svein and all his men."

The climactic confrontation between father and son took place at sea. Some of the sagas claim it was off Burgundaholm, that Danish Baltic island that Olaf had first raided on his return from Rus. The *Heimskringla* says it was in Ise fjord in Zealand, but little matter; the battle would have gone much the same either way. Vikings were not much for naval strategy or maneuvers. The objective was not to sink enemy ships, which were valuable prizes in themselves, but to capture them. To do so they fought at sea the way they fought on land: grappling their ships together and battling gunwale to gunwale until one side managed to board the other and kill the crews or drive them overboard. In that slow, bloody way Svein and Bluetooth and their men battled all day. The father lost ten ships, but the son twelve, yet the battle ended with Bluetooth dead or dying. Svein, now called *Tjuguskegg*, "Forkbeard," took over as King of Denmark, and immediately recanted his father's faith. Saxo Grammaticus lamented, "On Harald's death, Svein happily took the opportunity to attack religion, and tore up the whole tree of faith. The Danes had accepted Christianity, but under his reign they gave it up, and turned back to paganism all the more quickly as they well knew its bitterest opponent was dead."

Meanwhile Palnatoki ruled in Jomsborg. The *Fagrskinna* claims:

> There he quickly has built in his realm a seaside fortress, very large and strong, which was called Jomsborg. Inside he also has built a harbor that can hold 300 longships at the same time, all enclosed within the fortress.* The harbor entrance was designed with great ingenuity, built as if there was a door, with a great stone arch above it. At the entrance were iron gates which shut the harbor from inside. And upon the stone arch a big tower was built with catapults.

That sounds a bit farfetched, given what we know of Viking and Slavic architecture in those days, all wooden stockades and earthen parapets. (Stone fortifications date from closer to when the *Fagrskinna* was written, around AD 1220, and in Wolin none have been found to exist any earlier than the first half of the 14th century.) However, like the Volkhov flowing through Novgorod, at Wolin the Oder channel is just 350 feet wide. Log palisades extending into the water and heavy iron chains or wooden sea-gates across the gaps could certainly have walled off the passage. Furthermore, in conjunction with two islands lying side by side in the river next to it, Jomsborg sported a shoreline of some two and a half miles, which could have accommodated 360 ships as easily as did Constantinople.

Palnatoki, moreover, saw himself as more than a mere jarl of Jomsborg. If the sagas are to be believed, he took those disparate Wendish, Scandinavian, Slavic and Saxon warriors that Olaf had left

---

* Again, according to the Scandinavian "long hundred" of 120, this would actually come to 360 ships.

behind, and forged them into one of Europe's first military orders, predecessor of the Knights Templar, the Knights Hospitaller and the Teutonic Knights: the Jomsvikings.

Their historicity is on a par with Jomsborg itself, which is to say that many historians claim they never existed except as 12th-century fiction, because they were not referred to as Jomsvikings in their own time. Let us recall, though, that in those days literacy was a rare thing – very little Viking history was written down as it happened – and applying the same standard would render almost all of the sagas as fiction. It is reasonable to accept that there were Vikings on the southern Baltic coast, which would necessarily include Jomsborg; therefore, let us call them Jomsvikings.

They became so renowned in Scandinavian legend that they would inspire their own *Jomsviking Saga*, in no fewer than five versions, not to mention a drapa singing their praises and mentions by numerous skalds. They appear in both Odd's and Berg's versions of Olaf's saga, plus the *Fagrskinna*, *Heimskringla* and other tales. Their supposed law, the *Jomsvikingalog*, is at least useful as an idealized version of a medieval warrior code. Regardless of background, any man between the ages of eighteen and fifty could join their ranks, but only by defeating a Jomsviking in a duel. No women or children were allowed within their sanctum; no man could spend more than three nights outside. All were equals, obliged to defend each other, or avenge each other, as brothers. All loot was to be shared in common, on pain of exile. And all were decisively pagan. "They reside in the fortress on good terms and obey their laws properly," declares the *Jomsviking Saga*. "They leave the fortress every summer and go raiding everywhere and win great acclaim, and are said to be the greatest warriors, with nothing like their equals at the time. And they are forever called Jomsvikings."

Besides Palnatoki, their ranks included several warriors who would be remembered by name. There were Bui and Sigurd, sons of King Veseti of Burgundaholm, his grandson Vagn Akesson and Vagn's foster father, Bjorn *inn brezki*, "the Welsh". The Jomsviking who matters most to Olaf's story, though, is Sigvaldi Strut-Haraldsson.

(His father Strut-Harald was nicknamed for his *strut*, his cone-shaped hat or helm, with gold decorations worth ten marks.)

"Sigvaldi, son of Jarl Strut-Harald, had pallid features and a hooked nose," admits the *Jomsviking Saga*, "but he was very tall and nimble, with excellent eyesight. Thorkell, his brother, was strong and very tall. Both of the brothers were clever."

When, not long afterward, Palnatoki lay dying, it was Sigvaldi whom he recommended to King Burislav for command of the Jomsvikings. Their saga admits, however, "Sigvaldi had not been in command long before discipline began to loosen. Women stayed in the city for two or three nights at a time and the men also went outside longer than when Palnatoki had been alive. Sometimes men wounded one another and a few isolated murders took place."

As a leader Sigvaldi was less inspiring than wily. He desired Astrid, Burislav's daughter (and the late Geira's sister) for a wife. Berg described her much as the skalds did most female subjects – "a beautiful woman" – and in one way they rarely did – "very clever." As the price of her hand, she tasked him with either capturing Svein Forkbeard or at least getting him to release Wendland from paying the Danes tribute. Hard to say which job was more daunting, but Sigvaldi agreed to accomplish one or the other within three years.

He sailed for Denmark, where he lured Svein aboard his ship and kidnapped him. Rather than hand him over to Burislav's mercy, however, he struck a three-way deal. Svein would marry Burislav's remaining daughter, Gunnhild, with Burislav pledging that part of Wendland which she stood to inherit as her dowry. Burislav would marry Svein's sister, Styrbjorn the Strong's widow Thyri Haraldsdottir, with Svein forgiving Wendland's future tribute as *her* dowry. (Unlike her brother, Thyri was Christian, and would not be pleased to learn she had been auctioned off to a pagan, but that was a noblewoman's duty. More of her later.) Both kings saw the benefit in a treaty of marriage between them. And for his efforts Sigvaldi, of course, would receive Astrid's hand.

It was the kind of boldness and guile that Vikings admired, the kind that assured Sigvaldi a place in the sagas, perhaps as much as the roles he and Svein were to play in Olaf's. Yet the Norns had several other fateful threads yet to weave into the whole cloth. For now, Sigvaldi had connived his way into two royal families, but

Svein Forkbeard had gained something much more valuable: the fealty of the Jomsvikings.

According to their saga, not long after this Jarl Strut-Harald died. Svein summoned Sigvaldi and his brother Thorkell, "the Tall," and their men to Denmark for a funeral feast. The *Fagrskinna* attests, "King Svein readied the feast at Hringstad on Sjoland [modern Ringsted in Zealand, a traditional site of Danish thing meetings] making certain it lacked nothing that could make it most magnificent."

One of the most important traditions of such a feast was the drinking of *erfiol*, potent ceremonial beer, from a *bragafull*, a chieftain's cup, by which oaths were sworn before the gods. Svein took full advantage. "The first night, when King Svein and Jarl Sigvaldi were toasting their fathers," the *Fagrskinna* confides, "the king had servants give the Jomsviking leaders the strongest drink, to get them as drunk as possible."

Bjarni Kolbeinsson, the *byskup*, bishop, of Orkney from AD 1188 to 1223 and author of the *Jomsvikingadrapa*, the "Song of the Jomsvikings," confided, "I heard that troubles increased for some of them."

Once his guests were babbling drunk, Forkbeard led off with his toast: "This oath I swear, that I will drive King Aethelred out of his kingdom within three years, or else gain the kingdom by killing him."

By this time Aethelred II, about twenty years old, had sat on the English throne for some eight years, was newly married and enjoying relative peace in England. Scattershot, disorganized Viking raids were to him nothing more than a nuisance. Mercia, Wessex, Northumbria and the other great ealdordoms of England stood united against invaders, and even a concerted assault in the manner of the old days of the Great Heathen Army and Danelaw stood little chance of success.

An invasion of England, however, was not King Svein's intent. He called out, "And now, Sigvaldi, swear no less an oath than mine."

No less an oath than invading England? One can imagine Sigvaldi getting tipsily to his feet and raising the bragafull, trying to think of some way to one-up the king. There was one sure way, which the *Heimskringla* reports as common knowledge: "In those days the Danes were threatening to invade Norway against Jarl Hakon."

"I swear," Sigvaldi announced, "that I shall raid Norway before three years are out, with whatever force as I can gather for it, and shall either drive out Jarl Hakon, kill him, or lie dead there."

Sigvaldi's brother Thorkell, called *inn Havi*, "the Tall," was not to be outdone. "I swear that I will follow my brother Sigvaldi and not flee until I see his ship's stern. But if he fights on land I swear that I shall not flee while he still stands and I can see his standard before me."

And so it went, down through the ranks. Bui son of Veseti was said to be a man of few words, not handsome, but physically imposing and a great fighter; he had left his Danish lover behind in Burgundaholm to join the Jomsvikings. His brother Sigurd, on the other hand, had gotten all the good looks in the family, but could be cold and ill-tempered. They had gotten into a feud with Sigvaldi's father, Jarl Strut-Harald, from which Bui had retained two chests full of gold that were now rightfully his sons'. There was little love lost between the families, but as Jomsvikings Bui and Sigurd swore to follow Sigvaldi and Thorkell to Norway. "They made daring vows," wrote Bjarni. "I do not say they were only a little drunk."

Their nephew Vagn was not yet grown to manhood, but was already the wild child of the family, "so cruel that he spared no living thing." He had been admitted to the ranks of the Jomsvikings by defeating Sigvaldi in a duel, even though he was only twelve years old at the time. (Assuming that's true, in Sigvaldi's defense we should remember that, like Olaf, these characters were all very young; Sigvaldi may have been barely out of his teens, or not much older. Also, it didn't hurt that Vagn was Palnatoki's grandson.) Nor was he to be outdone. "I vow that I shall follow Sigvaldi and Bui, my kinsman, in this venture and stay while Bui lives. I also swear to bed Ingebjorg, daughter of Thorkell *leira* of the Vik, whether he and his family like it or not, before I come home."

What Vagn's quarrel was with this Thorkell leira ("Mudflat"), one of Jarl Hakon's landed men, has been forgotten; given the boy's nature, it's not unlikely that Ingebjorg had simply refused Vagn's advances. Whatever the reason, Vagn was backed in his vow by his fostri Bjorn the Welshman: "As long as I have the wit and bravery, I swear to follow my foster-son Vagn."

Forkbeard went to bed well satisfied, but in the morning when Astrid roused her husband and asked about it, Sigvaldi – his head no doubt throbbing – did not recall any of it.

"It will do no good to act like nothing happened," she told him. "We'll have to be prudent and plan ahead."

Sigvaldi said, "You are always clever. You will come up with something."

The next day, when King Svein brought up the oaths, Sigvaldi did as Astrid advised. He parried – "Ale is another man, and I would have said much less if I had not been drunk" – and riposted: "What are you going to give me to help me carry out my vow?"

Just as a vassal was obligated to serve his king, a king was obliged to support his vassal. Forkbeard pledged twenty ships.

Sigvaldi said, "That would be a fine offer from a farmer, but not from a king."

Give the man credit; he had nerve. Svein said, "How many would you like?"

"That's easily answered – sixty big ships. I shall provide the same, though smaller, as it's likely that many will not return."

To this Forkbeard agreed. But Sigvaldi wasn't finished: "Then all is for the best, and carry that out well as we will depart as soon as this feast ends."

"It shall be done as you propose," said the king, "though this is happening more quickly than I expected, and I hardly believed that you would be rushing off so fast."

Then Astrid – the mastermind – spoke up: "You cannot expect a victory over Jarl Hakon if you tarry until he hears of it and has time to prepare. You must act as quickly as you can so no news of it precedes you, and take him by surprise."

In the sagas women are often characterized as instigators, driving men to deeds they would not otherwise attempt. And every drapa repeats a *stef*, a refrain (else it would not be a drapa but a *flokkr*). In his *Jomsvikingadrapa* Bjarni's refrain laments,

"A certain nobleman's wife saddens me...The chieftain's kinswoman brings harsh torment upon me."

As it so happened, Jarl Hakon was attending a feast of his own in the south of Norway with his bastard son Eirik when a messenger arrived: "An army has landed in the east, in the Vik, ravaging and harrying without fear."

The jarl, known by now as Hakon *inn riki*, "the Mighty," or *inn illi*, "the Bad," did not wish to hear such tidings in the midst of his dinner. "This news is an evil lie. Norway would have been ravaged long ago if the Danes invaded every time it was said, and it will not stop until some rumor-monger is strung up."

He and Eirik, formerly a jarl of southern Norway under the late Bluetooth, had been reconciled; Eirik was a Norwegian jarl now, and Norway was at peace. But Eirik said, "This is no liar."

The messenger was one Geirmund, called *hviti*, "the White," a landed man of Tunsberg, modern Tonsburg down in Oslofjord. Six days earlier, he reported, around midnight, foreign invaders had stormed the town. He himself had survived only by leaping out a window as the attackers were battering down his door, and barely got away with his life.

"It is Sigvaldi who commands the army," he told Jarl Hakon. "But I heard named among the army both Bui and Vagn, and I have proof that I am not lying." He showed the jarl the fresh stump of his arm, cut off in his escape.

"You are gravely wounded," admitted Hakon. "Who did you that harm?"

"I have a good idea, Jarl," said Geirmund, "as they said 'You've got a good haul, Vagn,' to him who picked up the armlet which was on my arm. I think that they are known as the Jomsvikings."

"You are right enough about that," said Hakon, "and they are the last men I should wish to deal with."

He sent word north to his other sons to summon every available warrior and every available ship and make ready for war. After his years of promiscuity, Hakon had at least six sons. There was Eirik's brother Erlend, his half-brother Svein, all roughly Olaf's age, and the rest all the way down to Erling, just seven. Their fleets rendezvoused in the shelter of a fjord just east of the coastal island of Hod, modern Hareidlandet.*

While this was happening Sigvaldi and the Danish/Jomsviking fleet had been making their way north, landing to pillage as they went and seeking to learn Hakon's whereabouts. When they raided Hod, a local farmer told them the jarl lay anchored up the channel with a few ships. They took him aboard as a guide, but when they rounded the point, their saga says, "The Jomsvikings saw that the water was covered with ships, as far as the eye could see."

Probably inflating enemy numbers to flatter the Jomsvikings, their saga credits Hakon and Eirik with 360 ships, though not all dragon boats. The *Heimskringla* claims 150, and the *Fagrskinna* 180, "warships, longships, merchantmen and trading ships which Jarl Hakon had procured, with high freeboard, all well equipped with men, weapons and stones." In any case the Norwegians outnumbered the Danes and Jomsvikings, possibly two or three to one.

At the sight of them, the farmer promptly dived overboard and swam for it, but one of the Jomsvikings rewarded his treachery, sinking him with a spear in the back. There was nothing else to be done but prepare for a fight. "They immediately drew up their ships in battle order," records the saga. "Sigvaldi placed his ship in the middle, and his brother Thorkell the Tall put his ship next to him. And Bui the Stout and his brother Sigurd Cape placed their ships out on one end of the line, with Vagn and Bjorn the Welshman on the other end."

"Then," wrote Bjarni, "the Norwegian jarls forcefully bade their men to the spear-storm against those of the south."

Of the Battle of Hjorungavag the *Fagrskinna* declares, "This battle was exceedingly famous. The Danes never fought such a

---

* The exact location is not agreed upon, even among the differing versions of the *Jomsviking Saga*, and remains a matter of dispute among historians, with over a half-dozen sites suggested. The date, like that of the Battle of the Danevirke, is also disputed, with some sources claiming it as late as AD 995. All this said, in 1986 Norwegian King Olav I unveiled a memorial to the battle on Hareidlandet, commonly accepted as the site and 1,000th anniversary of the battle.

battle against Norwegians before or after, because the Norwegians had a greater force than they."

Besides the *Fagrskinna* and *Jomsviking Saga*, the battle is attested by Odd and Berg, Snorri in the *Heimskringla*, and Saxo Grammaticus, though he has Bluetooth still alive and in command. Hakon is said to have had no fewer than four or five skalds in attendance to record the event – Vigfuss Viga-Glumsson, Tind *inn froekni*, "the Brave" Hallkelsson, Thord *orvahond*, the "Left Handed", Thorleif *skuma*, "the Dusky" Thorkellsson and Einar *skjaldmeyjar* Helgason, "Einar of the Shieldmaiden."* These skalds were not mild-mannered singers of songs, however. They were warrior poets who fought alongside their lords. Thorleif the Dusky, for instance, armed himself with an uprooted tree, sawed off and fire-hardened into a club, which he named "Bui's bone-breaker, bane of Sigvaldi," and vowed that while he lived it would bring harm to Danes.

Berg wrote, "Both sides now raised their banners, and a fierce battle began, in which the first weapons used were stones and arrows."

According to the *Jomsviking Saga*, "Soon a furious battle was raging, with both sides fighting as hard as they could. It was said to be an even contest between Sigvaldi and the Jarls Hakon and Svein, who fought together, with neither side giving ground."

"As the combatants closed," wrote Berg, "there was great slaughter on each side, but especially among Jarl Hakon's men. Many heads and limbs, hewn off, were thrown overboard into the sea."

The *Heimskringla* records, "Many fell on both sides, but more of Hakon's men, for the Jomsvikings fought bravely and boldly and piercingly and shot right through the shields."

Berg agreed: "The Vikings shot so hard that neither shields nor armor could stand it. The missiles flew so thick around Jarl Hakon that his mail coat was rent and useless, and he cast it aside."

Bui the Stout's ships broke through the Norwegian line. Hakon's sons Eirik and Svein ordered theirs into the gap. The *Fagrskinna*

---

* Right before the battle, it's said, Einar took advantage of the crisis to complain that Hakon was not compensating him enough for his verse: "This jarl gives grudgingly, so I shall certainly join Sigvaldi, who can't do me less honor than the jarl does." It's a measure of the importance with which skalds were regarded that Hakon gave him a set of scales in gold and silver, with weights that tinkled musically, and Einar's nickname changed to *skalaglamm*, "Tinkle-Scales."

asserts, "The Danes got the best of it," and the *Heimskringla* tells us, "The Jomsvikings had bigger ships, standing higher out of the water, but both sides fought with bravery."

"Svein slowly withdrew his ships, and was about to flee," wrote Berg, "but his brother Jarl Eirik came to his aid, and pushed forward to the front of the formation."

Vagn and his men leaped onto the bow of Eirik's ship, *Jarnbardin* (Iron-Prow), recognizable by its metal-reinforced stem and figurehead of Thor. They battled their way down along the gunwales, both sides at once. "Then many fell in the slaughter," declares the *Fagrskinna*, "for both sides wielded sharp blades. Any cowards aboard had a difficult time."

The fighting was so close, so desperate, that Vigfuss the skald slew one of Vagn's men by grabbing up an anvil off the deck and crushing his skull. With his fire-hardened club Thorleif the Dusky shattered Vagn's helmet. Vagn warded him off with his sword, but the Dane and his men were driven back to their ship. Nevertheless, the *Jomsviking Saga* claims, "Jarl Eirik pulled *Iron-Prow* from the battle, for too many men in the bows had been slain."

Despite superior numbers, the Norwegians were losing. Jarl Hakon's pagan gods were failing him. He needed his patroness, and ordered Eirik and Svein to hold the line while he went to find her.

In the sagas he is said to have landed on a nearby island named Primsignd.* Hakon, his young son Erling and a few trusted men hurried inland, beneath the trees. There was no gilded, carven temple, no Christian-ish chapel to the gods, only a clearing in the forest. The Norse, who believed in *landvaettir*, land spirits – elves, dwarves, little people, associated with certain trees, plants and stones – held forest glades to be holy places, where the gods could not only be worshipped, but descended to interact with mortals. The *Jomsviking Saga* tells of Hakon: "He knelt down facing north to pray, calling on his protector Thorgerd Holgabrud, but

---

* There is no such island, but historians have pointed out that in the original sagas – Latinized translations of Old Norse – the island was named Vigdr; there was an island named Vigr, modern Vigra, just north of Hjorungavag. And, tellingly, "Primsignd" would seem to be an Old Norse version of the Latin *prima signatio*, implying some kind of holy place.

in her anger she would not hear him. She rejected all his offers of great sacrifices, and Hakon thought matters very bleak. He even offered her a human sacrifice, which she also rejected."

We don't have to believe Jarl Hakon personally conversed with his goddess. We can believe, however, that people of that time believed it, and that Hakon's faith in her drove him to extremes.

> The jarl thinks things will only get worse unless he can appease her. He begins to raise his offers, finally promising her any man except himself and his sons Eirik and Svein. But the jarl had a son who was called Erling, seven years old and full of promise for one so young. And it comes about in the end that Thorgerd accepts the jarl's offer of his son. When he sees that his prayers and oaths have been heard, and the outlook is improving, he has the boy given into the hands of his thrall Skopti, who puts the boy to death in the manner usual for Hakon and as he ordered.

"In the manner usual for Hakon." Particularly chilling, that, and perhaps deliberately left unspecified. Stabbed and strangled, as ibn Fadlan had seen done to the slave girl sacrificed along the Volga? Drowned, as Svyatoslav's Varangians had done to children in the Danube, and Vladimir's Rus in the Volkhov? Hung from a tree, as Adam of Bremen claimed the Swedes did nine men every nine years? Burned, as Thietmar claimed the Danes did ninety-nine people, horses, dogs and fowl after every Yuletide? In the end, it matters not. Dead is dead. We moderns can be repelled by Jarl Hakon's cold-blooded murder of his own son, and we can ridicule his belief in gods, let alone that Thorgerd spoke to him. What makes him most villainous is that, rather than give his son's life, he did not give his own.

The *Jomsviking Saga* resumes, "The fighting paused while the jarl was away, and while the lull lasted both sides had prepared to battle as most certain for success."

"Jarl Hakon now returned from the shore," wrote Berg, "and having reboarded his ship, urged his men on eagerly, assuring them that victory was theirs."

He had his ship rowed up against Sigvaldi's, pressing his attack with the certainty that Thorgerd was behind him. "Clouds gathered in the north," declares the *Jomsviking Saga*, "and soon covered the entire sky."

It was late afternoon. The prevailing winds over Norway are westerlies, coming in from over the ocean toward the northeast, but at unpredictable intervals the wind turns and polar winds blow down out of the northeast. Down from Thorgerd Holgabrud's Halogaland. "Then came lightning and thunder, and a violent hailstorm. The Jomsvikings had to fight into the wind. The hail was so fierce that men could hardly keep their feet."

"Holgi's bride brought down the terrible storm," asserted Bjarni the Christian bishop. "Cruel hail out of the north rang on shields, where the storm-driven cloud-gravel stung men's eyes."

"When the Jomsvikings hurled stones or threw spears," claims the *Jomsviking Saga*, "the storm blew it all back at them, together with their enemies' weapons."

Saxo heard this story too. "The enchanted tempest rained down unusually large hailstones on our people's heads, half blinding them as though shot from the clouds, and they felt the weather hitting them harder than the enemy."

All this sounds like the ancient scribes invoking the supernatural to explain the fortuitous arrival of a storm in the midst of battle. Yet the *Jomsviking Saga* would have it that one of Bui's men swore he saw Thorgerd Holgabrud herself, standing in the prow of Jarl Hakon's dragon ship and shooting arrows from her fingertips, each killing the man it hit. Others claimed to have seen her too.

Sigvaldi lost his nerve. "We can say that we are not fleeing men if we retreat. We did not swear to fight against monsters," he declared, and called to the Jomsvikings to abandon the fight.

In the *Fagrskinna* Vagn saw Sigvaldi's ship withdraw. "Why do you flee, evil dog? You are selling your men's lives too cheaply, and will go home shamed for life, and be remembered for it." He hurled a spear across the water at Sigvaldi, but missed and hit his steersman, killing him.

Thorkell the Tall and Sigurd Cape followed Sigvaldi in escape. Odd wrote, "But Bui remained, saying it was better to die like a man than to flee in utter terror."

A Norwegian named Thorkell *Midlangr* ("Long Waist") struck Bui in the head, so hard that the sword bit through his helmet nosepiece and sheared off the lower part of his face. "He cut off his entire mouth and chin, which slid down onto the deck," laments the *Jomsviking Saga*, "and his teeth fell out of his head."

Thorkell, however, slipped on the bloody deck and fell against the gunwale. Bui cut him in two, but was heard to say, "The Danish woman would be loath to kiss me in Burgundaholm, if we lived to return."

Berg claimed Bui had his hands cut off, despite which he took up the two chests of gold he'd stolen from Sigvaldi's father Strut-Harald in the stumps of his arms. Either way, leaping to the gunwale, he shouted, "Overboard, Bui's men!" and jumped to his death.

"Many of his men leaped over after him," wrote Berg, "and some were killed aboard, as there was no asking for quarter. The ship was cleared from stem to stern, and the other [Jomsviking] ships with it, one after another."

The *Saga* declares, "It is said that once Sigvaldi fled, the storm and lightning and thunder abated, and afterward the weather was clear and cold."

Saxo Grammaticus wrote, "So the Norwegians, more lucky than powerful, caused the Danes to flee for their lives, convinced that the gods were against them."

"Vagn defended himself most bravely, striking and slaying men to both sides," credited Berg, "but at last he was overwhelmed by numbers, his ship was cleared, and he himself taken captive with thirty of his men and put ashore."

"The Jomsvikings' ships were landed, and the property too, and the goods were all counted," reports their saga, "and Jarl Hakon and his men divided everything between them, as along with the weapons, and they thought they had won a total victory, since they had all the booty and captured the Jomsvikings, and driven the rest away, with greatest number of them dead."

Vagn and his surviving crewmen were bound by the ankles to a log by Hakon's thrall Skopti.* We might expect the child-killer to finish

---

* *Skopti*, Old Norse "head of hair," might be a nickname, as Berg and Snorri called him Thormod. He had another nickname, *Kark*, "thick skin," or "thick bark," or more ominously "to bind tightly"; it might be Celtic. Skopti Kark will play a small but critical role in our story.

off the prisoners as well, but come morning they faced a different executioner: none other than Thorkell Mudflat, whom Vagn had vowed to kill and whose daughter he had vowed to bed. Thorkell appears to have done nothing of note in the battle, but according to the *Heimskringla* he now said, "You vowed to kill me, Vagn, but now I think it more likely that I will kill you."

He proceeded to behead three helpless prisoners before turning to Jarl Eirik. "Do you think I have paled on account of this? Many say that happens if one beheads three men."

"We did not see your color change," Eirik told him, "but all the same you look different."

Thorkell worked his way down the line, striking off heads one after another, but allowing each victim a few last words. Some offered a final insult. One wished the blow to come from the front, to see his death coming and show no fear; this was done, and he did not. Another requested time to urinate, and while he did, wished aloud that he might have waggled himself thus to Jarl Hakon's wife, in bed. He did not get the chance. Another, it is said, jerked his head so that the man holding him by the hair had his hands cut off by Thorkell's blade. The Jomsviking laughed – "Whose hands are in my hair?" – and went happily to his death.

Then Thorkell came to Vagn.

The Jomsviking regretted aloud only that he had not fulfilled his oath to kill him.

Thorkell raised his blade. "I'll see to it you never do."

But Vagn's foster father Bjorn the Welshman kicked Thorkell's foot out from under him. Thorkell fell and dropped his weapon. Vagn grabbed it up and struck him dead, declaring, "Now I can die gladly, having accomplished at least half of my vow."

Jarl Hakon ordered him slain immediately, but Jarl Eirik stepped in. He had no love for Vagn. He had just come from finding the skald Thorleif the Dusky looking sick. "Thorleif, are you wounded?"

"I am not sure," Thorleif had said. "I think Vagn's sword-point tickled me a bit yesterday as I struck him with the club."

"It will be difficult for your father if you die," Eirik told him, but Thorleif had fallen down dead.

Yet now Eirik saved his killer, for to slay men in battle was no crime. Vagn was a good man, he declared, and Thorkell deserved death for being too glad an executioner. He granted Vagn, Bjorn and the rest clemency – in fact, granted Vagn Thorkell's land in Vik.

It is said that Vagn and Bjorn never rejoined the Jomsvikings. Bjorn returned home to Wales, to reappear later in our tale. And Vagn fulfilled the rest of his vow, taking Thorkell's daughter Ingebjorg with him as his wife, home to his ancestral lands in Denmark, thereby recasting himself as her rescuer instead of her ravisher. It's the kind of happy ending that all Vikings wished for their sagas – for themselves.

As for Jarl Sigvaldi, the saga reveals that on his return home his wife Astrid drew a bath for him, remarking, "I imagine there were some on the Jomsvikings' side in the battle who came away with skins more holed than yours, for it seems fit to keep wheat-flour in."

Sigvaldi snapped, "It might yet happen in my life that you have no such victory to celebrate, so think on whether you will prefer that."

Sigvaldi too will figure again in our saga. Regarding the Battle of Hjorungavag, it was Vagn of Burgundaholm who best summed things up, as Olaf might have heard it told during one of his visits among the Jomsvikings: "Sigvaldi led us straight into danger, then cravenly ran home to Denmark, looking forward to his woman's embrace; but brave Bui went over the broad gunwale."

In the 1920s Kung Tryggves Grav on the Swedish coast was rebuilt to resemble the Viking Age tomb, which originally dates from the Bronze Age. (Lise Ivanoff)

Some Vikings were both pagan and Christian. Viking smiths cast amulets of Thor's hammer Mjolnir in the shape of a cross. (Getty Images)

Constantinople's Hagia Sophia is today Istanbul's Aya Sofya, an Islamic mosque. Except for the Arabic symbols, the interior is much as Olaf experienced it. (iStock)

The hermitage of St. Elidius on St. Helens, Scilly Islands, where Olaf is said to have heard the prophesy of his life, and was also nearly killed. (Des Blenkinsopp)

The beach on Tresco, Scilly Islands. St. Helens in the distance. The Old Blockhouse at left was built circa 1550 to defend against French attack. (Alamy)

Ruins of the old abbey on Tresco. Olaf very likely walked under this arch as he underwent Christian baptism. (Stephen McKay)

The Viking fleet led by Olaf Tryggvason to ravage the English coast in AD 991 was the largest seen in decades. (Alamy)

Statue of Byrhtnoth, the Anglo-Saxon ealdorman who died fighting Olaf's Vikings at the Battle of Maldon, AD 991. (Oxyman)

Today the battlefield at Maldon is a tidal bog, but a thousand years ago was solid ground, ideal for Viking Age warfare. (Alamy)

At low tide the causeway to Northey Island lies exposed, but at high tide is underwater. (Trevor Harris)

The Battle of Maldon, AD 991. Viking raiders cross the causeway from Northey Island as their front ranks engage the Anglo-Saxon shield wall. (Artwork by Peter Dennis © Osprey Publishing)

Leif Erikson Discovers America by Hans Dahl. Sent by King Olaf to Christianize Greenland, Leif was blown off course and discovered the New World by accident. (Alamy)

Olaf Tryggvason's Last Stand at Svolder by Angus McBride. Whether Olaf survived the battle is still disputed and will probably never be resolved. (Artwork by Angus McBride © Osprey Publishing)

The Icelandic Thing by W. G. Collingwood. Icelanders decided to accept Christianity at their thing, which is still survives as the world's oldest parliament.
(© The Trustees of the British Museum)

England's King Aethelred II, reviled for paying Vikings danegeld to stop raiding, named Olaf his foster son to defend against other Vikings. (Alamy)

Statue of Olaf Tryggvason in Trondheim, Norway, where he is revered for bringing Christianity to the Vikings. (iStock)

XVII

The Prophecy

Three years I passed in Wendland, and the next four years in the British Islands, living as a freebooter.

King Olaf's Saga

AD 988

Loveless, godless, aimless, meaningless, living only for the moment. From 985 to 988, according to the various sagas – longer than he had been wed to Geira – Olaf Tryggvason wandered the western coasts: Bretland [Wales]; Kumraland [Cumbria]; even Valland [Gaul].* Berg would have it that Olaf himself later rued those days: "I had my freedom, but only in strange and foreign lands. To survive I had little but what I took, risking my life and my men's lives...Of this I will say nothing more, for we deprived many an innocent man of his property, and some of life too, as is the warrior's way."

The *Historia* laments, "Unthinking, the great sea-rover was moving further and further away from God."

Finally, as though seeking the ends of the earth, he went about as far west as he could go. Berg wrote, "The wind drove him off course, bearing him to the Scilly Islands, in the ocean west of England. Here he dropped anchor for a while."

---

* At this time Vikings raiding England were finding ready markets for their ill-gotten loot in Normandy, where the aristocracy had Viking roots and proved receptive. Olaf may have pioneered such trade.

About twenty-eight miles beyond Land's End, the far southwestern tip of England's Cornwall peninsula, lie over fifty small islands and rocky islets. The Cornish people, in their Brittonic tongue, called them *Enesek Syllan*, the Isles of Scilly, the meaning of which is lost. That whole southern end of England is gradually sinking as the northern, Scottish end rises from under the weight of retreating Ice Age glaciers, and it's thought that as late as AD 500 most or all the Scillies were one, *En Noer*, "the Great Island." It's hard to say how many islands existed when Olaf's little Viking fleet arrived there, driven before another fateful wind.

At the far end of Europe, this was a place of exile. In the 4th century a pair of Christian bishops were banished there as heretics, followers of Priscillian, a nobleman of Hispania, Roman Spain, who advocated a strict code of abstinence and asceticism, banned wine and meat, pleasures of the flesh and marriage, but believed in mysticism and prophecy. For that, he was persecuted, and executed, by the Church, yet his followers found sanctuary in the Scillies, which, on the receiving end of the Gulf Stream, boast a humid, mild and temperate climate.* By Olaf's time Priscillianism had largely died out, but that far from the Church's reach a small monastic community lingered on. Normally such a remote target would have been an enticing one for Vikings, but ascetics had little worth stealing, and after four years Olaf was seeking more than material gain. Perhaps he still recalled what Malusha, mother of Prince Vladimir, had foretold: *When at last he is grown to manhood he will return to his native land and gain the kingdom which is his by birth. As king he will shine with bright glory and become a savior to many men of the northern regions.*

After all this time Olaf must have wondered if that still held true. As Snorri wrote, "He heard that on the island was a certain prophet who foretold future events, and to many it seemed that these prophesies generally came true."

The prophet is not named in the sources, but is often taken to be one Elid, or Elidius, today venerated as St. Lide. He is said to have lived as a hermit on one of the northernmost of the islands, St. Helen's, the

---

* The similarity of "Priscillian" and "Scillian" appears to be coincidental; the islands were named long before the man.

name of which might be a corruption of his. (Some historians assert Elid resided there in the 8th century, well before Olaf's time, but the hermit of the saga could have been one of his followers.) Fortunately the ocean pool lying below St. Helen's, fifteen feet deep and sheltered from wind and swells by the surrounding islands, still offers the best anchorage in the whole archipelago. Odd wrote, "Olaf sailed his ships to that island. He who lived there knew of his coming through his gift of foresight. He bade all the monks there to dress their best and meet him on the beach with their holiest relics. Many monks, clerics, and servants of God were there, all dressed in fine clothing. It was early morning."

"The king was curious to put the prophet's gift to the test," wrote Berg. "So, choosing one of his tallest and most handsome men, he dressed him as magnificently as possible, and bade him go to the hermit and pretend to be king."

The *Historia* refers to Olaf's man as his *armigerum*, his armor- or weapon-bearer, a kind of proto-squire who would have been familiar with a kingly air of command. Perhaps he overacted the role. "On meeting the prophet, he said he was the king," wrote Snorri. "He was told, 'You are not the king, but I advise you to be true to your king.'"

"The messenger came back to the king, telling him what had happened," continued Berg, "so that King Olaf no longer doubted that the man really was a prophet, and wanted more than ever to meet him."

"Disembarking, Olaf saw a great company coming down to the beach," wrote Odd. "The morning sun shone on their fine clothes."

The Norns, busily spinning the thread of his life, must have looked down on Olaf and his men as they set foot on the granite quay (the remains of which still exist, though submerged at high tide), just as they had a generation earlier: armed Vikings climbing a windswept island toward an unknown fate. St. Helen's, less than fifty acres in size and not even 150 feet above sea level, is studded with Bronze Age stone cairns, like that faraway one under which lay King Tryggvi. Olaf, rather, might well have recalled the warrior priest Thangbrand of Saxony, and that monks' robes could conceal weapons and ill intent. None of that, however, was on offer here. "When Olaf saw they came in peace, he and his crew went to meet them and gave them a good welcome."

Today the path from St. Helen's beach leads up past the ruins of a 1760s "pest house," a quarantine station used to isolate plague victims before ships bound for England could land, as well as a graveyard for those who got no farther. At the foot of the hill are the even older ruins, overgrown stone walls three feet high, that were once the foundations of a church and houses clustered around the old hermit's cell, and that of a round hut that served as his oratory. In that stone circle a thousand years ago, king and prophet spoke of the future. Olaf the agnostic, the pragmatic, was more interested in learning whether he was destined to win a fortune, perhaps even a real kingdom. In Odd's telling, the hermit said only, "Not long ago, it was revealed to me who you are and who you will be. I am here to teach you the true faith and preach the name of the Christ and that baptism will bring you, and all who join the true faith with you, salvation."

The evolution of Olaf's saga at this point is notable, for it follows two paths. Odd and Theodoric, writing in the 1190s or so – about 200 years after the event – have little more to say about the prophecy. It was the anonymous authors of the *Agrip* and *Historia* who, about the same time, elaborated on it:

> You will be a great king and do great things, and convert many people to faith and baptism, and so do good for yourself and many others. And so that you do not doubt me, take this as a sign: at your ships you will meet with treachery and enemies. It will end in battle. You will lose men and yourself be wounded. As a result, you will be near death, and borne on a shield to your ship. But you will recover within seven nights, and soon afterward receive baptism.

Dead men carried on a shield – in the *Historia*'s original Latin, *scuto portaberis* – is a very Greco-Roman turn of phrase, harking back to the Spartans at Thermopylae, as told by Plutarch.* Clearly the unknown monk who wrote it was not only literate, but versed in the classics, and knew how to strike a tone, even if his Scandinavian readers didn't make the connection. The unknown author of the

---

* Never mind that Plutarch wrote his *Moralia* 500 years after Thermopylae; in those days dead Greek warriors were buried near the battle site, not borne all the way home on their shields.

Fagrskinna, circa 1220, didn't mention the prophesy or treachery at all. Yet, writing in those same years, secular, nonspiritual Snorri, who usually edited out the more fantastic aspects of the saga, chose to include this one in his *Heimskringla*. (Cynics claim the whole story is based on one told by Pope Gregory I, St. Gregory the Great, in his *Dialogues* of AD 593, about St. Benedict and the Gothic king Totila in Sicily, which the Icelandic scribes mistook for Scilly.) And of course the monk Berg, writing a hundred years after that, had Olaf meet nothing less than "an enemy fleet and many foes." With the hindsight of a thousand years, skeptics today can claim the "prophesy" is purely a literary invention, created after the fact of our hero's near-death experience.

And yet...

Any suspicion or premonition Olaf may have had of betrayal and ambush came true after all. There was promise of gain, the lure in a trap; a flurry of swords on a remote, barren island; men giving their lives in the service of their lord, only to die among stone graves dating from time immemorial. There is a feeling here of a story coming full circle – of the Norns steering a son inevitably, unavoidably into his father's footsteps. To his doom. And in that final moment, as he was being cut down, Olaf could only have put his faith in the prophesy, as set down in the Norwegian synoptics: "In a week heaven will heal you, and you will return to be bathed in the font of life."

Without any more description in the sagas, it's impossible to know the nature or extent of Olaf's wound. Viking swords, basically big double-edged clubs, were optimized for hewing and cleaving rather than fencing and stabbing; few wounds dealt by them were minor. That said, most cuts, if not to the throat, major blood vessels or organs, were theoretically survivable, but a strike to an exposed head was instantly incapacitating, usually fatal. In the event of amputation, either on the battlefield or during treatment, bleeding out was certain if not quickly controlled. Shock or infection meant lingering death.

We can surmise that none of those applied in Olaf's case, but that his injury was serious, potentially deadly. Luckily Vikings had generations of experience with combat medicine, and not all of it runes, chants and charms. Cleaning wounds, setting broken bones, suturing, poultices and cauterization were well known, and the use of plants was something of a science. Small doses of hemlock or belladonna could be administered as sedatives, yarrow stopped minor bleeding, chamomile reduced inflammation and swelling, plantain or honey served as antiseptics, and concoctions of various herbs as curatives.* Victims of abdominal wounds were fed broth of boiled leeks or onions; if the wound whiffed of it, the gut was holed, and the prognosis fatal.

Pagan Vikings believed one's end was predetermined, yet the seer had not foretold death for Olaf. We can imagine the survivors waiting all week to see if the prophesy bore out, to see whose god was more powerful. Was it the Valkyries, the Choosers of the Slain hovering over his sad bier, ready to bear him to Valhalla, Folkvang or Helheim? Or the Angel of Death, that rider on a pale horse, extending a skeletal hand to beckon him to the Christian heaven, or point the way to the Christian hell?† And why should a Viking – why *did* the Vikings – come to choose one over the other?

It was not only the Hebrew God who promised paradise or damnation. Whether in Odin's boisterous mead hall, Freyja's heavenly meadow, or Hel's icy underworld, Viking gods offered their worshippers afterlife as well. Notably, Helheim was for those who simply died of disease or old age, not exclusively reserved for punishing the wicked. Murderers, adulterers and oath-breakers went to Nastrond, "Corpse Shore," where the dragon Nidhogg gnawed on them until the end times. From this we might take it that pagan Vikings had a shorter list of deadly sins than the Israelites' ten, and

---

* In 2015 a 10th-century recipe of garlic, leeks, wine and bile from a cow's stomach, left to ferment in a brass bowl for nine days, resulted in a salve that proved 90 percent effective against the modern superbug, methicillin-resistant *staphylococcus aureus* (MRSA).

† By Olaf's day the 4th-century *Apocalypsis Pauli*, the "Revelation of Paul," said to have been written by Paul the Apostle, had already been scorned by the Church as a forgery, even heretical (and so is largely forgotten today), yet had become influential in medieval Christian thought, particularly among ascetics like the expelled Priscillians, whose lifestyle it commended. It promised the worst torments of hell to wayward Christians, but nonbelievers could still undergo conversion, and their souls be redeemed.

that their odds of spending eternity in relative comfort were much better for them than for Christians.

Yet in its heart, belief in Valhalla hid an overarching pessimism. Men reached it only when Odin withdrew his favor from them, leaving them to suffer defeat and death. To be taken into his army of the dead to drink and fight lasted only until Ragnarok, the end of days. Then all would battle against the *jotnar*, Loki's army of trolls and demons and giants, until the gods themselves were slain and the world was purified by fire and reborn. For Vikings, not even the afterlife was eternal. Whether Ragnarok or Revelations, all was prophesied.

But the Hebrew God's appeal for the Vikings was temporal as well as spiritual.

Gods gain followers when their followers succeed. At the beginning of the Viking Age, when they came boiling out of Scandinavia, Odin, Thor and the rest granted them victories. (There is a theory that those initial forays against Christian monasteries and abbeys were driven less by greed or population pressure than as attempts to forestall the relentless expansion of the new religion by striking at its heart.) By Olaf's day, though, the Vikings had been ejected from Christian England and utterly stopped by two Christian empires, the Holy Roman and the Byzantine, whose houses of worship were far wealthier than any pagan temples. Much as they loved robbing such places, the Vikings must have wondered whose deity was the more powerful.

At first, the notion of an invisible, immaterial god being beyond their conception, Vikings saw the Christ who walked the earth as God personified – one and the same – yet just another god among many. Evidence of this is the many necklace pendants found representing Thor's hammer Mjolnir but doubling as Christian crosses; a Viking could believe in and pray to both. By Olaf's day, however, the *Hvitakrist*, "White Christ," was elbowing aside the pagan gods, assuming his heavenly throne as the supreme deity: in the sagas, *heims drottinn*, "king of heavens," the *gumna valdr*, "ruler of men," the *alls drottinn*, "king of all things." He was not the same Christ as that of the Romans and Greeks – and this is crucial for modern readers, whether practitioners of Christianity or otherwise, to understand – nor was he the Christ worshipped today. Few of the Scandinavians first heard of the Christian God through scripture being read to them. They heard rumors of a foreign god, an aggressive god, a victorious god of war, imparting good luck and granting victory to his chieftains. Charity and humility were as foreign to him as to his worshippers, who served him as their own underlings served them, in a kind of spiritual feudalism. Vikings understood completely that, despite his omnipotence, he had permitted his son (or as they saw it, himself) to suffer and die on the cross, pierced by a spear, for the sake of his people. Odin, pierced by his own spear, had hung himself on the world-tree Yggdrasil in order to win knowledge of runes and mastery of their power and magic for the benefit of his people. And perhaps most importantly, the idea of one god to rule all coincided nicely with one king to rule all.

Lastly, as far as Vikings were concerned, to attain this mighty god's support and spend eternity in his paradise only required becoming his follower: to undergo *skirn*, baptism.

Christ arose from the dead after three days. Odin came down from Yggdrasil after nine. Olaf came back to life after a week.

Perhaps he was comatose the entire time, and had no recollection of it, or no dream he wished to retell. His biographers had curiously little to say about it. This was almost certainly not the first time he had been wounded, but it's the first time mentioned in the sagas, and assuredly the most serious. Anybody who's come back from such an experience, or even major surgery under sedation, knows that though survived, even unremembered, it's still a kind of death and rebirth, a turning point. Life goes on, but there's a before and after, and things will never be the same again. If Olaf's monkish chroniclers were to make up a passage about such a life-changing event – say, a dreamed-of ascent to heaven – this was the ideal episode in which to insert it. Yet they largely ignored Olaf's experience as secondary to the prophesy itself, as proof of which god was true.

Still, he does seem to have undergone some kind of revelation. Berg wrote, "He was fully convinced of the truth of what had been told him, and that the prophet was real, from whatever source he had received his gift of prophecy."

THE PROPHECY

He returned ashore to visit the seer again, who assured him his insight came down from God, and that Olaf's recovery was proof that his future as a king and warrior of Christ was certain, once he himself was baptized. To this Olaf, of course, agreed.

Odd and Snorri would have it that he was christened on the spot, then and there. Berg, writing centuries later, was perhaps better acquainted with the Scillies. The prophet on St. Helen's was not the high priest of the isles: "There was a famous abbot in the islands, the head of a great cloister, to which King Olaf sailed with his ships and all his men."

Theodoric gives the abbot's name as Bernard.* He would have resided just across St. Helen's Pool on Tresco (Middle English *Trescau*, "farm of elder-trees"), today the second-largest island in the chain, back then probably still called in Cornish *Ryn Tewyn*, "promontory of sand dunes." The "great cloister" was the Benedictine priory founded there a few decades back, the ruins of which still overlook the dunes and beach.† As before, the abbot and monks (who, after seven days, had surely been apprised of the situation) came down to the shore to greet the visitors and make them welcome. They knew how to make an entrance. "King Olaf came ashore with all his men," wrote Berg, "and seeing a great brightness in the distance, knew not what it was. It was the morning reflecting off the abbot and his clerks' fine garments."

Abbot Bernard and his priests escorted the Vikings up the dunes to the priory and administered a crash course in catechesis. Noah and the Flood, Moses and the Red Sea; the association of Christianity with immersion stretched far back before John the Baptist and Christ in the river Jordan. And *skirn* differed from *ausa vatni*, the Vikings' sprinkling of water on an infant. That was a washing of the body; this was to be a cleansing of the soul.

---

* Adam of Bremen jealously insisted that Olaf was not baptized in the Scillies at all, but much later, by representatives of Adam's archdiocese of Hamburg-Bremen.
† Today the ruins, bathed in the warmth of the Gulf Stream, are surrounded by famous tropical gardens founded in the 1830s: seventeen acres and almost 2,300 exotic species from as far away as the Mediterranean, South America, South Africa, Australia, New Zealand and Asia.

Hippolytus, the 3rd-century Bishop of Rome, advised initiates to be educated and trained in moral principles and virtues for three years, as a test of sincerity. Today the process can take just as long, with final preparation during Lent – forty days of prayer, purification and enlightenment – and the actual rite on Holy Saturday, the eve of Easter Sunday. The scribes do not record a date or timetable for Olaf's baptism, but if it wasn't performed on St. Helen's it was done just as swiftly on Tresco. As to whether it was conducted in the priory's baptismal font (if there was one) or down in the surf, the word "baptism" comes from the Greek *baptismos* – to submerge, to dip in water – and it's thought early baptisms were full-body immersions, the way John the Baptist immersed Jesus. As Cyril, the 4th-century Bishop of Jerusalem, explained: "Having gone down dead in sins, you come up quickened in righteousness…So you, by going down into the water, and being in a manner buried in the waters as He was in the rock, are raised again walking in newness of life."

Or, as Abbot Bernard of the Scilly Isles would have put it, "I baptize you in the name of the Father, and of the Son, and of the Holy Spirit."

It was a Viking who went under the waters. It was a Christian who arose.

A warrior of God.

XVIII

A New Beginning

Olaf long remained there with his men, learning holy doctrine and righteousness from that man of God and his brethren.

Berg Sokkason

AD 988–989

By all accounts that mention Olaf's time in the Isles of Scilly (and not all of them do), he stayed there as long as he could, absorbing the lessons and knowledge that today are imparted to initiates months or years in advance of baptism. "They resided on the island until they folded away their baptismal robes," wrote Odd, "strengthened each day by holy teachings. Olaf learned much, and in answer to his prayers God enabled him to become the enlightener of many."

Yet he could not remain in Scilly forever. His crews probably doubled the islands' population, putting undue strain on the monks' scant resources. At least some of Olaf's men were eager to depart. Even if bathed in holy water as he had been, they had not undergone his near-death revelation. Asceticism was not required by Christianity, nor was it much compatible with the Viking lifestyle. They felt less need of religious enlightenment than of wealth, and would need to earn it elsewhere than on that penniless cluster of rocks at the far end of the earth.

Olaf let them go. He had a new mission in mind. To replace his departed men, he even enlisted some of the monks of Scilly. According to Berg, they too were ready and willing to join him in God's work, back in the world again, and perhaps enjoy a little of his largesse after their long destitute exile. Berg wrote, "That autumn,

Olaf Tryggvason sailed from the Scilly Islands to England, taking along priests and other clerics. He anchored in a certain harbor on the English coast, his visit peaceful, for the land was Christian, and he was Christian as well."

Olaf's mission may have been peaceful, but he was not the only Viking in the vicinity. There are attacks recorded in Wales in 986 and 987; in 988 the Welsh king Maredudd ab Owain purchased the return of 2,000 captives at the cost of a silver penny each. And the *Anglo-Saxon Chronicle* records 988 (or 987, as usual, the different manuscripts vary on the date) as the year Watchet, across the Bristol Channel from Wales, was raided by Vikings. An English monk of the time recorded, "A vicious battle took place to the west, in which our Devonshire men, fighting bravely, won the victory and accompanying glory. A great number of our men fell, but many more of theirs." In the 12th century English monks at Worcester Priory, in their annals of the era, the *Chronicon ex Chronicis* ("Chronicle from Chronicles"), set the attack in 988: "Watchet was pillaged by Danish raiders, who even slew the thegn of Devon by the name of Goda...but the Danes lost more men killed, and the English mastered the field of battle."

The chronicles do not blame Olaf specifically, not for this raid, but the timing seems suspiciously coincidental. Watchet is just about as far from Scandinavia as one can get in England, but just off his return route from Scilly into his old stomping grounds in the Irish Sea. Whichever Vikings raided Watchet, the fact that they were driven off demonstrates a lack of manpower.

Lack of manpower was to become a concern for Olaf. It was in Wales, according to Berg, that he had his first inkling of his new God's plan for him: "While King Olaf lived in the British Islands it came to him to visit his kin and patrimony in Norway. He eagerly sought news of the chieftains in Norway and the lands to the east."

Berg has this news of Norway come from none other than Bjorn the Welshman, uncle and foster father of Vagn of Burgundaholm, both of whom had so narrowly escaped execution after their capture at the Battle of Hjorungavag. Bjorn had returned home to Wales, which in those days was a separate set of kingdoms, no more united than Ireland. From there fate brought him together with Olaf, to whom he related the defeat of the Danes and Jomsvikings. Victory, he said, had made Jarl Hakon and his son Eirik more popular than ever in Norway. According to Berg, much as he admired the Norwegians for their victory, Olaf worried that his homeland had fallen under the sway of a devil who would sacrifice his own son to pagan gods. He came to see it as his duty, as the son of a Norwegian king, to right such a wrong: "He became determined that, if by God's grace he won himself a kingdom in Norway, he would do his best to convert the people to the true faith."

That would not be easy. Considering that the Danes and Jomsvikings combined had been unable to defeat Jarl Hakon, the chances of Olaf doing so were close to zero. He had no support in Norway. As far as he knew, everyone there thought him dead. To conquer the country would require an army, and that required money, or at least the promise of it.

"As King Olaf deliberated these problems," wrote Berg, "he saw it would be impossible to conquer Norway, unless strengthened by the grace of God, and so he gave himself into the hands and the guidance of the Almighty Lord."

Here, unusually, it is Berg and Snorri who skip a section of Olaf's life in which Odd indulges: "He learned of a Jarl Sigurd ruling Northumbria."

At this time there was no such thing as a jarl of Northumbria; that was a Viking title, and Northumbria had not been Viking soil since the death of Eirik Bloodaxe in 954.[*] The jarl of the Orkney Islands, Shetland, the Hebrides, and a good bit of the north Scottish coast – for the Icelandic chroniclers two centuries later, perhaps synonymous with Northumbria – was Sigurd Hlodvirsson. Like the late Jomsviking Bui he was called *inn Digri*, "the Stout." As did Jarl Hakon in Norway, he held his lands in fealty to no overlord, but ruled as a king in his own right.

---

[*] The current ealdorman of Northumbria was one Thored, whose very Scandinavian name indicates his Viking ancestry, but who ruled as an Englishman; his daughter Aelfgifu was King Aethelred's wife.

Given the blurry political distinctions around the Irish Sea at this time, it's hard to say where the meeting of Sigurd and Olaf took place. The east coast of England is much smoother than the west, which is riven by what Scandinavians would have called fjords – Morecambe Bay, the river Duddon estuary, Solway Firth – and the western Scottish coast and Inner and Outer Hebrides are even rougher. Probably word had spread around the local parts of the whereabouts of Sigurd's main hideout, if anything else as a place to avoid. Odd wrote, "Olaf headed for this site, and when he reached land, he sailed up a fjord with great flair."

Like the priests on Tresco, Olaf knew how to make an entrance. He and his captains stood in the open on their ships' prows, dressed in their best finery, spears and bows stowed, swords sheathed, shields hung on the gunwales rather than in hand. Sigurd and his men, having just come back from a raid themselves, watched these strange ships cruise right up to their landing, drop anchor and raise shipboard tents – another peace signal, as in battle raised tents invited fire arrows. "They saw one man who was much taller and more striking than any they had seen before," wrote Odd. "He wore silken clothes and commanded the most beautiful ships."

Olaf and Sigurd were roughly the same age, Sigurd perhaps a few years older. The *Orkneyinga Saga* describes him as "a powerful man, and a great warrior," and Odd as "well known, powerful and popular." Impressed by the newcomers' entry, he asked their leader his name and whence he hailed.

In his past years of freebooting Olaf's name must have become notorious around the Irish Sea. He told Sigurd he was Oli the Wealthy, and that he was a trader. "But we all come from Rus."

The subterfuge perhaps shows a certain lack of confidence on Olaf's part. One would think a jarl and veteran fighting man like Sigurd, familiar with who was who around the Irish Sea, would see right through such a story. Was this the very same Olaf who had come raiding through Sigurd's Hebridean domain just those few years past, on his way around Scotland and down to points south? Probably the jarl knew full well whom he was dealing with, but just let it pass, unremarked. He may have needed new allies as well. The Irish *Annals of Ulster* record a "Danish" raid on the Isle of Man in 987, in conjunction with the Irish Vikings of Limerick, in which a thousand Manx were slain. Later that same year, however, the Vikings had gone it alone, farther north, on the isle of Iona off Scotland's northwest coast – closer to Sigurd's Orcadian domain – where they were repulsed with a loss of over 350 men.

A few boatloads of "Rus merchants" would help replace Sigurd's losses. As for Olaf's Christianity, well, Sigurd was doubtless already familiar with the Hebrew God. The Irish, English and Norse-Gaels were by now all thoroughly Christianized; Sigurd's mother was Irish, almost certainly Christian. The jarl himself, however, was still resolutely pagan. His standard was a *hrafnsmerki*, a raven banner symbolic of Odin, and he was said to be impervious while it flew, even though his flag-bearers were inevitably slain. Odd wrote, "They soon joined forces, combining their ships and men. They planned to attack the Vikings, raiders and plunderers who had seized large parts of that region. They believed that with their combined strength they could take it for themselves."

It is here that, abruptly – preposterously – Odd invokes the story of Harald Bluetooth, Jarl Hakon and Emperor Otto II at the Battle of the Danevirke. Never mind that by this time Bluetooth and Otto had both been dead for years, and that the battle itself took place about a decade and a half before that. (Recall that Berg and Snorri place the scene four years earlier in their telling, and still ten or so after the actual event.) Odd has Olaf, still using his alias, arrive fresh from Ireland – which itself has had so far only passing mention in Odd's account – offer his services to the emperor, and order barrels full of burning wood shavings and tar rolled up against the Viking wall, "until the entire Danevirke was burned down that same night." As with Berg's account, after pursuing and defeating Bluetooth and Hakon, Otto and Olaf, who has now admitted his true identity, share in a victory feast, and the emperor invites the Viking into his service. Olaf declines, preferring to continue his own personal crusade against the heathen, upon which "They parted on friendly terms."

The causes of these chronological errors, accidental or otherwise, have been noted. At this point there's no need to labor the point further, except to point out that Odd may have wanted to depict Olaf as a proto-crusader against the then-heathen Bluetooth and ever-pagan Jarl Hakon, in order to offset his dalliance with pagan Sigurd.

Odd resumed the saga where he left off – "Olaf and his men went on to harry the Britons, Irish, and Scots" – but insisted that they victimized pagans only, leaving Christians in peace.

That would have limited their income considerably. One would think that almost everyone around the Irish Sea being Christian would be good reason for them all to get along as God intended. Instead, everyone saw everyone else as lesser Christians, not their kind of Christian, not Christian enough. The commandments *thou shalt not kill* and *thou shalt not steal* served more as general guidelines, best practices, rather than rigid laws handed down from God. Killing in battle was not the same as murder, looting a vanquished foe was not theft, and since anyone could be pointed out as insufficiently Christian, anything could be justified in the name of God. If Olaf – Oli – had any qualms, any pangs of conscience about raiding his fellow Christians, well, then as now, godly virtue is easily rationalized away by expediency. A man's got to earn a living, and in reality Olaf knew no other way. Christian though he was, he was still a Viking. He would need a few victories of his own to prove his new God's worth.

It seems Olaf did somewhat victimize at least one pagan: his own partner, Jarl Sigurd. Odd wrote of a very unequal division of spoils, with Sigurd and his men receiving a share apiece while Olaf's men got two, and Olaf himself three: "The division was made in this way because at the outset Olaf and his men earned a larger share by virtue of their toughness and boldness." It stands to reason that such an unequal partnership could not last, and that eventually Olaf and his men would have to prove their toughness and boldness against Jarl Sigurd and his.

However, this chapter in Olaf's life is less about his continuing in his old ways than about new relationships, not just the one with God or the other with Jarl Sigurd. The scenes do not follow the same sequence in the various versions of his sagas, and some do not appear at all. Let us, then, perhaps take them in order of importance, as told by Odd, Snorri and Berg.

The first story comes to us via several sources. As Olaf's latest medieval biographer, Berg Sokkason probably got his version from the *Kristni Saga*, the 12th-century "Book of Christianity," which tells of the conversion of Iceland, but as the scene involves the cleric Thangbrand of Saxony and England, this seems the likeliest place to tell it.

According to that account, Thangbrand had used the silver Olaf paid him for his shield to purchase a woman, a comely Irish girl. (This does not necessarily mean she was a slave, but that he paid the accustomed bride price to her family, though some today would call it the same thing.) He took her home with him, where she caught the eye of an imperial official, who claimed her for his own. Refusing to give her up, Thangbrand was obligated to fight for her. "Thangbrand was tall and strong," wrote Berg, "well spoken, a good cleric, warlike and full of bravery, even though a priest – not aggressive, but hardhearted and steadfast in word and deed when angered."

In Germanic culture judicial duels, trial by combat, were described by the Roman writers Tacitus in the 1st century and Cassiodorus in the 6th. The idea was to limit blood feuds between families and clans to the immediate belligerents, rather than let them escalate to miniature wars that might go on for generations. The practice was confirmed in various medieval Germanic law codes and had been sanctioned as legal by Emperor Otto I back in the year 967.*

Thangbrand's unnamed opponent was described by Berg as "a very great champion and duelist," but the cleric nonetheless slew him. Winning God's decision gained him nothing. The killing of an imperial official obliged him to flee the country, evidently leaving his bride behind. Being familiar with England from his previous visit, he

---

* Thietmar of Merseberg recounted the story of Count Gero of Alsleben, arrested for an unknown crime in 979 by our old friend Margrave Dietrich of the Northern March and sentenced to trial by combat. Gero was knocked down by a blow to the helmet and could not continue, but had already dealt his opponent a couple of cuts to the neck, which turned out to be fatal. Though Gero won the duel, Emperor Otto had him beheaded anyway, which, as Thietmar noted, pleased no one.

returned there, and by chance or by plan found his way to his old friend Olaf, who, according to the *Kristni Saga*, welcomed him and took him on as his personal priest.

England and dueling introduce us to another new person in Olaf's life, this one of even more murky provenance but of more import. Odd told us, "In England was a widow, eminent because of her ancestral standing but also because she herself was exceptional. Her name was Gytha, a woman of great property."

Her name is significant. Gytha or Gyda is Scandinavian, a pet name for Gyrid, but that's a variant of Gudrid or Gudfrid, "beloved of God," indicative of Christian faith. Berg claimed, "As she had been wife of a high-ranking English earl who had died, she ruled in his place," but that does not help narrow down her identity. As has been noted, there was as yet no such thing as an earl in England. We might expect her to have been married to a noble of formerly Viking Northumbria, but Thored, the ealdorman up there, had ruled it since the 970s and was still alive. According to the *Anglo-Saxon Chronicle*, however, Aelfhere, ealdorman of Mercia, had died in 983, and his successor Aelfric Cild had been accused of treason, banished, and was thought to have died in exile in 985. If either of them had been Gytha's husband, she had spent the past few years running the ealdordom herself, which might explain why there is no ealdorman of Mercia recorded in this period. Anglo-Saxon widows were the most independent women in their society, able to inherit and manage large estates, to decide whether they would remarry, and if so to whom. Laws enacted by King Aethelred in 997 in part to formalize existing, unwritten legal tradition, decreed of them, "each should remain idle [i.e., without a husband] for twelve months, then choose what they truly wish." This decision was being forced on Gytha.

"In her domain there was a man named Aelfwine, a great champion and duelist," recorded the scribes. "He had asked for her hand in marriage, but she replied that she would be the one to choose her own husband." This Aelfwine – "elf friend," written variously as Alfvine, Alfuin, Alfwini, Alfini, Alvini, or even Alpin;

the Old English *w*, written as a *wynn*, p, was often mis-transcribed by later translators – may have been Aelfwine, son of the banished ealdorman Aelfric Cild, but if so had been passed over for his title. (Aelfwine was a common enough English name, and surely there were others, but few of such rank as to lay claim to the widow of an ealdorman.) In those days it would not have been unheard of for a son to take his widowed *steopmodor*, stepmother, to wife, particularly in an effort to keep an estate within the family, but it might account for Gytha's reluctance to accept Aelfwine's suit. He was, however, being polite in asking for her hand, for he might just as easily have simply taken it. Anglo-Saxon widows had all sorts of freedom, but they were at all sorts of risk too, depending for protection on God and the state, which is to say, effectively on their own. Abduction and forced marriage were not unknown. A propertied woman like Gytha needed a champion. Aelfwine wished to be that man, but she had convened something of a thing – very Scandinavian of her – in order to assess the competition.

Olaf and his men learned of the gathering and flattered themselves that they might meet with the lady's approval. Odd wrote, "Many of them prepared for the assembly and dressed in fine clothing, thinking they might be the chosen one." For his part Olaf is said to have merely worn a rough wool cloak, with the hood raised against the weather, or possibly to conceal his identity.

They found themselves outclassed in this crowd. Every lordling for miles around had come dressed in his best fur-trimmed cloak and tunic fastened with decorative brooches. Olaf and his rough-hewn sea rovers stood apart from the rest as Gytha made her entrance with thirty ladies-in-waiting. Odd declared: "She was the most beautiful of them all."

They rode past Aelfwine, likewise finely dressed and seated on something of a throne, plush, gilded and bejeweled, "like an idol set on an altar." He called out to Gytha as she passed: "Hear me, great lady. I bid you get down from your horse, come sit here next to me, and proclaim me as your husband and lover."

That was not why Gytha had summoned them all. As Odd went on, "She rode around the circle and looked over the assembled men, judging their looks and dress, but she did not find the suitable man she sought. She rode around a second time, assessing each man's face and form. The third time she went around, she came upon a large man in a cheap wool cloak."

Berg wrote, "She examined him from all sides, lifted his hood and looked into his face, asking, 'Who are you?'"

"My name is Oli," he said. "I am a stranger here."

The *Agrip* attests: "Olaf was a large man, tall and good looking, with straight blond hair and beard, and of all men he was the most accomplished in courtly behavior."

"I am a king's daughter from Ireland," she said. "I was given in marriage in this country to the jarl who ruled this realm. Since his death I have ruled here. If you will have me, I will take you for my husband."

Berg wrote, "She was young, and very pleasing to look upon." The scribes would have us believe it was love at first sight, but pragmatically Gytha's was not an impulsive choice. Perhaps she recognized Olaf as the wayward, up-and-coming Viking making himself known around the Irish Sea, whose wealth and power could augment hers. Even if not, here at least was an outlander who would be loyal to her amid the legendarily treacherous Anglo-Saxon aristocracy: along with his men, her own personal Varangian Guard.*

"I will not refuse that," replied Olaf. (Thus do the later chroniclers, Snorri and Berg, portray him as making the choice.) He asked after Gytha's good name and family.

The scribes would have it that, as Berg put it, Gytha was "sister to Olaf Kvaran, King of Dublin, in Ireland." Olaf Sigtryggsson, nicknamed *Kvaran*, was known in Irish Gaelic as Amlaib mac Sitric *Cuaran*, usually translated as "shoe" or "sandal," but *cuaran granda* meant an unsavory character. He had been baptized a Christian by England's King Edmund I in 943 and had ruled Northumbria as his vassal two or three times, and Dublin twice on his own, but is remembered mainly for having finally lost the former to Bloodaxe in 952 and the latter to the Irish in 980, dying in monastic exile that same year. The problem is that Cuaran's father (and so Gytha's supposed father) had died in 927. Cuaran's mother being unknown,

---

* In a more literary analysis, she is the third person in Olaf's saga – after Grand Princess Olava in Novgorod and the seer in the Scilly Islands – who recognizes his innate royalty on sight; for a medieval audience, proof enough it was true.

perhaps she was young enough to remarry, and Gytha was Cuaran's very much younger half-sister. Otherwise, she would have been in her sixties when making her appearance in Olaf's saga.* The general consensus among historians is that Gytha was not Cuaran's sister but, as she had told Olaf, "an Irish king's daughter."† In any case, Gytha's ancestry mattered less to Olaf's saga-writers than her marital status. As she put it, "Many have proposed to marry me, but I would not give myself to them."

They have the pair talk it over a bit before agreeing on betrothal, but Odd, who recorded the tale first, had Gytha announce her choice dramatically, as soon as she saw Olaf's eyes: "Of all those who have assembled here, this is the man whom I choose as my husband."

By Anglo-Saxon custom, a couple was betrothed the moment both accepted each other in front of witnesses. Odd confided, "Rejected, disgraced and deprived of this advantageous match, and with this stranger chosen instead, Aelfwine howled in anger, saying he would not enjoy his marriage for long."

The English and Irish being by this time almost entirely Christian, including Gytha's kin (father, brother, whatever), she almost certainly was as well. As yet, however, weddings were not church business. Our word "wedding" comes from the Old English *wedd*, meaning a pledge or contract, and in the early Christian era a marriage was more of a business merger between families. A priest's blessing was always nice to have, so weddings were conducted at church, but outside the

---

* There was another possible Olaf brother. In the original Old Norse Gytha's father is referred to as *skota konungs*, literally King of the Scots; in the Latin in which Odd wrote, *Scotti* meant Gaels, both Irish and Scottish. Amlaib (Olaf) mac Illuilb, the King of Alba (Scotland), had died in 977, but his father Illuilb not until 962, meaning his daughter, the Scottish Amlaib's sister, could have been about Olaf Tryggvason's age. And just to make matters even more complicated, over in Sweden there would be yet another King Olaf *Skotkonung* – "Tax King" – the son of Eirik the Victorious and Queen Sigrid, but he would not reign until AD 995.

† Assuming she was Amlaib Cuaran's daughter, Gytha had two sisters as well. Ragnhild ingen Amlaib ("Daughter of Olaf") had been married to a son of the High King of Ireland Conghalach Cnoghbha. That king had died, ambushed, in 956, and his son, her husband, in 976. The other sister, Mael Muire ingen Amlaib ("Servant of Mary") would eventually be married to Malachy II and reign beside him as Queen of Ireland.

entrance, not inside; financial matters such as the bride's dowry and groom's dower were public business and announced as such at the service, but were thought beneath God's concern.

All the assembled lords and ladies, including even pagan Jarl Sigurd, were invited to the wedding feast, which is said to have gone on for days. According to the scribes, the guests even got to enjoy a little extra special entertainment, when trouble arose. Odd wrote, "As Olaf enjoyed the feast, the champion Aelfwine came to him in a rage and challenged him to combat, saying he should prove his strength and bravery."

To refuse such a challenge marked a man as a *niding*: one without honor, a villain, weak and cowardly.

Odd wrote, "Olaf said he would come."

XIX

To the Death

It was then the custom in England, if two men quarreled about anything, that the matter should be settled by a duel.

Snorri Sturluson

AD 989

Here the later scribes date themselves. Despite their Germanic heritage, there is scant evidence that Anglo-Saxons settled matters through trial by combat; it was the Normans who brought that innovation to England after their conquest of 1066. However, this episode most likely taking place in what had formerly been the Danelaw, in Olaf's time judicial duels may have been conducted in England under Viking tradition. The Old Norse word for it was *einvigi* – single combat, duel – but Old English had a corresponding word, *anwig*, which would seem to indicate its speakers were familiar with the concept. An einvigi, however, was not a legal resolution. There were no judges, no rules regarding weapons or tactics. It was fairer than a stab in the back, but not by much. The loser's kin could still demand legal redress in the form of blood price or blood vengeance, which rather defeated the entire purpose.

It was the West Norse – the Norwegians, the Icelanders – who developed einvigi into what has come down through history as a duel. *Holmgang*, they called it, "island going," as such private matters were often settled in secluded places. There were rules, *holmgangulog*, not uniform everywhere but agreed upon by opponents prior to the fight. The *holmgongustad*, the little arena marked out by ropes or stones, counted as a court of law in which the outcome was regarded as divine judgment. Generally, one foot out of the ring was considered accidental, but two feet out amounted to defeat. Death in the ring was not murder, but the same as executing a criminal. Blood money might still be due, but the matter was considered settled. The victor won the dispute. The loser, if he survived – duels could be fought to first blood – might be ransomed by kin or, if dead, lost his possessions to his foe. (This had the unintended result of encouraging skilled swordsmen to enrich themselves by picking fights with wealthy but weaker victims, a kind of legalized robbery, which is why the practice was eventually abolished.)

Holmgang is attested in a number of 12th-century sagas, like Olaf's, recording deeds of the 10th. They are taken to be more than legend, as the characters interact with historic figures, including King Harald Fairhair, Aethelstan of England, Hakon the Good, Eirik Bloodaxe and his queen Gunnhild. *The Saga of Cormac the Skald* is the story of an Icelandic poet's duel with his lover's husband, ending in a draw. *The Saga of Gunnlaugur Serpent-Tongue* tells of two rivals fighting over a woman; they too battle to a draw in Iceland, but take it up again in Norway, where they kill each other. And *Egil's Saga* records two duels by the warrior poet Egil Skallagrimsson, in which he kills both opponents. Those duels took place in Iceland or Norway, but the *holmgang* between Olaf and Aelfwine is often cited as evidence for the practice in England. The Norwegian synoptics do not refer to this scene at all, but Snorri, and Berg following him, claim that Olaf and Aelfwine did not engage in single combat, at least not at first. "The time and place for the duel were decided," records the *Heimskringla*, "and that each man could bring twelve men with him."

And Odd agreed that Olaf came to the fight with eleven men, but claimed Aelfwine tipped the odds: "At dawn the next day Olaf arrived with eleven men," he wrote. "The champion came with twenty-four."

Again, shades of the ambush that claimed Olaf's father's life.

Olaf, though, was not his father.

"As Olaf's picked men prepared to fight, he gave them large axes, and told them to do as he did," wrote the scribes. "He too had a huge axe."

Interesting, in this age of the blade, that our hero chooses a Dane axe for personal combat. The sword, being all edge, was easier to master, more instinctive to use. The axe blade, of minimal edge, though weighty out there on the far end of a long wooden staff, required skill to put on target.

There is virtually no historical evidence regarding axe-fighting technique in this period, no instructional guidebooks, no treatises like the *Fechtbücher*, "fight books," the combat manuals of the later Middle Ages. Yet to this day the two fundamental concepts of fighting with edged weapons have always been *tempo* and *measure*. Tempo is the time it takes to make one move – to hit, to thrust, to swing or recover. Measure is the range to the opponent. Skilled fencers maximize measure and minimize tempo, maintaining just enough safe distance to carry out one move. Compared with a three-foot sword, a five- or six-foot Dane axe slowed one's tempo, but vastly increased measure, especially swung at arm's length, when all that angular momentum and weight out on the very end gave it the power to crack helmets and break bones through mail armor. And while a sword could be used to parry, cut or stab, the Dane axe could do all that, but also hook an opponent's body or shield to create an opening. It was the prototypical polearm, that in centuries to come would evolve into the even longer bill, halberd, poleaxe and more. It was versatile. It was light (less metal, more wood – as little as one and a half pounds overall, versus about two and a half pounds for a sword). It could be *fenced with*. The trick, as in all bladework, was to hit without being hit.

Considering Olaf's sorry clothes (though presumably he dressed up for his wedding), Aelfwine doubtless thought he was up against some poor sea rover, making a show with that big clumsy axe, and that he could end the fight with one swift stroke before it could even be raised against him. Berg wrote, "Aelfwine tried to strike Olaf with his sword."

The key word is "tried." In fencing, a too-impetuous attack invites not only a parry, but a riposte. An axe's broad, strong upper edge could catch and turn a sword, and the *oxarhamar*, axe hammer, the back side of the blade, was a weapon too. "With his axe," Berg continued, "Olaf knocked the sword out of his hands, and then with a second blow hit and stunned him."

In a holmgang, a downed opponent was as good as dead. In their duel Egil Skallagrimsson attacked the Swedish berserker Ljot the Pale as he was getting back to his feet and cut off his leg, killing him. And against Atli the Short, whose armor Egil's sword could not pierce, Egil is said to have dropped his sword and shield and leaped upon him. According to Egil's saga, "Atli fell backward, but Egil dropped on top of him and bit through his throat, and Atli died."

Olaf did not need to resort to throat-biting. "Olaf lowered his weapon," wrote Odd, "rushed the champion, grabbed him and threw him to the ground." According to the sagas, his men defeated Aelfwine's as well, all eleven (or two dozen) of them. Olaf was within his rights to have them all executed. But he was a Christian now. *Blessed are the merciful, for they shall receive mercy.* And in Germanic society there were worse fates than death. Odd wrote, "He securely bound the survivors, set the champion on a horse backwards, facing the tail, and drove him ahead, back to the town."

Berg added, "All Aelfwine's men were treated the same way, led conquered and bound to Olaf's hall."

When Jarl Sigurd and the other assembled chieftains and nobles beheld Aelfwine and all his men thus shamed and disgraced, they proclaimed Olaf a true champion. All the fruits of victory were his. "Olaf ordered Aelfwine to go away, never to return," records the saga, "and he claimed ownership of all his lands and property."

Now that was a wedding gift fit for an ealdorman.

XX

IRELAND

I have heard of towns set afire in past times in Ireland, where came the battle-furious prince. The sword rang out. Banners fluttered.

Olafsdrapa

AD 989–991

Although marrying the widow of an ealdorman did not make one an ealdorman, Olaf was now a man of means. Unfortunately, this period of his life is one of the least documented by his medieval biographers, possibly because it was the most boring. It requires a bit of educated guesswork to fill in the blanks. The sagas do not detail exactly where his new wife Gytha's lands lay, nor those confiscated from his defeated foe Aelfwine, but assuming the two tracts together totaled at least five hides (about 600 acres), they were enough to qualify Olaf as a *thegn*, a mid-rank nobleman, roughly equivalent to his Norwegian grandfather Eirik the Bald, the *stormann* of Oprekstad, or Eirik's Swedish friend Hakon the Old, the *lendermann* of Swedish Gotland. Not that this made Olaf anything special; in decades to come there would be some 5,000 thegns in England.

Olaf the English nobleman would undoubtedly have found his new life was nothing like that of a seagoing Viking. Certainly there was good living: wealth, steady income, fine clothing and jewelry, hunting in his own personal forest, and feasting, drinking, music and revelry in his great hall. Yet a medieval estate had to be run as a business. The "Ely Memoranda," six short texts of early 11th-century Old English, relate in tedious detail how the finances and lands of the monastery on the island of Ely in England's eastern fens were managed, which would have equally applied to any English landowner's holdings. Admittedly Olaf, who was not formally educated, or probably even literate, would not have kept the books himself. A well-run manor, as Gytha's was said to be, would include a man, likely a monk or priest, educated in numbers and letters and trusted to keep track of silver pence, ora (sixteen to twenty pence each), pounds (240 pence), gold mancuses (twenty pence), and even *feorm* (food-rent). Olaf's duty was defined by responsibilities to his household staff and all the farmers, villagers, herdsmen, craftsmen and families on his land and in his service. It was not just his Viking crews with whom he had to concern himself now; they were all his extended family, his men, his women and children, his slaves and fields and livestock, and they all required constant, careful attention. Then too, he was obligated to the nobility above him, if not to an ealdorman (and again, there are none confirmed in Mercia at this time) then to the king, to whom all loyalty and military service was owed. At sea Olaf had been a king in his own right. Here, he was in middle management, local government.

Life as a minor noble in Anglo-Saxon England, however, was hardly more secure than that of a Viking. Doubtless Olaf kept his former crewmen on as his personal retainers, his housecarls, or as the Anglo-Saxons might have called them, his *cnihtas*, his knights. Not everything a wealthy manor required could be grown or manufactured on site. Some had to be traded, bought or taken, and the only persons to whom Olaf owed nothing were his neighbors.

The ancestors of the most powerful English ealdormen had once been kings of their own realms, the Heptarchy: Northumbria, Mercia, East Anglia, Essex, Kent, Sussex and Wessex. Though now nominally subservient to the king in London, they were not above pushing each other around for territory, wealth, power and prestige. King Aethelred held his throne only by their mutual consent, and by maintaining an ever-shifting balance of power between them. Personal duels might not be in the Anglo-Saxon tradition, but generations-long feuds and constant mutual raiding certainly were. An Irish widow and her new Scandinavian husband might well attract the ire of Anglo-Saxon neighbors who within living memory had been subject to the tender mercies of Eirik Bloodaxe.

Olaf, however, had an advantage his English neighbors did not. "Having won Gytha in marriage," wrote Snorri, "Olaf sometimes lived in England, and other times in Ireland."

And why not? In England he was a minor noble at best; in Ireland he was now brother-in-law to a king.

This was a particularly fraught time for Gytha's Irish kin. The nobility of the Emerald Isle were so back-stabbing, double-crossing and murderous they made the treacherous Anglo-Saxons of England look like squabbling children. Since his defeat of Olaf Cuaran in 980, Mael Sechnaill (Malachy) II reigned as High King, but in name only. Anywhere more than a few miles inland from the Viking coast, Ireland was a lawless mayhem of battling Gaelic clans: the Ui Imair, Ui Neill, Ui Briuin, Eoganachta, Connachta, the Dal gCais. Petty kingdoms, ever feuding, shifting alliances, in constant conflict.

With his new wife, and lands on both sides of the Irish Sea, Olaf might be seen as a true heir of the Ui Imair, the sons of Ivar, once all-powerful but now fractured, with the kings of Dublin, Waterford, Limerick and others battling each other as well as the purebred Gaels. After Olaf Cuaran's defeat, abdication, exile and death in 980, rule of Dublin had passed to his son Gluniairn, in Old Norse *Jarnkne*, "Iron-knee." He had reigned as a puppet in the name of his father's conqueror, High King Malachy. (The fact that Malachy was both Iron Knee's half-brother and brother-in-law, not to mention currently wed to his stepmother, Cuaran's widow, demonstrates just how intertwined were the kinship ties of Vikings and Gaels.) The Dubliners' resentment of native Irish rule may have found expression in 989, when the 15th-century *Annals of Ulster* record, "Gluniairn, king of the foreigners (Irish Norse), was killed while drunk by his own slave."

Malachy punished the town for its crime. After almost three weeks of siege the defenders, reduced to drinking brine for lack of fresh water, submitted once again to the High King's overlordship and agreed to pay him an ounce of gold per household every Christmas Eve in perpetuity, a penance that would seem intended to keep the town economically weak. To make sure it was paid, it's thought that

Malachy also installed a new puppet king, once again drawn from his kinsmen among the sons of his late father-in-law Olaf Cuaran: his and Gluniairn's (and Gytha's) mutual half-brother, Sigtrygg Olafsson, called *Silkiskegg*, "Silkbeard."

Given Olaf's years of raiding around the Irish Sea, this was almost certainly not his first visit to Dublin. Some 150 years earlier Vikings had established a *longphort* there, a seasonal raiding camp where the rivers Poddle and Liffey came together, above a peat-stained tidal pond that the locals called *Duibh Linn*, "Black Pool." The settlement had been sacked by the Irish in 849, 902 and 944, when according to the 17th-century Irish *Annals of the Four Masters*, "its houses, suburbs, ships, and all other buildings were burned. Its women, boys, and commoners were enslaved. It was totally destroyed, three out of every four men killed, drowned, burned and captured, except a few who fled in ships and reached Deilginis [Dalkey Island, just down the coast]." As a result of this repeated destruction Dublin had been gradually but completely rebuilt along more modern lines: ground leveled, primitive dugout houses backfilled and replaced by some 600 rectangular post-and-wattle homes laid out on a Scandinavian street grid, very unlike native Irish wickerwork roundhouses and ringforts. In Olaf's time it was already the Emerald Isle's biggest metropolis, but still no more glorious than Vladimir's Novgorod or the Wends' Jomsborg: a village of a few thousand people, defended on three sides by water and on the fourth by an earthen rampart with a ditch and wooden stockade.

It's thought Sigtrygg's stronghold stood at the southeastern end of the gravel ridge where today Dublin Castle overlooks what was then the Black Pool and is today the castle garden. It was doubtless there that the new king and Olaf sat down to make plans. Sigtrygg was probably a few years younger, and his low profile in those early years might indicate he let his new brother-in-law take the lead.

The first problem was, as King of Dublin, Sigtrygg owed High King Malachy that ounce of gold per household every Christmas. As that was the price of a plot of land in Dublin, equivalent to eleven or twelve ounces of silver or the same head of cattle, the tax amounted to re-purchasing the entire city every year.

The second problem was, Ireland was not a great source of gold, or money in general. The Gaels used precious metals for adornment – armlets, neck rings, brooches, a "status economy" – but before the coming of the Vikings they had no concept of currency. Three-quarters of all Viking Age silver hoards in the Emerald Isle were buried after AD 940, the earliest consisting mostly of ingots, armbands, brooches and hack-silver – bits and pieces of cut-up jewelry and plate – indicative of a bullion economy. The gradual increase of Arabic, English and continental coins in these caches illustrates the final transition to a monetary economy, but also that the coinage came in from abroad, not from inland.

The Irish primarily measured wealth in terms of cattle. Beyond food – analysis of medieval Dublin graves indicates the occupants' meat intake was ninety percent beef – their milk, leather and labor served as currency, investments, debt settlements, and payments for food, rent, work and military service. Wealth and status were measured by herd size. Cattle rustling was less a form of theft than of economic competition – warfare by other means – a noble occupation for any warrior. Even the Church took a cut of the action, though priests were forbidden from actual pillage. (The Irish had converted to Christianity even prior to the English, but interpreted the commandments much as did Christianized Vikings. Any clan's monasteries were considered fair game for any others, the priests of which were only too happy to accept their brethren's looted goods. More Irish churches were looted and destroyed by other Irish than by Vikings.)

Evidently, Olaf had to start his Irish enterprise from the ground up, which leads to one of the sagas' few actual scenes of him in the Emerald Isle.

In his telling, Odd placed the tale prior to Olaf's meeting Gytha, and Snorri and Berg afterward, but then the order of events does not make much difference. The story has Olaf and his men on a seaborne raid off the Irish coast. They put ashore for a little cattle thieving. (As city folk, Dubliners did not raise their own cattle but got them from elsewhere, by trade or plunder. That Olaf could not or did not simply buy butchered beef in town might illustrate the point about money.) A poor farmer has the temerity to approach and ask for the return of his herd.

An old-school Viking would not only have kept the cattle, but slain the farmer as well for his effrontery. It's perhaps a demonstration of Olaf's newfound Christianity that he merely replies: "It would be impossible. We cannot find your cows among all the others." (This would have been a herd of old Irish breeds, uniformly black Kerry cattle, or black Dexters with perhaps the odd red or dun among them, all identical except for their brands.) "No man could single them out or separate them."

"Have mercy," the farmer pleads, "and let me keep the animals my dog finds for me."

"If your dog is smart enough to cull your cattle from the rest and bring them out by instinct and skill, I will grant your request, but see to it he causes us no delay."

At his owner's command, the dog plunges into the herd. To Olaf's amazement, it cuts out the exact number of cattle the farmer claims, all with his brand on them.

Olaf tells the farmer, "A very clever dog you have there, fellow. Will you sell him to me?"

The farmer, surely realizing he has pushed his luck about as far as it can go with Olaf, who could simply take his herd, his dog and his life, says, "I would rather give him to you."

But as he had done with the cleric Thangbrand and his shield, Olaf pays well for the dog – a gold armlet – and pledges the farmer his friendship going forward.

"The dog was named Vigi," wrote the scribes, in Old Norse meaning Fighter or Scrapper, "and all men agreed there has been no greater treasure in all the world than this dog." *

Herding dog or not, Olaf was no cattleman. Then as now, livestock were not the most fungible of assets – bulky, balky, difficult to transport, especially by boat – but ultimately Ireland simply had little else worth

---

* Vigi was probably not an Irish Wolfhound, at least not the giant breed we know today. Hunting dogs, war dogs, they largely died out in the 19th century after the last wolf was killed and there was no further need of them. The modern breed was later recreated using the blood of Scottish Deerhounds and Great Danes. Wolfhound-sized dog remains older than about AD 1200 have not been found in Ireland. More probably Vigi was an Alsatian-like herding dog, forerunner of today's Icelandic Sheepdog or Norwegian Buhund.

stealing. Once all the churches were cleaned out and their precious metals melted down, everybody was simply thieving the same stolen goods from each other, back and forth, over and over again, a kind of barter economy by force. There was, however, another commodity in Ireland, just as plentiful as cattle and simpler to turn into profit.

Slavery had been known among the Irish, though it's believed that until the coming of the Vikings the trade was not a goal in itself but an incidental byproduct of their incessant wars, not conducted in bulk but merely for luxuries: household servants, concubines, skilled labor. The Church was not against slavery, far from it; the testaments not only condoned it, but endorsed and regulated it. The average Irish household was too poor to support many slaves (or protect itself against them), but stone churches and monasteries were natural sanctuaries for refugees fleeing Viking raids, which made such places even more attractive targets for slavers. And the sea rovers had the means to ship great numbers of captives offshore for sale in markets as far abroad as Iceland, Muslim Spain and the Byzantine Empire.* Dublin, facing out onto the Irish Sea toward the rest of Europe, was the natural embarkation point for such an industry, but as late as the 960s, this potential was not fully exploited. (After capturing the town in 980, High King Malachy had ordered all its Irish slaves freed.) It was not easy to turn a profit at human trafficking if nobody had silver to buy slaves.

The third of Ireland's prime commodities, however, was another form of manpower: fighting men, and lots of them. Besides native warriors, from at least the 940s Vikings had been hiring themselves out as mercenaries in the island's incessant intertribal wars, but since High King Malachy's conquest of the Emerald Isle in 980 the market had dried up considerably. (Probably that was just one more reason Vikings resumed raiding England soon afterward. Mercenaries fight where the money is.)

Gytha's English estate would generate income through rents, taxes and trade, but legally, slowly. Olaf needed money now, for at some time in this period (as usual, the scribes offer no dates), Gytha bore him a son.

---

* The population of Iceland in 930 has been estimated at 20,000, of which 5,000 were Irish slaves.

In the old Scandinavian tradition, and just as Olaf had been named after his grandfather Olaf Haraldsson, son of Harald Fairhair, they named the boy Tryggvi, in hopes that the spirit of Olaf's father would live on in him. Olaf had, of course, inherited nothing but his name at birth, but every father wishes to pass on to his son a better lot in life. Together, Olaf's English estates might have amounted to an ealdordom, but his son was at least in theory an heir to two kingdoms, those of Ivar and of Tryggvi. He deserved something more than a Varangian father's bare sword and a command to make his own way in the world – something worthy of his forefathers. Perhaps even a real kingdom.

In Ireland, the way to achieve that was to go to England.

XXI

Maldon

*Then he stood on the shore, boldly calling out to the warriors,
a Viking messenger, speaking words of promise.
He offered a challenge from the sea-faring men,
an invitation to the ealdorman on the opposite bank.*

"The Battle of Maldon"

AD 991

Folkestone, Sandwich, Ipswich. And then, that August, a Viking warrior came out from among the fleet of beached dragon ships on the shore of Northey Island. (Olaf? The earliest version of the *Anglo-Saxon Chronicle* would have it so.) He shouted across the channel of the river Blackwater to Ealdorman Byrhtnoth of Essex: "We need not fight with each other. If you, as lord of these parts, agree to ransom your people and give these sea rovers what they want, tribute in exchange for truce, accept our terms. We will go back to our ships with our payment, and sail away in peace."

Byrhtnoth must have at least considered the offer. Judging by the dragon ships beached on the island – nearly a hundred – his army of local farmers and villagers was evenly matched, perhaps even outnumbered. Yet the English held the advantage of position. Even when the tide went out and the river went down, the Vikings could only cross the channel over the causeway connecting Northey to the mainland, which was less than ten feet wide. Numbers would count for nothing when only the front few ranks, a dozen or so men at a time, could actually engage. And even if they managed a crossing, these Vikings had so far had things their own way, surprising and slaughtering helpless villagers.

They had yet to face a real army – Anglo-Saxon housecarls, the likes of which had slain Eirik Bloodaxe, sent his horde back across the North Sea and reclaimed the Danelaw for England.

It seems Byrhtnoth put the question to his men, who gave a resounding answer. Raising his shield and spear for the Vikings to see, he called back:

> Sea-robber, do you hear this army's reply? They will give you tribute – spears with deadly points and swords as in the old days, weaponry of no use to you in battle. Messenger, take my answer, give your people this dire warning, that here with his men stands a leader of impeccable reputation, who will defend our homes, the country of Aethelred, my ruler, my people and land. You heathen will fall in battle. I would find it shameful for you to return to your ships with our treasure without a fight, having come this far into our country. You will not get rich so easily. Spear and sword shall settle our differences in a fierce game of battle, before we yield payment.

In his account of events, a contemporary English monk recorded, "Who, however well-spoken, could say how magnificently, how fearlessly, how audaciously the commander encouraged his men in the army?"

Byrhtnoth had bidden them to dismount and send their horses to the rear. (Anglo-Saxons and Vikings alike considered controlling a horse in battle to be a needless distraction.) Now the ealdorman and his warriors moved up to line the riverbank, waving spears, clashing swords on shields, hurling insults and giving vent to their own anger, eagerness, and yes, fear. Here and there arrows flicked back and forth over the water, and sometimes an inattentive man caught one, but the real battle could not commence while the river separated the armies.

All the while, however, the tide was going out and the water level fell, like the Red Sea parting for Moses, gradually revealing the sunken causeway that would soon bear men to their deaths, or victory.

With the exception of Hastings in 1066, probably no other battle in medieval English history has inspired a larger cottage industry among historians than Maldon, while raising more questions and yielding fewer answers. Everything we know about the battle comes to us from the Anglo-Saxon viewpoint. In their day Odd, Snorri and Berg had little or no access to English accounts of it; to them – to Olaf – Maldon was just another raid, beneath notice, left unrecorded. Even most English accounts give it little more than passing mention.

The earliest is included in the *Vita Oswaldi*, a biography of Oswald, Archbishop of York 972–992. Its author, Byrhtferth, a monk at Ramsey Abbey in what was then Huntingdonshire, about sixty miles from the battle, was a contemporary of Ealdorman Byrhtnoth, probably had met him personally, and composed his account partly in homage to him. The fact that he wrote it so soon after the battle gives it credence, as people alive at the time would have recognized and reviled any part that wandered too far from the truth. Unfortunately, the battle not being his main subject, he gave it little more than 300 words.

The *Liber Eliensis*, "Book of Ely," was written at Ely Abbey in the Cambridgeshire fens, closer to the battle geographically but further removed in time, being written some two centuries after the fact. In life Ealdorman Byrhtnoth had been the abbey's patron and benefactor; in death the monks revered and even embellished his memory. As a result their telling is more subject to induced error, for instance naming the ealdorman as *Northanimbrorum dux*, Duke of Northumbria, which he was not, and having the battle last a full two weeks when it almost certainly lasted no more than an afternoon. They even credited Byrhtnoth with defeating a previous Viking force at Maldon four years earlier, that he "slaughtered nearly all of them on a causeway above the water," and that they returned in 991 seeking vengeance on him. This earlier raid and supposed great victory are not recorded in any other accounts and are regarded as spurious, which casts doubt on the whole account.

The *Anglo-Saxon Chronicle* documents the battle, but as usual its various versions conflict. The earliest surviving edition gives the most detailed account, but does not give it even 500 words. Unfortunately, and possibly because the battle's significance was not realized until later – the entry was probably written at Canterbury sometime between the years 1000 and 1006 – the annalist belatedly entered it under the year 993. Three other editions, compiled later at Abingdon

Abbey, Worcester Priory and Peterborough Abbey, give less detailed accounts, but all date the battle correctly to 991. (Calendars from the Ely, Winchester and Ramsey abbeys narrow the date down further to August 991, but even they disagree on the exact day, whether the 10th or 11th.) Byrhtnoth's signature appears on no legal documents after 990, and he is assumed to have died soon afterward.

By far the most elaborate account of the battle comes to us from the famous Anglo-Saxon poem on the subject, but scholars dispute even that. Was "The Battle of Maldon" written soon after the battle? Might the author even have taken part in the fighting? Or did he not compose it until the 11th century, from hearsay and legend? Both the beginning and ending of the poem are lost; what might they have revealed? It's a piece of literature, not a historical record; unlike more clerical documentation of the battle, it does not concern itself with who fought on the enemy side. The Viking horde simply serves as an evil nemesis.

For the purposes of our story, the greatest mystery about the Battle of Maldon is whether Olaf Tryggvason was the "Anlaf" cited by the *Anglo-Saxon Chronicle* as the leader of the Vikings there, or for that matter whether he took part at all. Only the edition compiled at Winchester Cathedral mentions him by name. A strong case can be made, and has frequently been made, that because Olaf is known to have led Viking forays in England in these years, the annalist merely assumed he must have been at Maldon, or confused and conflated the campaign of 991 with others. Yet Winchester's edition of the *Chronicle* is the oldest of the many versions. Its author(s) must have been the most familiar with contemporaneous events like the battle, which though belatedly entered for 993 can be attributed to 991: "In this year came Anlaf with ninety-three ships to Folkestone, and harried outside, and sailed thence to Sandwich, and thence to Ipswich, overrunning all the countryside, and so on to Maldon."

Right or wrong, tradition has it that if any Olaf led the Vikings at Maldon, it was Olaf Tryggvason. (Technically, because of his marriage to Gytha and their English fiefdoms, he was a subject of King Aethelred, which would make him the leader of an English rebellion. Yet, as noted, English ealdormen were not above raiding each other. The 991 invasion was a local affair that barely warranted royal attention. And Olaf had married as Oli, the expatriate Rus; as far as the English knew, this Olaf the Viking leader, though well known, was not the same person.) And even if he didn't lead or even attend Maldon, the battle would affect his life just as did the battles of the Danevirke and Hjorungavag. Therefore let us recount it, as did the old English writers.

"The fight was near, glory at hand," declared the anonymous poet. "The time had come that fate would bring men down." Two age-old enemy hosts faced each other across a channel of the river Panta, the modern Blackwater. English warriors lined the south bank, while the Vikings held an island in mid-stream. Both sides wore similar, simple, conical helmets of leather or metal. They waved similar ash-shafted spears in the air, and clashed similar swords and axes on similar leather-covered, iron-rimmed round shields of linden wood. If not for the fact that they cursed each other across the water in two different languages, Old English and Old Norse, few could have discerned the difference between them. And all that separated them was the narrow causeway from the island to the shore, gradually being unveiled by the receding tide.

To block the way did not require Ealdorman Byrhtnoth's entire army. He chose just three of his best warriors. Wulfstan, son of Ceola, took position at the bridgehead, spear at the ready. At his side stood Aelfhere and Maccus, "two brave men," according to the poet, "who would not flee, but would stand firm as long as they had weapons with which to fight." Together these three would have to face the brunt of the enemy attack, but that was not so hopeless as it might seem.

To reach the enemy required the Vikings to cross 150 yards of slippery, silt-covered causeway. Armored men sliding off into deep water faced drowning in thick black ooze, and every second spent on the runway would bring them under ever-more accurate arrowshot from the landward shore. Yet they could not charge all-out in hopes of overrunning those few English holding the far end, for any men who managed it would meet certain doom, swallowed up in the main English army behind them. It seems the Viking leading the way

– evidently, not Olaf – did not even get that far. The poet recorded that Wulfstan "with his spear struck down the first man who boldly stepped onto the bridge."

This was not a game the raiders could win, and they knew it. Their island was not such an ideal base after all. Byrhtnoth and the English had bottled them up on it. If they were to fight, they needed to do it somewhere other than on that causeway, or else get back aboard their ships and sail off to find easier pickings.

Then again, there was no need to fight for the crossing if Ealdorman Byrhtnoth could be convinced to give it up.

"When they realized and saw immediately that they faced fierce bridge-guards," scorned the poet, "the hateful strangers turned to guile, asking that they might have free passage over the ford, leading the foot soldiers."

Why Byrhtnoth should have ceded his advantage to the enemy is argued by historians to this day. The Maldon poet accused the ealdorman of *ofermode*, the most contested word in the poem, perhaps even in all the Old English language. Its translation is straightforward enough – pride, arrogance, insolence – but its application to Byrhtnoth surely displays a misunderstanding on the poet's part of the military reality: Byrhtnoth *needed* this battle.

He needed to stop the Viking incursion then and there, at Maldon. If he did not, the raiders would indeed board their ships and sail off to surprise and victimize more helpless English towns before he could catch up to them again. As Ealdorman of Essex, defending the land was his primary duty to both his people and his king. If he and his army were slaughtered, or if the enemy withdrew without a fight, the outcome would be the same: The Vikings would be free to plunder England again. He had to defeat them, then and there, or at least kill so many of them that the rest wanted no part of England again.

"Now you are granted free passage," he called back. "Come swiftly to fighting, warriors, and may God alone decide the victor on the field of battle."

Byrhtnoth was gambling everything. His willingness to give battle implies the two armies were of comparable size, for to fight a hopeless action against overwhelming odds and be slaughtered would serve no purpose. Byrhtnoth had to believe he had a fair chance of victory.

Even if the numbers were against him, it was commonly said that one English housecarl was more than a match for two Vikings. Yet in the poet's verdict, the English lost the battle before it was fought: "He gave up too much ground to those wicked people."

That's about as much strategy and tactics as can be gleaned from the primary sources on the Battle of Maldon. To say any more about it requires supposition and inference, but as with most battles, geography, logic and common sense dictate how it must have gone.

Today the south bank of the Blackwater at Northey is salt marsh, cut up with treacherous hidden water channels. Even the fields behind it, assumed to be the area of the battle, are below sea level and protected by flood walls. As such, it's totally unsuitable as a medieval battleground. Yet it's thought that over the past thousand years the ground has subsided up to six feet, and back then was higher, drier and firmer, all grassy pastureland sloping gently down to the river – a wide expanse of smooth ground, perfect for two medieval armies to decide their differences. Compared with the Battle of the Danevirke, which was more of a siege, or the Battle of Hjorungavag, fought at sea, the Battle of Maldon would be more in the tradition of Germanic warfare, going all the way back to the Tollense Valley in the Bronze Age.

The Vikings – the poem's "slaughter-wolves" – now came across the bared causeway unimpeded, "heedless of the water." Byrhtnoth made ready to receive them in the traditional fashion, ordering his housecarls into a shield wall, with his *fyrd*, the great mass of his militia, behind it where they could lend their weight to any advance or hinder a threatened retreat. The poet, no tactician, gives no further detail, but it stands to reason that, to avoid being outflanked, in giving ground the shield wall would have formed a crescent, with its ends on the riverbank to either side of the causeway, and its concave side facing in toward the crossing to contain the invaders as they came. The ideal time to attack would have been as the enemy was making his initial deployment, spreading out from the bridgehead, but according to the poem Byrhtnoth was not of a mind to attack, possibly more concerned that his men would enclose the enemy onslaught. Offense was so far limited to spears and arrows lofted into the Vikings' vulnerable bridgehead. If the numbers on either side were more or less equal, the English, holding the exterior line, would have been stretched thin around the enemy. Their best hope, surrounding the Viking attack as they did, was an envelopment: containing the assault while launching barrages of spears and arrows from all sides into the concentrated enemy horde. The raiders would have of course immediately raised shields, forming a miniature, convex version of the English wall, that grew and expanded like a blood-red flower as the rest of their army crossed and filled in behind it, or perhaps, as the *Book of Ely* claims, a svynfylking fighting wedge to break through the English line. The pressure of the army behind them inexorably pushed their front ranks forward. They surged into the English army like a North Sea wave, and the battle – so far fought at a distance with javelins and arrows and hurled insults – now came down to swords, spears and axes. Hand to hand. Byrhtferth wrote, "When the honored leader of the field saw the enemies falling and his own men fighting manfully and seeing them fall in great numbers, he began to fight for his country with all his might."

Clashes with Vikings earlier in the decade had been little more than one-sided raids, skirmishes. England had not seen such a set-piece battle in generations, perhaps not since King Aethelstan had defeated the combined armies of the Scots and Irish Vikings at Brunanburh back in 937. The younger warriors in the English ranks would never have experienced warfare like this – men looking each other in the face while they hewed, gutted, amputated and beheaded one another. "They stood fast," said the poet. "Byrhtnoth commanded them, bidding each youngster who wished to win glory against the Danes in battle to remember his training."

The ealdorman led by example, fighting like a younger man himself. "He struck to his right side," declared Byrhtferth, "paying no heed to his swan-white hair, since alms and holy Masses consoled him. He protected himself to his left, ignoring his body's weakness, for prayer and kind deeds inspired him."

There was no mistaking Byrhtnoth on the battlefield. The *Vita* admits, "Of great height, he stood out above the rest." (This, at least, was not mythologizing; examination of the ealdorman's exhumed bones in 1769 revealed him to have stood six feet nine inches, in an age when few men reached six feet.) An enemy warrior wounded him with a spear. Byrhtnoth smashed his shield down on the shaft, breaking it, and drove his own spear into the Viking's neck, killing him. He killed a second with a thrust so hard it broke through his ring-mail armor to find his heart. "The nobleman was joyful, he laughed then," wrote the poet. "The brave man gave thanks to the Creator for the day's work that his Lord had granted him."

At that moment, however, he was hit with another spear. One of his retainers pulled it out and hurled it back, but Byrhtnoth was mortally wounded. He drew his sword, but was unable to hold it, or even to stand. The poet gave him last words as he dies in the arms of his men: "I thank you, Ruler of Nations, for all the joys I have experienced in this world. Now I have, gentle Creator, the greatest need that you grant my spirit your grace, so that my soul may travel to you, leader of angels, in peace. I am devoted to you, so that the dark enemies may not harm me."

The Vikings overran his position, killed the men with him and, according to the *Book of Ely*, took Byrhtnoth's head as a trophy. On seeing this, some of the English lost heart and fled, one of them on the ealdorman's horse. "An uncounted number of them [the men of Essex] and us [the men of Huntingdonshire] fell," lamented Byrhtferth, "and Byrhtnoth fell, and the rest fled."

But not all. Their leadership now fell to none other than Aelfwine son of Aelfric Cild, the very same who (perhaps, probably) had been defeated by Olaf in the duel for Gytha's hand. (His identity at Maldon is better confirmed than it is against Olaf.) Shamed by his loss he might have been, but here he reclaimed his good name for posterity. The poet gave him an even better speech:

Remember all our talk in the mead halls, boasting on the benches, champions telling of fierce battles. Now one may see who is brave. I wish all to know my kin are of the mighty Mercians. My grandfather was Ealhelm, a wise ealdorman, blessed in the world. Let no warrior in this land be accused of wishing to desert this host, to go home, now that my leader lies slain, cut down in battle. This is my greatest sorrow, for he was both my kinsman and my lord.

Spearing the nearest Viking, Aelfwine called on his fellow Englishmen to stand fast. Others rallied to him. The poet called them out by name, like the champions of Troy – Offa, Leofsunu, Dunnere and Aescferth,

Eadward the Long, Aetheric, Wystan son of Thurstan, the brothers Oswold and Eadwold – so that none would be forgotten: "The warriors stood firm in battle, brave fighters weakened by wounds. The dead fell upon the earth."

Intact, the Anglo-Saxon army might have held against the Viking onslaught, but too many men had fled on Byrhtnoth's death, and too many Vikings were still pouring over the causeway. Once a shield wall collapsed, the fight was over. "The Battle of Maldon" cuts off at Line 325, as though the poet himself was struck down on the field in the midst of battle (though the ending, like the beginning, was most likely lost over the ensuing centuries). It leaves the ensuing, disastrous aftermath to the imagination, but what has lasted in British memory is the courage of those who remained standing over the body of their dead ealdorman, even unto their own deaths. As the ealdorman's retainer Byrhtwold is said to have put it in their last moments:

> The mind must be stronger, the heart braver, and spirit greater even as our strength fades. Here lies our leader, all hewn down, a good man in the dirt. He who would now depart from this battle shall regret it. I am wise in years; I do not wish to depart, but think I shall lie down at my lord's side, along with my beloved men.

Where was Olaf Tryggvason in all this? Hard to say. We might wonder if he and Aelfwine saw and recognized each other on the battlefield, and even came to blows again, but we'll never know. Aelfwine was killed with the rest, and the Maldon poet, concerned only with his Anglo-Saxon heroes, did not care who fought or died on the Viking side. And that one version of the *Anglo-Saxon Chronicle* says only that "Anlaf" led the Vikings. He would have had a hard job ahead of him, for the invaders had not come through the battle unscathed. Byrhtferth contended, "They were scarcely able to man their ships." Or, for that matter, continue their depredations; good evidence of Byrhtferth's claim is that the town of Maldon was spared a sack.

There were plenty of less well-fortified towns in southeast England, though, and no English army left to defend them, even if small villages yield small pickings. At the end of four months and doubtless many more wasted lives, the Vikings and English finally arrived back at the same resolution that could have spared them both the savagery and losses at Maldon: "tribute in exchange for truce."

King Aethelred, only twenty-five or so, had already proven himself somewhat hapless at handling the Viking incursions of the 980s. Instead he had attempted to cut off the cross-channel markets for their ill-gotten loot. In 988, the year of the Watchet raid (which, recall, might well have been Olaf's doing), the king took Duke Richard I of Normandy to task for, in effect, receiving stolen goods. By 990 the enmity between the two rulers had turned so venomous that Pope John XV had intervened, sending a legate to make peace between them, declared by treaty in Rouen that March of 991. Rather than deal with the Vikings direct, Aethelred turned to some of his more elder statesmen.

Foremost among these was Sigeric, Archbishop of Canterbury in Kent, where this latest raid had begun. He was no fighting bishop in the tradition of Heahmund, the Bishop of Sherborne, who had died fighting for the first King Aethelred of Wessex against the Danes back in 871, but Sigeric, probably in his forties, was a bit more worldly than his Aethelred. The king had as yet never left England – throughout his reign, he would rarely even leave the South – but just the previous year the archbishop had received his pallium, his ecclesiastical vestment, from no less than Pope John XV in faraway Rome. To get there he had taken the arduous *Via Francigena*, the pilgrim's route through France, Switzerland and over the Alps to Italy, under constant threat of attack by local bandits and warlords or even wild animals, or dying of food- or water-borne disease. Sigeric was familiar with risk, but placed his faith in God. He was an adherent of the English Benedictine Reformation, which after the Viking decimation of English monasteries in the 9th century had endeavored to replace the Church's secular, often married lay clergy – administrators concerned with parochial, ministerial and more earthly duties – with more monastic, celibate monks to further religious education and thereby raise liturgical and spiritual standards. He lived by the motto of the

Benedictine order, *Ora et labora*, "pray and work," and would employ both in his negotiations with the Vikings.

Sigeric reasoned that the raiders had not necessarily come seeking death and destruction, nor even conquest, but merely to make themselves rich. In England, as in Ireland, wealth resided mostly in the churches and monasteries. Aethelred's nobles demanded that the king raise fresh armies to defend it. (For years these nobles had been manipulating the impressionable young king to permit their seizure of church properties; it wouldn't do to have the Vikings rob everything before they could lay hands on it.) After Maldon everybody could see the military response was ineffective. The defeat of Byrhtnoth and his men had destroyed morale; any surviving English who had felt they could defeat the Vikings, the way their fathers had, now feared them, the way their grandfathers had. Sigeric, on the other hand, was willing to lose a little of the church's wealth to preserve the rest of it. Folkestone and Sandwich, the Vikings' initial targets, were in his diocese, and there was no guarantee the raiders would not return to plunder there again, perhaps even ravaging Canterbury itself. His cathedral stood to lose all its treasure; better to save it by having all England purchase its safety. He advised Aethelred to simply pay the invaders *gafol* – tribute, but more ominously tax or rent – to go away.

The idea of buying off the enemy, as though already conquered, surely did not appeal to the king or his noblemen. Yet the archbishop had the support of two western ealdormen, Aelfric of Hampshire and Aethelweard of the Western Provinces (thought to be England's southwest peninsula), coastal lords, both of whom had prior experience of Viking depredations. Aelfric was recorded in the *Chronicle* as, like Sigeric, "one of those in whom the king had utmost trust." Aethelweard, the king's kinsman (his great-great-great-grandfather was King Aethelred I of Wessex, elder brother of Alfred the Great), had written a Latin translation of the *Chronicle*. He doubtless reminded the king that Alfred had paid off the Danish raider Guthrum, not as a long-term solution but to literally buy time to strengthen his forces, resulting in Guthrum's defeat at the Battle of Edington in 878 and ultimately the Viking's baptism as a Christian. The *Chronicle* records of 991, "In this year it was first decided to pay tribute to the Danes because of the many atrocities they committed along the coast."

Recall that back in 988 the Welsh king Maredudd had ransomed 2,000 of his people for a penny apiece, less than eight and a half pounds of silver total. These Vikings – perhaps many of them the same Vikings – were aiming for a bigger payoff. "In this first instance," continues the *Chronicle*, "it came to ten thousand pounds."

The gafol was measured in Saxon pounds of silver, at about eleven troy ounces each. Assuming 3,000 Vikings survived Maldon, and that everyone got an equal cut – doubtful, considering Olaf's past bargain with Jarl Sigurd – that came to 800 pence per man. (Presumably the Viking leaders received even more.) Not much, we moderns might say, for a man to risk dismemberment, disembowelment, decapitation and death in personal combat. Back then, however, silver had much greater buying power. One pence, at 240 to the pound, was worth anywhere from ten to thirty modern pounds sterling *apiece*, perhaps much more.* In the 930s King Aethelstan had fixed costs, which held, more or less, right up to the time of the Conquest: five pence for a sheep, ten for a pig, twenty for a cow, thirty for an ox, 120 for a horse and a pound for a slave. A hide of land, 120 acres or so, sold for anywhere from one to five pounds. Little to no monetary data exists for cash-poor Ireland at this time, but the Vikings could have assumed that silver would fetch even more there. They would return home rich as lords.

As for Olaf, this was raising his Viking career to a whole new level. Any Viking could lay waste a village and make off with its goods. This was robbing an entire nation – a sin lesser in violence, but greater in degree – and with his victims' blessing. What would his new God say about that? Perhaps Olaf consulted with his Scillonian priests. They would have told him God forbade extortion implicitly under the Eighth Commandment, and explicitly through the word of his prophets and his son.

---

* Today a silver penny from Aethelred II's reign is worth anywhere from $500 to $1,000 and up.

But this wasn't extortion. It was pillage by more polite means. Who was Olaf to deny what the English offered? Less sinful, surely, to simply accept tribute, rather than slaughter people to get it.

No surprise, then, that he and his men agreed to Sigeric's proposal. But neither the Vikings nor the archbishop realized that what they actually had done was set off a vicious cycle of extortion and destruction that would see *gafol* become better known as *Danegeld*, "Danish gold." This surrender would immiserate England for decades to come, stain Aethelred's reign for all time, and even 900 years later compel Rudyard Kipling to warn, "That if once you have paid him the Dane-geld/You never get rid of the Dane."

XXII

The Prince of England

*A general truce is to be established between King Aethelred,
his subjects and the entire fleet to which the king has paid tribute,
according to the terms which Archbishop Sigeric and Ealdorman
Aethelweard and Ealdorman Aelfric made when they received
royal permission to buy peace for the domains
over which, subject to him, they ruled.*

King Aethelred's Laws

AD 992–995

It stands to reason that the price of peace in England was not the same in Ireland. The impact of those 10,000 pounds of silver must have hit the Dublin economy with a splash like a boulder plunked into a still pond, turning what had been a burgeoning market village into an overnight boom town. Nobody spends more freely than soldiers just back from war, having lived to fight another day, with money to burn and memories to drown. Straight off the boats, the silver would have passed through the fingers of the barkeeps, barmaids and whores, out to the innkeepers and shopkeepers and marketeers, the traders, craftsmen, laborers and their families, all soaking it up the way Olaf's men soaked up Irish ale.

(As the Viking fleet arrived home around Christmas of 991, we might hope some of that surplus silver was put toward the annual tribute due to High King Malachy to relieve the tax burden on the citizenry. Without knowing exactly how many households there were in Dublin, and so how many ounces of gold were due, or for that matter the exchange rate of silver to gold – in this era, generally about eleven or twelve to one – there's no way of knowing to what degree that year's debt could have been paid off. Also, to assume the Viking chieftains were that selfless would be to give them more credit than most political leaders in history.)

The laws of economics are timeless, however, unchanging and unrelenting, and one of the most basic is that the more of anything there is, the less it's worth. All that silver, so precious when the Vikings loaded it aboard their longships in England, would have lost by far most of its value the moment it hit the Irish shore. Too much hot money chasing too few goods; a principle which, it would seem, even modern economists often fail to grasp, and in the 10th century hyperinflation, currency devaluation, market distortions and the like would have been understood even less. (It's the same principle that, six centuries later, saw the massive influx of South American gold and silver ultimately contribute to bankrupting the Spanish Empire.) Eventually prices rise to absorb surplus currency and the market, if lucky, returns to equilibrium, or else crashes. Either way it needs a fresh hit of cash the way Olaf's Vikings needed hair of the dog the next morning.

They had probably never expected to be simply handed 10,000 pounds of silver, and were only too happy with it at the time, but as their wealth dissipated it must have occurred to them – to Olaf – that they could have driven an even harder bargain. The English being willing to part with such a hoard, so easily, must mean they had much more where that came from.

By that time, however, word of England's capitulation would have spread across the Irish Sea, and even farther – across the North Sea, to Scandinavia.

The disastrous defeat of his fleet and his Jomsviking allies at Hjorungavag had far-reaching consequences for Danish king Svein Forkbeard. Sigvaldi and Thorkell the Tall apparently held his trickery in sending them to battle on his behalf, and his personal abstention from it, against him. As Vikings did, Denmark and Wendland soon fell to fighting each other, pagans versus pagans, with Svein getting the worst of it. As Adam of Bremen put it, "Divine vengeance punished him for his rebellion against God for, when he went to war against the Slavs, he was twice captured and led off into Slavia, to be ransomed by the Danes for a huge amount of gold." Saxo put the ransom at Svein's weight in gold, and twice as much in silver. Probably the only reason he wasn't murdered was that he and Sigvaldi were brothers-in-law, but around this time Svein's wife Gunnhild, sister of Sigvaldi's wife Astrid, was lost to him. According to some sources she remained in Wendish exile (which for her meant returning to her family), but according to others she died.

That was not the end of Svein's travails. Eirik the Victorious of Sweden still resented Denmark for backing Styrbjorn the Strong's invasion a few years prior. In 990 he had taken advantage of Svein's weakness to invade Scania, now southernmost Sweden but then part of Denmark. Adam sneered, "Abandoned by God, vainly trusting in his idols, Svein sailed to meet him. The two armies fought many naval battles, for that is how those folk prefer to fight, and the entire Danish force was defeated. Eirik took over Denmark and made it part of Sweden. A jealous God rewarded Svein for his sins, seeing him driven from his realm."

Outcast, like Olaf a vagabond prince, Forkbeard had likewise embarked on a piratical voyage. In the early 990s his name crops up in numerous chronicles. Snorri, in the *Heimskringla*, claims he raided Saxony, Frisia and eventually England. (We should remember that in 985 or '86 Svein had supposedly sworn before the Jomsvikings and his pagan gods to drive Aethelred off his throne within three years. He was behind schedule, but then the loss of his kingdom may have released him from that vow.) Arguments have even been made that it was he, and not Olaf, who led the Vikings in the battle at Maldon, but then it's not his name mentioned in the *Anglo-Saxon Chronicle*. That does record King Aethelred assembling a fleet at London in 992 to intercept and defeat Viking raiders at sea, but failing miserably.* In 993 Vikings laid waste to Bamburgh on the Northumbrian coast,

---

* To command this fleet he appointed his ealdormen Thored of Northumbria and Aelfric of Hampshire (who had backed the payment of gafol to Olaf after Maldon), but on the eve of battle Aelfric, that "most trusted" of the king's ealdormen, warned the Vikings of the impending attack and himself fled. For that Aethelred had his son blinded, but soon ran so short of commanders that he had to take Aelfric back into his service.

then came south and raided into the Humber estuary, and again the English commanders fled. Finally there is the example of Aethelric, a thegn of Bocking in Essex, who in these years was accused of plotting to actually assist Forkbeard in landing there. Aethelric died before Aethelred could punish him for treason. (Clearly most of the brave English had been killed at Maldon, and the rest were wavering in their loyalty to their king. By 993 Viking attacks were being seen as God's punishment for Aethelred's sins and his advisors' greed.) Finally, in 994 Svein is named in the Welsh *Chronicle of the Princes* as going all the way around to the other side of England, devastating the Isle of Man.

That would put him square in the middle of Olaf's Irish and English domains. One might think two such warlords would immediately square off and battle to the death like a pair of roosters in a ring. Yet history shows that Vikings readily set aside any differences, however temporarily, for mutual gain. Svein would definitely have been the junior partner in any venture with Olaf, but he had leadership skills and royal blood that men would follow. And Olaf could certainly use the help. His former cohort Jarl Sigurd had apparently gone home to the Orkneys, taking his crews with him. By this time, with silver running low in Dublin, Olaf had to be planning another run on England. It would not have required much urging on either man's part for Svein to join in.

But Forkbeard was not the only Viking to have heard of Olaf's exploits.

Norway was enjoying the fruits of victory. The *Fagrskinna* relates, "After the fight with the Jomsvikings and defeating such great chieftains, Jarl Hakon had achieved supreme power, and he had no need to fear any threat by the Danes."

According to Berg, he had more to fear from the fathers, brothers and husbands among his own subjects.

> As he grew older his evil treatment of women became worse, and got to the point that he had wives and daughters of powerful men seized and taken to his house to be kept a week or two. In this way

the Jarl became hated by their menfolk, and the landowners began to murmur in the way Tronders are wont to do whenever anything displeases them.

As far as Hakon was concerned, the cuckolds could grumble as much as they liked. They had no leader. Yet. In the back of his mind he must have never forgotten that though he ruled Norway as king, he was only a jarl, lacking royal blood. The *Agrip* confirms, "Jarl Hakon did not rule Norway by right of descent from kings before him, but rather through strength and force, and because he was shrewd, though he used his wisdom for evil."

And the line of Harald Fairhair had not been eradicated. Snorri wrote, "Jarl Hakon heard some rumor about a man across the western sea who called himself Oli, who had been taken as king there, and the jarl suspected from these stories that he must be of the Norwegian royal family."

This "Oli" claimed to be of the Rus, but Hakon wasn't fooled. He had not forgotten the son of Tryggvi who had escaped him and gone east to be raised by his uncle Sigurd and Prince Vladimir, and he must have regretted not carrying out Gunnhild Konungamodir's contract when he'd had the chance. Perhaps he even heard of Olaf's aspirations toward Norway. It was a small, faraway threat, but history teaches that devious, conniving leaders, particularly those with guilty consciences, have a way of magnifying small threats into immediate ones and out-thinking themselves – what we moderns recognize as paranoia. Norway's malcontents might see a great-grandson of King Harald Fairhair as having a better claim to the throne than a jarl of Lade, and with less claim to their women. Odd wrote that Hakon "began to ponder how to keep Olaf from depriving him or his sons of the realm through some sudden or unanticipated trick."

It was going to be much harder to kill the man than the boy, not least because Olaf was in far-off Ireland. To get him there would require a full military expedition, all the way around the other side of England. If Hakon or his sons Eirik and Svein left the country with all their fighting men, however, there was even better reason to be afraid: They might find Norway rising up behind them. The jarl would need to lure Olaf within reach, and kill him before the farmers could proclaim him king. The trick would be to bring Olaf quickly, before he was ready, before he could raise a proper army of his own sufficient to do what the Danes and Jomsvikings had not. What – who – could entice Olaf into such an overshoot?

There was a longtime raider and trader in Norway, Thorir, called *Klakka*, said to have been Olaf's "great friend" and "sworn brother."* Then there were Olaf's uncles, his mother Astrid's brothers Jostein and Sigurd Karlshofud, still living in Rus. (Where Jostein was all that time while Olaf was growing up there goes unmentioned.) The sagas differ on how they came together, but in the end all three ended up before Hakon's *thing* in Lade. Evidently Thorir and Olaf weren't such good friends and brothers after all; Klakka agreed to betray him for money. As for Jostein and Sigurd, Hakon ordered them to swear they would go along with Thorir to Ireland and trick their nephew into returning to Norway: "Olaf will more readily trust your story, as his kinsmen, than in that of strangers."

Berg credited them with refusing: "We shall never allow ourselves to be so shamefully disgraced, as to so wickedly betray our kinsman."

"If you do not like this idea, you have another choice," Hakon told them, "to be tortured to death in agony before this assembly. If on the other hand you fully carry out our command, you will earn our friendship, and be well rewarded."

Sadly, there was another tool of persuasion available. Their sister, Olaf's mother Astrid, last seen being carried off into slavery aboard an Eistlander pirate ship, had been found.

"There was a man of the Vik country named Lodin, rich and of good name," wrote Berg. "He often went on trading voyages, and sometimes on Viking raids."

Snorri continued, "One summer he sailed on a merchant trip with many goods in his own ship. He went first to Eistland [Berg says Wendland] and visited a market. Many merchant goods were brought there, and many thralls or slaves for sale as well."

---

* His nickname is obscure, meaning "lump" or "clump" or "like a saddle-peg"; surely a comment on his appearance.

It was in this unknown eastern slave market that Lodin, being from King Tryggvi's former realm, came across a familiar female face. Berg wrote, "Upon seeing her, he recognized Astrid Eiriksdottir, the former wife of King Tryggvi Olafson."

"But now she was nothing like the last time he had seen her," added Snorri, "for now she was pale, haggard and dressed in rags."

Lodin, naturally enough, asked what had happened to her. She told him, "It is a sad tale, for I was abducted into slavery, and have been brought here to be sold again." Yet she recognized Lodin as more than just another buyer – as one of her late husband's subjects – and implored him to purchase her.

Lodin gave her a choice. "I offer you freedom and will take you home with me, if you will marry me."

She could have done worse. Berg wrote, "Since Astrid had little choice, and knew moreover Lodin was brave, wealthy and of the nobility, she pledged to marry him in order to gain her freedom. So Lodin bought Astrid and took her back to Norway where, with her kinsmen's consent, he married her."

Since then Astrid had been reunited with her daughters, Olaf's sisters Ingebjorg and Astrid, and she had given Lodin three more children, son Thorkell and girls Ingerid and Ingegerd. This all must have transpired some ten or fifteen years past already, for as shall be seen even the younger sisters were already of marriageable age. But given Jarl Hakon's predilection for the wives and daughters of his noblemen, in Norway none of them were as safe as they might have hoped.

"Not daring to oppose him," wrote Theodoric of Jostein and Sigurd, "they promised they would go, but only if they could reveal the jarl's treacherous plan once Olaf had come past Agdanes to the place called Thjalfahellir."

To this Hakon readily agreed. Agdanes, modern Agdenes, "Agdi's headland," is a promontory that slopes into the sea at the mouth of Trondheim fjord; Thjalfahellir is thought to have been the name of a cave about a mile and a half farther down the coast. Neither was much more than about thirty miles from Hakon's capital of Lade. If Olaf was tricked into coming that close, Hakon was sure to capture him.

"In the end," concluded Berg, "they agreed to the deceitful task, swearing to Jarl Hakon and all the chiefs present to do as the Jarl commanded, rather than disobey and be put to the harsh treatment he had threatened."

To Vikings a man's oath was a pact with the gods; to break it made him no better than a murderer or adulterer, and condemned his soul to the dragon Nidhogg's slavering jaws for all time. Jostein and Sigurd were putting their own honor above their nephew's life.

Odd, in his usual roundabout way, has them all sailing to England to meet "Oli," only to learn he had returned to Russia, and so sailing to meet him there, then everyone returning west again. According to Snorri and Berg they found him in Dublin, which makes more sense. In any case, on their meeting Thorir was welcomed by his "old friend" Olaf, and soon apprised him of goings-on in Norway – Jarl Hakon's tyranny, the unrest among the people, the opening for a new ruler.

Olaf asked, "Thorir, if I went to Norway, do you think the yeomen would willingly accept me as king over the land?"

Berg had Thorir answer:

You did well, Olaf, to not conceal yourself from me any longer, for I have heard many tales of your fame, and so have many others in Norway. In truth, I came here to the British islands with a special task. I was asked by the Upland chiefs and other nobility, your kinsmen, to learn who might be this Oli of Garda, of whom such famous deeds were told; and if I could get proof that you were Olaf Tryggvason, as I have done, I am to request on behalf of your kinsmen, and of all Norwegians, that you come home as quickly as possible, and be made king over the land.

When at last he is grown to manhood he will return to his native land and gain the kingdom which is his by birth. As king he will shine with bright glory and become a savior to many men of the northern regions, old Malusha had prophesied. *You will be a great king and do great things, and convert many people to faith and baptism, and so do good for yourself and many others,* the hermit of the Isles of Scilly had said.

And, Thorir added, it just so happened that he had brought two men from Norway who could vouch for such a venture: in fact, two uncles of Olaf Tryggvason. Berg wrote, "As soon as Olaf heard this, he sent for them and welcomed them with greatest joy."

"Olaf asked his uncles if what he [Thorir] said was true," wrote Odd. "They looked at the ground and answered quietly and reluctantly, but said it was. Olaf now believed the truth of it because they all said so, though he and many others wondered why Karlshofud and Jostein were so downcast on such a splendid occasion."

Olaf probably assumed they were simply unenthusiastic about his chances. And they were right to be. All his life, power had been given him by others – his uncle Sigurd, Grand Prince Vladimir, his wives Geira and Gytha. Even with his lands in Ireland and England, his noble blood and his royal in-laws, Olaf was no match for Jarl Hakon, who to judge by the Battle of Hjorungavag had old gods on his side.

If Olaf wished to bully rulers, best to start with a weak one.

In its entries for AD 994 the *Anglo-Saxon Chronicle* reels out the story: "In this year, on the Nativity of St Mary [September 8] Anlaf and Svein sailed to London with ninety-four ships, making a continuous attack on the city with the intention of burning it."

At up to 5,000 men, this was the greatest invasion England had seen in half a century, not because it was much larger than that of AD 991, but because it was led by two kings.* Admittedly Forkbeard was a former king and Olaf so far only a king of sea rovers, but both were veteran warriors, practiced conquerors. And they were aiming high. He who conquered London conquered England, though if the *Chronicle* is to be believed the Vikings

---

* It's surely more than coincidental that the Viking fleet consisted of ninety-three ships at Maldon and ninety-four just three years later. We can easily suppose a tired, eye-weary monk transposed the number from AD 991 to AD 994 or vice versa in the manuscripts. Then again, it was simply the same fleet, any losses in manpower filled out with fresh Danish reinforcements from one year to the other, and with one additional ship, doubtless Svein Forkbeard's.

wished to impress King Aethelred not by conquering his capital, but by burning it to the ground.

London, then called Lundenburh, was no wooden-walled town like Sandwich, Ipswich or Maldon. The stone walls of old Roman Londinium still stood, and had been repaired and strengthened by Alfred the Great a century past, with an encircling trench or moat as well, much more formidable than the Danevirke, or the walls of Kyiv, Jomsborg or even Dublin. It was more than enough to hold off a Viking horde. Sleets of arrows, spears and stones, boiling water, flaming oil; a city was not as easy to defeat as an army in the open. The *Chronicle* sneers of the Vikings, "They suffered more wounded and killed than they had thought a garrison would ever inflict upon them."

Olaf and Svein backed off, bloodied but wiser. In the end it wasn't necessary to destroy London to make their point to Aethelred. It was just as effective to lay waste the rest of England, a task which they undertook with such ferocity that it was still recalled with horror by the monks Florence and John of Worcester Abbey, 125 years later:

> In their fury and grief, they drew off to instead overrun the coasts of Essex and Kent, and after that Sussex and the province of Hants [Hampshire], burning villages, laying waste the countryside, putting many men and women to fire and sword, and carrying off an immense booty. Finally, seizing horses, they swept wildly through the land, slaughtering entire populations with savage cruelty, sparing neither the women nor young children.

And God rewarded their depredations. Utterly unable to stop this rampage militarily, Aethelred fell back on the stratagem that had worked in 991: "The king and his advisors agreed to send word to them, offering tribute and provisions, if they would stop their harrying."

That was surely what Olaf and Forkbeard had intended in the first place. There was no point in destroying London. A dead cow can't be milked, and if either of them was interested in conquest, it wasn't England they had in mind. Accepting Aethelred's offer, the fleet put in at Southampton for the winter, where the English supplied and paid them for their trouble. The amount of 16,000 pounds is given in several versions of the *Chronicle*, but these differ in whether it was all *gafol*, coin, or the total value of gafol and *metsunge*, provisions. Either way, that was over half again the size of the take from the Vikings' 911 raid. Olaf's get-rich scheme had paid off nicely, and he wasn't done yet.

Neither was Aethelred the Unready, who was not so unready this time around. With the Vikings still in his backyard, he wished to bargain further. "The king sent Bishop Alfheah and Ealdorman Aethelweard to king Anlaf, and hostages to the [Viking] ships," continues the *Chronicle*, "and Anlaf was shown with great ceremony to meet the king at Andover."

Aethelweard we have already covered, as having a hand in the agreement of 991. Alfheah (or Alphege), Bishop of Winchester, was a junior signatory to this 994 agreement but in 1006 would be Archbishop of Canterbury, in 1012 slain by Thorkell the Tall's Jomsvikings, and canonized in 1078.* There were signatories missing from the Viking side as well; fortuitously, around this time Eirik the Victorious of Sweden passed away, and Forkbeard hurried home to take back Denmark, leaving negotiations in England to Olaf. Aethelred must have breathed more easily without the baptized but relentlessly pagan Dane in the mix. It seems likely that he had learned of Olaf's professed Christianity, and intended to make the most of it.

In the spring of 995 Olaf journeyed some thirty miles up the river Test from Southampton to meet the king on his own ground. He was surely hesitant to do so without an army at his back. Aethelred had only achieved his throne through the betrayal and murder of his older half-brother Edward the Martyr in 978, but that was thought to have been his mother's doing, the king being only about twelve at the time. With English hostages of appropriate value left with the Vikings as insurance for his safety, Olaf did not go alone. He took with him his uncle Jostein and one Guthmund, son of Stegita, otherwise unknown

---

* For more on Alfheah, Thorkell and the Vikings, see *Battle for the Island Kingdom: England's Destiny 1000–1066*, by the same author.

but thought to have been a Dane, probably acting as Forkbeard's representative in any negotiations.

Andover (said to derive from the Celtic or Brittonic *on dubr*, "ash tree stream," or *afon dwfr*, "river water") dated back to pre-Saxon times. Since 950 English kings had maintained a hunting lodge there, which is probably where the details of the pact were hammered out. The treaty itself survives in the form of a 12th-century manuscript, referred to as "II Aethelred," the second of eight sets of laws still extant. It's been argued that it is actually the treaty of 991, mostly because decades later the Worcester monks wrongly claim it was Jostein and Guthmund and not Olaf who led the Vikings at Maldon, and that it mentions Archbishop Sigeric, architect of the 991 agreement. Sigeric, however, died before II Aethelred could be signed.* The text of the 991 treaty has not survived, but it was a local agreement between the Vikings and the provinces of Suffolk, Essex and Kent, by Aethelred's permission but without his participation as a signatory. The 994 treaty is an extension, an enlargement of that: an agreement of Olaf, Jostein and Guthmund with King Aethelred II, in person, by name, negotiating on behalf of his entire kingdom, governing relations between Vikings and Anglo-Saxons henceforth, across all England.

In it, the king does not simply agree to pay Olaf and his men to leave his kingdom. The treaty invites them – requires them – to defend it as well, to become his allies against all other invaders: *If any hostile fleet harries in England, we shall have their help, and we shall be obliged to supply them, as long as they side with us*. Aethelred, whose commanders had proven so ineffective, was following the same precedent set by the Rus and the Byzantines: He was buying his own Viking army. The price was to be 22,000 pounds, and not in supplies and provisions, either. In gold and silver.

This was beyond tribute. This was sharing the wealth. It was making Olaf and his Vikings real English subjects, with all the benefits. And, as recorded in the *Chronicle*, to seal the deal Aethelred made it a personal pact between him, Olaf and their mutual God:

---

* "I Aethelred" deals with punishment of criminals and has nothing to do with Olaf, Vikings, or 991.

"The king sponsored him at confirmation, and bestowed royal gifts on him."

In 10th-century England, confirmation was the final covenant of Christian initiation. Baptism was a rebirth, a washing away of sin, but in itself did not guarantee salvation. Confirmation was required; the initiate had to actively choose his new God.

Just a few years earlier Olaf the homeless, wandering marauder had been baptized at the far end of the earth and sent back out into the world a changed man. Since then he had sinned, yes, but despite that had become wealthy, a husband, a father, brother-in-law to an Irish king and friend to an English one. All this he could easily put down to the blessings of his new God, and as he aspired to even greater heights, he would have ever more need of such favor. He had every reason to see his conversion through to the end.

The Christian sacrament would not have been performed in the Andover hunting lodge. The current church in town, St. Mary's, was raised in the 1840s on the site of a crumbling Norman-era edifice, which had replaced the Anglo-Saxon church that stood from at least 950. Nothing remains of it, but English churches of that era followed rather standardized plans. Those in the north were of the simple old Celtic design: tall naves, rectangular chancels and no side chambers. Those down in the south followed the Roman model introduced by St. Augustine, with chambers on either side of the nave, the chancel to the east, and in later builds a sturdy tower that doubled as a lookout and refuge against Danish attack.

Details of Anglo-Saxon confirmation are sparse, but the central ritual dating from Roman times still involves the laying-on of hands by a bishop or priest, and anointing with holy oil. We might imagine Olaf kneeling before Bishop Alfheah, the very personification of once-pagan savagery totally submitting to God, as overseen by King Aethelred while a choir sang Latin hymns and his old friend Thorir and uncle Jostein looked on with wonderment, perhaps pondering the treachery in their own hearts.

It's been posited that King Aethelred did not have entirely pure motives in this either. When the *Chronicle* says he *his onfeng æt bisceopes handa*, "received him at the bishop's hands," it's generally taken to mean he served as Olaf's *godfaeder*, godfather, literally his "father in God." In Anglo-Saxon England, going at least as far back as the 7th century, godparents played a much more important role than today, and the English practiced fosterage much as did the Vikings; for them, godparenting was a kind of adoption. By standing sponsor for Olaf at his confirmation, and even though he was probably a few years younger, Aethelred was asserting himself as the Viking's spiritual parent, the way Alfred the Great had over Guthrum the Dane, and Aethelstan over his foster son Hakon the Good. Furthermore, by creating and treating Olaf as his godson, Aethelred elevated him far above being a simple thegn of Mercia or even a brother-in-law of Sigurd of Dublin. Olaf was now an adoptive prince of England, a son of the royal house, with princely duties. And it was his king who would define those duties.

To have the Viking army remain in England would have been beyond foolish. Despite the stipulations of the treaty just signed, the English simply could not afford to provision them forever. Sooner or later there was bound to be trouble. An invincible army is a dangerous thing to keep around when there is no war.

Aethelred intended for the Vikings to make war elsewhere.

The best place for England to fight Viking invaders was over on their side of the North Sea, before they ever set foot on English soil. By the Treaty of Rouen in 991 Aethelred had deprived them of their illicit marketplace in Normandy, driving a wedge between the Normans and Norsemen. Forkbeard had his hands full trying to regain Denmark. That left Norway.

In 934 Aethelred's granduncle Aethelstan had furnished Olaf's granduncle Hakon the Good with the ships and men to oust Eirik Bloodaxe and conquer Norway, eliminating its Vikings as a threat to England. Since then Jarl Hakon had led the country's descent back into paganism – an affront to all Christian lands – but Olaf's aspirations toward the Norwegian throne were by now no secret. By equipping him to carry them out, Aethelred was sending a Viking invasion the other way. Not only might Olaf turn Norway into an English ally, but any other Vikings with designs on England would have to come through Olaf first.

Whether or not this next-level strategy was apparent to Olaf, or explained to him, did not matter. What mattered was that he now had a patron, and money, and a cause. The *Chronicle* attests, "Anlaf promised, and kept his word too, that he would never return to England intent on war."

Of course he wouldn't. He was a prince of England.

Now to make himself King of Norway.

XXIII

Crusade

Thorir ardently urged him to this task, and avidly praised him and his abilities. Olaf now grew very eager to visit his father's land.

Snorri Sturluson

AD 995

It's surely no coincidence that in the mid-990s, while Olaf was based there, Dublin began its rise toward becoming one of the most important cities of the Viking Age. Its economy still depended on the slave trade (and would, well into the next century), but the export of native Irish prisoners had attracted buyers from far and wide, and to feed the ever-increasing demand outlanders were bringing in captives from England, Wales, the Continent and – if the references to "blackmen" in the chronicles is taken at face value – even North Africa. Slaves were such a prime commodity that the word for a female slave, *cumal*, became a standard unit of value, even in land transactions.

Nobody fretted about all this human misery when in exchange they were enjoying imported luxuries, wine, silks, crafts and jewelry. Exports of leather and beef were still strong. Access to high-quality oak from Wicklow, just down the coast, was feeding a nascent Irish shipbuilding industry of *longa fada*, longships based on the Viking design. And over the short term Olaf's fresh injection of all those thousands of pounds of English silver and gold into the economy couldn't have hurt either.

Evidence that Dublin was booming is that in the last decade of the millennium King Sigtrygg founded the town's first mint. Minting their own coins gave medieval kings a measure of control over their free-market economies, plus the advantage of seigniorage – profiting off the difference between a coin's face value and the cost of making it – and charging moneyers for the right to operate mints. (Not to mention, stamping one's image on the face of one's coins lent one a certain air of legitimacy.) The Irish had no concept of minting prior to the arrival of the Vikings, but the Hiberno-Norse had been minting their own money in their Northumbrian realm as far back as the 920s. Gytha's father Olaf Cuaran had set up a mint in York during his first reign in the 940s, and again during his second in the 950s. The fact that the first Dublin pence were modeled on those of King Aethelred, and even used dies from Watchet in England – where Olaf might well have purloined them in the late 980s – is probably due less to any of Olaf's doing than Sigtrygg wishing his Irish coins to be as widely accepted as Aethelred's English ones.

Bitter experience, however, taught that the good times would not last. The money would eventually run out again. Right now Olaf was flush with cash, enjoying a reputation as a conqueror, and even renewed status as royalty. If he was to make a play for Norway, there was no better time than the present.

It would be no small undertaking, not like bullying helpless villagers or even a king of England out of some pocket change. Now Olaf would be playing for the very highest stakes, and as Harald Bluetooth and Sigvaldi the Jomsviking had learned to their regret, Jarl Hakon was no easy victim. There was every likelihood of Olaf running into another Battle of Hjorungavag, and of never returning.

It would be no place for women and children, no place for a wife and son. Icelandic monks, hardly romantics, were interested in female characters and love angles only to the extent they affected their champions. Given, however, that one child in perhaps half a decade of marriage was below the average for those days, we might suspect trouble between Gytha and Olaf. His biographers would not have recorded such if it cast our hero in a bad light, but the *Fagrskinna*, not so much taking his side, insinuates of little Tryggvi, "some said he was the son of a priest, and not the king's."

Among Viking cultures adultery was a serious, even capital offense, particularly for women. In Scandinavia Olaf would have been within his rights to kill Gytha and her lover. But he was in Ireland, with an Irish wife. Under Irish law, adultery was more like theft – property or reputational damage – and did not call for such severe punishment, but more often simply confession and penance, maybe a fine paid to the wronged spouse or family. Perhaps for Olaf that wasn't enough.

For Vikings, divorce was as easy as betrothal: simply declaring such before witnesses. In Christian Ireland, under Gaelic law, it was hardly more complicated. Marriage was a private contract, not a sacrament, and divorce likewise required no church approval. Both parties kept their personal goods and wealth. As a highborn lady of property, widow of an English ealdorman and sister of a king, Gytha may have felt she brought more to the marriage than her vagabond Viking husband, who may have served her purpose simply by getting her out of her marital predicament with the lord Aelfwine.

In any case, it would have been one more reason for Olaf to leave Ireland, and for Gytha and her son to drop out of the sagas. So let us simply assume that Olaf bade his brother-in-law Sigtrygg good luck, and his wife and son goodbye, and left them all standing there on the pier at Dublin as his longships pulled away and raised sail, bound for Norway.

"He sailed with five ships from Ireland to the Sudreys [Hebrides], and from there to the Orkneys," wrote Berg. "His uncles and Thorir escorted him on the voyage."

Five ships sounds rather thin for a task force bound on invasion. It might refer only to those ships of the fleet which Olaf actually owned, but he doubtless had fewer overall than on his English expedition. Hiberno-Norse mercenaries, like all mercenaries, sailed and fought for personal gain, but a Norwegian conquest offered much risk for little return. Many of them would have been all too content to stay home and spend their loot in Dublin rather than risk losing the rest, and their lives to boot, in pursuit of Olaf's dream of conquest. So it's hard to give a count of his ships and manpower in this venture, except to point out that even the ninety-odd dragon boats he'd led to England fell far short of the Jomsviking fleet at Hjorungavag, let alone the Norwegian fleet – in the old accounts, variously 120, 180 or even 360 ships – with which Hakon had defeated them. Whatever the size of his navy, Olaf had no hope of vanquishing the jarl in open battle. He would need to raise by far most of his army in Norway, sparking a rebellion among the commonfolk, subtracting their numbers from Hakon's and adding them to his.

"Because Pentland Firth was impassable," continued Berg, "he dropped anchor in Asmundarvag [Osmondwall] Bay, by Rognvaldsey [South Ronaldsay Island] in the Orkneys."

In Viking days Pentland Firth was *Petlandsfjord*, "the fjord of Pictland," but it is technically not a fjord, or a firth, but a strait separating the northernmost Scottish mainland from the Orkneys, and the Atlantic Ocean from the North Sea. Just six miles wide at its narrowest, often swept by gale-force winds, this oceanic crossroad is infamous for violent seas, sixteen-knot tidal races and deadly whirlpools, including the dreaded "Swelkie," which in their day the Vikings knew as *Svalga*, "the Swallower." In bad weather Olaf would not have been blamed for seeking shelter among the islets just to the north and waiting for smoother passage.

He was not the only one. "It so happened that Jarl Sigurd Hlodvirsson was there in the bay aboard a single warship, intending to cross over to Caithness [on the Scottish mainland]," wrote Berg. "When King Olaf learned it was Jarl Sigurd anchored before him, he sent word for him to come talk with him."

Sigurd, said to be present at Olaf's wedding to Geira, was notably unmentioned in his English raids, but then those raids received little coverage from his Icelandic biographers. Given their rather unequal past partnership, it may well be that Sigurd had gone his own way. Being outnumbered and summoned aboard Olaf's flagship like a lowly vassal surely did not fill him with confidence, and he was right to worry. The *Orkneyinga Saga* records, "King Olaf threatened the jarl's life if he did not embrace the true faith and undergo baptism, become his man and declare Christianity across the Orkneys."

Odd, who as usual placed this scene implausibly elsewhere in his narrative, requiring Olaf to double back after his arrival in Norway, nevertheless related, "King Olaf preached the word of God to him and exhorted him by way of good reasoning, from first thing in the morning until last thing at night, and with great passion." He apprised the jarl and his men of the torments of hell, and that the only way to save their souls was to destroy their pagan idols and become followers of Christ.

Sigurd replied, "I know of no better faith or tradition than that of my ancestors and most highborn of my kinsmen." On top of that, as he saw it, Olaf was not the King of Norway, and had no business dictating religion to, or demanding the fealty of, the Jarl of Orkney or his people.

Berg had it that Olaf recounted the history of the islands from the 870s, when King Harald Fairhair appointed Sigurd's great-grandfather Rognvald, "the Mighty," to rule them as his jarl, down to Sigurd's father Jarl Hlodvir Thorfinnsson, the point being that all Sigurd's forefathers had ruled on behalf of Norway, by the leave of Norwegian kings. "You, Sigurd, are jarl of this realm, which I now claim as my birthright, as I claim all the other domains that King Harald Fairhair, and his descendants, all down the line, inherited."

He offered the jarl two choices:

> One, that you accept God, and permit yourself and all your subjects to be baptized. You may then expect to retain your jarldom under my sovereignty, and what is more important, you may hope to reign with Almighty God forever in heaven if you keep the commandments. The other, a very unhappy course, unlike the first, is that you die, and after you are dead I will go over these islands with fire and sword, laying waste the entire realm, unless the folk worship the true God. If that is the course you choose, after a quick death you will suffer terrible torture with the devil in the fires of hell for the rest of time, like all others who worship carved idols.

Put that way, it wasn't much of a choice at all, but according to Theodoric, "Sigurd even declared that he would accept Olaf as king, if he would not force him to adopt Christianity."

That was not enough for Olaf. He already saw himself as king, and Sigurd as rebellious subject. An example needed to be made. Seeing that the jarl found his gods more important than his life, Olaf followed Jarl Hakon's lead. He took Sigurd's three-year-old son Thorfinn, called *Hundi* or *Hvelp* ("Hound", "Whelp") in hand. Odd wrote, "King Olaf laid him across his ship's prow, drew his sword and asked the jarl if he wished to see his son beheaded before him, if he denied the faith, or to be joined in friendship with him, and to have his son back and at the same time accept Christianity."

"But I tell you," he swore, "if you don't, your realm will be destroyed."

Perhaps he was bluffing. By now, however, Sigurd recognized that this was not the same Olaf who had spared his opponent Aelfwine's life in the *holmgang*, spared the Irish farmer rather than kill him for his dog, or given the English at Maldon a chance to save themselves by avoiding battle. This Olaf had a merciless god behind him. If he was willing to sacrifice a child in that god's name, then he was no better than Jarl Hakon.

But Sigurd had no choice. "Finding himself in a difficult position," related Snorri, "he chose to accept baptism."

"So by believing, or rather by agreeing," wrote Theodoric, "he was baptized, and all his subjects with him."

That, however, did not gain his son's return. Olaf knew the minute he was over the horizon Jarl Sigurd, like Jarl Hakon, would renege on his conversion. The *Orkneyinga Saga* says of Olaf, "He kept his son Hundi or Hvelp hostage."

"He then sailed off from the Orkneys, leaving behind clerics to reform the people and teach them sacred doctrine," concluded Berg, insisting, "King Olaf and the jarl parted company in friendship."

That's got to be the biggest fiction in the entire saga.

"King Olaf and his men continued on to Norway before a favorable wind," wrote Odd. "He sailed happily, the sleek ships racing each other."

With Sigurd's jarldom of the Orkneys, Hebrides and Shetlands now bowing to him, Olaf must have felt that half his work was done. "He was in a good mood," added Berg, "for he did not suspect any plot against him, or danger from his kinsmen or the others in his company. At the same time, it puzzled him that his kinsmen Jostein and Karlshofud stayed silent, unhappy ever since they met him in Ireland."

The fleet landed in the southwest Norwegian coast on the island of Mostr, modern Moster in Hordaland, the "Land of the Hordar," a Germanic tribe thought to have migrated there back in Roman times. The first order of business upon setting foot ashore was the conducting of a mass. "It was easy to worship there," asserts the *Agrip*, "with God's help and because men had grown tired of Hakon the Evil's tyranny. The people there accepted the faith and Olaf as king." Afterward he ordered the ground there consecrated with a church.* "He appointed Thangbrand [the Saxon] to conduct mass on the island, and bequeathed him a homestead and lands."

Then it was time to strategize. The conquest of Norway was not going to be like raiding Ireland and England. Those lands were already Christian. Here the goal was not just to conquer the people, but to change their religion. For Olaf, who had never believed in the old gods in the first place, there had been little trouble adopting a new one. His crusade would require pagans to renounce everything they believed in. Olaf could give them no choice, which meant he needed to quickly get the upper hand. Berg wrote, "Thorir Klakka advised that the king's best strategy was to keep his identity secret, and to proceed as rapidly as possible to Trondheim and take Jarl Hakon by surprise."

In fact, as Berg points out, Thorir knew full well that they had landed well north of Olaf's most likely support, which was all down in his father Tryggvi's former domain, the Vik. As soon as his kinsmen learned that Olaf had landed, they would rise to his banner and come storming northward to back him. Trondheim, on the other hand, was Jarl Hakon's stronghold. By hurrying Olaf north, Thorir was sending him practically alone, ahead of any help, into the enemy's den. Once there – assuming Thorir hadn't already found an opportunity to assassinate him – it would be a simple matter for Hakon to capture and kill him.

---

* Old Moster Church, dating from the 12th century and one of the oldest stone churches in Norway, still stands on the site where Olaf raised the original wooden post church.

That the scheme obviated the need for a large army or decisive battle, however, was a point in its favor as far as Olaf was concerned. He didn't need kinsmen when he had God on his side. Berg admitted, "The king thought this strategy well planned and clever, and acted accordingly."

The fleet put to sea again, circling out beyond sight of land, making its way north, anchoring at night on the far side of the outermost islands to avoid detection, until at last they put in at Agdanes, within striking distance of Trondheim. Thorir Klakka went ashore to get the latest news from the locals.

Imagine his shock on learning that the Tronders had already risen against Jarl Hakon, who had abandoned his throne and fled.

On seeing Thorir off to dispose of the greatest threat to his reign, Hakon had felt safe to indulge his devotion for Thorgerd Holgabrud to the extreme. "Hakon put more faith in sacrifice than anyone," wrote Odd, "overdoing it until his lust grew hot to the point of debauchery. He kept men's wives, even those of high rank, and numerous maidens with him for a week or a month, sending them back to their families in disgrace."

Berg told the tale of Brynjolf, a wealthy and powerful landowner of Gaulardale, the modern Gauldal Valley near Trondheim, who was literally in bed with his wife when the jarl's men came to take her away. "This jarl leaves little evil unsaid or undone," Brynjolf told them, "and he is so set in his evil ways that his reign must be soon overthrown, and him miserably slain, for his subjects are greatly oppressed and troubled. As for you, his underlings, choose quickly to withdraw, or suffer the fate which is certain to befall you."

Unsettled, Hakon's men returned to him emptyhanded, upon which he said simply, "This can only go one of two ways for Brynjolf. He shall either surrender the woman or be killed."

He sent back more men, too many for Brynjolf to resist. "I haven't the men to fight you now," he said, "despite which, the jarl will eventually be disgraced and shamed for such tyranny and outrage."

While the jarl was bedding his wife, Brynjolf called together his fellow landowners. "I now ask your help," he told them. "Let us assemble an army and march on the jarl, and either fight him, or burn down his house overhead. We deserve utter disgrace if we dare not drive off such evil from among us."

"Because he was formidable and well-liked and of illustrious ancestry," wrote Odd, "many men joined him in fiercely opposing the jarl."

And Berg added ominously, "Little more was necessary to induce open rebellion among them."

But Hakon was already onto his next conquest: Gudrun, so beautiful she was called *Lundasol*, "Sun of (the village of) Lundar." She was the wife of another wealthy landowner, Orm Lugg or Lyrgja, "Loafer," whose farm was just west of Trondheim. When Hakon's thralls arrived Orm actually invited them in for dinner, but meanwhile summoned his neighbors to outnumber them. That done, wrote Snorri, "Orm said Gudrun would in no way go with the slaves."

And Gudrun spoke for herself: "Tell the jarl from me that I will not be his unless he sends Thora of Rimul to bring me."

Snorri confided of this Thora, "She was a rich woman, one of the jarl's mistresses," but this was most likely Hakon's long-suffering wife Thora Skagadottir. Little wonder that after all these years she lived apart from her lord, and as Gudrun knew full well, the odds of her delivering another bedmate to him, or of Hakon even asking her to, were nil.

"We will be back," Hakon's men said, "and you both will think it better to obey the jarl's will."

Orm didn't give them the chance. As soon as they left, as Snorri put it, "Orm called up the warriors from all around the land, saying that everyone was to take up arms against Jarl Hakon and slay him."

"Early that morning the sentries entered the jarl's hall and warned him that a large force was coming from all directions," wrote Odd. "When the jarl heard this, he guessed that it would do no good to seek help from his neighbors because they would all oppose him." Like most strongmen down through history whose people have finally had enough, Hakon realized he wasn't so strong after all, and his best option was to flee.

"When Thorir Klakka heard all this, he was much amazed," wrote Berg, "as he had expected the news to be quite different." What were the odds, that after victory over the Danes and Jomsvikings and years of iron-fisted rule, Jarl Hakon would face a popular uprising at the precise moment an otherwise powerless king arrived to lead it? A religious man might have seen the hand of a god at work. Thorir simply summoned Jostein and Sigurd to make emergency plans.

That evening the brothers armed themselves, rowed a small boat over to Olaf's longship, boarded it unobserved, and made their way to where their nephew lay sleeping. It would have been a simple matter to stick a dagger in him, end his campaign on the spot, and save themselves and their sister.

Instead they shook him awake and convinced him to come ashore with them. Trusting them completely, Olaf did as they wished, and rather than murdering him they proved themselves worthy of his trust. Odd had them confess, "We both deserve death from you, and we now put our lives in your hands because of our treachery. Here, kinsman, you are meant to be murdered."

Jostein elaborated. "Last evening, when Thorir heard what happened here, he talked with us both, and thanked us for keeping our word with Jarl Hakon. He and Hakon planned your death before they parted." Now that Hakon had more pressing matters at hand, it was left to Thorir to carry out the deed. "They figured you would be slain before we reached land, and now that we have set foot on the mainland, we are both free to reveal their plot."

Olaf replied, "I cannot be angry with you for what you have done, because I believe this, like everything else, has happened according to God's will. I will spare your lives and forgive you, but tell me what to do now."

According to Odd, they told him of a hermit, a local prophet of the Saami folk, the nomadic hunters, fishermen and reindeer herders of Scandinavia's far north. The Norwegians called them Laplanders (today regarded as pejorative) and regarded them as shamans and mystics. (Gunnhild Konungamodir was said to have learned sorcery from two Saami wizards.) The prophet would, Jostein and Sigurd promised, know what was to come, and what was to be done.

"I am reluctant to meet and seek help from such men," admitted Olaf, "but because you think it best, let it be God's will."

The three made their way overland by night, Olaf at one point sinking up to his knees in a marsh and complaining, "This is just what I deserve for seeking help from Lapps."

They persevered, however, and soon saw light shining from within the hermit's hut. Having foreseen their coming, he greeted them at the door but denied Olaf entry: "You need not enter my house, for I have had a dire premonition ever since you landed. Momentous spirits precede you, powerful wraiths accompany you, and I cannot endure their company because I am of a different sort."

Olaf said, "Tell us, Lapp, what we are to do and what is to come, and whether I am likely to attain this realm."

According to Odd, the hermit, like the one in the Isles of Scilly, revealed Olaf's future. In the morning Thorir would attempt to kill him, but Olaf would kill him first.

> Hakon will die, and you will reign. You will proclaim a new and unfamiliar religion in the land, and before you die the majority of your followers will accept it. If what I say comes to pass, you should not force me to accept any religion other than my own, for I cannot convert to another belief or form of existence. I cannot help you in any way unless your dog is wounded. Then you should send him to me and I will heal him.

Interestingly, although Olaf's main biographers all related the Scilly prophecy, secular Snorri left this episode out of his account entirely, and Berg edited out the Saami, leaving it to Jostein and Sigurd to come up with a plan themselves, though much as the wizard foretold. Possibly the Scilly hermit, being Christian, was palatable to all three, but only Odd, in his earliest telling, was comfortable with a pagan prophet, which in later, more Christianized times Snorri and Berg found less believable, or even sacrilegious. (Even more curious is having the Saami mention Olaf's dog Vigi and promise he will live. More of that later.) In any case, things go very much as the hermit predicts, or as Jostein and Sigurd plan.

In the morning, Olaf and his uncles having returned to their ships, Thorir came to Olaf and requested the two of them go ashore alone to make plans. Olaf agreed. No sooner were they both seated, however, than both signaled to their men in the nearby forest. Thorir's men had lain in wait to assassinate Olaf. Olaf's men were Jostein and Sigurd. Odd claimed the uncles chased Thorir's men away; Berg said they killed them. Either way, they and Olaf killed Thorir too. Back at the ships, the traitor's crew begged for quarter, which Olaf granted on condition they converted to Christianity and swore allegiance to him. "When Olaf saw how he had been tricked but had nevertheless been saved by God's mercy," wrote Odd, "he gave thanks to God."

Now to finish the job.

As is so often the case, the sagas vary on Jarl Hakon's escape. The earliest account, Odd's, has him racing down to the waterfront where his son Erlend has a pair of longships waiting. (Of all Hakon's multitude of children, only Erlend was present; Odd explained that the eldest, Eirik and Svein, "were not in the country when these events took place.") They set off down the fjord toward the open sea, but before they could escape they beheld dragon ships ahead, Olaf's, coming up the fjord toward them. Astern, rebel boats blocked any retreat. Hakon told his son, "Launch a small boat. I'll take a few men and head for shore. You stay behind, for you are popular enough that you will be spared. Many of the people are friendly toward you, and none will attack you if I am not on hand."

For Snorri and Berg, Hakon ends up the same way, fleeing overland with his thrall Skopti Kark, figuring to rendezvous with Erlend's boats later, and meanwhile heading for his mistress Thora's farm at Rimul, in the valley of the river Gaula. As they cross the iced-over river, the jarl's horse falls through. They leave it there, along with Hakon's cloak and sword, to make any pursuers think he has drowned, and take shelter in a cave (which still exists, called the *Jarlshola*, "Jarl's Cave") where they try to sleep. Skopti awakens with a start and tells the jarl he dreamed. "We were in this cave. I saw a big evil-looking dark man approach, and we were afraid he would enter. I dreamed that he stopped at the entrance and said, 'Ulli is dead.' Then he went away, and I awoke."

"Ulli" was Erlend's nickname. Hakon says, "My son must have been slain."

Indeed, out in the fjord, pinned between two hostile fleets, Erlend had turned for shore. Olaf, thinking Jarl Hakon was aboard, gave chase. Erlend's crews ran their ships aground, leaped overboard and swam for shore. Olaf's ships came up and the sagas claim he brained one of the swimmers with his ship's tiller.* The surviving prisoners revealed the dead man was Erlend, and when the rebel ships arrived, Olaf announced himself as the son of King Tryggvi. "You are certainly welcome here," they told him, "because we have awaited you for a long time. We eagerly accept you as our king, as is your right. Let us now all be after the jarl and finish him."

In the cave, Skopti had started awake again. This time, he told Hakon, "I saw the same man descend the mountain to our cave, and he said to me, 'Tell the Jarl that all the straits are closed.'"

Hakon said, "This means we have only a short time to live."

Odd saved this exchange for a little later, when sagas converge again as Hakon and Skopti reach Thora's farm and ask her to hide them. One would think, after all those years, she would have been sorely tempted to tell Hakon to go call on Thorgerd Holgabrud for rescue, but she said, "This will not be easy. Your enemies will seek you here, every nook and corner of this place, since many people know that I will eagerly help you as best I can. There is only one place on my farm where I would never think of looking for such a great a chieftain. That is in the pigsty."

Again, one might suspect she was at long last taking her revenge for all Hakon's past transgressions against her, but what choice did he have? He said, "A man's life is more important than worrying whether his quarters are worthy of him."

Her slaves dug a pit in the sty, and after Hakon and Skopti went in, covered it with planking, covered that with dirt, covered that with pig manure, and drove the pigs in to trample it all up. When Olaf, his men and the Tronders arrived – having known better than to be fooled by Hakon's cloak and sword in the river – they

---

* Here the scribes date themselves; in Europe the center-mounted rudder and tiller did not replace the side-mounted steering oar until the early 13th century.

searched the entire farm, including the pigsty, but failed to find the fugitives.

Olaf climbed atop a large rock next to the sty. (A thousand years later a working farm still exists on the site, and the large stone as well.) "We have searched for Jarl Hakon and have not found him," he admitted. "Let it be known that I will reward the man who brings me his head."

After the pursuers were gone, Hakon whispered to Skopti Kark, "This man Olaf is impressive, and a great speaker. I have been in danger many times and cannot be called fearful, but the very sound of him troubles me greatly." He saw Skopti's face change color. (Evidently their pit was well lit.) "Why are you pale one moment and black as earth the next? Is it that you wish to betray me?"

"Not I," answered Skopti, "but perhaps you may believe that I, too, am made fearful by this man's voice."

Hakon believed it, all right. Berg confided, "This slave had been given to Hakon when he was a babe cutting his first tooth. They were of the same age."

He reminded Skopti, "We were both born on the same night. There will be as little time between our deaths."

"He believed the slave would betray him," wrote Odd, "and did not trust him enough to fall asleep, so he was on his guard and intent on staying awake all night. The slave, however, slept a long while and deeply."

Again Skopti came awake. "I have dreamed again, lord. We both were aboard a ship, and I was steering it."

Hakon said, "By this you see that both our lives depend on you. Be faithful now, so that you enjoy many good days ahead."

Skopti drifted off, but soon woke again. "I dreamed I was at Lade, and Olaf Tryggvason placed a golden necklace around my neck."

Hakon said, "Be warned, Olaf will cut your throat if you meet him. But I will treat you well, as you have always been, so don't betray me."

Once more Skopti fell asleep, and wakened. "I dreamed Olaf gave me an enormous horse."

Hakon warned, "He will hang you from the highest gallows he can find. Take care not to betray me, otherwise you will not have long to live."

"They both now remained awake, distrusting one another," wrote Berg, "but near dawn the jarl fell asleep. He slept restlessly, shouting in fear and jerking his whole body, as though about to rise."

All this awakened Skopti, who feared Hakon's noise would give them away.

So he drew his knife, stabbed his master in the neck, and sliced his throat from ear to ear.

"That," declared the scribes, "was the death of Jarl Hakon."

Not the end of his story, however.

Berg wrote, "Kark then sawed off the jarl's head and hurried off with it, arriving at Lade the next day. He brought the head to King Olaf, to whom he told everything that happened during his flight with the jarl."

Olaf asked, "Why did you betray the jarl?"

"I did it mostly for the reward you promised to whoever should kill him, and secondly because I hardly knew what else to do, lest he betray us in his sleep."

Olaf said, "I will keep the promise I made on this, and reward you as suits your work, and so keep those who come after from betraying their liege-lords. Though you served a wicked man, he was still your master, and you should have remained faithful to him, and refrained from betraying him, as if he had been a good lord."

He ordered Skopti to be hanged: "He betrayed Jarl Hakon, and will betray me if he gets the chance. This is how to prevent the betrayal of a lord."

Hakon's and Skopti's heads were taken out to the island of Nidarholm, modern Munkholmen where the river Nidelva lets out into Trondheim fjord. Snorri explained, "In those days that little island was where they executed thieves and criminals. A gallows stood there." The heads were mounted on stakes, facing out into the fjord as a warning to visitors. The people stoned them as they would have any other criminals. A detachment went back to Rimul, dragged Hakon's corpse out of the sty and burned it. (If his widow Thora was punished for helping him, it went unrecorded.)

The skald Tind the Brave, who fought alongside Hakon at Hjorungavag, lamented, "People will recall the life of generous Hakon, who supplied to the ravens aplenty, as long as men inhabit Odin's land."

"Jarl Hakon was a most generous man," admitted Snorri, "but the kind of ruler who experienced the worst luck until his last day. And the main reason it happened was, that the time had come for pagan worship and pagan worshippers to be condemned, and their place taken by the holy Faith and Christian morals."

And Berg agreed: "The day had come, as foretold by Almighty God, for idolatry and pagan worship and Jarl Hakon, the devil's evil minion, to be condemned, and in their place Holy Truth should arise, and a genuine faith flourish in splendor over all northern lands, through the benevolence and efforts of Olaf Tryggvason, the messenger of the blessed lord God."

Odd had nothing good to say about Jarl Hakon, in fact nothing more to say about him at all. What mattered to him was that everything was transpiring just as Malusha of Kyiv, the Scillian prophet, and the Saami hermit had foretold: "When the news spread across the land that Jarl Hakon had been slain and that Olaf Tryggvason stood in his place, all the chieftains and wise men came from Trondelag, nobles and commonfolk together. They agreed that everyone wanted him as their king and asked him to rule over all."

PART THREE

*King Olaf answered: "I command
This land to be a Christian land;
Here is my Bishop who the folk baptizes!*

*"But if you ask me to restore
Your sacrifices, stained with gore,
Then will I offer human sacrifices!"*

*…King Olaf from the doorway spoke.
"Choose ye between two things, my folk,
To be baptized or given up to slaughter!"*

*And seeing their leader stark and dead,
The people with a murmur said,
"O King, baptize us with thy holy water."*

Longfellow, "The Saga of King Olaf"

XXIV

King Olaf I

He was the first Norwegian king to keep the proper belief in God, and during his reign Norway was completely converted, but much happened before Christianity prevailed.

Odd Snorrason

AD 995–998

As with much of his saga, Olaf's reign as King of Norway has become jumbled and disordered by his biographers and their later interpreters and translators. Odd, Snorri, Berg, Theodoric and the rest placed events in different orders. Dates become approximate, estimated. We do know that Olaf attained the throne in AD 995. After that, we can order events only in what seems the most logical progression, which is that relations between the king and his subjects started out well, but didn't end up that way.

With Hakon dead and his sons Eirik and Svein doubtless somewhere plotting a vengeful comeback, Norway needed a leader. People in those days found it inconceivable to not have someone lording over them. But, as Hakon had learned to his detriment, no Scandinavian could rule without the consent of his subjects. Odd recorded, "The farmers supported the king in large numbers and put their great martial strength behind the kingdom. The king in turn was expected to render outstanding leadership in all circumstances and battles."

While Olaf was settling in to Hakon's former lodgings at Lade, the chieftains of the nearby families and clans assembled to make everything official. A thing was convened at nearby Ora, where

Norwegian kings going back to Hakon the Good and even Harald Fairhair had traditionally been crowned. According to Berg, Olaf gave a speech, recounting his life story as a series of wrongs and hardships suffered at the hands of the sons of Gunnhild and Jarl Hakon. "I now believe that there is no man here who by right and ancestry has better claim to the crown than I, if that is the will of the chiefs, and the consent of the people."

"They declared Olaf Tryggvason king at the Orething," wrote Odd, "and he in turn swore to uphold the law and traditions of the land. Each would now be obliged to support the other."

So far, however, he ruled over only a small part of Norway. Many people of the far hinterlands would not yet even have heard the news of Hakon's death, nor of Olaf's succession. As far as they knew, Hakon's sons Eirik and Svein would have inherited the kingdom. They still might. Snorri wrote, "Jarl Eirik Hakonarson and his brother Svein, their kinsmen and friends fled the country, eastwards to Sweden, where King Olaf *inn Soenski* ["the Swede," son of Eirik the Victorious and Queen Sigrid] welcomed them."

The Hakonarsons' self-exile meant peace and security for Olaf's subjects, but he was less worried about the threat to their lives than the one to their souls. Snorri affirmed that under Hakon's rule, "The Norwegians who had adopted Christianity had turned back to the pagan rites of prior days."

Becoming King of Norway had been easy. Not so easy would be Olaf's royal, and indeed holy, duty: getting the Norwegians to drop their pagan deities for the one true God. Hakon the Good had not been able to do it. Harald Greycloak and his brothers had not been able to do it. Harald Bluetooth had not been able to do it. People hardened in their beliefs would not simply come to God overnight, on the king's say-so. There were too few priests and clerics to spread the word, and even fewer who spoke Norwegian, and as a result they were distrusted by the commonfolk.

But Olaf had no choice. Theodoric wrote, "He saw that the heathens' hearts were wild, and that only an iron hand could lift them out of the age-old, deep-rooted lack of faith and inborn paganism which they had been fed like mother's milk."

He began with his own family. According to Snorri, he sailed down the coast to visit his ancestral homeland, the Vik. He had many kinfolk there, and many more people had known his mother and father, who would welcome him as their king.

It must have been quite the family reunion, what with Olaf not only seeing his mother Astrid and sisters Astrid and Ingebjorg for the first time in some thirty years, but also meeting his new stepfather Lodin, his half-brother Thorkell, called *Nefja*, "Beaknose," and half-sisters Ingerid and Ingigerd. His uncles Thorkell, Jostein and Sigurd joined them. On top of that, two local chieftains, the brothers Thorgeir and Hyrning, also came to visit and welcome the king. According to Berg, Olaf addressed the menfolk:

> I want to let you know of my wish to begin preaching Christianity here, and that I will either succeed in converting all of Norway, or die trying. I want your support in my effort, and aid going forward with all your might in this noble endeavor, that the good project meets success. I have told you this before anyone else, because with power and influence behind it I think this proselytizing is very likely to succeed, if you brothers Thorgeir and Hyrning are willing to help. As for my kin, I have great trust in their good will, and also that of Lodin, my stepfather.

Naturally Olaf's family stood with him in this, and to his gratification the brothers as well, but for a price. According to Odd, they told him, "Lord, you speak well, and your word is good and true. However, if we are to give up our kinsmen's faith, we brothers wish to have your blessing to wed your sisters Ingigerd and Ingerid. If you allow us such power, we will use all our honor and make every effort to furthering your cause."

Considering Olaf's kingly status, his sisters' weddings were matters of state. They would have been assigned husbands for the maximum benefit of their families anyway; it was just that their value in such business had suddenly, vastly increased. In any case, by their silence in the sagas we can assume they were either all for marrying Thorgeir and Hyrning or – equally likely – nobody asked them. Berg wrote, "It was decided that the brothers would wed Lodin and Astrid's daughters, and that the wedding feast would be held in the Vik in early summer."

And with their backing he began his crusade then and there, among the people of the Vik. "The king offered them two choices," declared Snorri, "to either accept Christianity, or to fight. But the farmers saw they could not fight the king, and so all decided to agree to be baptized."

By the time the royal fleet sailed back up around the curve of southwest Norway in the spring of 997 Olaf's reputation preceded him. Odd reported, "When the people there learned of Olaf's coming, the leading men there summoned a great assembly and convened the Gulathing."

Held at what is now Gulen in Norway's Vestland, the Gulathing was another of the country's major political assemblies. The people there had already agreed among themselves to welcome a new king, but not a foreign god. The chieftains were reluctant to abandon the gods of their ancestors, and required something of equal import in return.

It's a measure of Olaf's good will thus far that he deigned to haggle with his subjects. "What would you have of me, to best seal the compact between us?"

"Mainly," said their spokesman, "that you wed your sister Astrid, King Tryggvi's daughter, to our kinsman Erling Skjalgsson, whom we uphold as the most promising young man in all of Norway."

Had Olaf driven the bargain himself, he could not have wished for a better outcome. By virtue of his birth, this Erling was not only a leading local citizen but one of the keys to the entire kingdom. His great-grandfather had fought for King Harald Fairhair and been well rewarded for it in captured estates, to this day some of Norway's richest farmlands. Since then, the clan had done nothing but grow in power. The ancestral farm at Sola, farther down the southwest coast at the entrance to the huge, complex Boknafjord, may well have been where Vikings departed to attack Lindisfarne Abbey in England in 793; over the next two centuries it had developed into what amounted to a Viking naval base. Erling's ancestors were *hersirs*, barons, landowners wealthy and powerful enough to lead raids on their own. Through their merchant fleet they dealt on equal terms with foreign rulers across the North Sea and Baltic. On top of that, Erling's sister Sigrid had married into the Trondenes clan, an equally powerful faction up in northern Halogaland. If through marriage they all became Olaf's in-laws, his authority would triple.

There was, however, the matter of Astrid. Perhaps a full sister's opinion mattered more to Olaf than his newly met half-sisters'. (Though Odd had this marriage proposal preceding the other, so maybe Olaf learned a lesson from it.) Berg had him answer, "Doubtless such a match would be suitable and worthy, for Erling is prosperous, of good name, and very handsome, but the answer is up to Astrid. I will ask her what she thinks, for I must do everything I can to further Christianity."

When he put the proposal to her, however, Astrid turned up her nose. She was, after all, two years or so older than Olaf – if she had not already been through a marriage, a veritable spinster – and likely some fifteen years older than Erling, who may only have been about twenty. (Besides, Berg confided, "He was also said to be very domineering.") And she was well aware that with Olaf's rise to power her worth had risen as well: "What good is it for me to be a king's daughter and a king's sister, if I'm to be given to a man of low rank? I prefer to wait for a better offer, even if it takes years."

Having given her the chance to see reason, Olaf did not argue with her. He had more effective means of persuasion.

Birds of prey were of great value to Scandinavians. To pagans they personified Vedrfolnir, the hawk that sat between the eyes of a great eagle at the top of the world-tree Yggdrasil, symbolizing wisdom and knowledge, and they were also symbolic of the goddess Freyja, whose cloak of hawk feathers gave her the power of flight and to transform into a giant raptor. Even among Christian Vikings, hawks were prized for hunting and sheer status. The snowy white gyrfalcon was worth more than its weight in gold, and captive birds were traded as far away as the Middle East. Astrid owned one. It would have been one of her most prized possessions.

Olaf ordered all its feathers plucked out.

It was still living, probably, when returned to her, but having live feathers plucked is like having hair pulled from all over the body.

It can bleed a bird to death, and if not, the extreme stress and trauma can kill it from sheer shock. In any case, the sight of her noble pet reduced to a naked, bloodied, dazed, pink-skinned chicken, barely alive, apparently sent the proper message to Astrid: "My brother is angered with me."

She hurried back to Olaf, willing to accept marriage to whomever he wished. He told her, "I should think I can ennoble anyone in the land."

It was agreed that Erling and Astrid would be wed, and furthermore that Erling and all his people would be baptized as Christians. "No one," Snorri admitted, "was confident to oppose it."

The ceremony was held that summer. Perhaps as a wedding gift, Olaf offered to name Erling a jarl. He declined the honor. "My kinsmen have been *hersirs*," he said. "I do not aspire to a higher title than that. What I would like from you, my king, is that you make me the greatest *hersir* in the land."

So it was done. Olaf returned north, leaving his new brother-in-law Erling to rule over a domain the size of Belgium. A Christian domain.

These were tumultuous years across Scandinavia. In Denmark, Svein Forkbeard had succeeded in winning back his kingdom from Sweden's new king Olaf Skotkonung, son of the late Eirik the Victorious. Skotkonung may have been unable to defend his foreign conquest, for like the Norwegian King Olaf he was busy at home, undergoing religious strife with his subjects and trying to legitimize his rule. Like King Sigtrygg Silkbeard in Dublin, he was minting his own silver pennies, modeled on those of England's King Aethelred; their Latin inscriptions OLAF REX implying that, like Sigtrygg and Aethelred, he ruled in God's name, even if his subjects were unbelievers.

Skotkonung's own mother Sigrid remained stubbornly pagan. As with the other widows in our story, Geira and Gytha, though wealthy, she would of necessity have needed a husband to maintain her own standing. Odd recorded, "The eastern king Vissivald and Harald *Grenske*, king of Uppland, came calling for Sigrid's hand.

But she thought it unbecoming to be wooed by such petty kings, and presumptuous of them to aspire to such a queen."

Vissivald being a Baltic version of the Slavic Vsevolod, this otherwise unknown ruler was probably some minor Eistland pirate king. Harald Grenske, "the Greenlander," a great-grandson of Harald Fairhair, had been raised across the seas to keep him safe from the murderous sons of Gunnhild Mother of Kings. (His father, Gudrod Bjornsson, had been cousin to Tryggvi Olaffson, and like him killed in their purge of rivals to the throne; Harald the Greenlander was Olaf Tryggvason's first cousin once removed.) He was also Sigrid's foster-brother, not to mention already married – in fact his queen Asta was pregnant – but despite all that he pursued Sigrid with a passion.

Snorri wrote, "She told him it was nonsense, that he was already well married and well-matched. Harald replied that Asta was a good, noble woman, 'But she is not as high-born as I am.'"

Sigrid replied, "Perhaps you are of greater ancestry than she, but I should think you would both be very happy together."

Snorri continued of Vissivald and Grenske:

> The kings and all their men were put up in a large, ancient hall with luxurious comforts. There was plenty of drink that evening, so strong that everyone became completely drunk and their sentries outside fell asleep. Then Queen Sigrid ordered a night attack with both fire and sword. The hall burned and the people inside with it, and those who escaped were killed. Sigrid said this would make petty kings stop coming from other countries to ask for her hand.

"Afterwards," Snorri continued, "she was called Sigrid *inn storrada* ["the Haughty"]."

Olaf was by now well practiced at marrying-up with rich and powerful widows. (The fate of his second wife, Gytha, is unknown. Last seen in Ireland, she makes no more appearances in her husband's saga. She had either remained in Dublin, died, or at least had no say in his further wedding plans.) He was not put off by his predecessors' fate. They had been little kings.

Olaf considered himself to be a great king, and not just as measured by conquests and conversions.

For instance, in all the years he had reigned from Lade, Jarl Hakon had never bothered to develop Trondheim, the island trading post just two and a half miles down the fjord, where the *Fagrskinna* records there had been nothing but a single hall. Olaf, on the other hand, pictured it as a kind of Norwegian Jomsborg or Dublin. "He was establishing a market town there, and building a hall for himself," wrote Berg. He named it *Nidaros*, "mouth of the river Nid," the modern Nidelva in which the island stood. "That autumn he also had a church built there. On the riverbank he had the ground partitioned and assigned to those he thought fit and willing to build houses on them."

Olaf had furthermore ordered the pagan temple at Lade – Hakon's temple, the temple of Thorgerd Holgabrud – destroyed, but not before he looted everything in it, right down to the adornments on the idols and a huge gold ring that Hakon had specially ordered as a door knocker. Then the temple and idols were burned together.*

Yet such a great king needed a great queen. Olaf considered Sigrid the perfect match. By marrying her he would acquire not only a great queen, but all her lands with her.

Messengers passed from Trondheim down to Gotland with the king's proposal. They returned with word that the queen was not opposed to the idea. Olaf gifted her the great gold ring ripped off the temple door at Lade, which achieved the desired effect. Odd attested, "Now she was very keen to marry such a king."

A meeting of the royal couple was arranged at Konungahella, near modern Kungalv in southwest Sweden, on the Gota Alv River that drains the Vanern, the country's largest lake, into the Kattegat. In the future this would serve as a kind of neutral ground between Norway and Sweden, the site of multiple treaties between them, one of which would be agreed between Sigrid's son King Olaf and the son of her late suitor Harald the Greenlander.

---

* Olaf the Swede had similarly Christian intentions for the bloodstained pagan temple at Uppsala, but according to Adam of Bremen his subjects nearly rebelled and forced him to set up his private Christian domain at Skara in Vastergotland, modern West Gotland, way down on Sweden's southwest coast.

(Now follow this, for it is of import to Norway's future: Olaf had actually met the boy – his kinsman, first cousin twice removed – also named Olaf, now about three, at Hringariki, modern Ringerike, not far from the Randsfjorden where King Olaf had been born. Little Olaf's widowed mother Asta had married another petty king, another great-grandson of Harald Fairhair, Sigurd Halvdansson, called *Syr*, "Sow," as in female pig; he was a renowned farmer. On King Olaf's arrival, Sigurd, Asta and little Olaf were all baptized, with the king standing as godfather to the boy. Little Olaf was just one among many of King Olaf's converts to the new faith, but in decades to come he and his as-yet unborn half-brother, Harald Sigurdarson, would have at least as great an effect on Norway and the Viking Age.)[*]

The boy's murdered father, Harald the Greenlander, may have been on King Olaf's mind when it came to meeting Sigrid the Haughty. And she now had cause for misgivings herself. Olaf himself probably knew no better, but it had turned out that the great gold door-ring or knocker commissioned by Jarl Hakon to decorate the temple of Thorgerd Holgabrud was not solid gold, but merely gilded iron and brass. Perhaps that was why the goddess was annoyed with Hakon and demanded the sacrifice of his son at the Battle of Hjorungavag; Queen Sigrid reacted no better. "The queen was angered," recorded Snorri, "saying that Olaf must be tricking her in more than just this," and Odd claimed she went so far as to declare, "I will have no marriage with him."

Still, for both sides the pluses of such a match outweighed the negatives. Given time to cool off, and each perhaps assuming the other had good reason – or at least good excuse – for their actions, both sides proceeded to the nuptial summit at Konungahella. Snorri enthused, "They met and discussed marriage as had been proposed during the winter, and everything seemed to be going well."

That is, until it came to the matter of religion. Of course Olaf, converting his subjects as quickly and forcefully as possible to

---

[*] Olaf Haraldsson was also said to have been baptized years later in Normandy, but that might have been more of a confirmation, like the one between Olaf and King Aethelred. For more on Olaf Haraldsson and especially Harald Sigurdarson, see *The Last Viking* by the same author.

Christianity, could not be seen to have a pagan queen. According to Snorri, he took it as a given that Sigrid would be baptized and accept his faith. According to Berg, he demanded it.

But Sigrid was not yet his wife, to be ordered around like a housemaid. The sagas credit her with at least seeking a middle ground: "I will not give up the faith that I have held to now, and my kinsmen held before me. You may believe in whatever god you like."

That was basically the same argument Jarl Sigurd of Orkney had given Olaf, but Sigrid had no son at hand for him to threaten; her son was sitting on the Swedish throne. Sigrid had already been old enough to be married to Eirik the Victorious, back when Olaf was only three. In those days, that perhaps meant no more than a dozen years between them. But he was around thirty-five now, which meant she was pushing fifty – back then, more like our eighty. Still, diplomacy and simple good manners might dictate a civil reply. But, according to Berg, Olaf was speaking on behalf of God, and gods need not be diplomatic.

"Do you imagine, you wrinkled thing," he told her, "that I will marry you, a worn-out old hag, and a pagan bitch to boot? Don't even think it, and don't presume as to ever again blaspheme in my hearing the name of the Lord in your heathenish tongue, when referring to the sublime King of Heaven, whom I worship as God."

And, with his glove, he slapped her across the face.

In centuries to come, such a gesture would be a literal challenge, resulting in a duel to the death, or at least it would between two men. A woman had no such recourse. We can well imagine Sigrid's cheeks reddening, and not just from the mark of Olaf's glove. She said, "This shame and dishonor, Olaf, might well cost your life."*

"With that they ended their discussion, both in fury," Berg put it mildly. Between two heads of state, such an incident would almost certainly have resulted in war, which furthermore would likely have started then and there. Sigrid, however, could not speak for Sweden; she was a queen mother, not the wife of the king. That said, she and

---

* Saxo Grammaticus claimed that Sigrid was climbing the gangway to board Olaf's longship when she fell or was tipped into the water and laughed at by the Norwegians, which would have been just as great an insult.

Olaf would surely both have employed armed escorts, bodyguards, and for them the urge to draw sword and wade in among each other must have been strong. That everyone came away alive indicates both Olaf and Sigrid held both their emotions and their men in check. War was averted.

For the time being.

XXV

Hammer of God

After this, the king determined, with all his strength and heaven's aid, on driving idolatry and devil-worship from the land.

Theodoricus Monachus

AD 998–999

Olaf had to have left Konungahella in a vile mood, feeling as though the old gods had taken vengeance on him. He'd finally found a queen worthy of his new royal status, and the curse of paganism had destroyed their union. And after three years of rule he had not been able to eradicate it in his own kingdom. It was time to stop asking his subjects to worship God and start telling them.

On his return to Lade he summoned all the local chieftains to a feast in his great hall. News had spread of Olaf's destruction of Jarl Hakon's temple, which the pagans knew did not bode well for them. Yet Olaf made them welcome, and when they had assembled he admitted that he was Christian and wished all his subjects to give up the old gods, which stood between him and them. Nevertheless, he had arranged this feast in order to honor their gods in the ancient manner. According to Odd, he announced, "You say no sacrifice so pleases them as the killing of men, who then feast with them in Valhalla in Odin's hall. I will then offer you as sacrifices, to ensure peace for myself and eternal honor for you."

He called out ten of the pagan leaders by name. His retainers entered the hall and took them in charge. Faced with being marched out to their deaths, they suddenly lost some of their enthusiasm for human sacrifice.

"Why now are you so unhappy?" inquired Olaf. "Do you fear death, thinking it is not such a good thing after all? Then either accept baptism or go join your gods."

The chiefs admitted that they would rather obey the king and accept his faith. According to Odd, they and their followers were baptized on Christmas Eve, though which year he did not specify. Olaf went on with the great feast to celebrate the occasion, before sending the new Christians home with gifts of money. Snorri, however, added that just to be sure, "The king kept all who attended his feast as hostages, until they provided him their sons, brothers, or other family members."

Back in the year 950 King Hakon the Good had summoned the Norwegians to a thing at Frosta, across Trondheim fjord from Lade, and tried to persuade them to accept Christ. They had forced him to back down. Almost fifty years later, King Olaf called on them once again to meet with him atop Tinghaugen, "Assembly Hill." By now, everyone was wary of this king, and they all came armed, some 300 warriors.* When the assembly was complete, the king addressed the people, asking them to accept God. He had not talked long, however, when according to Snorri the farmers shouted back, telling him to shut up, for if not they would attack and drive him off: "We gave King Hakon, King Athelstan's foster-son, the same choice when he preached this religion to us. He took our protest in good spirit, we made peace, and both sides held to it. We do not regard you as better than him, and you would best follow that good king's example."

Their leader was a local landowner named *Jarnskegg*, "Iron-Beard," from down near the mouth of Trondheim fjord. Snorri recorded, "Skeggi spoke first against King Olaf at the assembly, and was the leader of those opposing Christianity."

(His reasons may have been more than religious. Odd confided, "King Olaf had an affair with the daughter of Jarnskeggi of Yrjar.")

---

* In Old Norse long hundreds, 360.

"If you do not stop this preaching, you will suffer the fate of Jarl Hakon," he warned Olaf. "Our desire, lord, is for you to offer sacrifices, as other kings have done in the past."

Snorri wrote, "The farmers applauded his words loudly, saying that they wanted everything as Skeggi said."

Olaf had God on his side, but not enough men. Much as King Hakon had before him, he relented: "It is not proper for me to raise my hand against you, for you are powerful. It seems to me much more kingly to increase the sacrifices rather than decrease them, and so it shall be done from now on."

He agreed to attend their next sacrifice, farther inland at a temple dedicated to Thor.

Odd recorded, "When the king arrived a human sacrifice was prepared, and they intended to force him to participate. A great crowd had come."

Before the ritual could take place, Olaf asked to see inside the temple. He went in accompanied only by a few of his men, a few of the farmers, and a priest to explain the proceedings. Adam of Bremen described what must have been a very similar temple and rites at Uppsala in Sweden.

> In this temple, entirely decorated in gold, the people pray to the idol of three gods. The mightiest of them, Thor, sits on a throne in the midst of the chamber. Odin and Frey sit to either side. The importance of these gods is as follows: Thor, they say, reigns over the air, which brings the thunder and lightning, the winds and rains, fair weather and crops. Odin – that is, the Furious – conducts war and gives a man strength against his enemies. The third, Frey, bestows peace and pleasure on men. They fashion his idol with an immense phallus. But Odin they carve with weapons, as our people prefer to depict Mars. Thor with his hammer is said to resemble Jove.

Adam explained, "Against plague and famine threaten, a toast is drunk to Thor; if war, to Odin; in celebration of marriage, to Frey." The temple was also where, every nine years, the Swedes celebrated their festival of death. "Of every living thing that is male, they offer nine heads, the blood of which is customary to please these gods."

Of the Norwegian temple, Berg agreed, "In the center, the place of honor, sat Thor, a huge idol all adorned in gold and silver."

No one went armed into the temple, but for ritual purposes the king carried a gilded ceremonial axe. He, however, intended a very different ceremony. Odd wrote, "King Olaf went to where Thor was sitting, raised the ax, and struck Thor's ear so that he crashed forward onto the floor."

Snorri wrote, "Then the king's men leapt forward and pulled all the gods off their pedestals."

"And while this went on inside the temple," added Berg, "outside at the door, the king's men slew Iron-Beard."

While all the people were still speechless with surprise and shock, Olaf emerged from the temple with axe in hand and Jarnskegg's body at his feet, a king who had defiled a god. He gave no one time to think, but ordered them all to sit. "Submit yourselves to peace and friendship with me. Believe in the God who sends the sun to shine on both the just and unjust and the rain on the good and the evil," he told them. "I command you all to accept Christianity here and now, or else ready yourselves to fight with me."

Bereft of their leader, no one dared raise a hand or even speak out against the king for fear of likewise being slain. Snorri wrote, "Then King Olaf had everyone there baptized, and took hostages from the farmers to ensure they held to their Christianity." Odd claimed that 600 men, women and children were baptized on the spot, and could count themselves lucky to be alive, having threatened to rebel against their king.

Others would not be so lucky.

When Trondheim was only just becoming a village, and Oslo did not yet exist, Tunsberg, "mountain fort," modern Tonsberg down near the mouth of Oslofjord, was one of the closest things in Norway to an actual town. Today regarded as the oldest city in Norway, it had been founded by Harald Fairhair back around 871 to support his southern campaigns. In the two centuries since, given its easy access from points both north and south, it had grown into a vibrant market center. It was also the site of Hauger farm, "hill" or "burial mound," and the Haugathing, the political assembly for southern Norway. Like the Orething and Frostathing, it was an ideal place for Olaf to spread God's word to the people. "The king went to Tunsberg," wrote Snorri, "and convened a thing, at which he gave a speech declaring that any men known beyond doubt to have dealt with evil spirits, or in witchcraft, or in sorcery, were to be banished from the land."

Odd claimed this took place in the vicinity of Nidaros, but agreed, "King Olaf banished anyone who practiced magic and the old superstitions, and most especially those men or women whom the Norwegians call *seidmenn* [sorcerers]." He had all such folk brought together and gave them his ultimatum: baptism or banishment, forfeiting their wealth and property.

These pagans had chosen as their spokesman one Eyvind *Kelda*, "Bog". Odd asserted, "He had a distinguished ancestry, the third or fourth generation down from Harald Fairhair."

But Snorri added, "Eyvind was a sorcerer, very skilled in witchcraft."

According to Berg, Olaf told him, "I sincerely hope that if possible you will submit to my authority. Forsake your old creeds and accept Christianity instead, with honest faith in Almighty God. You may then retain your homes and estates, happy and esteemed by us, with such power and honor as I see fit to bestow, and nearly as great as you may ask."

Eyvind answered, "You need not ask, O King. Neither false words nor harsh treatment will cause us to abandon our faith or ways."

What could Olaf do, but throw up his hands and wish the pagans well on their way?

> Your leaving greatly harms me and my people, and in our parting I may lose more than I gain, because you take with you all the ability and power in which you are greater than other men. But because our task and preaching here have such a great success that Christianity is triumphant, it becomes necessary that you and your kind should leave this land. However, I hope you do not become my enemies and use your power in rage against my rule. Now, before you board your ship, I invite you to a feast that I have arranged with the best available provisions.

But Olaf hadn't forgotten Sigrid the Haughty's method of dealing with troublemakers. Snorri recorded, "The king let them all be seated in one room, which was well decorated, and gave a great feast for them, with plenty of strong drink."

"In this way they became so drunk that they all fell asleep where they sat," wrote Berg.

That night Olaf ordered the building set afire.

"Burning brands flew everywhere inside, and there was a great and horrible turmoil, with both men and women weeping and grieving," wrote Odd.

Theodoric recorded, "People numbered them at eighty altogether, men and women."

Only Eyvind Kelda escaped the flames, leaping out of an upper window. In the morning, on the road, he crossed paths with travelers coming to meet the new king. According to Berg, he told them, "That is lucky. Do me the favor of taking him a message from me, that Eyvind Kelda escaped the fire, and will never again put himself in King Olaf's power. He will practice his sorcery and witchcraft he always has, but with extra purpose."

"The King was not happy to hear Eyvind was still alive," wrote Berg, "and said that if he were caught again, he would not boast like that again."

Eyvind was not idly boasting. He acquired a longship and crewed it with fellow sorcerers and wizards, intent on waging unholy war against the king. That Easter, when Olaf feasted at Ogvaldsnes on Kormt Island, modern Avaldsnes on Karmoy, at the mouth of the vast Boknafjord, they approached by night and landed close ashore. Odd said of Eyvind, "He meant to attack King Olaf and kill him along with all his men."

The sorcerer and his crew set about doing this by black magic. Berg wrote, "Eyvind gave them helmets to make them invisible, and called up a thick dark fog, so that the King and his men would not see them."

Odd attested, "They disembarked and went ashore to where the king and the bishop and all the Christian people were attending church. But when Eyvind looked upon the holy church, he and all his men went blind and were left wandering back and forth on the island."

This sounds rather like the monks coming up with a supernatural cause for Eyvind and his men simply losing their way in a night fog, but what matters is that their magic was not powerful enough to keep them from blundering into Olaf's sentries, who captured them and brought them before the king.

Olaf would not have been surprised that their wizardry had failed them. "Eyvind, since you have learned that your witchcraft and sorcery bring you and your followers nothing but trouble, surely you will all be willing to give up your false ways, and come at last to believe in the true God."

But Eyvind and his companions still refused baptism. So the next day Olaf had them taken aboard ship and bound down on a skerry [Old Norse *sker*, a rock protruding from the sea] north of the promontory at the end of Karmsund, which was under water at high tide. (The rock still exists in Karmoy harbor, even more prominent today; a thousand years ago the water level was some five feet higher.) Snorri wrote, "Eyvind and all with him died on this rock, the skerry still called *Skrattaskjaer* [Sorcerers' Rock]."

Olaf's marriage of his sister Astrid to Erling Skjalgsson had not paid off quite so handsomely as Olaf had hoped. Erling's sister, married into a clan up in northern Halogaland, had not been enough to sway its chieftains over to the king's side. In fact, the first time he made a foray in that direction, they banded together against him, ready for war.

There were three principal chieftains up there: Harek Evindsson, from the island of Tjotta, who might be called the money; Thorir *Hjort*, "Hart" or "Stag", who lived even farther north, on Austavagoy, Eastern Inlet Island, in the Lofoten archipelago, and provided the army; and another Eyvind, called *Kinnrifa*, "Torn Cheek," also said to be a sorcerer who could invoke evil spells. All were heathen, unwilling to give up the old gods. Unable to defeat them all at once, Olaf resolved to do it piecemeal.

Harek of Tjotta was basically kidnapped and delivered to the king. Harek had started as a small-plot farmer, and through his own wit and wisdom had soon come to own the whole island of Tjotta. He was respected for his shrewdness and his royal lineage, being descended from Harald Fairhair, which made him Olaf's distant kinsman. This entitled him to good treatment, and according to Odd rather than strong-arm him Olaf appealed to his self-interest. He offered Harek control of a pair of provinces, each of which could supply a dozen ships fully armed and crewed with sixty to seventy men apiece. Shrewd businessman that he was, Harek held out for four such provinces before Olaf sent him home, swearing him to secrecy.

According to Snorri and Berg it wasn't as easy as all that. Harek refused to convert. Olaf did not force it, telling him, "Go home. I shall not harm you for now, because we are related, and because you will claim that I captured you by deceit. But be certain, I intend to come up north and visit you Halogalanders. Then you will learn how I punish those who refuse Christianity."

He even furnished Harek with a ship and a thirty-man crew. In this version of the story, as soon as he arrived safely home Harek sent word to Eyvind Torn Cheek to come quickly so they could plan for Olaf's invasion. But Olaf's crew were watching Harek's estate on Tjotta, and the moment Eyvind arrived they kidnapped him too. (In Odd's version, it was newly Christianized Harek who betrayed and kidnapped him.)

Either way, Eyvind's interrogation did not go as well as Harek's. Olaf began browbeating him with God's word, imploring him to renounce his gods. Eyvind refused. Olaf offered him high position and great honor in the kingdom. Eyvind refused. Olaf promised him gifts, money and rule over five provinces, more than he had promised Harek. Eyvind refused. Finally Olaf threatened him with painful death. Eyvind refused. The man could not be bargained with, and was a sorcerer besides.

Odd wrote, "The king ordered a flaming brazier to be set on his belly. When he began to burn, the king asked whether he would accept Christianity."

Eyvind did not, even as the bowl full of hot coals seared its way through the skin of his stomach, which burst open. At this they both knew his life was at an end, but Eyvind managed to speak. "Take off the bowl. I have something to say before I die."

As the brazier was lifted off him Olaf said, "Now, Eyvind, will you believe in Christ?"

"No," Eyvind said, "I cannot accept any baptism."

Odd and Berg gave him an impossibly long speech for a man whose belly has been burned open, explaining that his parents had been unable to conceive except by Finnish magic, on condition that his life be dedicated to Thor and Odin unto death. Eyvind had been taught from birth that he was not human: "I am a spirit, conceived in a human body by Lappish sorcery."

With that, he died.

We moderns can take Eyvind's story with a grain of salt. What makes it worth the telling is not so much what he believed as how steadfastly he believed it – and that people back then could well believe he believed it, even in the face of hideous, painful death. His conviction, it must be said, made him immortal. Today he is revered as something like a saint, a martyr, by practitioners of modern Nordic paganism – Asatru, Vanatru, Disitru, Rokkatru, *Forn Sidr*, "the Old Way."

Olaf had just had a new longship built, a *snekkja*, "snake." "It numbered thirty rowing benches," wrote Snorri. "It had a high stem and stern and was not of exceptional capacity. The king named it *Traninn* [Crane]."

In the spring after Eyvind Kinnrifa's death, the king used it as the flagship of the fleet in which he sailed north to subdue Halogaland. "Wherever he put ashore he convened a thing," wrote Berg, "calling upon one and all to be baptized and accept the true faith. No man was brave enough to speak against him, and wherever he went the land became Christian."

Harek of Tjotta had learned not to defy the king. He feasted Olaf in his hall, where he and all his men were baptized. Harek presented Olaf with gifts and swore allegiance, and in turn was acknowledged as the king's man.

The last holdout was Thorir Stag. Faced with the loss of two-thirds of his triumvirate, he recruited another half: Raud, called *inn Rami*, "the Powerful." "Raud was a very wealthy man and had many warriors in his service," wrote Snorri. "A large number of Lapps came when he called them."

Berg added, "Raud was a dedicated worshipper of the old gods, completely practiced in witchcraft."

When they learned Olaf and his army were approaching, they mustered their army and warships. Raud's ship in particular was well known for its size – thirty rowing benches, with room for more – and its gilded dragon head.

The two fleets met in a great battle, with many casualties, but greater on the northerners' side. As more and more of their ships were cleared, panic set in. Raud raised sail and fled out to sea. (Snorri confided, "Raud always had a favorable wind when he sailed, as a result of his magic.") Thorir headed for shore, beached his ship and fled on foot. Olaf landed as well, and leaped down to give chase, but Thorir the Stag was too fast.

Olaf told his dog, "Catch the hart, Vigi."

Vigi quickly dragged Thorir to a stop. Odd claimed one of Olaf's men killed the Stag with an arrow between the shoulders, but that wasn't heroic enough for the later sagas. Both Snorri and Berg claimed Olaf himself killed Thorir with a spear in the armpit that came out his other side, but not before Thorir stabbed Vigi. Odd saved his mythmaking for the dog, claiming a deer was seen to leap from Thorir's body and gore Vigi before it was brought down. Luckily Olaf remembered what to do. Odd wrote, "They took the dog aboard ship, wrapped in a cloth. The king had him sent to the Lapp they had visited before, asking that he heal the dog. It so happened that in a few months the Lapp healed the dog and returned him to the king."

In the sagas Vigi becomes something of an instrument for the king's less Christian impulses. When a member of his bodyguard was murdered by an Icelander, even though his own men pleaded for mercy, Olaf ordered the killer stripped and set upon by dogs: "This will deter others from killing my men." Even the king's bishop sent word urging him to show mercy, but Olaf just said, "A bishop cannot judge a man better than I. Strip him at once."

Even naked and bound, the prisoner was so intimidating – or the punishment unjust enough – that the dogs would not attack him. Odd wrote, "The king called upon his greatest dog, Vigi, patting him two or three times, urging him to bite the man. Finally, at the king's command, he made one leap forward, bit the man's stomach, and returned to the king."

Disemboweled, the victim fell dead. When the bishop heard of it, he admonished the king so sternly that Olaf repented, knelt before him and confessed his sin. "The king paid heavy penance for it," admitted Odd. But Vigi the dog answered for nothing.

"King Olaf and his force sailed north along the coast, making all the people Christian wherever he landed," wrote Berg. "On reaching the firth of Salpti in this northern progress, he tried to enter it to visit Raud, but met only gales and squalls."

Berg recounts two versions of the king's encounter with Raud, differing mainly in their outcome. In each, the royal fleet is unable to penetrate Salpti, "strong stream," the Old Norse name for the Saltfjorden, near modern Bodo. It is bisected by a strait less than two miles long and just 500 feet wide, through which the tides rip at up to twenty-five miles an hour. The whirlpools formed can be over thirty feet across and fifteen feet deep, and in Viking times were thought to be the work of the gods.

Secure behind this natural defense, Raud visits his temple to Thor, but finds the god in a melancholy mood: "I am greatly troubled by the approach of some coming here, for whom I have a terrible hate." Told it is Olaf Tryggvason, Raud advises the thunder god to close off the fjord with wind and wave.

Out in the fjord, Olaf orders his priest to conjure up a counter-spell. "So, having dressed himself in all his vestments, he went up into the prow of the king's ship. Here he set up a crucifix, lit wax candles, burned incense, and after having read aloud the Gospel and many prayers too, sprinkled holy water all over the ship." (Christian magic was just fine with the monks writing the sagas.) The waters calmed and Olaf's longships rowed through, all this probably just the scribes' exaggerated way of saying they waited for slack water at the changing of the tides. In one version Olaf, arriving at Raud's hall, summons him and his people to be baptized. Raud not only refuses, but challenges Olaf to defeat Thor himself in a wrestling match.

Now, it's easy enough to think Raud simply passed off the biggest, strongest man in his domain as the thunder god in order to bluff the king.* According to Berg, Olaf was not intimidated. "I fight, however, on the condition that neither Thor nor I spare the other's life when the fateful moment comes, nor shall any person help he who is beaten."

King and god fight around a great fire, over which Thor trips and falls, burning to death. "It is now apparent to all," proclaims Olaf, "it is groundless faith to trust in Thor, seeing as he cannot even save himself from burning." He takes the unrepentant Raud prisoner until he finally relents and accepts God.

The other version is more violent. Olaf and his men leap ashore and break into Raud's house.

The king has Raud dragged before him, ordering him to consent to baptism: "Then I will not take your property, but instead be your friend."

"But Raud adamantly refused," testified Berg, "swearing many terrible blasphemies and saying he would never believe in Christ. At this the King became angry, saying that Raud should die the worst possible death." Raud was tied down on his back, with his mouth forced open. Berg recorded,

> A viper was put to his mouth, but shrank back without entering, because Raud coughed it out. Then the King ordered a hollow angelica stalk, or a trumpet, as some say who tell the story, to be inserted in his mouth. Into this stalk went the viper, driven with a hot iron bar into Raud's mouth, from where it passed into his breast to his heart, forcing its way through his left side. In this way Raud died.

Whether the snake bit Raud internally, or he simply choked on it, or it was a total fiction, those of his subjects who still lived and heard the story were willing to be baptized and spared. The rest were put to death. Berg wrote, "From this King Olaf acquired great riches in gold, silver, and other transportable property, in weapons and many valuable goods." He also confiscated Raud's ship, it being much larger

---

* He may not have had to rename him. The list of Scandinavian names that are variations of "Thor" – Thorbjorn, Thorkell, Thorleif, Thorsten, Thorvald – runs to over 180. (Odin, notably, was not so popular.)

and better than the *Crane*, and renamed it *Ormrin*, "Serpent" or "Dragon," for the dragon-wings motif on its sail. "It was the finest ship in all of Norway."

Odd himself admitted, "These sorts of tales about such phantoms and phenomena as have just been recorded may certainly seem unbelievable, but everyone knows that the devil always opposes Almighty God, along with those wretched men who reject God." As an enlightened man of the 12th century, he felt the people of the 10th were a little too gullible, too superstitious – just as we might consider him, and Snorri, and Berg – and felt he needed to justify the retelling. "In regard to such tales and examples, we do not judge the events we have related to have truly happened, but instead we believe they appeared to happen, because the devil is full of trickery and evil."

Snorri told only the version with the snake, and at that thought it best to move his *Heimskringla* along: "King Olaf made the entire fjord Christian, afterward returning south along the coast. On that voyage many things happened that have been retold as trolls and evil spirits playing tricks on his men and sometimes on him as well," he wrote. "But we want instead to write about King Olaf making Norway Christian, and the other countries to which he brought Christianity."

XXVI

God's Viking

He was the first king of Norway to keep the true faith in God, and by his guidance and power the entire kingdom of Norway became Christian, and Orkney, the Faroes, Shetland, Iceland and Greenland as well.

Fagrskinna

AD 999–1000

Iceland had theoretically been Christian since the arrival of the first permanent settlers there in the 770s, Irish monks who had learned of the temporary hunting, fishing and whaling camps there and made the voyage to practice their faith in seclusion. That was 200 years before Olaf's time and a hundred years before the first Scandinavian settlers arrived, as Ari the Wise, in his *Islendingabok*, "Book of the Icelanders," recorded: "There were once Christians here, whom the Northmen call *papar* [fathers], but they eventually left, because they did not wish to live here with heathens. They left behind Irish books and bells and staffs. From these it was apparent they were Irishmen."

In another century's time most of Iceland that could be farmed was being farmed, the *Althing* had been founded (still the world's oldest surviving parliament) and settlers were pressing even farther west to Greenland. All this was accomplished by pagans.

It was probably in the 970s that Harald Bluetooth, after his and Denmark's conversion to Christianity – and his failure to convert Jarl Hakon and Norway – explored the idea of conquering and converting Iceland, which was largely populated by expatriate Norwegians.

He scouted the island by the most un-Christian means. Snorri wrote, "King Harald sent a warlock to Iceland in altered form, to see what he could learn there, and he set out in the form of a whale."

In this guise he is said to have completely circumnavigated the island, but every time he attempted landfall he was put off by supernatural beings – here a dragon, there a giant bird, a hill-giant taller than the mountains – before he returned to Norway, reporting nothing but sand, deserts, rough surf, all across an ocean so hazardous ships could not cross it. The fact that both Norwegian and Irish ships had been making the crossing for generations rather makes the case that the warlock never actually made the trip himself. Nevertheless, Bluetooth gave up on Iceland.

Around that time an Icelander, Thorvald Kodransson, called *inn Vidforli*, "the Far Traveller," started out as a Viking raider. In Saxony he met a Bishop Fridrik who baptized him. In 981 they both went to Iceland to convert Thorvald's family and anyone else willing to convert. Since Bishop Fridrik did not speak the language, Thorvald did the preaching. Things started out well enough. They built a church and made a few converts, but as usual folk were reluctant to give up the gods of their fathers. Children began to openly make fun of the Christians, two men were killed in religious squabbles, and the church was destroyed. Thorvald and Fridrik were stoned, proclaimed outlaws and driven off the island.*

Iceland being part of Norway, Olaf felt it his duty to bring God to the heathen there. (Contrary to Odd, who only now had the king sail to the Orkneys to convert Jarl Sigurd, Olaf did not yet dare leave his kingdom unattended and conducted his crusade from home, sending missionaries to convert the overseas parts of his realm.) As his evangelist he had chosen one Stefnir Thorgilsson, an Icelander who had converted in Denmark and traveled with Thorvald before joining up with Olaf in England and accompanying him on his conquest of Norway. Making no more progress than Thorvald, Stefnir adopted Olaf's example in his treatment of pagans. He broke up their idols and

---

* Thorvald went on to visit Jerusalem and Constantinople, where Emperor Basil II appointed him as church ambassador to Rus. He ended up in Polotsk, where he built a monastery in honor of St. John the Baptist which stood until the 15th century, and served as its spiritual leader until his death in 1002.

destroyed their temples, provoking a backlash. The Althing passed a law, the *fraendaskomm*, "kin shame," calling for the prosecution of Christians and even their families if they blasphemed against the gods. Stefnir's own family conducted his prosecution. Stefnir returned to Norway, reporting the poor reception God received from the islanders, and that converting Iceland would be no easy thing.

Meanwhile Olaf's Saxon priest Thangbrand had been making the most of his posting to the church on Mostr Island. He was extravagant, a gift-giver whose funds soon dried up, so he acquired a ship and turned to pillaging the heathen for a living. According to Berg, Olaf called him to account: "Your methods have changed for the worse. You undertake plundering raids like a pagan Viking, supporting you and yours by theft and robbery, when you ought to be serving God as his priest. You will certainly receive no further honor from me. You must leave the kingdom."

"I have done wrong," admitted Thangbrand, "yet I would beg you, lord, to show mercy. Assign me some hard duty as a penance, rather than banishing me or driving me out. I would do all that I can gladly, to turn your anger away from me."

Olaf replied, "If you value my friendship, then you will go to Iceland and, God willing, convert all the people there to the true faith. If you succeed, you may hope to receive from me such honor and rank as you enjoyed before, and even more."

"I will go wherever you send me," answered Thangbrand, "and strive to do God's work and yours, but I know not what success I shall achieve."

Like Stefnir before him, Thangbrand made a few initial converts, but soon found the island rising against him. Being a warrior priest, he retaliated, killing one man in a duel, murdering another for libeling him, and killing a third in a fight, and like Stefnir was ultimately forced to flee. Back in Norway he reported, "Other than a few, the people of that nation will certainly never accept the faith."

Icelanders at court who had seen the priest at work disagreed, telling the king, "Thangbrand behaved just as badly there as here. He killed several men. People found that hard to take from a foreigner."

"The king went into a furious rage," wrote Berg, "and instantly convened a thing, summoning all the Icelanders in town or aboard ship. Then he ordered all of them who were heathen to be seized, plundered, maimed, or slain."

Their leaders begged for mercy. One of them, Hjalti Skeggjason, had been converted by Thangbrand, and in fact outlawed for blasphemy for speaking out at the Althing, saying, "I don't wish to bark at the gods, but to me Freyja seems a bitch."

Nevertheless he and his fellow islanders told Olaf, "We Icelanders here are all willing to accept the true faith and undergo baptism, and we will find a way to introduce Christianity to Iceland. There are many powerful Icelanders who have sons here in Norway, and for their sake will greatly help its spread."

The king chose the most prominent of these sons. "I shall hold these hostages until the Christian faith is either instituted by law in Iceland, or else totally rejected." What would become of them in the latter case did not need to be said.

And just to increase the pressure, he initiated a trade war against Iceland, forbidding merchant ships to do business there, refusing Icelandic ships entry into Norwegian ports, and confiscating Icelanders' property. Norway was the island's prime trading partner, and many islanders had kin on the mainland. They had to wonder why their gods weren't protecting them from the Christian menace. Iceland came near to civil war between the religious factions before the matter was submitted to the lawspeaker Thorgeir Thorkelsson. He was pagan, but open to the new faith, and split the difference. The *Islendingabok* records, "Thorgeir proclaimed that everyone in Iceland should be baptized and believe in one God, but the old laws regarding the exposure of children and the eating of horseflesh should stand. People could sacrifice in secret if they desired, but would be punished as minor outlaws if witnesses came forth."

Those pagan provisions later were abolished as well, but history marks the year 1000 as when Iceland converted to the new faith. As for Thangbrand the Saxon, he appears no more in the sagas, and it can be assumed that Olaf was finally through with him.

It was another courtier of Olaf's who, though we have heard from him already, enters Olaf's life in this period. Hallfred Ottarsson had left Iceland after a bad love affair, traveled as a trader, fighting man and poet, and briefly served as court skald to the late Jarl Hakon. He would himself be the subject of a saga, but for now had been one of those Icelanders trying to escape Norway, only for his ship to be driven back to Nidaros. Berg described Hallfred as "tall, strong and manly. He was a little swarthy, and had a thick head of brown hair, and though handsome enough, had an ugly nose. As he matured he was thought to be very whimsical. From early on he was a poet, much given to satire, and was not popular."

According to Snorri, Olaf drafted Hallfred into his service: "You will desire to become Christian and afterward become my follower."

Hallfred said, "I will be baptized on one condition: that you, king, be my godfather. I will accept no one else."

Olaf agreed, and after it was done, said, "Will you now be my follower?"

Hallfred was wary of royal beneficence. "I was once a follower of Jarl Hakon. So I will not enter your service, nor that of any other rulers, unless you promise me that I shall never be judged guilty of anything that will cause you to drive me away."

"Under that arrangement," said the king, "you might get away with much, for there is little you will not do. Stories of your temper are common, which will probably lead to deeds on your part that I cannot possibly tolerate."

Hallfred said, "Then kill me."

"You are a *vandraedaskald*," said Olaf – a troublesome poet – "but you will now be my follower."

"But if I am to be known as the Troublesome Poet, what gift do you give me in honor of the new name?"

Olaf gave him a fine sword. "You will find it troubling as well, for I give you no scabbard for it. You must keep it unsheathed three days and three nights without injuring any man."

Hallfred took good care of the sword, but soon lived up to his nickname. Some men of the king's bodyguard resented him for his new standing. The matter came to blows and Hallfred killed one of them in the royal hall, a capital offense. He threw himself on Olaf's mercy: "I pray you, lord, remember your promise never to cast me off. Do not make yourself an oath-breaker towards me, or we shall part sooner than I would like. Also, there is the matter that you are my godfather."

Olaf relented. "We shall be reconciled, but you are not free of punishment. Do not carry your sword to table, or in church, or on other occasions when men do. At this, you have been forgiven more easily than most."

Berg wrote, "The king appointed his maternal uncles Karlshofud and Jostein to teach Hallfred the Apostle's Creed and the Lord's Prayer." Despite his new faith, Hallfred remained sympathetic to pagans. Ordered by the king to go slay or blind a heathen worshipper, Hallfred took only one of the man's eyes, then stopped on the way home to take an eye from one of his own rivals and pass them off as a set to the king. Olaf was not fooled, but neither did he punish the poet. On the strength of his verse, Hallfred was honored to remain in the king's service. He was said never to blaspheme the old gods, and when other men did, merely chided, "It is not necessary to blame them, if men are unwilling to believe in them." His verse does sometimes betray a certain sense of regret:

> *The religion of the King of Sogn* [fjord, Norway's largest] *forbids sacrifice. We reject the long-worshipped Norns, and the fate they spin. All men have stopped praying to Odin's race. Forced from the children of* [the old Vanir god] *Njord, I pray to Christ.*

Still, it is Hallfred the Troublesome Poet's verse about Olaf's exploits that formed the very basis of the king's sagas. Snorri freely admitted, "It is from Hallfred's verse that we learn and confirm what is told about King Olaf Tryggvason."

Another former protégé of Jarl Hakon soon arrived at Olaf's court. His story didn't make it into Snorri's *Heimskringla*, but Berg must have read it in the anonymous *Faereyinga Saga*, the story of the Faroe Islands, written around AD 1200. He incorporated it into his version of Olaf's saga, in places almost word for word.

Like Olaf, the Faroese Sigmund Brestisson had as a young boy lost his father to murder – had in fact witnessed it – been sold into slavery, traveled east (though in his case, to the Vik and Denmark) and eventually freed. According to the saga, that was right around the time Harald Greycloak was killed and Jarl Hakon took over Norway, so in a few years Sigmund gravitated to the jarl's court and befriended his sons Eirik and Svein. In time they each furnished him with a ship and men, a force that Sigmund soon enlarged into his own Viking fleet. He made a name for himself in raids against Eirik the Victorious in Sweden, in the Orkneys (where Jarl Sigurd the Stout had not yet come to power), and captained a ship for Hakon at the Battle of Hjorungavag. (According to the *Faereyinga Saga* it was Sigmund who cut the hands off Bui the Stout and forced him to jump overboard.) When Sigmund had desired to return to the Faroes and avenge his father's murder, Jarl Hakon had taken him to the temple of Thorgerd Holgabrud and given him the goddess's armlet for luck and protection. It must have worked, for he soon took over the Faroes and ruled there as Jarl Hakon's vassal. It was not unexpected that after Hakon's death King Olaf would summon him to Nidaros. "The message came with a promise," wrote Berg, "that the voyage would bring Sigmund honor. The King would make him chieftain in the Faroes if he became his vassal."

Olaf had heard that, like himself, Sigmund had never worshipped graven images, and hoped that he would accept Christianity for himself and all his people. He pointed out the similarities in their lives to this point, that each had regained their rightful inheritances, and that they should now work together. "I sent for you mostly because I heard much of your valor and deeds," Olaf told him, "and I will gladly be your steadfast friend if you will heed me in affairs that I regard as important."

Sigmund acknowledged having been a loyal follower of Jarl Hakon: "He did me great honor, and I was very happy with my post. He was loyal and a helpful advisor, liberal and agreeable to his friends, although he was harsh and treacherous to his foes. Your beliefs, however, differ greatly." Still, he recognized that there was a new king and a new god in Norway, and was willing to accept both. "I will eagerly follow your counsel and win your friendship. I would not like to worship graven images because I saw long ago that that religion was good for nothing, though I knew nothing better."

"At the King's orders Sigmund and his men were then baptized, and taught holy principles," wrote Berg. "The King then appointed him to rule over all the Faroes, furnishing him with priests to baptize and instruct the people."

Back home Sigmund convened a thing. He told the assembly that Olaf had retained him as his vassal over the islanders, which was welcomed, and that he had become a Christian and that all the Faroese were expected to convert as well, which was not so welcome. The opposition leader was none other than Sigmund's kinsman Thrand of Gata, who had taken part in Sigmund's father's murder and had wanted to kill young Sigmund as well. He said, "We landowners have all agreed not to change our religion for any reason, and we will attack you in the Assembly, and kill you, unless you desist from this, and promise firmly to never again bring this up in these islands."

Outnumbered, Sigmund backed down and bided his time. In the spring he attacked Thrand at his home, took him prisoner and, against his own men's advice, mercifully offered him the choice of baptism or death. Thrand of course chose the former, and was freed on condition that he remained both Christian and loyal to Sigmund and King Olaf.

When Sigmund reported back to Olaf, the king said, "It is too bad that Thrand did not come to see me, and it is a great obstacle to your living out there on the islands that he is not banished, for I believe that there lives one of the very worst men in the North."

Then Olaf saw Sigmund wearing the armlet of Thorgerd Holgabrud. He said, "Let us see the ring," and when Sigmund took it off and handed it to him, "Will you give me this?"

Sigmund said: "Lord, I intend never to part with it."

"I will give you another in exchange, which will be the same size and just as fine."

But Sigmund said, "I'll not part with this one. When Jarl Hakon generously gave me this ring I promised that I would not part with it, and I shall keep that promise, for I found the jarl to be a good man, who always treated me well."

The king reddened. "You may think as much of the ring and Hakon as you like, but it is bad luck and means your death. I know this as surely as I know how you received it and where it came from. I do not wish to own it, but I want to shield my friends from trouble."

With that the matter was dropped, but things had soured between them. Sigmund soon departed for the Faroes for good, and never saw the king again. He retained the armlet of Thorgerd Holgabrud that he had kept from King Olaf, but the king's prophecy bore itself out. Sigmund's kinsman and archfoe Thrand of Gata never gave up their feud. In 1005 he and sixty men assaulted Sigmund's house. To escape, Sigmund was forced to swim the channel to a neighboring island, where he dragged himself onto the beach so exhausted that a local farmer, coveting his gold armband, decapitated him with a wood axe.

By now King Olaf had spread Christianity across half the North Atlantic. By some accounts the opportunity arose to spread it the rest of the way, when a visitor from faraway Greenland arrived at court. According to the saga written about his father Eirik Thorvaldsson, called "the Red" – either for his coloring or for his bloody past as an Icelandic murderer and outlaw – Leif Eiriksson hailed from Brattahlid, modern Qassiarsuk, the settlement his father had founded, at the southern tip of the island his father had discovered. In the warm climate of those days the island's population was well on its way to its peak of some 5,000 sheep and cattle herders, fishermen and seal hunters, all pagan. The *Graenlendinga Saga*, "Saga of the Greenlanders," admits, "Greenland was then still a heathen country."*

Leif, according to the sagas, did not come to Norway seeking religion. He was a country boy in his twenties, wanting to get off

---

* Some historians have asserted that, because the *Graenlendinga Saga* makes no mention of him, Olaf's involvement in its Christianization is an invention of the later Icelandic monks crafting his story. Scholars still debate which saga was earlier, the Greenlanders' or *Eiríks saga rauda*, the "Saga of Erik the Red," which does credit Olaf with bringing God to the island. Whether or not the monks used later information which has since been lost, or made up the story of Leif and Olaf to glorify the king, it is part of his saga, and so recounted here.

the farm to go visit the big city. The Greenlander saga records, "Leif was tall, strong and very impressive. He was shrewd and always mild-mannered."

His first stop was in the Hebrides, where he got the daughter of a local lord pregnant, declined to marry her, and abandoned her to continue on his way. This does not seem to have harmed his reputation. He crossed Pentland Firth and the North Sea to Norway and met King Olaf, who preached the gospel to him much as he did other pagans. Leif was a ready convert, being baptized along with his crew and residing in Nidaros for the winter. But Olaf had more use for a Greenlander in Greenland than in Norway. At one point he asked Leif, "Do you intend to sail to Greenland in the summer?"

Coming from the king, this was probably more a suggestion than a question. "Yes, if you approve."

"I think it would be a wise idea for you to go there on a mission from me, to preach the faith in Greenland."

Leif agreed, but felt it would be no easy task. And that was assuming he even made it back alive. To traverse the North Atlantic in a medieval longship, let alone a cargo *knarr* or even smaller boat, was to challenge fate. Berg asserted, "From Stad in Norway west to Horn in eastern Iceland is seven days' voyage, and to Greenland, from Snaefellsness, the westernmost point of Iceland, is another four days' west across the ocean." That's over a week in a small boat, in frigid northern seas, out of sight of land, completely at the mercy of wind and wave. Eirik the Red's saga records that when his fleet had departed Iceland to colonize Greenland, back in 985 or 986 – the short four-day leg of the crossing – half never made it: "Twenty-five ships sailed…but only fourteen succeeded. Some were driven back, and others lost at sea."

This, of course, was nothing to the king, especially in the service of the Lord. Leif had already made the crossing once; who better to make it again? "Your luck will see you across."

Leif replied, "Only if I have yours too."

History records that Leif indeed became known as "the Lucky." Snorri documented, "Out at sea he rescued the crew of a ship which had been lost, who were clinging to the wreck. He also discovered

Vinland the Good [modern Newfoundland], arrived around harvest time in Greenland, and brought with him a priest and other instructors, with whom he went to Brattahlid to reside with his father Eirik."

He began preaching the faith to the Greenlanders in their remote fjords. Eirik the Red had doubts, but according to the saga Leif's mother Thjodhild was an immediate convert. She had a small church built a short distance from the family farmstead where she and the other new Christians could pray.* On the other hand, after she converted she refused to live with her pagan husband, which did not endear him to the new faith. He thought Leif not so lucky after all. Berg confided, "Eirik said that his good luck in saving the lives of a ship's crew was offset by his bringing the juggler to Greenland." (At the time the sagas were written, *juggler* meant a jester or clown, but also a wizard or sorcerer.) "That is what Eirik called the priest."

With or without Leif's help, Greenland was made Christian, and around the same time as Iceland, in the year 1000. From its struggling presence in Norway five years earlier, King Olaf had spread the word of God completely across the North Atlantic, even to the New World.† The old gods were in full retreat, but according to legend they did not give up easily, and the king's struggles with them elevated his saga into myth.

Odd tells the story of two of the king's retainers who overheard a pack of demons in a cave, sitting around a fire complaining to each other of their suffering at Olaf's hands. They had appeared to him invisibly or in human guise – as beautiful women – seeking to do him harm, but he always found them out and sent them packing. When

---

* Thjodhild's Church – more of a small chapel, sixteen by eight feet, with turf walls four feet thick – was uncovered in 1962, about 200 yards from Eirik's house and hidden from it by the terrain.
† The Vikings did not think of Greenland or even Vinland as part of a new continent, the way southern European explorers would, centuries later. To them the western islands were not a new world, but simply the farthest reaches of theirs.

his men reported this to the king, he said it was all true. "Even so, I do not want you going out again at night because it is asking for trouble to go on such unnecessary trips all alone."

Yet he often left his ships and went into the forest alone at night, his guards oblivious until his return, with dry feet leaving no tracks in the morning dew. After persistent pleading from his third uncle, Thorkell Short Tail, Olaf took him along on one of these midnight sojourns. Years later Thorkell swore that, in a forest glade, Olaf prayed until a bright light shone down on him and two figures appeared, laying hands on his head. On their return to the ships in the morning the king swore him to secrecy, which Thorkell held until years after the king's death.

Even unflattering stories evolved to reflect better on the king. Berg related that once, while sailing in his longship *Serpent*, Olaf spotted a man in a rowboat near the shore. Ordering his men to their oars, he attempted to overhaul him, but the rower could not be caught. The king called, "Stop there, tall one! Don't row away! We only want to speak with you."

The boatman answered, "By your treatment of all our friends, I do not wish to speak with you, nor shall I wait for you…You will never have me in your power." So saying, he overturned his boat and drowned himself.

But Berg also told the story – which may be the same story, so greatly embellished as to become legend – of another man who flagged down the *Serpent* from shore. "He was a young-looking man, tall and handsome, with a red beard."

Once aboard, he immediately belittled Olaf's crew: "You are not worthy to serve so famous a king and so fine a ship. This dragon was better manned when it was Raud the Strong's. He did not require the help of men like me for their strength, but only for entertainment and advice, and compared to me you are a feeble lot."

He was taken aft before the king, who demanded to know who he was. The stranger spoke of olden times, of how the land had once been inhabited by giants until humans came from the east, when the last two giants, both female, lorded over them. "This evil continued until the people called on Redbeard for aid. So I took my hammer and killed both the giants. And from that day, when in need the people have called upon me for aid, O King, until now, when you have so greatly wasted all my friends in a manner that calls for vengeance."

"Having said this," wrote Berg, "he looked over his shoulder at the king, and at the same time, with a scornful smirk, leaped overboard, swift as lightning into the deep, and was not seen again."

By his giant-slaying and hammer, the stranger was no less than Thor himself, who famously hated giants and wielded his hammer Mjolnir against them. But the point of the story – of the treatment of friends and threatened vengeance – was that the old gods would not soon forget the harm Olaf had done them.

The king stood unafraid. "See how boldly the fiend came openly before us in broad daylight," he told his men. "And though devils are bold enough to tempt us, all the same they greatly fear Christians who trust in God and holy baptism."

The gods were not always so obvious in their schemes. All three of the king's biographers tell the story of a visitor to one of the king's feasts. Odd wrote, "When the people took their seats that evening and the drink was prepared and they awaited the king's table to be set up, an old one-eyed man entered the hall. He had a broad hat on his head."

Berg continued, "He came forward to speak to the king, who enjoyed his conversation, for he spoke of all lands, old tales as well as new. The king had many questions, and the stranger had answers for them all." He spoke of the long-dead ruler who had once owned the hall in which they feasted, of how he died in battle and was buried on the grounds. "Many such tales the stranger told of events long past and of olden kings."

The feast went on long into the night, well past when everyone had gone to sleep. Olaf went to bed too, but had the one-eyed man brought to his bedside. His stories went on until the king fell asleep. When he awoke, the stranger was gone, and could not be found. It was revealed, however, that he had gone to the royal stewards and cooks and criticized the meat being prepared for the feast: "Come with me. I will show you good, delicious meat fit for a king."

He led them to two thick, fat sides of beef. The cooks had duly butchered them and mixed them into the day's fare. When he learned this, Olaf realized the visitor's identity.

"Throw this meat into the sea so that no man partakes of it," he ordered. "If a man so much as tastes it, he will suffer a quick death...I think that devil was Odin."

Why a father-god would need to resort to a method as mundane as poison to do away with mortals perhaps in itself demonstrates Odin's impotence against a king chosen by God, but that's beside the point. The moral of the story was that Olaf was too smart to be deceived by the most powerful of pagan gods, that they were well and truly beaten. It's worth repeating because his Christian biographers were willing to give credence to Odin walking the earth. Either they believed the old gods were real, but simply evil, or were including the old tales to demonstrate our hero's triumph over their ancestors' superstitions.

The schemes of the old gods, however, mattered less to Olaf's reign than the schemes of men. For Gudrod Eiriksson, the last surviving son of Eirik Bloodaxe and Gunnhild Mother of Kings, still had designs on the Norwegian throne. "This same Gudrod," wrote Odd, "along with his brother King Harald [Greycloak] and with the schemes of their most evil mother, had betrayed King Tryggvi. He had a large army and sixty ships to see whether the chieftains in Vik wished to do battle with him, or accept him as their king."

XXVII

Kings and Queens

God himself shows in these stories that he aids and rewards men for the good deeds they perform, but that he scatters and brings to nothing the evil plans and cruelties of the wicked, who often perish in the traps they have laid for others.

Berg Sokkason

AD 999–1000

Gudrod did not dare take on Olaf directly, but instead employed the strategy with which the king had overthrown Jarl Hakon. Berg recorded, "Hoping to avoid meeting King Olaf, when he neared Norway he turned south along the coast, then east to the Vik. As soon as he landed he began to plunder everyone and subject them as their king."

Sixty ships full of armed men was no token force, and the people of the Vik put up no fight. Perhaps Gudrod expected them to join in his conquest of Norway, for this was where his first conquest had started all those years ago, after the murder of King Tryggvi. But the Vik was the land of King Olaf's kin, and such an endeavor was not to be undertaken lightly. The king's brothers-in-law, Hyrning and Thorgeir, agreed to accept Gudrod over them, but requested that a thing be convened to gain the approval of the people. To this Gudrod agreed, provided that he and his men were well fed and lodged in the meantime.

Word went out for the people to assemble. Tragically, when Thorgeir arrived he brought terrible news, that his brother Hyrning had suffered a fatal fall from his horse: "My brother is dead, and I and all our men grieve for him. I ask, lord, that you give us permission to bury him honorably. We planned a happy reception for you at our hall, but if you agree to wait, we will convene a second assembly and honor you then."

To this Gudrod also agreed, doubtless wishing to show himself to his new subjects as a kind and merciful king. He went to the feast and got drunk. Meanwhile Hyrning, who had not been killed at all, arrived with the fighting men he had been gathering from across the Vik. They made a night attack on Gudrod's feasting hall, killed the would-be king and all his men, then went to his ships and killed the guards as well. Snorri wrote, "Now all the sons of Eirik [Bloodaxe] and Gunnhild were dead."

"And when King Olaf received word of this," concluded Berg, "he was very happy it had been done, and thanked his brothers-in-law for the daring and bravery they had shown."

Those final months of the First Millennium were the peak of Olaf's reign, as a king and as a man. Even Adam of Bremen recorded that during his reign, "Almighty God showered such good fortune over the land in every way, causing the earth to be fruitful and the climate to be mild, that never before or afterward were known such favorable times."

A king's renown being measured in part by the number and greatness of his ships, Olaf determined to have the most and the best. He already had the *Crane* and the late Raud the Strong's *Serpent*. Now he commissioned what was to be the greatest of all. The master shipbuilder was to be Thorberg, called *Skaffhogg*, "Shave-Stroke."

"But many others worked on it," wrote the scribes, "felling the trees, shaping the planks, forging the nails, bringing up the timber, and whatever else was needed. Everything was done with elaborate detail. The ship was both long and broad, with high sides, and large timbers."* To judge by later descriptions of the ship in action, it even

---

* The Viking Ship Museum in Denmark, in recently reconstructing a Norse longship, required 7,000 nails totaling 880 pounds of iron. In the old days, when Scandinavian blacksmiths got their supply from iron-oxidizing bacteria in bogs and swamps, that would have required the smelting of thirty tons of raw ore.

featured raised castles, fighting platforms at the bow and stern to allow archers to shoot down on enemies. These were common features on later medieval ships, and dated as far back as Roman times; Viking *knarrs* had raised cargo decks fore and aft as early as the 8th century, but fighting decks were not typical of low, sleek longships. Either Olaf was ahead of his time, or his medieval biographers were crediting him as such.

Unfortunately, while the ship was under construction, Thorberg was called away home. On his return, he and the king looked over the near-finished hull, which everyone agreed was larger and finer than any before it: a true *drakkar*, "dragon-ship." Olaf went home pleased.

By the next morning, the ship had been vandalized. Somebody had gone along the gunwales with a wood axe. Olaf raged, "I will pay a gold mark to him who kills the man who has so marred my ship and caused me harm and disgrace."

"Lord, I will tell you who has done it." Thorberg said. "I have done it."

"Why would you do this?" Olaf demanded.

"Because it appeared misshapen to me, and I saw it would be better if the gunwales were lowered," said Thorberg. "If you wish me to repair it, I will make it the most beautiful and splendid of all."

"You shall make amends by making this ship as good as it was before, if not better," commanded Olaf. "Your life depends on it."

Thorberg took a plane to one rail and smoothed out his cuts, which lowered the gunwale. The king and his court agreed it was a vast improvement. He bade Thorberg finish the other side too, and paid him well for his work.

"It was a dragon ship, like the *Ormr* which the king had brought from Halogaland, but this one was much larger and more ostentatious in every way," recorded Snorri. "He called it *Ormr inn langi* ["Long Serpent"], and the other one *Ormr inn skammi* ["Short Serpent"].* The *Long Serpent* had thirty-four rowing benches [for sixty-eight rowers]. Judging by the 9th-century Viking burial ship unearthed at Gokstad,

---

* Odd claimed the *Short Serpent* was a separate ship from Raud's *Serpent*, built after the *Crane*, but Raud's *Serpent* and the *Short Serpent* do not appear together in the sagas, leading historians to consider them one and the same.

Norway in 1880 – seventy-eight feet long with thirty-two rowers – the *Long Serpent* would have measured almost 150 feet in length. "The figurehead and stern post were gilded. The sides were as high as those on ocean-going ships. This was the finest vessel in Norway, and the most expensive."

Kings were not judged merely by their ships, and if scribes are to be believed, Olaf I excelled by every measure of the day. By his biographers' exorbitant praise a kind of medieval cult of personality was established. "Of all eminent Northmen, King Olaf was the most athletic," wrote Berg. "Many stories are written of his great strength and agility."

Snorri told us, "While his men were rowing on *Long Serpent*, King Olaf was known to walk on the oars over the side, and to juggle three daggers so one was always in the air, every time catching the handle. He fought just as well with either hand and could throw two spears at the same time."

Odd likewise attested, "When he fought under his flags, he caught flying spears and arrows with both left and right hands and threw them back with either hand. He was the quickest and most agile of all men, the boldest and most steadfast in battle."

Not just in ships, and not just in battle was he said to be the greatest of Norwegian kings. Berg insisted, "King Olaf was jovial and the most cheerful of men, moderate and deferential, generous and benevolent, most intuitive in many things, and much given to appearances and regalia. In battle he surpassed everyone; he was the harshest of men when angered, and a great harrier of his foes…In this way he became loved by his friends, and feared by his enemies."

"If one searched the entire earth, one would not find in the north his equal in valor and accomplishments," agreed Odd. "In many ways his luck far exceeded that of others."

It must be said that the popular regard for the king was not universal. After the murder of Jarnskegg of Yrjar outside the temple of Thor, Olaf had attempted to reconcile with the dead man's kin by agreeing to marry his daughter Gudrun and make her his queen. We might recall his rumored dalliance with her, which may have been at the root of all the trouble, but in any case, upon her father's death it seems the girl had no love lost for the king. "After the wedding feast," wrote Berg, "when they were together and Gudrun thought the King was asleep, she tried to stab him to death."

Perhaps recalling Grand Prince Vladimir's Polotskan victim-wife, Gorislava, and her similar attempt, Olaf slept with one eye open. Snorri wrote, "He took the knife from her and got out of bed and called his men, telling them what happened. Gudrun then collected her clothes and all her servants who had come with her. They went their own way, and never again did Gudrun bed King Olaf."

But Olaf was not the only Viking ruler with woman trouble.

In Wendland, old King Burislav was feeling cheated. He had made a deal with Sigvaldi the Jomsviking to marry Forkbeard's sister Thyri, daughter of Harald Bluetooth, and for her had given up as wives his daughter Astrid to Sigvaldi and Gunnhild to Forkbeard. But Thyri had not been party to the agreement. Unlike her brother, she was a dedicated Christian, and utterly refused to be wed to an old Wendish pagan.

Years passed, and Burislav had come to realize Forkbeard had reneged on the deal. He summoned Sigvaldi and demanded that he go to Denmark and fetch his bride. Sigvaldi and Forkbeard had been on the outs ever since their mutual defeat at Hjorungavag, but they were still brothers-in-law, and the message may have passed from one wife to another. As Sigvaldi's wife Astrid doubtless well knew, Forkbeard's wife Gunnhild resented the fact that Thyri remained living on lands that had been promised to her as her dower, while under the agreement Gunnhild's former lands in Wendland were Thyri's as well. Sigvaldi also made the none-too-subtle point that the marriage agreement had sealed the peace between Denmark and Wendland, and unless Svein wished for war he should see to it that his sister did her royal duty. "King Svein relented," wrote Odd, "and sent messengers to Thyri saying that he wished to meet with her. When she arrived, he had ships and crews prepared and sent Thyri to Wendland."

"Thyri wept inconsolably and went very much against her will," wrote Snorri. "And when she and the jarl [Sigvaldi] reached Wendland, King Burislav held his wedding and married Queen Thyri."

That was hardly the end of the story. Thyri had followed her king's command, but she had no intention of doing anything more. She neither ate nor drank at the wedding feast, nor for the next week. Odd says eleven days, at the end of which Burislav admitted defeat. "I see now that you would rather die than be my queen, so I will give you men and ships and let you go." (Snorri and Berg claimed she simply ran away at night.) Knowing her brother would send her straight back to her husband, she and her party soon made for Norway.

"King Olaf gave them hearty welcome, and they lived there in good cheer," wrote Berg. "Thyri told the King of her troubles, and asked him for help, begging him for asylum in his kingdom. Thyri was a well-spoken woman, and her talk greatly pleased the king. She was also beautiful and courteous."

Snorri continued, "He saw she was a good-looking woman, and it occurred to him that she would make a good match, so he turned the conversation to that, and asked her to marry him."

Considering her circumstances, Thyri had little choice. On the other hand, she could consider herself lucky to be married to such a powerful king, and a good Christian at that. She and Olaf were wed at a great celebratory feast. Olaf, on the high seat with his chieftains and retainers, sent a man to the queen, seated with her ladies: "Lady, my lord has sent me to inquire whether he should give you a bridal gift fit for a maiden, or one becoming a woman that has been married?"

She answered, "Go tell your lord to ask himself which would be the better gift, had I been his wife for seven days as I was another's, and then let him choose what is most honorable for both of us." Olaf gave her an ornamented cloak of fine furs. She, in turn and in time, gave him a son. Odd recorded, "King Olaf and Queen Thyri had an exceedingly handsome son, whom they baptized Harald after her father [Bluetooth]. He was most loved by the king and queen, and their subjects well expected he would rule the realm after his father."

Olaf must have felt that he had accomplished all that had been prophesied for him. What more could there be?

Sometime in this interim, Svein Forkbeard's wife Gunnhild had died. In casting about for a new queen Svein hit upon the same conclusion as Olaf had, that Sigrid the Haughty of Sweden would make quite the catch, not to mention form a familial alliance with her son, King Olaf Skotkonung. A proposal was made and duly accepted, for although baptized as a child at the orders of Holy Roman Emperor Otto II (and bearing his name), Svein was well known for having forsaken Christianity and, unlike Olaf of Norway, did not insist on Sigrid's adherence to it. Like Gunnhild, Sigrid would bear him children, but the sources are unclear about which wife was the mother of sons Cnut and Harald and daughters Gytha and Estrid. It seems certain that Gytha at least had been born to Gunnhild, as she could have been at most fourteen or fifteen when Svein found her a husband: Jarl Hakon's son, Eirik.

After the death of Jarl Hakon, his sons Eirik and Svein had fled to Sweden. Little is said in the sagas of Svein's doings there, but Eirik set himself up as an independent Viking raider. "Many who fled the country because of King Olaf Tryggvason went to Jarl Eirik," records the *Heimskringla*, "and the jarl decided to prepare ships and go a-viking, to acquire wealth for him and his people."

At first he had stayed local, haunting the waters around Gotland, plundering the Wendish coast and returning to winter in Sweden. The next year he crossed the Baltic and Gulf of Finland and sailed up the Neva River to enter Lake Ladoga and the mouth of the Volkhov River. There, Aldeigiuburg [modern Staraya Ladoga] had been old Rurik's first capital in Rus, and though Vikings had raided it before it was still the gateway to the lands of Grand Prince Vladimir. Eirik laid siege to the fortress until it fell, then raided deeper into Vladimir's lands. It had been several years before he returned to Sweden, plundering Adalsysla and Eysysla in Eistland along the way, a man of substance and proven ability, a jarl by right of primogeniture from his late father. When he, too, sought a wife worthy of him, he went to Denmark, where he courted Forkbeard's daughter Gytha. "His proposal was accepted, and Jarl Eirik married Gytha," wrote Snorri, "and a year later [probably 997] they had a son, named Hakon."

Around this same time Eirik's brother Svein wed Holmfrid, the daughter of Swedish King Skotkonung. The brothers could have lived out their lives in peace, comfort and happiness, but not while Olaf of Norway lived. Odd wrote, "They bore great hostility and hatred toward King Olaf due to their father's murder, because of which they could not live in their homeland. They desired to take both King Olaf's land and his life."

For Sigrid the Haughty in Denmark the pieces were all coming together. With these two Norwegian exiles and her new Danish husband available to do her bidding, it was not long before she got around to addressing old slights. Snorri admitted, "Sigrid was King Olaf Tryggvason's greatest foe."

Olaf must have had a sense of his old sins coming back to haunt him when God called away his son Harald. Odd lamented, "The people loved him, but he lived barely a year before he departed this world for eternal glory."

At this point in the sagas, Queen Thyri, who so far has been willing to defy her royal brother Forkbeard and her royal husband Burislav, and has been unafraid to take her life into her own hands to escape from Wendland to Norway, undergoes a rather stark personality change. Snorri wrote, "Queen Thyri often protested to King Olaf, weeping plaintively, that she who had so much property in Wendland had nothing in Norway suitable for a queen."

These Wendish properties were the lands that had been Queen Gunnhild's and, along with other gifts and money, were supposed to have become Thyri's as her bride-price. She told Olaf, "You can see, my lord, what great properties I had in Wendland, but no one has had the authority or will to demand compensation for my loss. Many days I weep to think how shamefully I have been deprived of what was mine."

Surely this mourning of material loss was just her way of coping with personal loss, but anyone who has lost a child through stillbirth or otherwise might recognize the symptoms of postpartum depression or simple overwhelming grief. The queen could not be consoled. Snorri continued, "Sometimes she movingly begged the king to retrieve her money, saying that King Burislav was such a great friend of King Olaf that once they met, he would grant Olaf everything asked."

Olaf's friends and courtiers did their best to talk him out of that. It was true enough that Burislav had once been Olaf's father-in-law, but that was almost fifteen years in the past. He owed Olaf nothing, and surely owed Thyri nothing either. It was not common practice in those days, what with the difficulty of travel and the risk of rebellion in their absence, for kings to leave their realms and show up on fellow kings' doorsteps. For Olaf to suddenly appear and throw himself on Burislav's hospitality might itself cause offense. Moreover, visiting Wendland meant transiting the Oresund, the narrow channel from the Kattegat into the Baltic between Denmark and Sweden, practically within bowshot of Svein Forkbeard's royal hall, and would require most if not all of the Norwegian fleet to sail as Olaf's escort.

Before it came to that, Olaf sought to cure his wife's sadness, but in a most hapless, husbandly way. Berg wrote, "It is said that as King Olaf was walking the street on Palm Sunday, he came across a man carrying a number of angelica plants, extraordinarily large for that time of the year." Besides being eaten as a sweet treat, angelica, in Old Norse called *hvonn*, was thought to ward off sickness and infection with its bittersweet smell. Its stalks, growing up to nine feet tall, were made into flutes and toys, but also into charms against evil spirits and burned as incense. "The King took a stalk home to his hall, where he found Queen Thyri in her sitting-room, weeping. He said, 'See this fine stalk of angelica I give you.'"

She slapped it out of his hand. "Harald Gormsson was more generous, and did not fear to go abroad and get his property the way you now fear. This he proved when he came here to Norway and laid waste most of it, taking all the tribute and taxes. Yet you do not dare to sail Danish waters because of my brother King Svein."

Now, it was a bit of a stretch to claim old Bluetooth had conquered Norway, when at most he had merely enabled the sons of Bloodaxe and then Jarl Hakon to do the bloody work. And Olaf had sailed Danish waters often enough in his old Viking days in complete defiance of Bluetooth or Forkbeard or whoever ruled there, though without dragging the entire Norwegian fleet along with him. And as far as Thryi's lost property in Wendland, well, she had only herself to blame for that, having abandoned the husband who had gladly bestowed it on her.

But the sagas make clear that even a king of the Vikings found it impossible to argue with a weeping woman, especially when she challenged his manhood. Olaf rose to his feet and swore, "I will never travel in fear of your brother King Svein, and if we ever meet, he shall be the one to yield."

Snorri recorded, "King Olaf soon called a town assembly to inform everyone that he was taking an army abroad that summer, and he wanted each district to contribute ships and men, stating how many ships he wants from there in the fjord. Then he sent messengers north and south along the coast and inland to call out troops."

They were going to Wendland.*

First Astrid with Sigvaldi, then Thyri with Olaf, and now Sigrid the Haughty with Forkbeard; one wonders if the Vikings would ever have gone anywhere or gotten anything done, had their wives not hectored them into it.

According to the scribes, Sigrid took care to nag her husband not in private, but before an audience. "Lord, how long will you tolerate the humiliation you have suffered?"

Forkbeard replied, "What humiliation, lady, am I suffering with no remedy?"

"It was humiliating and shameful that you were not esteemed enough to be consulted about the marriage of your sister Thyri to King Olaf of Norway, and you have done nothing about it since."

---

* It should be noted that many modern historians consider this motivation for Olaf to go to Wendland to be implausible, a later, rather romantic invention, when Olaf may simply have been set on establishing an alliance with the Wends against the Danes.

"How is that humiliating me? Is Olaf Tryggvason not the most distinguished of all kings? Could I marry my sister to a better king if I chose? Even if my realm were at its height, she would be married with sufficient honor."

Sigrid did not deny that. "But he has shamed you more than that," she said. "Without your leave, he has taken over your dependency, land that is rightfully your inheritance, and now holds the kingdom of Norway, without paying you tax or tribute. Your ancestors would not have suffered such slights, one after another, but you act as though you are unaware of any disgrace."

In truth, Berg maintained – and as Sigrid doubtless knew full well – Forkbeard did hold it against Olaf for conquering Norway, which before had been Jarl Hakon's and technically a vassal state of Denmark, though it had been many years since he had paid any Danes tribute. But Forkbeard said, "I believe this injury and humiliation are things I must accept. That is also wise, since King Olaf is powerful. My strength is not equal to his, and I cannot avenge this insult."

Sigrid wagered all. "If that is how you want it, you will be a petty king all your days. But if you wish to be the kind of king your ancestors were, you will not endure this shame and degradation. I speak truly, that if you desire to be such a nobody that you will not dare avenge such an offense, I will divorce you and remain here no longer."

Evidently Forkbeard had grown no more adept at recognizing being manipulated by a woman since his sister-in-law Astrid, Sigvaldi's wife, had masterminded his previous failed invasion of Norway. "With King Olaf being so powerful, how should I seek vengeance?"

Now she had him. "You can overcome him with guile, in your own good time. I will see to it that you need not attack King Olaf in Norway, nor will you lack an army to lead against him, if you are brave enough."

"Advise me how I should bring about his downfall."

(Berg confided, "Queen Sigrid often had this kind of tongue in her mouth.") "That is easily done. I have learned that King Olaf prepares to depart Norway with a small naval force, intending to sail south to Wendland come summer." The various scribes recorded slight differences in her schemes, but taken together the plot becomes clear.*

> Let my son King Olaf send word to Norway that Olaf Tryggvason should join him in proclaiming God's word and popularize Christianity in his realm. For this cause, he will go at whatever cost to preach God's name. We can then easily lure him into an ambush. If Jarl Eirik joins with the Danes and Swedes, and you three still fear to face him, then send word south to Jarl Sigvaldi in Wendland. You have rightfully outlawed him from your realm. Let him buy peace with you, regaining his possessions and lands in Denmark, by visiting Olaf Tryggvason and tricking him. Let him either draw Olaf's army away from him, or bring Olaf unsuspecting within your reach, for if the king has only a small force, it will be no great task for you with yours to take his life. If King Olaf Tryggvason departs Norway and transits the Oresund unimpeded, with no interference from you, he will not suspect trickery. But, King Svein, you will show how petty you are if you let him return in peace, unhindered.

Sigvaldi jumped at the chance to regain the Danish properties and titles Svein had confiscated after his defeat at the Battle of Hjorungavag. As an excuse to visit Norway, he first went to Sweden, and divulged Sigrid's plan to her son King Olaf. Skotkonung, who also blamed the Norwegian Olaf for his mother's treatment, readily agreed to go along with the plot: "I have a great shame to avenge."

With that assurance, Sigvaldi now sailed back around the southern tip of Sweden and up through the Kattegat to Norway. He arrived at Nidaros in time for Christmas and spent the holiday there, passing along the Swedish king's "message."

To convert Sweden as he had Norway was an opportunity beyond even Olaf's wildest dreams. He was going to Wendland anyway, which

---

* Again, many historians consider this version of events to be a romantic fiction. Adam of Bremen and Saxo Grammaticus, writing from the Danish viewpoint, depict Olaf as pre-emptively attacking the alliance of Danes and Swedes. Forkbeard and Skotkonung may simply have considered Norwegian incursion into the Baltic as an infringement on their territory, and teamed up to put a stop to it.

was halfway around Scandinavia to the Swedish capital at Sigtuna; how fitting it would be to continue on up the coast and further God's work! He told Sigvaldi he would do whatever he could to accomplish it. He would assemble a fleet that winter, and in the spring sail to meet the Swedish king at Brenneyjar, an archipelago near Goteborg, modern Gothenburg, down on Sweden's western coast, back then the frontier between Norway and Sweden. They would lay plans for the conversion of Sweden. Olaf would stop off in Wendland along the way, regain his wife's property, then rendezvous with his counterpart in Sigtuna.

Sigvaldi returned to Denmark, reporting to Sigrid and Forkbeard that Olaf had taken the bait and would come south in the spring. They upheld their end of the bargain, making peace with the jarl and giving back his ancestral lands.

In early spring Forkbeard sent men to Sweden to inform Skotkonung and Jarl Eirik of King Olaf's upcoming trip to Wendland. He proposed that they both should bring their armies south to Denmark that summer. Once Olaf had passed, they could in essence blockade the entire Baltic, waiting to catch him on his return trip, cut him off from home and destroy him in a titanic sea battle.

Sigrid's plan was coming to fruition.

XXVIII

The Trap

The king of the Swedes and Jarl Eirik sailed to meet the king of the Danes, and all together they had an immense force.

Snorri Sturluson

AD 1000

"Spring came to a close as King Olaf was fitting out his ships at Nidaros," wrote Berg, "He decided to steer the *Long Serpent* himself, as it was the biggest and best warship in Norway." He manned it with a select crew, no man older than sixty, and none younger than twenty, including his personal housecarls and bodyguard, with the rest hand-picked. "It was commonly said that the crew chosen for the *Serpent* bettered all others in appearance, strength, and valor, just as the *Long Serpent* bettered other ships."

Queen Thyri of course came aboard, as well as Olaf's last unwed sister Ingebjorg. His half-brother Thorkell Beaknose was given command of the *Short Serpent*; his uncles Thorkell and Jostein captained the *Crane*. His brothers-in-law Hyrning and Thorgeir each brought a warship of their own. Snorri credited the fleet with sixty ships, the same as that with which Gudrun Eiriksson had of late tried to invade Norway, and doubtless with many of the same ships; Odd, twice as many. Either way, it was a formidable fleet that would dare Forkbeard's ire, passing through the Oresund, and Olaf would pick up more ships and men along the way.

However, the king's skald, Hallfred the Troublesome Poet, begged off the trip. He still pined for his lost love in Iceland, and was determined to go settle the matter one way or the other.

THE TRAP

Berg wrote, "When ready to go, he went to see the king to take leave, and it was plain how deeply their parting affected Hallfred." Olaf told him:

> I have found you to be a fine fellow, and knowing your temperament, I fully imagine the day will come when you wish to be at my side again rather than in Iceland or anywhere else. As we may not meet again, I will give you a velvet cloak, a helmet, and an armlet weighing six ounces. Keep these treasures always, in remembrance of your service to me. Have them buried with you at church, or put in the coffin with you if you are buried at sea.

The loss of Hallfred was softened for the king when the fleet arrived in the lands of his brother-in-law Erling Skjalgsson. Besides a large ship of thirty benches, Erling offered a great feast to welcome the king to his barony. One of the invitees was Ragnvald Ulfsson, Jarl of Vastergotland or Ostergotland down in southern Sweden. Over the winter Ragnvald had made a proposal of marriage to Olaf's sister Ingebjorg. Recall that Olaf's eldest sister Astrid had belatedly been married to Erling, right there a few years prior; Ingebjorg was almost as old, a year or so older than Olaf, nigh-on forty. She had once been married, but her husband had been killed and she had long been in mourning; one saga claimed she loved an Icelander, one of Olaf's hostages, and was heartbroken when he chose to return home. Olaf had arranged other marriages for her, but she had not accepted, telling him, "When you lost your wife it grieved you so badly that you wept loudly enough for your grief to be heard all across Norway."*

Still, time heals all wounds, and a Swedish jarl's interest in Ingebjorg was not unwelcome to her. Olaf consented to the marriage, on the condition that Ragnvald converted to Christianity, and have his subjects do so as well. The jarl agreed. He and his party were baptized on the spot, and Erling's feast became a wedding banquet. "Now King Olaf had given away all his sisters in marriage," wrote Berg.

---

* Whether this was in reference to Geira of Wendland or Gytha of Dublin is not specified in the sagas; the passage does not appear in all of them.

"The jarl and Ingebjorg prepared to journey home, and King Olaf supplied them with clergy to Christianize the Gotland folk, and teach them the true faith. The king and jarl separated on happy terms."

Besides a happy ending for Ingebjorg (and the closure of one of the last loose ends in the saga), it was a good head start on helping King Olaf Skotkonung bring the people of Sweden to God, and Olaf must have been in good spirits as the fleet set sail. Before continuing south, however, they doubled back a short distance across the wide-gaping mouth of the Boknafjord, to Mostr, the island where Olaf had begun his conquest of Norway. There was someone there he wished to see.

"On this island there was an old blind man," wrote Berg, "who was said to have great foresight and powers of prophecy."

Given his experience with it, it's understandable that Olaf would have put great stock in prophesy. This was not necessarily a pagan attribute – the Bible is full of prophets and augury – but some of his less Nordic biographers would fault him for it. Saxo Grammaticus wrote that Olaf "was so given to believing auspices and omens that, even after being baptized and learning the beginnings of religious faith, neither pious examples nor devout authorities could prevent him from heeding augurs' warnings or seeking wizards to know the future. Thus he was not truly holy, but merely aped the words, belying his professed faith with superstition.'"

And Adam of Bremen recorded, "Some say that Olaf had been a Christian, others that he had forsaken Christianity [though Adam is the only source to make that claim]. All, however, confirm that he was skilled in divination, an observer of the lots, and had placed all his hope in the prognostication of birds. Because of all this he was called by the nickname Craccaben."*

On landing the king took a handful of men and proceeded ashore to the prophet's hut, where they passed themselves off as traveling merchants.

According to Odd, the old man asked, "What can you tell me of the king's fleet and troops?"

---

* To the Norse the *Krake*, crow, symbolized wisdom; *ben*, leg bones, would have been used in cleromancy, divination by the casting of lots, as practiced by Hebrews in the Bible and Germanic peoples from Roman times well into the Viking Age.

They replied that the king and his entire fleet were anchored offshore. At this the prophet lamented, "Alas, great misfortune will befall us now that our king readies to leave us. We will lose four of our country's treasures that are much greater and worthier than anything else we have had."

> First is King Olaf Tryggvason, who all agree has never been equaled. To lose such a chieftain will be a great loss, for no king ruled over all the people so honorably and so hopefully as King Olaf. Second I deem Queen Thyri, for everyone declares that Norway has never had a queen of such wisdom and kindness. The third is King Olaf's ship the *Long Serpent*, which all agree is the greatest ship ever built in Norway. Fourth is the king's dog Vigi, naturally more intelligent and cleverer than any other dog in the land. I fear that we are not fated with the luck to have such precious things here, for it often happens that the greater things are, the sooner one loses them.

That was certainly not the prophesy Olaf wished to hear, but according to the chroniclers he did not contest it. He simply told his men, "Let us return to our ships."

But as they passed on their way the old man was said to mutter: "It happens to everyone who grows old that not only do we lose our sight, but our minds also dim. I did not know I was talking to the king himself. If I had known, I would not have been so talkative."

There was no reason to expect trouble. Olaf and King Burislav were not enemies. He was not going to Wendland on a mission of war, and if he had been, he had the entire Norwegian fleet to help him fight it.[*] Neither were he and Olaf Skotkonung enemies, but when Olaf arrived at the appointed meeting place on the Brenneyjar archipelago the Swedish king was not there. The Norwegians waited two weeks, after which the promised rendezvous had still not taken

---

[*] Adam of Bremen and the Norwegian synoptic histories tell this setup differently. Adam claimed that Olaf was incensed by the alliance of Olaf of Sweden with Svein Forkbeard, and sailed to attack Denmark directly. The *Agrip af Noregskonungasogum* and *Historia Norwegiae* agree, but claim the majority of the Norwegian fleet did not gather at all, requiring Olaf to go to Wendland for support.

place. Olaf could not wait forever. It was now well into summer, and he had that pressing business in Wendland. It was decided to move on. The Norwegian fleet put back out to sea, bearing south for the Oresund. The king could hardly guess that the Swedish Olaf was hosting a meeting of a quite different kind. Odd wrote, "King Olaf suspected nothing of the betrayal and trickery being organized against him."

Even as Sigvaldi had departed for Norway, Jarl Eirik had sailed for Sweden to discuss plans with its king Olaf Skotkonung. (Eirik's brother Svein, not much of a raider, would fight under Skotkonung's command, but little is heard of him in this affair.) He reported that Svein of Denmark would muster thirty ships full of warriors. To this King Olaf agreed to match him with thirty Swedish ships. Jarl Eirik would contribute his pirate raiding fleet, twenty-two ships. Eirik's otherwise unknown skald Halldor, called *okristni*, "the Unchristian," recorded, "The prince-striker, eager for battle, summoned a large troop from Sweden and steered south to battle. Every freeborn warrior wished to accompany Eirik."

Berg wrote, "When the king of the Swedes and Jarl Eirik were ready for the voyage, and had gathered together a large Swedish naval force, they sailed south to Denmark, where they arrived after King Olaf had already passed through, headed eastward."

Had Olaf's fleet been challenged by the Danish on his way to Wendland, or met the Swedes and jarls coming the other way, or even met them all together, history would certainly have changed. The Norwegians would most probably have defeated the enemy piecemeal, or even the combined fleets at the same time. But, having threaded the Oresund channel without incident or even sighting enemy ships, Olaf arrived safely in his old Wendish lands, oblivious to the danger. Odd wrote, "In Wendland he met many old friends and received an honored welcome from them. He spent much of the summer there. King Burislav's daughter Astrid, wife of Jarl Sigvaldi and sister of Geira the Wise, King Olaf's late queen, came to see him, and Dixin as well."

Regardless of Queen Thyri's history with King Burislav, her dowry proved to be no impediment between him and King Olaf. Astrid acted as go-between to get the whole matter settled amicably. Burislav agreed to convert Thyri's lands into an equal value in movable goods, which would have been not only silver and gold but native leather and furs, grain and salt, along with imported Byzantine silks and spices, glass beads, Frankish and Saxon wine, silver and jewels.

Business concluded, it must have been like old times for Olaf in Wendland. Fifteen years since Geira's passing; time enough for that pain to have healed. (The recent loss of his infant son Harald would still have been a fresh wound, but then between stillbirths and infant mortality the odds were against every Scandinavian newborn and, Thyri's grief notwithstanding, parents would have necessarily hardened their hearts to the possibility of losing them.) How much had changed since! Olaf of Norway was a far greater king than he had ever been in Wendland. And Christian, too. We can assume the Wends, having pushed the Saxons and their German god farther west in the recent Great Slavic Revolt, still held to their pagan deities. Surely the matter of religion came up, but the scribes do not mention Olaf making any attempt to undertake or, God forbid, force Burislav's and Astrid's conversion, let alone the Wends as a people. It appeared he was going to have a hard enough time converting Sweden as he had pledged to do; besides, to berate his hosts would have spoiled the reunion. Odd wrote, "King Olaf resided there a long time."

In Denmark Forkbeard, Olaf of Sweden and Jarl Eirik were losing their nerve. At its narrowest the Oresund is just two and a half miles across. The Swedish and Danish coasts can be seen from each other, and the passage of the Norwegian fleet would have been easily visible from either. Forkbeard and possibly Olaf Skotkonung surely had men posted to count the number of ships, and whatever the total, it was enough to intimidate them. Odd recorded, "When they all heard that King Olaf Tryggvason had reached Wendland with a great army, they were very worried and believed he would be hard to overcome."

Victory would require deceit. For that, Forkbeard called once again on the Jomsviking Jarl Sigvaldi.

He had evidently not returned to Jomsborg, and was probably reacquainting himself with his Danish domains when he got the summons. Forkbeard instructed him to return to Wendland, learn King Olaf's plans and lure him into their trap.

A trickster's work is never done. Snorri wrote, "Jarl Sigvaldi went on his mission to Wendland, went to Jomsborg and then on to meet King Olaf Tryggvason [presumably in Burislav's city of Stargard, forty miles inland]. They met as friends. The jarl worked his way in close to the king."

Just in time. A story had been spreading in Wendland that a trap was waiting for Olaf on his return to Norway. Sigvaldi told the king, "This baseless rumor is nothing but a monstrous lie. Your fleet is so big and well-equipped that King Svein and his Danes would not dare seek battle with you. However, if you are concerned about a fight, let my force escort you, for it is always helpful for Jomsvikings to accompany kings. I will give you eleven well-crewed ships."

Berg added, "Earl Sigvaldi, shrewd and sagacious, meddled in the king's plans and greatly delayed his departure through one pretext or another. King Olaf's force, anxious to go home, grew impatient with the long delay, as they were quite ready to go, and the wind was favorable."

Olaf's Norwegians had not spent the time in Wendland that he had. Queen Thyri had her dowry, and the conversion of the Swedes had been put on hold. The mission was complete. It was time to go home. When Olaf learned of the discontent in the ranks, he assembled and addressed them: "It is understandable that you resent being delayed here so long, and so we will permit those men who wish to leave to go home, but I will show my gratitude to those who stay, though it will have to be later."

A few of the men thought it their duty to remain at the king's side however long he wished, in case danger threatened. But there was no obvious threat, and the vast majority elected to go. Odd wrote, "The next day, when the king and his retainers arose, they found the fleet breaking up, most of the men having emptied their tents and raised

THE TRAP

sail. Only eleven ships remained. But King Olaf was not yet ready to leave and stayed behind a while."

The number of ships remaining after most of his fleet had already sailed is open to dispute. Most sources claim just the eleven, but some seventy-one, though these probably included Sigvaldi's and most of those which had already sailed. It's known that Olaf kept the biggest – the *Crane*, the *Short Serpent* and the largest of all, his *drakkar*, the *Long Serpent* – with him. It was not until the first week of September that he finally made preparations for his return to Norway.

As the last of the fleet prepared to sail, Jarl Sigvaldi came alongside and advised the king to follow in his wake: "I am well acquainted with the channels between the islands, and your large ships will need deep water."

Olaf had been threading the Oder River channels to and from Jomsborg since years before Sigvaldi got there. The jarl's motive was clearly to keep Olaf behind him, in order to lead him into the trap. Yet the chronicles don't record the king objecting to, or suspecting, anything.

Sigvaldi's wife knew better. According to the sagas, although not accusing her husband by name, Astrid had a premonition there was treachery ahead, and warned Olaf to beware of a trap.

The king replied, "I cannot let mere rumors turn me from my path if they are not true in fact. Good Sigvaldi would surely reveal any plots against me. And even if you convinced me it was true, I would not avoid battle with my enemies, for it is in God's power to bestow the kingdom on whom he wills."

"I ask you, then, to accept whatever help I can give, in the event you need to retire from the battle." She volunteered to send a few ships of her own along behind the Norwegian fleet.

Olaf said, "I will accept your help, if it is needed."

If the old chroniclers giving him voice are to be believed, the king sounds blindly oblivious to Sigvaldi's treachery. But Odd, for one, believed God had planned it that way: "King Olaf believed Sigvaldi because Almighty God allowed him to be tricked and betrayed with hatred and lies, so that he lost his kingdom against his will. Betrayed by his enemies, he no longer ruled his earthly realm, so he could become a man of heaven rather than of the earth."

As king he will shine with bright glory and become a savior to many men of the northern regions, old Malusha had foretold. *You will be a great king and do great things, and convert many people to faith and baptism, and so do good for yourself and many others*, the Isles of Scilly hermit had prophesied. But the blind man at Mostr had predicted Norway would not see its King Olaf again.

None of them had promised him a long life.

XXIX

The Battle of Svolder

There was little wind, but it was favourable.
The king ordered the fleet to cast off and the trumpet to signal departure.
Men raised their sails and, the small ships sailing faster,
they put out into the open sea.

Snorri Sturluson

MONDAY, SEPTEMBER 9, 1000

Theodoric wrote, "This battle was fought aside the island called Svolder, which lies near Slavia, what we in our mother tongue call Wendland." And the *Fagrskinna* calls it "an island off the Wendish coast...This island is called Svolder." The whereabouts of this island is the subject of much contention among historians, as no such island exists today. The narrow Oresund would be a natural location for Forkbeard and Skotkonung's seagoing trap – the *Agrip* and *Historia Norwegia* locate it off the island of *Sjoland*, Zealand – with perhaps the islets of Ven and Saltholm or even the far side of the channel used to hide their ships. One Danish annal goes so far as to place the battle in the inlet of the Schlei, the narrow fjord leading from the Baltic to Hedeby, far to the west of the Wendland–Oresund route. However, the sagas refer to the Wendish coast and that Forkbeard, Skotkonung and Jarl Eirik would be able to watch the Norwegian ships pass while they themselves remained hidden. Many historians favor the island of Rugen, about fifty miles northwest of Jomsborg off Germany's Pomeranian coast, with a number of bays, lagoons and inlets that could hide the combined fleets while the Norwegians passed. However, there might be an even better candidate.

A little over eight miles southeast of Rugen and five miles off the German coast lies the tiny island of Greifswalder Oie. Less than a mile long, a third across, and just 130 acres in area, other than the 1850s lighthouse and infrastructure left over from World War II (when the island was a launch site for V-2 rockets), the *oie*, islet – the farthest from the mainland German Baltic coast – is today a nature reserve. Over half of it is forested in beech, hornbeam, oak and elm, its floor carpeted with flowering Eurasian garlic. It was named for the nearest mainland town, Grypswold, modern Greifswald, "Griffin's Forest." (The town as such wasn't founded until about 1200, but legend evidently had the griffin inhabiting the woods long before that, where an imperial trade route passed near a natural salt evaporation pond – a medieval resource – and it's not hard to see Old Norse *Svolder* as short for Old German *Grypswolder*.) September is when the Baltic subspecies of the grey seal comes to give birth; every offshore boulder becomes a sunning spot for a 400- or 500-pound pinniped, and the rocky shore is littered with helpless, white-coated pups, prey for white-tailed sea eagles, great black-backed gulls and, a thousand years ago, hungry Vikings.

Greifswalder Oie's name does not often come up in discussions of the possible sites of the Battle of Svolder, but it does come up, and with good reason. It is only about thirty miles from the outlets of the Oder. Its southwest tip now boasts a small harbor protected by rocky breakwaters, but back then its mile-long western shore offered plenty of room to land the ships of the Danish-Swedish fleet, completely hidden from the east, while the higher northeastern tip, with its sixty-foot chalk cliffs, would have given Forkbeard, Skotkonung and Jarl Eirik the vantage point from which the sagas report they spotted the approach of King Olaf's fleet. "These chieftains had an invincible army," relates the *Fagrskinna*, "lying in a harbor on the side of the island toward the mainland. King Olaf's ships passed on the far side. From the island, the leaders watched the fleet approach from the east."

Local sunrise in early September being about 6.30am, and assuming the Norwegians did not attempt the Oder channel in the dark and departed at sunup, at a longship's unhurried seven and a half knots they would have arrived off Greifswalder Oie in some three and a half hours, around midmorning.* Their approach out of the sun, however, would have been visible long before that, particularly with the smaller, faster ships – and Sigvaldi's – separating themselves ahead and the rest of the fleet stringing out in trail. The *Heimskringla* reported, "The weather was fine, with bright sunshine."

As with so much of Olaf's saga, his biographers differ in their descriptions of the battle. Events are disordered or even omitted from one version to the next. Any attempt to assemble one story out of them is bound to disagree here and there with all of them, but Odd, Snorri and Berg all recounted the conversation of the kings watching from the clifftop as they spotted a big dragon ship among the rest. Forkbeard and Skotkonung both said, "That is a large ship and very beautiful. It must be the *Long Serpent*."

"That is not the *Long Serpent*," Jarl Eirik told them. "Though that one is well built, you will see the *Serpent* is much larger and grander."

Sure enough, an even larger ship soon appeared. Forkbeard said, "Olaf Tryggvason must be fearful, for he has not sailed with the dragon figurehead on his ship."

But Jarl Eirik said, "That is not the king's ship either, for I recognize the colored stripes on its sail. That is Erling Skjalgsson's. Let him pass, for it is better for us that ship is far from Olaf, well-equipped as it is."

Olaf Skotkonung grumbled, "We should not be too cautious to fight King Olaf, even if he has great ships. People would think it a shameful disgrace for us to remain here with an enormous army while he passed by for all to see."

"Lord, let that ship pass," said Eirik. "I assure you that King Olaf Tryggvason has not sailed by. You will have a chance to do battle with him today. There are many chieftains in his fleet, and I expect they will give us a hard enough fight before it is over."

---

* To the mouth of the Oresund is about 125 miles, over eleven and a half hours, meaning they would have arrived shortly before sunset. As the chroniclers do not describe the battle as a night fight, that's another factor favoring Greifswalder Oie, or at the outer limit the island of Rugen, as the island of Svolder.

At this point Jarl Sigvaldi, having sailed ahead, arrived at the island. Berg reported, "As soon as Earl Sigvaldi neared the island of Svolder, he was met by the crew of a skiff, who confirmed that the Danish and Swedish host lay in the harbor before him. The Jarl took in sail and had his ships slowly rowed under shelter of the island."

Where Sigvaldi was, King Olaf would not be far behind. When the kings saw three large vessels approaching, Forkbeard ordered his men to go to their ships, certain that the largest was the *Long Serpent*.

Jarl Eirik cautioned, "They have many great and regal vessels besides the *Long Serpent*. Let us wait a bit."

There was muttering among the assembled Vikings: "Jarl Eirik dares not fight and avenge his father. What a shame that it will be said that we lay here with such a fleet, while the King of Norway, with only a handful of men, escaped to sea as we watched."

Eirik bristled, "Though you Danes and Swedes may question my courage, I expect you will be just as weary of the fighting before sundown this evening."

And just before the conspirators could fall to fighting among themselves, the tail end of the Norwegian fleet hove into sight: the *Crane* and the *Short Serpent*. The last of these ships, and the largest – a *drakkar* larger than any the Vikings had ever seen – glittered and gleamed in the morning sun, its prow bearing a gilt dragon figurehead.

"Stand up now," said Eirik, "for we no longer need argue whether this is the *Long Serpent*. Now you will meet with King Olaf Tryggvason. This magnificent ship suits him, for he is as much superior to other kings as it is superior to other ships."

Some of the Vikings were taken aback by the sheer size of this floating fortress. Forkbeard, however, arose boasting, "The *Long Serpent* shall bear me high this evening when I captain it."

But as he and his men turned down the hill toward their ships, Jarl Eirik, a true Norwegian, was heard to remark, "Even if King Olaf had no bigger ship than that, King Svein would never win it from him with an army of mere Danes."

With the enemy fleet hidden behind the island, there was every likelihood the Norwegians, under full sail, would simply have breezed past and continued on their way – as indeed most of them already had – requiring the conspirators to mount a stern chase. That might have worked, leaving the *Long Serpent*, big but slow, to be caught all alone, from behind. There was a risk, though, that it would gain too much of a lead before the conspirators could come out in pursuit. Somebody had to slow Olaf down. Jarl Sigvaldi took his longship out to the fleet, raising a white shield in signal.

Commanding the *Crane*, Olaf's uncle Thorkell Short Tail hove to and called out, asking why the jarl had stopped. Sigvaldi replied that he wished to wait for King Olaf's arrival: "I believe there to be a hostile fleet ahead."

Sigvaldi either wished to catch the king and all his kinsmen together, or was betraying both sides to see which one came out on top. He advised Thorkell to shorten sail and heave to in the lee of the island, out of the wind, and wait for Olaf to come up. He and Thorkell lay adrift off the island as Olaf's half-brother Thorkell Beaknose came up in the *Short Serpent*. On heeding the warning, he too lowered sail to await the king. When, in the *Long Serpent*, Olaf saw their ships lying offshore with lowered sail, he realized something wasn't right, and came in among them. "King Olaf demanded to know why they were not under sail," wrote Odd. "They explained the situation and urged him to flee."

"I will not," said the king. "I would rather fight. Let God see to my life. It is no true king who runs from his enemies in terror."

"Then," wrote Berg, "the whole hostile fleet rowed out from behind the shelter of the island, the chiefs delighted to see King Olaf had fallen into their trap."

The *Fagrskinna* relates, "King Olaf and his men saw they were betrayed. All around them the sea was crowded with warships, while King Olaf had only a small force."

Now that most of his fleet was out of the fight, and not counting Jarl Sigvaldi's ships, Olaf is said to have commanded eleven ships at Svolder; the attackers, at least seventy, perhaps twice that.

There was still time to avoid a fight. Aboard the *Long Serpent* Olaf's uncle Thorkell Short Tail said, "Lord, the foe is too numerous to be fought. Let us raise sail and follow our fleet out to sea. We can easily do it while our enemies prepare for battle. It is not thought cowardly of any man to act prudently for himself and his people."

But for a Viking to avoid danger was to be seen as *argr*, unmanly, a *niding* without honor. Olaf ordered, "Bind the ships together, draw your swords and prepare for battle. Men of mine must not think of flight."

"Hallfred testified to these words," wrote Odd.

As noted, Hallfred the Troublesome Poet was in Iceland at the time of the battle, but spoke to many of the survivors afterward in composing his verses on the life of King Olaf. He recorded, "One must mention the speech with which the king reportedly addressed the warriors at the battle. He asked his men not to think of escape. This ruler's forceful words live on."

The Battle of Svolder is a turning point not only in our story, but in the history of the Vikings, as it involved warriors of all three Viking homelands, Norway, Denmark and Sweden. (Though according to Saxo and Adam, writing from the Danish viewpoint, the Swedes took little or no part.) Still, even taking the Norwegian accounts at face value, Olaf does not always come off well. The battle should never have happened, when the trap laid for him might so easily have been evaded. A good king should not have run from a fight, but nor should a good king have risked disaster. By letting most of his fleet run out ahead of him, halfway to the Oresund, Olaf had practically invited his enemies to cut him off with only a fraction of his force available to fight. By the time the lead Norwegian ships got turned around and came back to the rescue – if they even learned there was a battle behind them – it would be too late.

The first thing to admit is, it could simply have been a fatal blunder. Olaf is remembered as a great king, but in retrospect he was not a great military commander. In Russia he fought at the command of Grand Prince Vladimir. In Wendland he is said to have overcome several walled towns on Queen Geira's behalf, but that called for no great strategic genius. The Viking victory at Maldon was not a result of superior tactics, but of guile and sheer numbers. His successes around the Irish Sea and even in England after Maldon were those of a typical Viking raider, hitting defenseless villages fast and hard and being gone before enemy armies could arrive. He conquered Norway with hardly a fight, which may have had the most effect on his military thinking, assuring him that God was on his side. That certainty had to be a big reason why, though he had the opportunity, Olaf did not flee the trap at Svolder. We are left to believe either he had fallen for Jarl Sigvaldi's lies and did not expect battle, or he expected battle but did not fear it since God would see him through to victory, or he fully expected battle, and his own death, and simply did not seek to avoid it.

There is, however, a certain degree of fatalism here, like worshippers of Odin needing to die in battle to reach Valhalla, or Jesus in the garden of Gethsemane willing to die on the cross in order to carry out God's will. Martyrdom requires death. It's very likely that Olaf Tryggvason, having fulfilled the prophesies of his life, went into the Battle of Svolder believing even defeat, even death, would mean final victory.

"King Olaf ordered his eleven ships to be laid side by side," recorded Berg. "The king's ship was the center, with the *Short Serpent* to one side and the *Crane* to the other, and the remainder placed next to them, four on either side."

With these ships all lashed together the Norwegians formed a fortress on the water, with the huge *Long Serpent* a kind of high ground at the center, its bow and stern extending out beyond the others like bastions. "Lay the big ship more in front," commanded Olaf. "My place in this army is not behind all my men, furthest to the rear when battle begins."

The king's standard-bearer, Ulf *inn Raudi*, "the Red," would be defending the high forecastle. It would be more or less safe from direct assault, but a big target for arrows and spears. He said, "The *Serpent* extends beyond the other ships by as much as it is bigger and longer. There will be hard fighting in its prow."

"I ordered the *Serpent* built longer than other ships so it would stretch more boldly beyond them in battle, and be easily recognized in a fight or under sail," said Olaf. "But I did not know that I had a deck hand both red and fearful."

"While defending the stern, O King, do not show your back before I in defending the prow." That was bold talk to a king. Olaf had his bow in hand, and nocked an arrow in Ulf's direction, but Ulf said, "Not at me, Lord, but shoot at your foes, where it is needed more.

What I win in the fight, I win for you. It may be by evening you will not have men to spare."

That was true enough. Saving his anger for the enemy, Olaf went to the traditional king's post on the quarterdeck in the ship's high stern, from which to direct the battle. He carried a gilt shield and wore a helmet inlaid with gold, with a red surcoat over his mail byrnie or hauberk. With him, and similarly dressed, stood his *stallari* – his marshal, his military commander – Kolbjorn, "Black Bear." The *Historia* records of the *Long Serpent*, "It had room for 160 oarsmen if rowers occupied all the half-bench spaces together, and in the battle all of them are said to have worn coats of mail. There were also forty clerics in the thirty half-bench spaces in the stern, but not being educated in war, they prayed harder than they fought."

In this last moment before battle commenced, one of the little Wendish ships that had followed the *Long Serpent* out from Jomsborg was seen to row up beneath its stern where stood the king. "A man came aboard and spoke to King Olaf in an unknown language," recorded Odd. "The king replied likewise, so that the Norwegians did not understand."

"After they had talked a bit, the little ship rowed close to shore, and the crew dropped anchor," reported Berg. "When the king's men asked who the strangers were that had been speaking to him, he replied, 'They are our Wendish friends.'"

(This cryptic little passage did not make it into Snorri's account, but Berg took Odd's word for it. It made for a better story.)

The two fleets deployed for combat. Olaf's fleet was so small, and the enemy's so large, that they could not all attack at once; there simply was no room for all their ships to get at the Norwegians. According to the sagas, the chieftains had drawn lots to determine who would lead the attack. The first chance had fallen to Forkbeard, then Skotkonung, and lastly, if necessary, Jarl Eirik. Each would keep whatever ships he took from the Norwegian fleet. (Having done his part by luring King Olaf into the trap, Jarl Sigvaldi is said to have stood off with his ships and taken no part in the fighting.) As for Norway itself, Snorri wrote, "It was agreed by the rulers, King Svein, King Olaf and Jarl Eirik, that if they brought King Olaf Tryggvason down each would get a third of Norway, and whichever one boarded the *Long Serpent* first should have all the booty captured on it, and each of them should keep the ships he himself disabled."

"Now the kings' forces split up," wrote Odd. "The Danish army went to one side, the Swedish army to the other, and Jarl Eirik with his army to a third."

Most of the scribes agree that Forkbeard attacked first. Seeing his ships approach, Olaf inquired, "Which is the chief whose banner is nearest?" Told it was King Svein, he scoffed, "We do not fear those cowards. Danes are no braver than wild goats. They have never triumphed over Norwegians, and will no more conquer us today than they have in the past."

On hearing this, Queen Thyri is said to have wept, knowing either her husband or her brother would meet defeat and likely death by nightfall. Olaf sent her below: "There is no cause to weep, for today I will retrieve the dowry your brother owes you."

As the distance closed, arrows began arching over the water between the ships, and then spears and javelins. "From the big ships in the king's formation there was no shortage of missiles," recorded Odd. "They inflicted deadly wounds on the Danes, some of whom were killed."

Berg wrote: "King Svein's men maneuvered their boats as closely as they could against both sides of the *Long Serpent*, which stretched out past King Olaf's other ships." The bow and stern of the great Norwegian *drakkar* towered like fortresses over the Danish boats. "As the Norwegians' bulwarks were much higher, their weapons had the advantage of striking from above."

On the flanks the ships were more evenly matched, with the smaller Norwegian boats forming salients that Forkbeard's fleet could surround. The nearest Danes bound themselves fast to the Norwegians and clambered over the gunwales with swords and shields to get at the enemy. The battle front extended the length of the outermost Norwegian ships, where blades threshed limbs and lives. Skotkonung's Swedes and Jarl Eirik's ships stood off at a distance, but within bowshot, launching barrages of arrows into the center of the Norwegian formation. From behind their shield walls, Olaf and his housecarls popped up to fire back. The air was filled with a crisscrossing rain of deadly points. The warriors' chain mail over layered, quilted, stiffened cloth and leather could blunt arrow strikes to some extent, but everywhere decks became cluttered with wounded and dead men. "The battle grew most fierce, and many were killed," wrote Berg. "All the men on the *Serpent*'s bow, within reach of the foe, fought hand to hand, while King Olaf himself and those in the stern shot arrows and threw daggers, slaying as many Danes as they could, and some they wounded."

"This battle was very savage and deadly," recorded the *Fagrskinna*. "The Danes suffered most because they had closed with the Norwegians. They could not stand fast, but sailed out of range, acting as Olaf Tryggvason predicted, without honor."

Berg wrote of Olaf's men, "They then cleared all the Danish ships which managed to grapple, and King Svein and those of his crews who could, escaped to other ships where, wounded and exhausted, they withdrew out of range."

Those Norwegians who had survived the Danish attack on the outlying boats now cut them loose and abandoned them. "It is said that when the Danes withdrew, King Olaf's men climbed from the smaller ships onto the larger," reported Odd. "The crews of the larger ships welcomed them aboard."

They got no respite. Another wave of enemy boats was already closing in. Olaf said, "Which chief is that whose standards fly there to the right?" Advised it was Olaf of Sweden, the king told his men, "The Swedes will think it easier and more pleasant to sit at home making sacrifices than to board the *Long Serpent* today against your weapons. I don't think we need fear these horse-eaters."

Again the enemy ships came up under the *Long Serpent*'s bow. "Now a very murderous struggle developed between the like-named kings," recorded Odd.

"The fiercest and sharpest of battles resumed," agreed Berg. "A deafening clamor arose as men urged one another on with loud shouts, and weapon clashed on weapon. King Olaf defended himself bravely, his men supporting him like heroes."

The Norwegians were already battle-weary, and the Swedes fresh, but the height of the big ship's upraised bow and stern gave the defenders the advantage. Men hacked and stabbed and fought and died underneath the great gilded dragon-head like sacrifices to the old gods, and as Christian kings the two Olafs must have been gladdened to see so many willing to give their lives for their God as well.

Around the periphery of the Norwegian fleet the fighting was just as relentless, and there the Swedes, like the Danes, whittled Olaf's warriors down a little more, the Norwegians unable to rotate fresh ships and crews into the battle. Still, the *Serpents* and the *Crane* lay undefeated at the center. "Once again Norwegian king's men fled from the smaller ships to board the *Long Serpent*, seeking to escape death there because it was so much longer and higher in the sides than other ships," wrote Odd. "That made it a good fighting platform, like a fort. There were now so many warriors on the *Long Serpent* that able-bodied men could hardly strike a blow for all the crowding."

Meanwhile, Odd recorded, eighteen of the Swedish ships, over half his fleet, had their crews slaughtered until they were useless and adrift. "The Swedes lost many of their men as well as their biggest ships, and most of the survivors were wounded," attested Berg. Skotkonung decided it was better to retreat than attempt to board the *Long Serpent*, and commanded his oarsmen to back their ships to safety, "having added nothing to his reputation, and glad to escape the battle with his life."

Forkbeard, Skotkonung and Jarl Eirik now stood off to regroup. The kings were both beaten, but the jarl had so far been in reserve and was eager to attack. His was the smallest force of the three, but the kings agreed to provide him some of their men, on the condition that if victorious he would keep the *Long Serpent* and rule over two-thirds of Norway, but pay both of them tribute as their mutual vassal. This was agreed.

Eirik's ship was *Jarnbardin*, Iron-Prow, the same as he had sailed at the Battle of Hjorungavag, the one with the figurehead of Thor on its metal-clad stem. "It was a big ship, exceptionally well armored," conceded Odd. "Bow and stern were both strongly reinforced with iron and sharp spikes." Some historians take this to mean it was equipped with a ram, which was certainly not a standard Viking weapon. In Odd's telling Eirik sailed as though it did, setting a collision course with the *Long Serpent*. Seeing its approach, Olaf asked who was making such an unorthodox attack.

His men said, "Lord, we think that is Jarl Eirik Hakonarson and the *Iron-Prow*."

Olaf said, "We may expect the sharpest conflict with these men, for they are Norwegians like us and have often seen bloody swords and many battles. They will also think it fit to fight us, and so it is. He is not holding a slow course toward us, and is doubtless eager to avenge his father."

If Eirik did indeed try a ramming attack, it was ineffectual. The *Long Serpent* was tied up between the *Crane* and *Short Serpent*, with only its bow and stern, the strongest parts, exposed. Even a head-on impact would likely have glanced off. Odd attested that the *Serpent* took damage in the collision, but not enough to sink it. "The jarl advanced boldly against the *Serpent* and would have taken it if possible, but King Olaf and his men defended themselves well and with indescribable bravery."

Berg, on the other hand, had Jarl Eirik, like the Danes and Swedes before him, assaulting the smaller ships out on the sides of the Norwegian formation, which he may have done after his initial strike failed: "He attacked the outermost of King Olaf Tryggvason's ships to one side of the *Long Serpent*."

The Icelandic and Norwegian writers praised Jarl Eirik for doing what the Danes and Swedes had not. Snorri wrote:

> Jarl Eirik laid *Iron-Prow* alongside the furthest of King Olaf's ships, stripped it and at once cut its cables, then attacked the one next to it, and fought until that was stripped. Then his men jumped off the smaller ships, up onto the bigger ships, and the jarl cut each from its cables the moment it was cleared. The Danes and Swedes moved into range all around King Olaf's ships, but Jarl Eirik always lay alongside them and fought hand-to-hand. As men fell on his ships, Danes and Swedes took their place.

(Berg, typical Icelander, called them "Danish and Swedish leeches who had been lazing, unfatigued and unwounded.")

"On the *Serpent*," wrote Odd, "many men had been wounded by projectiles or axes or stones. Not many had died yet, but all were weary and at the end of their strength." King Olaf is said to have stood on the quarterdeck, hurling spears with both hands, catching those aimed at him and throwing them back. His brother-in-law Hyrning stood at his side, and young Einar Eindridesson stood amidships firing arrows into the attackers. Einar was a descendant of the jarls of Lade, which made him a distant kinsman of the jarls Eirik and Svein, but he had cast his lot with King Olaf, and even though he was only eighteen he had won his place among the *Serpent*'s crew by being the strongest bowman.

"Finally, all King Olaf's ships had been captured but the *Long Serpent*," wrote Snorri. "All his men who were still able to fight had come aboard it."

Yet Eirik and his remaining men could not take the Norwegian flagship. Its gunwales, even as lowered by Thorberg the shipwright, stood too high to climb while the defenders hacked away with their swords and stabbed down with their spears. The jarl ordered his ships back to shore to offload the wounded and take on fresh fighting men.

Seeing the jarl's retreat, Olaf cried to his men, "What? Have you hurled the jarl back off the *Serpent*? A heroic deed, as to be expected. He will never defeat us as long as he bears Thor on his ship's prow."

While there was a pause in the action Olaf had the damaged *Short Serpent* and *Crane* cut away from aside the *Long Serpent*, ordering his uncle Thorkell to take the wounded aboard the *Crane* out of harm's way. "Because of this royal order," wrote Odd, "Thorkell succeeded in escaping the battle."

The Norwegians were down to the last and greatest of their warriors. There was Ulf the Red, the king's brothers-in-law Hyrning and Thorgeir, his marshal Kolbjorn, Einar Eindridesson and a few more. While there was still a chance, and given how much was at stake, they again asked their liege to flee the battle. "It is not for me," Olaf answered, "and I cannot believe they will take the *Serpent* as long as so many valiant champions defend it."

And once more the Wendish boat put out from shore to arrive under the *Serpent*'s stern and inquire if the king wished to escape, or whether the Wends should board and fight alongside him, even to the death. Olaf replied, "It will not help for you to board this ship, but if you go back where you were before, you might still be of assistance."

Meanwhile Jarl Eirik felt victory slipping away. He told the surviving fighters, "It will be an eternal shame to us, and to the Danish and Swedish kings, each and every time there is mention of King Olaf Tryggvason, if we cannot defeat him. I have never witnessed such a disgrace, considering that he has one ship and we have a numberless army."

The kings and the jarl talked each other up, reassuring each other they would conquer in the end. Eirik had the dead and wounded taken off *Iron-Prow* and brought aboard fresh Swedes and Danes. In case that was not enough, he consulted Jarl Sigvaldi's brother, the wise Thorkell *inn Havi*, "the Tall." "I have often fought in battle, but I have never fought braver or more spirited warriors than King Olaf and his men, nor seen a ship as hard to take as the *Long Serpent*. Thorkell, if you are as wise as people say, think of some way to overcome the *Serpent*."

A true Jomsviking, mercenary to the end, Thorkell had no ideas to tell until enticed with a payment of gold and silver. Then, Odd admitted, "In return he came up with a clever and ingenious stratagem."

He advised Eirik to erect a kind of siege tower on *Iron-Prow*, then use it to swing heavy beams over onto the *Serpent*, causing her to list that way until her rails were low enough to climb. That sounds entirely too elaborate and farfetched to be true – Snorri omitted it – but also sounds like a tale that over the centuries had outgrown its origins, which might have been far more realistic: to drop wooden planks or beams across from one ship to another as gangways, allowing the jarl's men to run up and over onto the *Serpent*'s deck.* Their weight on the *Serpent*'s rails would certainly have given the ship a list, if the damage from *Iron-Prow*'s ram had not. Spare planks from some of the defeated, damaged longships could have been hoisted or propped lengthwise up against the *Iron-Prow*'s mast, ready to be tipped down onto Olaf's ship.

And just to be sure, Eirik sought the higher power that so far had assisted King Olaf. He had heard the king's taunt about *Iron-Prow*'s figurehead of Thor. Now he had it taken down and broken up, raising a holy cross in its stead and vowing to accept holy baptism if God granted him victory.

---

* The tactic had been in use at least as far back as the Romans, who dropped such boarding ramps from their triremes onto opposing Carthaginian galleys in the First Punic War in order to board and fight land battles at sea.

When Olaf saw Eirik coming out to renew the fight, he mused, "Thor is gone from *Iron-Prow*, and the holy cross put in his place. The Lord Jesus would presumably rather have two kings than one."

The jarl had just five ships remaining. One would think he would attempt another ramming, but the scribes do not claim so; lightly built Viking longships were too flimsy for ramming, and *Iron-Prow* may have taken damage as well on its first attempt. In any case, Eirik is said to have come up alongside the *Long Serpent*, the side bared by the departure of the *Crane*. The two longships scraped hulls. Grappling irons flew. Battle resumed.

"There was such a heavy rain of weapons on the *Long Serpent* that hardly any cover could be found," wrote Berg, "spears and arrows flying thick because enemy warships were attacking the *Serpent* from all sides."

"This battle was so hard-fought that it was a sight to behold," declared Odd, "not just because of the attack but mostly because of the defense. Eventually the *Serpent* was surrounded on all sides, but its crew defended it so well that they had no regard for their lives, leaping over the gunwales with their weapons as though fighting on shore."

Jarl Eirik ordered that the beams or planks be dropped from the *Iron-Prow* onto the *Serpent*. Even with the gangways, there was hard fighting; Snorri wrote the jarl and his men needed three attempts to board the king's ship. Berg declared, "The *Serpent*, it is said, would never have been taken except by this tactic advised by Thorkell the Tall."

"Men fell first amidship, where the rails were lowest," records the *Fagrskinna*, "while forward around the prow and to the stern, in front of the raised decking, men held out longer."

Snorri added, "But because so many men had fallen on the *Serpent*, in many places the gunwales were undefended, and here and there the jarl's men began to board. The men still defending the *Serpent* made their way aft on the ship to the king's position."

Young Einar Eindridesson spotted Jarl Eirik and targeted him with his bow. The arrow just missed the jarl's head. Eirik was about to ask where that came from when another passed between his arm and his body. "I will not wait for a third," he said, and having spotted Einar, told one of his own archers to shoot him. Just as Einar raised his bow Eirik's man let fly, and hit it. The powerful bow broke in two with such a loud crack that King Olaf looked around and – in probably the most famous scene of the battle – demanded, "What just broke so loudly?"

Einar answered, "Norway, O King, from your hand."

"Find no such great meaning as that," snapped the king. "My realm does not depend on your bow, for it is in God's hand. Take mine, and shoot."

But when Einar drew the king's bow he could pull it back past the length of the arrow. "Too weak, the royal bow is too weak!" He threw it back and resorted to sword and shield.

"By this time many of the jarl's men had boarded the *Serpent*, as many as the ship could hold," wrote Berg, "and the jarl's ships lay about on all sides. And as the *Serpent*'s defenders were fewer compared to the great number of their foes, many of the king's champions, though both strong and valiant, soon fell."

"Finally," wrote Theodoric, "because the enemy could constantly relieve each other and replace wounded men with fresh, the king's army was not so much vanquished as worn down. His foes, however, by no means won a clean victory, for every one of their bravest warriors either fell in the battle or was badly wounded."

It's said Olaf was down to his last eight men, though as with everything else about the battle, the scribes disagree on which eight. His kinsmen Hyrning and Thorgeir were both dead, as was Ulf the Red. Einar Eindridesson was still alive, and Olaf's half-brother Thorkell Beaknose as well, and even his uncle Sigurd Karlshofud. Kolbjorn the king's marshal still stood at the king's side, their shields bristling with enemy arrows. Olaf chided them all, "I see that you are taking many wounds and some of you are dying on the deck, but your enemies still stand, even though they must wield their weapons overhead."

Kolbjorn said, "Not so strange, lord, that the swords are dull. They have taken many blows today, and many have been broken for nothing."

Olaf threw open a sea-chest full of fresh, sharp swords and passed them out in preparation for their last stand. As he did so blood was seen dripping down his right arm from under his mail shirt. No one knew when or where the king had been wounded, and there was no time to ask. The end of the battle came when Olaf spotted Jarl Eirik and, using both hands, threw three spears in succession at him, but missed him with all three.

"Never up to now have I missed a man like that," said the king. "Great good luck is on the jarl's side. God now wishes him to have both the kingdom and the land."

These are said to have been his last words at the Battle of Svolder. The *Long Serpent* was good as taken. Jarl Eirik, known for mercy, would surely grant the survivors quarter; for their sake Olaf surely thought of surrender. After his treatment of Norwegian pagans, however, he himself could expect little more than similar punishment from a son of pagan Jarl Hakon: drawn-out, torturous death. And they would surely try to take him, though wounded and bleeding, alive.

Unless, like Bui the Stout at the Battle of Hjorungavag, he refused to give them the satisfaction.

"Of the events which then occurred," admitted Berg, "there are several versions." Though muddled and confused in the retellings, it has passed into the legend of the Battle of Svolder.

Odd Snorrason recorded that as Jarl Eirik and his warriors advanced into the *Long Serpent*'s stern to finish it, a bright light shone down, and when it faded the king had vanished. Everyone thought he must have jumped overboard, but did not see him in the water. The men he left behind, including Einar and Kolbjorn, all jumped in after him.

Snorri, as was his way, disregarded the heavenly light and had it that Olaf and Kolbjorn leaped over the sides at the same time, on opposite sides of the ship. Some of Eirik's men tried to grab the king, but he held his shield overhead to prevent it.

Einar Eindridesson reported seeing blood running down Olaf's cheek from under his helmet. As they were awaiting Jarl Eirik's final attack, Einar was hit in the side of the head by a thrown rock and briefly knocked unconscious. When he came to, the king had vanished. Einar jumped the rail.

Berg quoted Kolbjorn, who admitted to a touch of fear at seeing the *Serpent* literally filled with enemy warriors. Looking back, he saw the king was gone, and jumped over the side himself. In the water he recalled seeing the king's shield underneath him and a man, presumably the king, swimming beneath it, but that was the last he saw.

Odd even retold the enemy viewpoint, that of Skuli Thorsteinsson, who was one of Jarl Eirik's fighters but later became a skald of some repute. He recalled pressing forward with Eirik at the end, but the *Long Serpent*'s deck was cluttered and jumbled with bodies, according to him "the dead so thick underfoot, that it was difficult to advance." He remembered seeing King Olaf on the quarterdeck, but knelt to roll some of the bodies out of the way, and when he looked up again the king was gone.

The other Norwegians were fished out of the sea by Jarl Eirik's men, but King Olaf Tryggvason was not found. Having jumped into the water in full armor, the victors claimed, he could only have sunk to the bottom of the sea and drowned.

Odd summed up the Battle of Svolder thus:

This battle is the most celebrated ever fought in the North, firstly because of how hard the *Serpent* was defended and secondly because of how a ship that no man thought could be taken while still afloat was won. But most of all it became famous because of the king whose ship it was, the most famous man wherever Norse is spoken: King Olaf.

EPILOGUE

THE SAGA OF KING OLAF

There is told a wonderful tale,
How the King stripped off his mail,
Like leaves of the brown sea-kale,
As he swam beneath the main;

But the young grew old and grey,
And never, by night or by day,
In his kingdom of Norroway
Was King Olaf seen again!

Longfellow, "The Saga of King Olaf"

"People say Olaf Tryggvason's life was divided into three parts," wrote Odd. "During the first he was enslaved, greatly oppressed and disgraced. In the second his life shone with great brilliance and good deeds. The third was a time of honor and glory, and a great wish to make reparations for many wrongs."

More than a thousand years after his passing, Olaf Tryggvason is reckoned one of the most important rulers in Viking history. More than any other, and though he did not always do it by loving and peaceable means, it was he who was responsible for bringing Norway to God. Eirik Bloodaxe may have died a Christian, but not until he lived in England, after being evicted by Hakon the Good. Hakon was definitely Christian, but he failed to convince his subjects to convert, and abandoned Norway to the old gods. Harald Greycloak and his brothers were also Christian, and tore down the heathen idols, but ruled so abominably that their subjects held God responsible for their misery. And of course, Jarl Hakon was a diehard pagan. So Olaf may not have been the first Christian king of Norway, but he was the first king of a Christian Norway. He founded the country's first church, at Moster in Vestland. He destroyed pagan idols wherever he found them. He built up a collection of fishing shacks and traders' huts into the town that would become Trondheim, Norway's capital for 300 years. And he did all this in the course of a very short reign: just five years, AD 995–1000, accomplishing more for God than did Hakon the Good in his reign of twenty-seven years (934–961) or even Harald Greycloak in nine (961–c. 970).

One of Olaf's earliest biographers, the 11th-century Icelandic priest and historian Saemund Sigfusson, "the Wise," attested, "King Olaf forcefully stopped robbery and theft and killing, and gave the people just laws and a true religion."

None of Olaf's main biographers, Odd, Snorri or Berg, were at pains to make Olaf out to be a saint. Or a monster. They describe his torture of Eyvind Kinnrifa, the burning of Eyvind Kelda's sorcerers, the drowning of Kelda himself, without judgment. Such acts were mere necessity, the deaths of nonbelievers being of no consequence. Berg conceded of Olaf, "He had great success in spreading Christianity and in other matters, both at home and abroad, because some did his bidding out of friendship and kindness, and others because of fear."

And yet, as is the eternal way with kingdoms and empires, when the founder passes on the realm swiftly goes to pieces. Odd, Snorri and Berg documented the dissolution of King Olaf's reign as something like the moral of the story. As Odd put it, "Because the labor was hard and the time short to gather the sheep into the flock of Almighty God, it was as if God's work was left unfinished."

Just as he had done with Vagn Akesson and his Jomsvikings after the Battle of Hjorungavag, Jarl Eirik granted his prisoners quarter. He could afford to be magnanimous. As agreed with Forkbeard and Skotkonung, he took possession of the *Long Serpent*, plus the other ships he had cleared, and all the weapons and gear of the crews captured or killed aboard them. He even took his kinsman Einar Eindridesson back to Trondheim to begin his own rise, where he became known as *Thambarskelfir*, "Bowstring Shaker."

Eirik's benevolence extended even to Olaf's wife, Queen Thyri, but she, already racked with grief over the death of her infant son, was inconsolable after the loss of her king. Berg wrote, "When the slaughter aboard the *Serpent* ended and the ship was searched and cleared of dead bodies, Queen Thyri was brought up from below deck, her face swollen with grief, weeping bitterly." Jarl Eirik tried to comfort her, assuring her that she would lose nothing in rank or honor under his reign, but she replied, "I would accept your kindness and willingly live on if I could, but my heart is so badly broken with grief that I have no hope of living." So saying, she stopped taking food and water, and died just nine days later.

Nor did Olaf's great ship, the *Long Serpent*, long outlive its king. It had been irreparably damaged in the battle, possibly from the ramming encounter with the *Iron-Prow*. It acquired a list and would not answer its steering. After fighting it up through the Oresund to the Vik, Eirik had it broken up and burned.

Finally, on the arrival of the jarls Eirik and Svein in Trondheim, they found Olaf's dog Vigi awaiting his master's return at the foot of his throne. According to Berg, it was Einar Eindridesson who broke the news to him – "We've no master now, Vigi" – upon which the dog is said to have bayed mournfully, run out and lay down on a nearby hillock as though it was the king's burial mound. Like Queen Thyri, he refused all food and water and, like her, died within days.

As with all the prophecies in Olaf's saga, the one by the blind man of Moster, about Norway's four losses, came true.

As per their agreement, the victors of Svolder divided up Olaf's united Norway between them. Forkbeard reclaimed the southernmost lands that King Olaf had taken from him. Jarl Eirik ruled the greater part of the country in the manner of his father Hakon, as a vassal of Denmark. His brother Svein ruled the smaller part in the name of Sweden. As for Christianity, they ruled as had Hakon the

Good. Snorri wrote, "The jarls Eirik and Svein both had themselves baptized in the true faith, but while they ruled in Norway they let every man do as he wished in regard to Christianity. They obeyed the ancient laws and customs of the land and were popular and good rulers."

Forkbeard invaded England in 1013, and conquered it, but died after just five weeks on the throne, passing the crown to his son Cnut. In 1015 Jarl Eirik joined Cnut in his retaking of England, for which Cnut, on its success, named him Earl (yes, not Viking jarl, English earl) of Northumbria. While he was out of the country, his son Hakon and brother Svein ruled Norway, until both were defeated in battle and exiled by none other than Olaf Haraldsson.

The last time we saw Olaf, the son of the late King Harald Grenske, "the Greenlander," who was burned to death by Sigrid the Haughty, he was about three years old, being baptized by his kinsman King Olaf Tryggvason. Since then he had grown up and joined Forkbeard's invasion of England, but became an archfoe of Cnut and put his efforts into the conquest of Norway. The ensuing decades would be a continuation of the power struggle between the descendants of Harald Fairhair, including both Olafs, and the jarls of Lade, descendants of Hakon the Good's Jarl Sigurd Hakonarson. With the latter driven out, Olaf Haraldsson seized the throne of Norway as King Olaf II and reinstated Christianity, though he did so in the same merciless way as his predecessor Olaf I: by destroying pagan idols and blinding, maiming and killing reluctant heathens. He went to war with Sweden's Olaf Skotkonung, but peace was brokered, in part by Olaf I's brother-in law, Ragnvald Ulfsson, his sister Ingebjorg's husband. Skotkonung died around 1022. Jarl Svein died in Sweden. Sometime after 1023 Jarl Eirik died of medieval surgery, bleeding to death after his uvula was cut, and in 1030 his son Hakon drowned in the whirlpools of the Pentland Firth, the last of the jarls of Lade.

After Olaf Tryggvason departed for Norway, Dublin under King Sigtrygg Silkbeard flourished economically, becoming the biggest slave market in Western Europe. Sigtrygg led several revolts against Ireland's High King, the legendary Brian Boru, including the one that ended in Brian's death at Clontarf in 1014. Besides constantly battling other Irish kings in the decades following, Sigtrygg was a benefactor of the Church, even making a pilgrimage to Rome in 1028. After an exceptionally long reign of forty-six years, in 1036 he was forced by a rival to abdicate, and died in exile in 1042, aged seventy-two.

Nothing more is known of Sigtrygg's sister, Olaf's wife Gytha, except that her son is said to be the "Tryggvi the Pretender" who mounted an invasion of Norway in 1033. By that time the country was ruled by Cnut's son Svein; the two met in battle on Tungenes peninsula where it projects into the mouth of the Boknafjord. The *Fagrskinna* relates, "Throwing two spears at once, Tryggvi said, 'See how my father taught me to say mass.' In this boast he claimed to be more Olaf Tryggvason's son than that of the priest [said to be his real father]. Tryggvi fell there, and did no more brave deeds in Norway."

Stefnir Thorgilsson, the failed missionary to Iceland, had gone to Wendland with King Olaf and was on one of the ships that returned home ahead of him. News of the king's death hit him hard and he resolved to leave Norway. According to the *Islendingabok*, "Thorvald Kodransson and Stefnir Thorgilsson met up after the disappearance of King Olaf. They traveled both together far and wide around the world and all the way out to Jerusalem, and from there to Miklagard and then to eastern Koenugard along the Dnieper." Stefnir eventually returned to Scandinavia, where in Denmark he crossed paths with Jarl Sigvaldi, and composed a verse: "I will not name he who kidnapped King Svein and drew the son of Tryggvi into a trap, but I will say the traitor's nose is hooked."

For that accusation, Sigvaldi murdered him. The jarl never paid for his multiple treacheries. He ruled his domains in Zealand for many years, and may have been part of the force with which Forkbeard invaded England. Possibly because Sigvaldi was killed there, his brother Thorkell the Tall is known to have taken part in the invasion, as commander of the Jomsvikings. Thorkell was said to have foster-fathered Forkbeard's son Cnut, who made him briefly Jarl of Denmark, but he died there in 1021 – according to some, murdered on Cnut's orders.

Olaf's kinfolk – his brother-in-law Thorkell Beaknose, his uncles, mother and sisters – all faded from history, their fates unknown.

His sister Astrid's husband Erling Skjalgsson profited by the partition of Norway, his family holdings and manpower strong enough to sustain him against the brother jarls. He even supported Jarl Svein against Olaf Haraldsson, but in 1028 Olaf defeated him in battle and, though captured alive, Erling was killed. Cnut's Norwegian noblemen, however, chased Olaf back out of the country to Kyivan Rus – the court of Grand Prince Vladimir's son, Grand Prince Yaroslav.

In 988, on accepting the Byzantine princess Anna Porphyrogenita as his wife, Vladimir had been baptized, taking the Christian name Basil. He had his subjects likewise baptized in the Dnieper, destroyed all the pagan idols and founded churches, including the Church of the Tithes on the site of the martyrdom of Feodor the Varangian and his son Ioann. After Vladimir died in 1015, Yaroslav even had the bodies of his uncles, Yaropolk and Oleg, exhumed and baptized. He gave asylum to his kinsman Olaf II (both being married to daughters of Olaf Skotkonung).

When Olaf attempted to retake the Norwegian crown in 1030 (urged on, it was said, by Olaf I in a dream) he was killed – martyred, according to some – at the Battle of Stiklestad. Yet Olaf II won the recognition that Olaf I never got: A year after his death he was canonized as St. Olaf, the patron saint of Norway.*

The thing is, if we give all legends the same hearing we've given them so far – as being as much a part of history as fact – Olaf I might have lived to see it.

"Now we will tell of the matter which some doubt," wrote Odd, "namely that King Olaf stripped off his armor underwater and swam to the ship we mentioned as having come from Wendland."

Berg admitted, "Although men of repute who were at the battle related what each in the last moment saw of Olaf, still no one seemed able to say for certain whether or not the King escaped."

"Most people would not hear of his falling," attests the *Fagrskinna*, "instead saying that he was in Wendland or southern Europe, and

---

* For more on Forkbeard, Cnut and Eirik in England, and Olaf Haraldsson in Norway, see *Battle for the Island Kingdom* and *The Last Viking* by this same author.

many tales are told of that, but his friends feared it was untrue. That is said by Hallfred Vandraedaskald, who had so greatly loved the king that after the king's death he grew sick from grief, illness he suffered to his dying day."

"Though one man makes little difference, it was an evil, harmful thing that I stood far from the warrior where steel weapons clashed," Hallfred would write. "I have lost a godfather mightier than every warlike prince under the northern sky."

Recall that Hallfred had gone to Iceland that summer prior to the battle at Svolder, intent on killing the rival in love who had driven him out years before. The night before the *holmgang*, however, King Olaf appeared to him in a dream and advised him to back out of the fight and instead pay compensation for the wrongs he had done: "Another matter will then come to be more important to you than a duel."

"Let men think what they will of me," Hallfred told his friends. "I shall take King Olaf's advice. It will prove best for me now, as it has in the past. Perhaps the prophecy which he voiced before we last parted is about to come true, and I will soon see it would have been better for me to stay with him than come here to Iceland."

In the morning came news of Olaf's death at Svolder. Halldor gave up his plans and returned to Norway, where he heard the details of the battle and the king's end, and composed his verses about Olaf. His *Erfidrapa Olafs Tryggvasonar*, "Memorial Song for Olaf Tryggvason," may be the earliest mention of the rumor of Olaf's survival, and its first dismissal. "People say Olaf escaped the blizzard of steel weapons. Men guess [things] further from the truth; it is not so good as that," he wrote. "Fate would not have allowed it, when retainers attacked the invincible lord. I deal with words. It seems to me that men do not speak of a likely thing, that the magnificent lord would escape such an attack."

Finding no peace, Halldor traveled aimlessly around Scandinavia for some time, even briefly serving as skald to Jarl Eirik, before raising sail for Iceland again. However, the voyage was rough, he took sick and soon lay dying. Giving the sword which Olaf had gifted him to his son, he had the rest of the king's presents put in his coffin and was buried at sea, covered over by the waves much as he always believed had been his king.

When the cheer of triumph was raised across the water at Svolder, Jarl Sigvaldi ordered his ships out from their anchorage by the shoreline where they had spent the entire battle, to join the victors in celebration. On the other hand, the lone Wendish galley that had repeatedly visited the *Serpent* during the fight was said to have picked up a passenger. Odd reported, "Some of the jarl's men said they saw a man in a red tunic swimming toward the Wendish ship, and when he was taken aboard, it immediately made off."

Theodoric concurred, "Some say the king escaped aboard a skiff, and went on to foreign lands seeking salvation for his soul. Others say that he plunged into the sea in full armor. I dare not say which of these reports is the truth."

All the witnesses agreed that Olaf went into the water wearing his mail armor. Byrnies, or mail hauberks, might weigh anywhere from fifteen to thirty pounds and were fastened by multiple lacings, not quick to get off. (In a bit of foreshadowing, Odd did posit early in his saga "the very notable manner in which King Olaf often swam in his armor and took it off under water.") The fact that the man swimming to the Wendish boat was said to be wearing a red tunic or surcoat, which would have been worn over the armor, adds more doubt to the story, but let's go with it. Odd wrote, "Astrid and Dixin, as mentioned, were aboard and had ridden at anchor all day, but as soon as the battle ended they sailed away as though planned."

The king was said to have taken multiple wounds, the most serious of which were a stone hit to the forehead and an arrow through his mail sleeve into his arm. Astrid cured him of these in Wendland, where many people were said to have recognized him and even offered to help him mount an expedition to reclaim Norway from the jarls Eirik and Svein. He refused: "I believe it is God's will that they now rule the kingdom of Norway. I also fear that God has been unhappy with my reign."

Astrid (who gives the impression of regretting that she married the wrong man) is said to have offered Olaf her Wendish estates, over which Earl Sigvaldi had no control, he having gone back to

EPILOGUE

Denmark. Olaf refused them as well. She suggested they both go to England to visit his old friend King Aethelred, but he declined even that. She said, "What help can I give that you will accept from me?"

Olaf wished to go to Rome. So Astrid equipped him with a horse and money and followers, accompanied him as far as the Rhine, and saw him on his way. Olaf is said to have traveled as a pilgrim to Rome and even to have visited Pope Sylvester II. From there, Berg recorded, he sailed to Jerusalem and visited the city's patriarch and king. The Kingdom of Jerusalem would not be established until 1099, after the First Crusade; in those first years of the new millennium the Holy City was part of the Muslim Fatimid Caliphate, an Isma'ili Shi'a dynasty. Their kings, caliphs, were tolerant of Sunni Muslims, Christians and Jews, and though Olaf's supposed visit may not have been as momentous as claimed in the sagas, it certainly could have been done.

"After that," wrote Odd, "King Olaf did not associate with commonfolk, but communed only with God and his holy men."

Years later a traveler arrived in the court of Erling Skjalgsson with word that Olaf was still alive and living as a monk in a monastery, as proof offering a knife and a gold ring, which Erling's wife Astrid recognized as her brother's. And sometime during the reign of Olaf II (1015–28) the skald Thord Sjareksson, who was court poet to both that king and to Jarl Eirik, and whom Berg highly respected as a source, returned from a pilgrimage to the Holy Land reporting meeting a tall man in Syria who recognized the pilgrims as Scandinavian. Speaking Danish, he warned them off going all the way to Jerusalem. "Turn back, the road is unsafe. Foes lie ahead."

This part was true enough. In 1009 the "Mad Caliph," al-Hakim bi-Amr Allah, had suddenly turned on the Christians in his realm, forbidding pilgrimage to the Holy Land and even ordering the demolition of the Church of the Holy Sepulchre in Jerusalem.

Learning that Thord was an Icelander, the stranger asked who ruled in Norway, and was happy to learn it was Olaf II and not the jarls of Lade. He asked Thord if he knew Hjalti Skeggjason, the Icelandic chieftain who had supported Christianity there and called the goddess Freyja a bitch. Thord replied that he was in fact kin to Hjalti by marriage. (Hjalti had gone on to serve as part of Olaf II's peace delegation to Ragnvald Ulfsson and Olaf Skotkonung.) The stranger said, "Bear my greetings to Hjalti on your return to Iceland."

"What should I say to Hjalti of he who sends greetings?"

"I will not disclose my name, but you may say that I spoke with him at Lade in Norway. I held a sword, and Hjalti took it in his hands between mine. He then went out to Iceland, and we never saw each other again."

"When he [Thord] arrived in Iceland," recorded Berg, "he told his story to Hjalti, who said that event had been chosen by him and King Olaf Tryggvason before they parted at Lade, to signify the truth of any message that might eventually pass between them."

And no less than King Aethelred was said to have received from a recently returned pilgrim a book sent by his former vassal Olaf, telling of the ex-king's life after Svolder, which he took as proof that Olaf was still alive. This book was handed down to his son Edward, who later became King Edward the Confessor (r. 1042–66). Every Easter, related Berg, Edward read Olaf's story to his courtiers, because "Olaf Tryggvason was as much greater than other kings as Eastertide is superior to any other day of the entire year."

Finally, Berg recounts the story of Gaut, a pilgrim who visited Einar Thambarskelfir in 1046 with a tale of a desert monastery and a tall, elderly cleric who spoke Danish and was eager for news of Norway. By that time the jarls Eirik and Svein were dead, Erling Skjalgsson was dead, Olaf II and Tryggvi Olafsson were dead – "On hearing this story the old man grew very sorrowful" – and Magnus Olafsson and Harald Sigurdarson, the son and half-brother of Olaf II, reigned as co-kings. The monk had heard much of King Magnus, called the Good, from Norwegian travelers, and was pleased to learn he was king, but had also heard of Harald Sigurdarson's exploits while he served the Byzantine emperor, and considered him no more than a pirate. "But tell me, do the Northmen still remember Olaf Tryggvason?"

"His memory," said Gaut, "is glorious, and he is held in high honor, because he brought the Christian religion to Northern lands."

"Tell me, what is said to have been Olaf Tryggvason's fate in the fight on the *Long Serpent*?"

"Men believe differing accounts. Some say that he jumped into the sea, severely wounded, and wearing his mail-shirt and other armor, sank down and died."

The monk thought the king would have preferred death in battle to drowning, and that he was reputed to be skilled enough in the water to shed his mail coat.

Gaut said, "Others think that God in his might took the king to himself, or put him in some other place, at the instant when the great light was seen around him."

The monk thought this doubtful as well, for though the king had done good deeds, he had committed many sins as well, but because of his humility, with God's help he had escaped.

Gaut admitted, "Some say that, as he was swimming, he was rescued and taken ashore by the same ship that lay all day not too far from the battle."

The monk preferred to believe that, rather than having gone to heaven, Olaf was still alive almost fifty years after the battle. He asked after Einar Thambarskelfir, whom Gaut said was still the greatest chieftain of Trondheim, the favorite and chief advisor of young King Magnus and, in his name, practically the ruler of Norway. Married to the daughter of old Jarl Hakon, the sister of jarls Eirik and Svein, he was now a fat old warrior in his sixties, his nickname taken less to mean "Bowstring Shaker" than a pun on the "belly" of the bow: "Paunch Shaker."

The old man mused, "I saw Einar Thambarskelfir aboard the *Serpent*, fighting with the strongest, young though he was, for though he was only eighteen years old he was a match for the most heroic of the king's champions."

By now this venerable monk had very much captured Gaut's interest. "When I was a young boy," he said, "I saw King Olaf Tryggvason. You look much like him, though old. Tell me now. Are you King Olaf?"

The monk said, "I do not claim the glory or the name of King Olaf."

He was then called away by the ringing of the church bells to conduct services, and Gaut was unable to learn more. But when he was ready to leave, the old man gave him a valuable knife and belt. "Mention me to Einar Thambarskelfir when you return to Norway. Tell him I bear witness that no one on the *Serpent* fought more bravely than he. As a proof that you bear a true message, give him this knife and belt."

This Gaut did, and on his return to Norway and delivering them, found that Einar, now in his sixties, broke into tears: "Believe me, brother Gaut, you certainly met with Olaf Tryggvason, who sent me these gifts."

Einar had supported King Magnus the Good over King Harald Sigurdarson, but the next year, 1047, Magnus died. And around the year 1050 Harald, called *Hardrada*, "Hard Ruler," had Einar murdered.

"There are many men who found these stories suspect, and many still doubt," admitted Odd. "I however consider it certain that it is true that Olaf survived the battle and devoted himself to God, inspired by the Holy Spirit and dwelling in a monastery in Greece or Syria, repenting the misdeeds of his youth."

It is certainly comforting to think that Olaf did indeed live on for many years, and perhaps comfort is all the king's followers sought from the stories of his survival. As Theodoric wrote, "I prefer to believe no more than this: that he now enjoys perpetual peace with Christ."

And yet…

It's a fact that the Greifswalder Oie is not so much an islet as the exposed, farthest end of a submerged sand bar, the Oier Reef, extending over two miles southwest toward the mainland. Even today its crest runs less than three feet beneath the surface, and a millennium ago the sea level in the southern Baltic was even lower. The sagas state that Jarl Sigvaldi lured Olaf's ships right in to the lee of the island of Svolder, where shallow-draft Viking longships would easily have dropped anchor in less than six feet of water. It is entirely possible that a man jumping the *Long Serpent*'s gunwale might have waded in a crouch along the bottom, ducking under the lashed-together raft of longships overhead and raising his head above the surface only enough to catch quick breaths of air, keeping to the reef until he could finally shed his armor and be taken aboard a friendly nearby Wendish boat.

We will never know. It's one of the possibilities that makes Olaf Tryggvason's saga – arising from legend to itself become legend – perhaps the greatest Viking saga of all.

SOURCES

ADAM OF BREMEN was an 11th-century German historian. His *Gesta Hammaburgensis ecclesiae pontificum* ("Deeds of Bishops of the Hamburg Church"), written c. 1073–1076, primarily chronicled the history of the Hamburg-Bremen diocese, partly in an effort to preserve its ecclesiastical claim over Scandinavia and keep it from being subjected to the archbishopric of Cologne. In doing so, however, Adam included a history of medieval Northern Europe, including Christian missions to Viking Scandinavia and even the Viking discovery of North America.

The *AGRIP AF NOREGSKONUNGASOGUM* ("Summary of the Norwegian Kings' Sagas," though not so named until 1835) was composed in Old Norse around 1190 by an anonymous Norwegian author, probably in the vicinity of Nidaros, modern Trondheim. Along with the works of Theodoric Monachus and the *Historia Norwegiae* (see below), it is one of the oldest Norwegian synoptic histories.

AHMAD IBN FADLAN ibn al-Abbas al-Baghdadi was a 10th-century ambassador of the Arab Abbasid Caliphate, who famously documented his mission to the Bulgars living along the Volga River and the Varangian Vikings living among them.

AHMAD IBN RUSTA Isfahani was a 10th-century Persian explorer and geographer who traveled extensively among the Rus and other northern peoples. His *Kitab al-A'laq al-Nafīsa*, "Book of Precious Records," relies on second-hand reports, but tells of the Khazars, Slavs and Bulgars, and even mentions what he knew of Anglo-Saxon England.

The *ANGLO-SAXON CHRONICLE*, also known as the *Old English Royal Annals*, is a record of yearly events begun in the reign of Alfred the Great (871–899). The original manuscript is lost, but copies were made, sent and continued in various monasteries across England. Nine still survive, which often disagree on events and even the year they took place, but taken together they are the first post-Roman European history written by a people in their own language.

ARI THORGILSSON, called Ari *frodi*, "Ari the Wise," was an Icelandic chronicler of the late 11th and early 12th centuries. His *Islendingabok*, "Book of Icelanders" (see below), mentions King Olaf in passing, but he is thought to have written a more comprehensive, lost biography of the king in Old Norse. Ari and his contemporary Saemund Sigfusson (see below) were cited as sources by Odd Snorrason when writing his early version of *King Olaf's Saga*.

"THE BATTLE OF MALDON" is a poem in Old English, thought to have been written in the late 10th or early 11th century. The only original manuscript, already missing its beginning and end, was lost in a fire in 1731. The 325 surviving lines, all from the Anglo-Saxon viewpoint, name many characters whom scholars accept as real people, and the poem can be taken as evidence of medieval tactics, motivation and valor.

BERG SOKKASON was in 1316 a Benedictine monk at the monastery of Thingeyrar (Thingeyraklaustur) in northwest Iceland, and by 1322 prior of the monastery at Munkathvera in northern Iceland, where he twice served as abbot, 1325–1334 and 1345–1350. A scholar and prolific chronicler of sagas, he is named in one manuscript as the compiler of *Olafs saga Tryggvasonar en mesta* ("The Greatest Saga of Olaf Tryggvason"), the latest, enlarged and most embellished version of *The Saga of Olaf Tryggvason* by Odd Snorrason (see below).

BYRHTFERTH OF RAMSEY was a monk at Ramsey Abbey in what is now Huntingdonshire around the dawn of the Second Millennium. His *Vita Oswaldi*, a biography of Oswald of Worcester, the Archbishop of York, contains a passage about the Battle of Maldon, which occurred during his lifetime.

The *FAEREYINGA SAGA* was written anonymously in Iceland in the early 13th century, but relates how the Faroe Islands were converted to Christianity during Olaf Tryggvason's reign.

The *FAGRSKINNA* ("Fair Parchment," so named in the 17th century for the condition of the vellum on which it was written), was known in the Middle Ages as *Noregs konunga tal*, "Enumeration of the Kings of Norway." It was written in Norway, probably in the Trondelag region, around AD 1220, the unknown author drawing upon the *Agrip af Noregskonungasogum*, the *Jomsviking Saga* and Odd Snorrason's *Olafs saga Tryggvasonar*. It was a direct source for Snorri in writing his *Heimskringla* (see below).

The *GRAENLENDINGA SAGA*, "Saga of the Greenlanders," written in the late 13th or early 14th century, tells the story of the Icelanders who settled Greenland and the coasts of North America around AD 1000.

GUNNLAUG LEIFSSON was a Benedictine monk, scholar, author and poet at the Thingeyraklaustur in northwest Iceland in the late 12th and early 13th centuries. He was a monastic brother of Odd Snorrason (see below) and translated and expanded his biography of Olaf Tryggvason, written in Latin, into Old Norse. Both versions were since lost, but were used as source material by Olaf's later biographers Snorri Sturluson (below) and Berg Sokkason (above).

HALLFRED OTTARSSON, called *Vandraedaskald*, "Troublesome Poet," served as skald, court poet, to Jarl Hakon Sigurdarson, then Olaf Tryggvason and lastly Eirik Hakonarson. He composed praise poems and dirges about Olaf, including his own distress over being forced to adopt Christianity at the king's command. Much of his work was incorporated by Odd Snorrason (see below) into *The Saga of Olaf Tryggvason*.

The *HEIMSKRINGLA*, the most famous of Old Norse kings' sagas, was compiled in Iceland c. 1220–1230, most likely by Icelandic poet and historian Snorri Sturluson (see below). It recounts the stories of Swedish and Norwegian kings from the semi-mythical Yngling dynasty up to the Norwegian civil wars of the 12th century. It was untitled until the 17th century, when it was named from its first two words, *kringla heimsins*, "the Circle of the World." Its version of Olaf's saga is much more secular than the monks' sagas.

SOURCES

HELMOLD OF BOSAU was a 12th-century Saxon priest and historian. His *Chronica Slavorum* drew heavily on Adam of Bremen (see above) in covering the Saxon conquest and conversion of the Slavic people from the reign of Charlemagne, c. 800, to 1171.

The *HISTORIA NORWEGIAE* ("History of Norway") was written in Latin by an anonymous monk, probably in eastern Norway. Written around 1220, but possibly as early as 1150, it is believed to be the earliest of the three synoptics, the oldest preserved kings' sagas, the others being the *Agrip af Noregskonungasogum* (see above) and that of Theodoric Monachus (see below). It comprises a geography of Norway and discussions of the jarls of Orkney and kings of Norway.

IBRAHIM IBN YAQUB, called *al-Tartushi* (from Tortosa in Spain), was a 10th-century Jewish Arab merchant who journeyed north on business and documented his travels, notably regarding the people of medieval Germany, Poland, Denmark and the Czech Republic.

ISLENDINGABOK, the "Book of Icelanders," written by early 12th-century Icelandic priest, Ari Thorgilsson (see above), describes early Icelandic history, including Olaf Tryggvason's influence on it.

The *JOMSVIKING SAGA* is the story of a semi-legendary order of pagan Viking mercenary fighters who operated out of Jomsborg (thought to be modern Wolin in Poland), in the 10th and 11th centuries. Composed in Iceland during the 13th century, the saga exists in no fewer than five different manuscripts that vary wildly in their retelling, leading many historians to regard them all as a mix of history with sheer fiction.

KRISTNI SAGA, the "Book of Christianity," was probably written by the 13th-century Icelandic chieftain, lawspeaker and historian Sturla Thordarson. It tells of the Christianization of Iceland in the 10th century. It incorporates the work of Ari Thorgilsson (see above) and Gunnlaug Leifsson's 12th-century version of King Olaf Tryggvason's saga (see below).

The *LAXDAELA SAGA* is a story of the people of western Iceland from the late 9th to early 11th centuries. It was composed around 1245 by an anonymous author who, judging by its unusually romantic theme, historians speculate may have been female.

The *LIBER ELIENSIS*, "Book of Ely," was composed at the Benedictine abbey on the island of Ely in the Cambridgeshire fens. Drawing on earlier English histories like the *Anglo-Saxon Chronicle* (see above), it is a monastic history of eastern England from the mid-7th century to the mid-12th, including the Battle of Maldon, the hero of which, the ealdorman Byrhtnoth of Essex, was a patron of the abbey.

ODD SNORRASON was a 12th-century Benedictine monk at Thingeyraklaustur in northwest Iceland. His version of King Olaf's saga, written in Latin, is thought to be the earliest full-length Icelandic king's saga. Though the original is lost, it was expanded on by Odd's brother monk, Gunnlaug Leifsson (see above), and later included in the *Heimskringla* of Snorri Sturluson (see below) and was used as a source for the early 14th-century *Olafs saga Tryggvasonar en mesta*, "The Greatest Saga of Olaf Tryggvason" (see below).

The *OLAFSDRAPA*, or more formally *Olafsdrapa Tryggvasonar*, "Song of Olaf Tryggvason," is a praise poem long thought to have been composed by Olaf's skald Hallfred Vandraedaskald (see above) around 996. Based on style and language, it is now believed to have been written by an anonymous author no earlier than the 12th century.

The *RUSSIAN PRIMARY CHRONICLE* or *TALE OF BYGONE YEARS* is a chronicle of medieval Russia from about the mid-9th to early 12th century. It was long attributed to the Kyivan monk Nestor, called "the Chronicler" or "the Hagiographer," but of late is thought to have been written by Abbott Sylvester of St. Michael's Monastery near Kyiv, or else is the work of an anonymous author edited by him. It is notoriously bad with dating, beginning with a ten-year error in start date, then discrepancies with other sources and even internal contradictions, but is a valuable source for medieval Slavic history if cross-referenced with other documentation.

SAEMUND SIGFUSSON, called Saemund *Frodi*, "Saemund the Learned," was an Icelandic scholar and priest of the late 11th and early 12th centuries. He wrote a history of Norwegian kings in Latin which is lost, but is thought to have been used by the anonymous author of the *Agrip af Noregskonungasogum* (see above). Saemund and his contemporary Ari Thorgilsson (see above) were acknowledged as sources by Odd Snorrason when writing his early version of *King Olaf's Saga*.

The *SAGA OF OLAF TRYGGVASON* (*Olafs saga Tryggvasonar*) comes down to us in multiple versions, with most of the later ones feeding off the earlier. The initial transcript, since lost, was written in Latin by the Icelandic monk Odd Snorrason (see above) sometime around 1190, a compilation of tales probably originating with Olaf's court poet, Hallfred Ottarsson (see above). Said to be the first full-length Icelandic saga, it was enlarged by Odd's fellow monk Gunnlaug Leifsson (see above), whose version was also lost, but in the early 13th century incorporated into the anonymously written *Fagrskinna* and the *Heimskringla* by Snorri Sturluson. Finally, an extended biography of Olaf in Old Norse, called *Olafs saga Tryggvasonar en mesta* ("The Greatest Saga of Olaf Tryggvason"), is thought to have been translated from the Latin and compiled around 1300 by the Icelandic abbot Berg Sokkason (see above) at Thingeyraklaustur in northern Iceland. He based it on Snorri's version of *Olafs Saga*, but incorporated material from the late-12th-century *Orkneyinga Saga*, the 13th-century *Jomsviking Saga* and *Laxdala Saga*, the 13th–14th-century *Landnamabok*, and the 14th-century *Hallfredar Saga*. The *Greatest Saga* was included in the late-14th-century *Flateyjarbok*.

SAXO GRAMMATICUS, "Saxo the Grammarian," was probably a clerk or secretary to the 12th-century Archbishop of Lund, across the Oresund from Denmark in what is now Sweden, but incidentally a theologian and historian. The sixteen books of his *Gesta Danorum* ("Deeds of the Danes"), which also cover early Estonia and Latvia, are some of the oldest and most important records of Danish history.

SNORRI STURLUSON, 12th–13th-century Icelandic historian, writer and politician, either wrote or compiled the *Heimskringla* (see above), the most famous of the Old Norse kings' sagas, around 1230. His account therein of the life of Olaf Tryggvason was a major source for the 14th-century "Greatest Saga of Olaf Tryggvason" (see above). As Snorri was not a man of the Church, his version of Olaf's saga is much less hagiographic than those written by Icelandic monks.

THEODORICUS MONACHUS, "Theodoric the Monk," was a Benedictine monk at Nidarholm Abbey on the island of Munkholmen in Trondheim fjord. Between 1177 and 1188 he wrote the Latin *Historia de Antiquitate Regum Norwagiensium* ("Ancient History of the Norwegian Kings"), one of the earliest kings' sagas, which may have provided source material for Odd Snorrason when writing his version of Olaf's saga (see above).

THIETMAR OF MERSEBURG was a Saxon bishop, historian and loyal supporter of the Ottonian dynasty. Named Prince-Bishop of Merseburg in 1009, he composed his *Chronicon Thietmari* in eight books, covering the history of the empire from 908 to his death in 1018. As both an advisor to Emperor Henry II and a onetime hostage of the Northmen, he had a unique view of events.

WIDUKIND OF CORVEY was a 10th-century Benedictine monk and chronicler who wrote the three-volume *Res gestae Saxonicae sive annalium libri tres* ("The Deeds of the Saxons, or Three Books of Annals"), a history of Germany and the Holy Roman Empire up to the death of Emperor Otto I.

WULFSTAN OF HEDEBY was a 9th-century traveler and merchant, possibly English but probably Danish, who documented his journeys and the peoples around the Baltic coast. His account was included in the *Old English History of the World*, a travelogue and geography possibly commissioned by King Alfred the Great.

BIBLIOGRAPHY

Alvarez-Pedroza, Juan Antonio, ed. *Sources of Slavic Pre-Christian Religion*. Brill, 2020.

Anders, Andrén, Kristina Jennbert and Catharina Raudvere, eds. *Old Norse Religion in Long-Term Perspectives*. Nordic Academic Press, 2006. https://bora.uib.no/bora-xmlui/bitstream/handle/1956/3273/Old%20 Norse%20Nordeide.pdf

Andersson, Theodore M. "The First Icelandic King's Saga: Oddr Snorrason's 'Óláfs Saga Tryggvasonar' or 'The Oldest Saga of Saint Olaf?'" *The Journal of English and Germanic Philology* 103, no. 2 (2004): 139–55. http://www.jstor.org/stable/27712412

Andersson, Theodore M. "The Viking Policy of Ethelred the Unready." *Scandinavian Studies* 59, no. 3 (1987): 284–95. https://www.jstor.org/stable/40918864

Atherton, Mark. *The Battle of Maldon*. Bloomsbury Publishing, 2020.

Bachrach, David S. *Religion and the Conduct of War, c. 300–1215*. Boydell Press, 2003.

Bachrach, David S. *Warfare in Tenth-century Germany*. Boydell Press, 2014.

Bagge, Sverre. "The Making of a Missionary King: The Medieval Accounts of Olaf Tryggvason and the Conversion of Norway." *The Journal of English and Germanic Philology* 105, no. 4 (2006): 473–513. https://www.uio.no/studier/emner/hf/iakh/HIS1110/h11/undervisningsmateriale/HIS1110s%C3%A6remne_Sverre_Bagge.pdf

Barnett, Elnathan. "Family, Feud, and the Conduct of War in Anglo-Saxon England." The University of Southern Mississippi, 2011. https://aquila.usm.edu/cgi/viewcontent.cgi?article=1235&context=masters_theses

Beard, David. "The Battle of Maldon." *Medieval World* 1, July/August 1991. http://archeurope.com/@pdf/battle_of_maldon.pdf

Blake, Ernest Oscar. *Liber Eliensis*. Camden Third Series. Vol. XCII. London: Offices of the Royal Historical Society, 1962.

Bloomfield, Morton W. "Beowulf, Byrhtnoth, and the Judgment of God: Trial by Combat in Anglo-Saxon England." *Speculum* 44, no. 4 (1969): 545–59. https://www.jstor.org/stable/2850382

Brückner, Dr. Ludwig. "Rethra Lag Auf Der Fischerinsel in Der Tollense." *Jahrbücher Des Vereins Für Mecklenburgische Geschichte Und Altertumskunde* 59 (1889): 153–67. https://mvdok.lbmv.de/mjbrenderer?id=mvdok_document_00002989

Bugge, Alexander. "Sandhed Og Digt Om Olav Tryggvason." *Yearbooks for Nordic Antiquities and History.* Copenhagen: The Royal Nordic Antiquities Society, 1910. https://heimskringla.no/wiki/Sandhed_og_digt_om_Olav_Tryggvason

Byock, Jesse L. *Medieval Iceland: Society, Sagas, and Power.* University of California Press, 1990.

Byrhtferth of Ramsey, and Michael Lapidge. *Byrhtferth of Ramsey: The Lives of St Oswald and St Ecgwine.* Clarendon Press, 2009.

Dasent, Sir George Webbe, trans. *The Story of Burnt Njal.* T. Fisher, 1911. https://archive.org/details/cu31924080933728

Dejevsky, Nikolai J. *Novgorod in the Early Middle Ages: The Rise and Growth of an Urban Community.* BAR International Series. Oxford: BAR Publishing, 2016.

Ditucci, David. "Deadly Hostility: Feud, Violence, and Power in Early Anglo-Saxon." ScholarWorks at WMU. Western Michigan University, 2017. https://scholarworks.wmich.edu/dissertations/3138

Duk, Dzianis V. and Aliaksei L. Kots. "New Archaeological Research on the Territory of Zapolotsky Posad of Ancient Polotsk (End of 10th – First Half of 12th Century)." *Stratum Plus. Archaeology and Cultural Anthropology* 2013 (5): 83–90. https://www.ceeol.com/search/article-detail?id=648024

Ellis, Caitlin. "Reassessing the Career of Óláfr Tryggvason in the Insular World." *Saga-Book of the Viking Society for Northern Research*, No. 43, January 1, 2019, pp. 59–82. https://www.academia.edu/42252994

Ellis, Hilda Roderick. *The Road to Hel: A Study of the Conception of the Dead in Old Norse Literature.* Cambridge University Press, 1943. https://books.google.com/books?id=aLA8AAAAIAAJ

Fairweather, Janet, trans. *Liber Eliensis: A History of the Isle of Ely from the Seventh century to the Twelfth.* Boydell, 2005.

Faulkes, Anthony, trans. *Faereyinga Saga.* Thorisdal, 2016. http://www.vsnrweb-publications.org.uk/Faereyinga%20saga.pdf

Faulkes, Anthony and Alison Finlay, eds. *Íslendingabók – Kristni Saga: The Book Of The Icelanders – The Story Of The Conversion.* Translated by Siân Grønlie. Viking Society for Northern Research Text Series. Vol. XVIII. University College London: Viking Society for Northern Research, 2006. http://www.vsnrweb-publications.org.uk/Text%20Series/IslKr.pdf

Fellows-Jensen, Gillian. "King Olaf Tryggvason and Sir Edward Elgar." *The Elgar Society Journal*, Vol. 11, No. 4 (March 2000): 202–217. https://www.elgarsociety.org/wp-content/uploads/2014/04/Vol.11-No.4-March-2000-Compressed.pdf

Flateyjarbok: A Collection of Norwegian King Sagas. Vol. 1. Christiana: P. T. Mallings Publishing Bookstore, 1860. https://archive.org/details/flateyjarbokens01ungegoog/

Franklin, Simon and Jonathan Shepard. *The Emergence of Rus, 750–1200.* Longman, 1998.

Garmonsway, George Norman, transl. *The Anglo-Saxon Chronicle.* Everyman's Library, Vol. 624. Dent, 1967.

Goeres, Erin Michelle. "The Many Conversions of Hallfreðr Vandræðaskáld." *Viking and Medieval Scandinavia* 7 (2011): 45–62. http://www.jstor.org/stable/45019149

Gordon, E. V. "The Date of Æthelred's Treaty with the Vikings: Olaf Tryggvason and the Battle of Maldon." *The Modern Language Review* 32, no. 1 (1937): 24–32. https://doi.org/10.2307/3715138

Gordon, E. V. *The Battle of Maldon.* Methuen & Co., 1949.

Grønlie, Siân. "'Þáttr' and Saga: The Long and the Short of Óláfr Tryggvason." *Viking and Medieval Scandinavia* 9 (2013): 19–36. http://www.jstor.org/stable/45020169

Halldórsson, Ólafur. *Text by Snorri Sturluson in* Óláfs *Saga Tryggvasonar En Mesta.* Viking Society for Northern Research: University College, London. 2001. http://www.vsnrweb-publications.org.uk/Olafur2.pdf

Halsted, Christopher. "How Saxon Was the Saxon March in the Tenth Century?" *Online Archive of University of Virginia Scholarship*, Corcoran Department of History, University of Virginia, 2017. https://libraetd.lib.virginia.edu/downloads/mp48sd106?filename=1_Halsted_Christopher_2017_MA.pdf

Helmold of Bosau. "*Chronicle of the Slavs – Book I.*" Jassa.org, 2024. https://www.jassa.org/?page_id=10175

Heslop, Kate. "Anonymous, *Poem about Óláfr Tryggvason*" in Diana Whaley (ed.), *Poetry from the Kings' Sagas 1: From Mythical Times to c. 1035. Skaldic Poetry of the Scandinavian Middle Ages* 1. Brepols, 2012, p. 1061. https://skaldic.org/m.php?p=text&i=1096

Heslop, Kate. "'Hallfreðr Vandræðaskald (Erfidrápa Óláfs Tryggvasonar, Hákonardrápa); Anon., Óláfs Drápa Tryggvasonar; Anon., Verses from Óláfs Saga Tryggvasonar En Mesta; Poetry by Skúli Þorsteinsson and Þorleifr Járlsskald Rauðfeldarson (74 Verses Total)." *Academia.edu*, 2013. https://doi.org/1050987/1312526/s200_kate

Hilen, Andrew. "Longfellow and Scandinavia Revisited." *Papers Presented at the Longfellow Commemorative Conference.* National Park Service, Longfellow National Historical Site, 1982. http://npshistory.com/publications/long/symposium82/sec1.htm

Holm, Poul. "The Slave Trade of Dublin, Ninth to Twelfth Centuries." *Peritia*, Vol. 5, 1986. https://web.archive.org/web/20170118054303/http://static.sdu.dk/mediafiles//Files/Om_SDU/Institutter/Ihks/Forskningsenheder/CMRS/Materials/Holmslavetrade.pdf

Howard, Ian. *Swein Forkbeard's Invasions and the Danish Conquest of England, 991–1017.* Boydell Press, 2003.

Hudson, Benjamin T. *Viking Pirates and Christian Princes : Dynasty, Religion, and Empire in the North Atlantic.* Oxford University Press, 2005.

Hurstwic Viking Combat Research, https://www.hurstwic.org/

Iceland Review. "A New View on the Origin of First Settlers in Iceland." *Iceland Review.* June 4, 2011. https://www.icelandreview.com/news/a-new-view-the-origin-first-settlers-iceland/

Jackson, Tatjana. "The Role of Óláfr Tryggvason in the Conversion of Russia." In Magnus Rindal, ed. *Three Studies on Vikings and Christianization*, 1994, pp. 1–17. Academia.edu, The Research Council of Norway's Research Programme for Culture and Tradition (KULT). https://www.academia.edu/23704863/The_Role_of_Óláfr_Tryggvason_in_the_Conversion_of_Russia_In_Magnus_Rindal_ed_Three_Studies_on_Vikings_and_Christianization_Oslo_1994_pp_1_17

Jones, Gwyn. *The Legendary History of Olaf Tryggvason.* Jackson, Son & Company, 1968.

Jones, Gwyn. *A History of the Vikings.* Oxford University Press, 2001.

Jones, Prudence and Nigel Pennick. *A History of Pagan Europe.* Routledge, 1997.

Keraliumes, Simas. "The Information on the Aistians in *Óláfs Saga Tryggvasonar* and Its Importance for the History of the East Baltic Region." Akureyri, Iceland: International Saga Conference, 1994. http://sagaconference.org/SC09/SC09_Karaliunas.pdf

Kerr, Thomas R., Finbar McCormick and Aiden O'Sullivan. "The Economy of Early Medieval Ireland (Early Medieval Archaeology

Project (EMAP 2) Report 7:1)." *Internet Archive.* Irish National Strategic Archaeological Research (INSTAR) programme, 2013. https://web.archive.org/web/20170323110350/http://www.emap.ie/documents/EMAP_Report_7_2013_The_Economy_of_Early_Medieval_Ireland.pdf

Killings, Douglas B., trans. *The Laxdaela Saga.* The Medieval and Classical Literature Library, 1997. http://mcllibrary.org/Laxdaela/

Korpela, Jukka. *Prince, Saint, and Apostle: Prince Vladimir Svjatoslavič of Kiev, His Posthumous Life, and the Religious Legitimization of the Russian Great Power.* Harrassowitz, 2001.

Kovalev, Roman K. "The Mint of Al-Shāsh: The Vehicle for the Origins and Continuation of Trade Relations between Viking-Age Northern Europe and Sāmānid Central Asia." *Archivum Eurasiae Medii Aevi* 12 (2002–2003). Edited by Th. T. Allsen et al. Harrassowitz Verlag, 2003, pp. 47–79. https://www.academia.edu/11769778/_The_Mint_of_al_Shāsh_The_Vehicle_For_the_Origins_and_Continuation_of_Trade_Relations_Between_Viking_Age_Northern_Europe_and_Sāmānid_Central_Asia_Archivum_Eurasiae_Medii_Aevi_12_2002_2003_

Kowalewska, Joanna. "Ritual and the Socio-Religious in the Cultures of the Celts and Germans." *Język – Szkoła – Religia* 13, no. 3 (2018). https://czasopisma.bg.ug.edu.pl/index.php/JSR/article/view/1880

Krakow, Annett. "The King and His Retainers. Some Notes on Interpolations in the *Flateyjarbók* Version of *Óláfs Saga Tryggvasonar En Mesta.*" *Średniowiecze Polskie I Powszechne* 11 (2019). https://doi.org/10.31261/spip.2019.15.02 or https://core.ac.uk/download/270093418.pdf

Laborde, E. D. *Byrhtnoth and Maldon.* William Heinemann Ltd., 1936.

Longfellow, Henry Wadsworth. *Tales of a Wayside Inn.* Ticknor and Fields, 1863. https://archive.org/details/talesofwayside00long8

Longfellow, Henry Wadsworth. *The Letters of Henry Wadsworth Longfellow.* Edited by Andrew Hilen. Vol. IV, 1857–1865. The Belknap Press of Harvard University Press, 1972.

Lynch, Joseph H. *Christianizing Kinship: Ritual Sponsorship in Anglo-Saxon England.* Cornell University Press, 2019.

Mägi, Marika. *In Austrvegr: The Role of the Eastern Baltic in Viking Age Communication across the Baltic Sea*, in the series *The Northern World: North Europe and the Baltic c. 400–1700 AD, Peoples, Economies and Cultures.* Vol. 84. Brill, 2018.

Mägi, Marika. *The Viking Eastern Baltic*, in the series *Past Imperfect.* Arc Humanities Press, 2019.

Magnus, Leonard Arthur. *The Tale of the Armament of Igor. A.D. 1185. A Russian Historical Epic.* Oxford University Press, 1915. https://archive.org/details/taleofarmamentof00magnuoft

Marchant, Francis P. "The Vikings and the Wends." *Saga-Book* 8 (1913): 108–29. https://www.jstor.org/stable/48611691

Melnikova, Elena. "How Christian Were Viking Christians?" *Ruthenica: Journal of East European Medieval History and Archeology*, vol. 4, no. 4, 2011, pp. 90–107, history.org.ua/JournALL/ruthenica/ruthenica_2011_suppl4/9.pdf

Melnikova, Elena A. "A New Runic Inscription from Hagia Sophia Cathedral in Istanbul." *Futhark: International Journal of Runic Studies* 7 (2016, pub. 2017): 101–10. https://uu.diva-portal.org/smash/get/diva2:1087633/FULLTEXT01.pdf

Miller, William Ian. *Bloodtaking and Peacemaking: Feud, Law, and Society in Saga Iceland.* University of Chicago Press, 1990.

Mishin, Dmitrij. "Ibrahim Ibn-Ya'qub At-Turtushi's Account of the Slavs from the Middle of the Tenth Century." In *Annual of Medieval Studies at the CEU 1994–1995*, edited by Mary Beth L. Davis and Marcell Sebök, pp. 184–99. Central European University, 1996. https://ams.ceu.edu/1994_5/Mishin.pdf

Monachus, Theodoricus. *Historia De Antiquitate Regum Norwagiensium: An Account of the Ancient History of the Norwegian Kings.* Translated by David and Ian MacDougall. Viking Society for Northern Research Text Series, Vol. XI. University College, London: 1998. http://www.vsnrweb-publications.org.uk/Text%20Series/Theodoricus.pdf

Mundal, Else. "The View of Blood Vengeance in Medieval Norwegian Sources." *Scandinavistica Vilnensis* (2009): 139–52. https://www.researchgate.net/publication/335265032

Nader, Laura. *What the Rest Think of the West: Since 600 AD.* University of California Press, 2015.

Niedorf, Leonard. "II Aethered and the Politics of the Battle of Maldon." *Journal of English and Germanic Philology.* University of Illinois Press, 2012. https://citeseerx.ist.psu.edu/document?repid=rep1&type=pdf&doi=11a789382fe05d1b6a9f1915ea29e14f82f3aa50

Noonan, Thomas S. "The First Major Silver Crisis in Russia and the Baltic, c. 875–c. 900." *Hikuin* 11 (1985): 41–50. https://tidsskrift.dk/Hikuin/article/view/151100

Nossov, Konstantin S. *Medieval Russian Fortresses AD 862–1480.* Fortress 61. Osprey Publishing, 2012.

Olley, Katherine. "Labour Pains: Scenes of Birth and Becoming in Old Norse Legendary Literature." Cambridge Colloquium in Anglo-Saxon, Norse and Celtic, 2018. https://www.repository.cam.ac.uk/items/9ce7ba7f-4cb4-4e94-bb15-314b066e1fdd

Owen-Crocker, Gale R. and Brian W. Schneider, eds. *Royal Authority in Anglo-Saxon England*. Oxford: British Archaeological Reports, 2013.

Perrie, Maureen, D. C. B. Lieven, and Ronald Grigor Suny. *The Cambridge History of Russia*. Cambridge University Press, 2006.

Petty, George R. and Susan Petty. "Geology and the Battle of Maldon." *Speculum* 51, no. 3 (1976): 435–46. https://www.jstor.org/stable/2851706

Rappoport, Pavel. "Russian Medieval Military Architecture." *Gladius*, Vol. 8. Spanish National Research Council (CSIC), 1969. https://gladius.revistas.csic.es/index.php/gladius/article/view/175

Rębkowski, Marian. "On the Origins and Chronology of the Wolin Emporium." Institute of Archaeology and Ethnology PAN, 2020. https://www.researchgate.net/publication/357293562_On_the_origins_and_chronology_of_the_Wolin_emporium

Regia Anglorum, https://regia.org

Rivers, Theodore John. "Widows' Rights in Anglo-Saxon Law." *The American Journal of Legal History* 19, no. 3 (1975): 208–15. https://www.jstor.org/stable/844882

Robertson, A. J., ed. and trans. *The Laws of the Kings of England from Edmund to Henry I*. Cambridge University Press, 1925.

Røthe, Gunnhild. "The Fictitious Figure of Þorgerðr Hǫlgabrúðr in the Saga Tradition." The International Saga Conference, 2006. http://sagaconference.org/SC13/SC13_Roethe.pdf

The Russian Primary Chronicle, Laurentian Text. Samuel Hazard Cross and Olgerd P. Sherbowitz-Wetzor, eds. The Medieval Academy of America, 1953, www.mgh-bibliothek.de/dokumente/a/a011458.pdf

Samarrai, Alauddin Ismail. "Arabic Sources on the Norse English Translation and Notes Based on the Texts Edited by Alexander Seippel in Rerum Normannicarum Fontes Arabici." University of Wisconsin, 1959. https://minds.wisconsin.edu/handle/1793/21462

Sawyer, Peter. "Ethelred II, Olaf Tryggvason, and the Conversion of Norway." *Scandinavian Studies* 59, no. 3 (1987): 299–307. https://www.jstor.org/stable/40918866

Schaeken, Jos. *Voices on Birchbark: Everyday Communication in Medieval Russia*. Brill, 2018.

Scragg, Donald. *The Return of the Vikings: The Battle of Maldon 991.* Gloucestershire: Tempus Publishing Limited, 2006.

Sephton, John, trans. *The Saga of King Olaf Tryggwason who Reigned Over Norway, A.D. 995 to A.D. 1000.* David Nutt, 1895. https://books.google.com/books/about/The_Saga_of_King_Olaf_Tryggwason_who_Rei.html?id=fZwTAAAAMAAJ

Sheehan, John. "The Form and Structure of Viking-Age Silver Hoards: The Evidence from Ireland." In *Silver Economy in the Viking Age*, edited by James Graham-Campbell and Gareth Williams, pp. 143–54. Left Coast Press, 2007. https://cora.ucc.ie/server/api/core/bitstreams/092752f1-2f7d-46dd-bcaf-bf570b9af42e/content

Short, William R. and Reynir A. Oskarson. *Men of Terror : A Comprehensive Analysis of Viking Combat.* Westholme Publishing LLC, 2021.

Slupecki, Leszek P. "Facts and fancy in Jómsvíkinga saga." Durham/York: International Saga Conference, 2006.

Snorrason, Oddr. *The Saga of Olaf Tryggvason.* Translated by Theodore M. Andersson. Cornell University Press, 2013. https://www.google.com/books/edition/The_Saga_of_Olaf_Tryggvason/fLdcDwAAQBAJ.

Stenton, F. M. *Anglo-Saxon England.* Clarendon Press, 2001.

Sturluson, Snorri. *Heimskringla.* Translated by Alison Finlay and Anthony Foulkes. Vol. I: *The Beginnings to Olafr Tryggvason.* University College, London: Viking Society for Northern Research, 2011. http://vsnrweb-publications.org.uk/Heimskringla%20I%20revised.pdf

Svärdström, Elisabeth. "Runorna I Hagia Sofia." *Fornvännen* 65 (1970): 247–49. https://www.diva-portal.org/smash/get/diva2:1225042/FULLTEXT01.pdf

Thompson, James Westfall. "The German Church and the Conversion of the Baltic Slavs." *The American Journal of Theology* 20, no. 2 (1916): 205–30. http://www.jstor.org/stable/3155462

Thorgilsson, Ari. 2006. *Íslendingabók – Kristni Saga – The Book Of The Icelanders – The Story Of The Conversion.* Translated by Siân Grønlie. University College London: Viking Society For Northern Research. https://vsnr.org/translations/islendingabok-kristni-saga-the-book-of-the-icelanders-the-story-of-the-conversion/

Troianovskii, Sergei. "The Great Bridge of Novgorod: Republican History through Material Evidence." European University at St. Petersburg. https://eusp.org/sites/default/files/archive/RESPUBLICA/RepTradition/02.Troyanovsky_-_Great_Bridge_of_Novgorod.pdf

Tvauri, Andres. *The Migration Period, Pre-Viking Age, and Viking Age in Estonia.* Tartu University Press, 2012. https://www.academia.edu/2237217

Uhlirz, Karl. *Jahrbücher Des Deutschen Reiches Unter Otto II. Und Otto III. Auf Veranlassung Seiner Majestät Des Königs von Bayern.* Vol. 1. Bd: Otto II. 973–983. Duncker & Humblot, 1902. https://archive.org/details/bub_gb_UfoOAAAAYAAJ

Unger, Richard W. "Warships and Cargo Ships in Medieval Europe." *Technology and Culture* 22, no. 2 (1981): 233–52. https://www.jstor.org/stable/3104899

Vernadsky, George. *The Origins of Russia*. Oxford University Press, 1959.

Vernadsky, George. *A History of Russia*, Vol. II: *Kievan Russia*. Yale University Press, 1966.

Volkoff, Vladimir. *Vladimir, the Russian Viking*. The Overlook Press, 1985.

Voytovych, L. V. "Holmgard: Where Did the Russian Princes Svyatoslav Igorevich, Volodymyr Svyatoslavich and Yaroslav Volodymyrovych Rule?" *Ukrainian Historical Journal*, 2015, no. 3 (2015): 37–55. http://resource.history.org.ua/publ/UIJ_2015_3_5

Wareham, Andrew. "Peacemaking after Defeat in England in 991 and Northern Song China in 1005." *Medieval Worlds*, Volume 18 (2023): 108–136. https://www.medievalworlds.net/0xc1aa5572%20 0x003e5882.pdf

Warner, David A. *Ottonian Germany: The Chronicon of Thietmar of Merseburg*. Manchester University Press, 2013.

Widukind of Corvey. *Deeds of the Saxons*. Translated by Bernard S. Bachrach and David S. Bachrach. The Catholic University of America Press, 2014.

Williams, Mary Wilhelmine. *Social Scandinavia in the Viking Age*. Macmillan, 1920.

Yanin, V. L. and M. X. Aleshkovsky. "The Origin of Novgorod." *History of the USSR* Vol. 2 (1971): 32–61. http://archnov.com/wp-content/uploads/2016/01/V.L.YAnin.-M.H.Aleshkovskij.-Proishozhdenie-Novgoroda-k-postanovke-problemy.pdf

ACKNOWLEDGMENTS

The brothers Gunnlaug and Odd report that these people provided most information about King Olaf Tryggvason: Gellir Thorgilsson, Asgrim Vestlidason, Bjarni Bergthorsson, Ingud Arnorsdottir, Herdis Dadadottir and Thorgerd Thorsteinsdottir. Later Gunnlaug said that he showed the saga of King Olaf to Gizur Hallsson and that Gizur kept the book for two years. When it was returned to Brother Gunnlaug, he amended it as Gizur thought necessary.

So wrote the monks Odd Snorrason and Gunnlaug Leifsson in the monastery at Thingeyrar in Iceland around AD 1200. Eight hundred years later, I can do no less than to thank them as well, and Snorri Sturluson, and Berg Sokkason, and Theodoric and Adam and all those who told King Olaf's story before me, and Hallfred Ottarson and Ari Thorgilsson and Saemund Sigfusson and the others who told it before them.

I of course once more thank the editorial team at Osprey Publishing: Kate Moore, Publisher for the General Military List, Managing Editor Gemma White, Senior Desk Editor Kezia Johnson, Copyeditor Julie Frederick and Proofreader Sharon Penlington. This is my fourth book with Osprey (more to come), and the process is now as smooth and sharp as a fresh sword, which is to say, the cuts are almost painless.

And, as always, greatest thanks to my agent, Scott Mendel, Managing Partner at Mendel Media Group LLC, who took a small author of magazine articles and fulfilled his dream of becoming an Actual Writer.

INDEX

Figures in **bold** refer to illustrations.

Adalsysla ("the heart of the sea") 63–64, 319
Adam of Bremen 25, 42, 47, 51, 53, 57–58, 61, 65–66, 89, 92, 107–108, 138, 148, 150–151, 153, 155, 159, 188, 201, 242, 282, 288, 314, 324, 328–329, 366, 369
Aelfwine 11, 17, 210–211, 213–214, 216–219, 235–236, 258, 261
Aethelred II, "the Unready" 8, 17, 166, 181, 239, 252
Aethelstan, King 41, 216, 234, 239, 254
afterlife 54, 77, 170, 198–199
Africa 169
  North 59, 256
  South 201
agriculture 65, 102
Agrip af Noregskonungasogum ("Summary of the Norwegian Kings' Sagas") 12, 24–25, 33, 37, 40, 45, 53, 68–69, 84, 90, 141, 175, 196, 212, 245, 262, 329, 335, 366, 368–370
Akesson, Vagn 16, 136, 179, 182–185, 187, 189–192, 204, 354
Alfred the Great 142, 166, 238, 250, 254, 366, 372
Althing, the 299, 301–302
amulets 7, 102
Anglo Saxon Chronicle, the 11, 20, 23, 25, 173, 204, 210, 227, 229–230, 236, 243, 249, 366, 370
Ansgar, the "Apostle of the North" 51, 54, 61
archaeology 92, 113, 139
archers 94, 177, 315, 350
archipelago 31, 195, 292, 325, 329
Asgard (the "City of the Gods") 58, 121
Asia 61, 123, 201
Astrid, daughter of King Burislav 140, 180, 183, 192, 243, 317, 322–323, 330–331, 333, 360–361
ausa vatni 45, 201

axes 32, 60, 62, 71, 79, 83–84, 95, 100, 102, 112, 116, 153, 216–217, 231, 234, 289, 346
  Dane axe 60, 82, 84, 216–217
  wood 307, 315

Baltic Sea/coast 32, 46–48, 51, 56, 59, 63–64, 66–67, 92, 106–108, 120–121, 131, 135–138, 144, 151, 153, 157, 163, 165, 174, 319, 321, 324, 335–336, 372
baptism 7, 35, 92, 98, 126, 196, 200, 202–203, 238, 248, 253, 259, 261, 287, 290, 292, 294, 297, 302, 306, 311, 334, 348
barbarians 138, 145, 149, 158
Basil II, Emperor 121, 300
bastions 93, 149, 341
Benedictine monastery/nunnery 20, 24, 201, 238, 370
  monks 367–368, 370, 372
  Reformation 237
Bernard I 16
Bernard, Abbot 201–202
bishoprics 149, 157–158
Bjorn "the Welsh" 16, 179, 183, 185, 191–192, 204
Bjornsson, Eirik "the Victorious" 15, 53, 85, 106, 108, 213, 243, 251, 276, 280, 284, 305
Bjornsson, Gudrod (King of Vestfold) 14, 36, 41, 43, 45, 48, 69, 281
Black Sea, the 79, 121, 123
"Blud", General 118–119
Boknafjord 278, 291, 328, 357
Bornholm 135–137, 163
Bronze Age, the 7, 31, 39, 65, 148, 152, 195, 233
Bulgars 75, 78, 101, 111, 366
Burgundaholm ("Mountainous Island") 135–136, 168, 177, 179, 182, 190, 192, 204

Burislav, King 15–16, 140–141, 164, 177, 180, 317–318, 320–321, 329, 331
Bygone Days 114, 119, 121, 123, 126, 128
Byrhtferth of Ramsey 229, 234–236, 367
Byrhtnoth of Essex, Ealdorman 17, 21–23, 227–235, 236, 238, 370
  Statue 8
Byzantine Empire 76, 79, 102, 150, 225
Byzantine(s) 59, 76–77, 86, 101, 104–105, 107, 121, 124–126, 128, 140, 151, 199, 252, 331, 358, 362
Byzantium 76–77, 111, 122, 124

cairns 31–32, 38–39, 195
Cantwaraburh (Canterbury) 167, 229, 238
  Archbishop of 237, 251
cavalry 92–96, 101
Charlemagne 148–149, 165, 369
chieftains 15–16, 22, 33–34, 37, 52, 65, 72, 75, 140–142, 145, 151–152, 157, 163, 170, 181, 184, 200, 204, 218, 242, 244, 268, 271, 275, 277–278, 286, 292, 305, 312, 318, 329, 336–337, 342, 362–363, 369
Christianity 8–9, 25, 34–35, 41, 45, 52, 66, 90–92, 104, 109, 118, 126–127, 129, 138, 140, 145, 149, 151, 158–159, 162, 164, 167, 170–173, 178, 199, 201, 203, 207, 209, 223–224, 251, 259–261, 267, 275–279, 284, 287, 289–290, 293, 298–299, 302, 305, 307, 319, 324, 327–328, 354–356, 362, 367–368
Chrobry, Boleslav "the Brave" 140
Chronica Slavorum 145, 369
Chronicle of Vladimir-Suzdal 115–116
Church, the/churches 123–127, 130, 150, 157–158, 162, 164, 167, 174, 194, 196, 198, 213, 223, 225, 237–238, 253, 258, 262, 282, 291, 300–301, 304, 309, 327, 354, 357–358, 363, 371
  Anglo-Saxon 253
  Christian 54, 148
  Church of God's Holy Wisdom 124
  Church of the Holy Sepulchre 361
  Church of the Tithes 358
  English 167, 253
  Irish 223
  Old Moster Church 262
  Russian Orthodox Church, the 77, 130
  Thjodhild's Church 309
clerics 78, 102, 159, 167, 195, 204, 209, 224, 261, 276, 342, 362
Colchester 21–22
compensation 87, 320, 359
concubines 107, 128, 225
Constantinople 76–77, 111, 117, 121–123, 126–128, 137, 167, 172, 178, 300

craftsmen 82, 87, 115, 117, 124, 220, 241
Crane, the 294, 298, 314–315, 326, 333, 338–339, 341, 345–347, 349
Cnut the Great 22, 319, 356–358

Danavirki (the Danevirke, "Danish Works") 92–94, 96–97, 150, 161, 164, 250
Battle of the Danevirke 89, 94–96, 99, 123, 150, 164, 172, 185, 207, 231, 233
Danelaw, the 19–22, 181, 215, 228
Danes, the 15, 19, 33, 52, 68, 89, 91–93, 96, 149, 161, 166, 171, 173, 176, 178, 180, 182, 184–188, 190, 204–205, 234, 237, 239, 243–244, 246, 265, 322–324, 326, 332, 338, 343–346, 348
Denmark 15–16, 20–21, 25, 31–33, 42, 51, 56–57, 59–60, 67–69, 89–93, 96–98, 110–111, 135–136, 139, 164–166, 171, 173, 176–178, 180–182, 185, 190, 192, 204, 206, 238, 240, 242–243, 249, 251, 253–254, 280, 299–300, 305, 314, 317, 320–325, 329–332, 335–336, 338, 340, 343–344, 346–347, 355, 357, 361–362, 369, 371–372
Dereva 77, 104–105
Dietrich of Haldensleben, Margrave 16, 150, 152, 155, 158, 161, 164, 209
divorce 54, 144, 258, 323
Dixin 141–142, 145, 330, 360
Dnieper, the 77, 79, 82, 105, 117, 119, 137, 357–358
Dobrynya 15, 77, 86–87, 100, 102, 105, 108, 115–116, 129
dowry 180, 214, 331–332, 343
drapa (praise poem) 69, 91, 179, 183
Drevlians 76–77
dromund (merchant vessel) 59–61
druzhina 71, 86, 105, 119
druzhinnik 14, 73, 105, 127–128
druzhinniki 74, 78, 104, 113, 130
Dublin 10, 16, 174, 212, 221–223, 225, 241, 244, 248, 250, 254, 256–258, 280–282, 327, 356
Dubliners 221, 223

ealdorman/ealdormen (elder man/elder men) 8, 17, 21–22, 205, 210–211, 218–220, 227–232, 234–236, 238, 241, 243, 251, 258, 370
earthquakes 123, 126
East Anglia 20, 220
Eiriksdottir, Astrid 14, 37, 40–52, 55–58, 60, 62, 67, 72–73, 246–247, 277
Eiriksdottir, Ingebjorg 37, 41, 49, 182–183, 192, 247, 277, 326–328, 356

INDEX

Eiriksson, Gudrod 31–32, 36–38, 40–42, 312–314
Eiriksson, Harald "Greycloak" 14, 31, 40, 45, 68–69, 109, 276, 305, 353–354
Eiriksson, Jostein 47, 246–249, 251–253, 262, 265–267, 277, 304, 326
Eiriksson, Olaf (*Skotkonung*, "Tax King") 15, 213, 280, 319–320, 324–325, 328–331, 335–337, 342–343, 345, 354, 356, 358, 362
Eiriksson, Sigurd *Karlshofud* ("Carls' Chief") 47, 56, 72–74, 78, 80–81, 83–88, 100–101, 105, 108, 119–120, 245–246, 249, 262, 304, 350
Eistland ("East Land", Estonia) 58–59, 62–63, 65, 70, 74, 108, 246, 281, 319
Eistlanders 10, 59, 61–62, 65–66, 71–73, 83–84, 108, 136, 246
Emerald Isle 174, 221–223, 225
emissaries 74, 78, 104, 106, 113, 123, 125–127
England 8, 10, 15, 17, 19–24, 32–35, 107–108, 142, 166, 171, 173–175, 181, 193–194, 196, 199, 204, 206, 209–210, 212, 215–216, 219–221, 225–226, 228, 230, 232, 234, 237–238, 240–245, 247–257, 259, 262, 278, 280, 300, 340, 353, 356–358, 361, 366–367, 370
English, the 17, 19, 22, 33, 173–174, 204, 213, 223, 227, 231–235, 240, 242, 244, 251, 254, 261
envoys 32, 76, 92, 115
Eirik, *Bjodaskalle* ("Bald Head") 47, 72
Essex (Eastseaxe) 17, 21–22, 220, 227, 232, 235, 244, 250, 252, 370
Estonia 58, 61–65, 67, 80, 107, 371
Europe 42, 45, 51, 54, 79, 82, 100–101, 117, 123, 135–136, 138, 148, 151, 162–163, 165, 169, 177, 179, 194, 225, 268, 309, 356, 358, 367
  Northern 9, 10, 25, 43, 174, 366
excavations 39, 139, 143–144, 153
Eysysla 63–64, 319

fabrics 120, 124, 141
Fadlan, Ahmad ibn 71, 74, 120, 128–130, 137, 170, 188, 366
Faereyinga Saga, the 304–305, 367
Fagrskinna ("Fair Parchment") 25, 34, 37, 53, 67, 69, 109–110, 176, 178–179, 181, 185–187, 189, 197, 244, 257, 282, 299, 335–336, 339, 344, 349, 357–358, 368, 371
Fairhair, King Harald *Harfagri* 32–33, 44–45, 52–53, 110, 174, 216, 226, 245, 260, 276, 278, 281, 283, 289–290, 293, 356

famine 67–68, 119, 288
farmers 20, 22, 32, 35, 46, 67, 108–109, 117, 137, 220, 227, 245, 275, 278, 287–289
farmsteads 65, 143, 309
fealty 89, 141, 150, 181, 205, 260
fisherman/fishermen 117, 153, 265, 307
Flanders 165–166, 175
Folcanstan (Folkestone) 19–20, 227, 230, 238
Folkvang 122, 198
Fowler, Henry the 89, 93, 97, 149, 158
Franks, the 92, 139, 148, 165
Freyja 43–44, 109, 122, 145, 198, 279, 302, 362
Frisians 10, 89, 92, 165–166, 171
Funen 93, 110

Gaels, the 174, 207, 213, 221–222
  Foreign (Norse-Irish) 174
Gardariki ("land of cities") 56, 108, 111
Geira, Queen of Jomsborg 16, 140–147, 155–156, 160, 163, 168, 171, 177, 180, 193
Germany 16, 25, 42, 57, 90, 135, 137–138, 144–146, 148, 150, 165–166, 331, 335–336, 366, 369, 372
God 122, 125–127, 129–130, 136, 148, 151, 157, 159, 161, 167, 169, 172, 193, 195, 198–199, 201–203, 205, 207–208, 210–211, 232, 237, 239, 243, 250, 252–254, 260, 263, 267, 271, 275–276, 284, 286–290, 292, 297–302, 307, 309, 311–314, 320, 328, 331, 333, 339, 341, 344, 348, 351, 353–354, 360–361, 363–364
  Christian 66, 92, 125, 127, 167, 199
  Hebrew 198–199, 207
gods 25–26, 34–35, 45, 53, 55, 66–67, 70, 77, 86, 91, 102–103, 107, 109–110, 114, 122, 124, 127, 129–131, 136, 138, 143–145, 148, 150, 153, 155, 167–168, 170, 172, 175, 181, 187–188, 190, 198–200, 248–249, 261–262, 265, 278, 284, 286–289, 292–293, 295–297, 300–302, 304–305, 309, 311–312, 331, 344, 353
  pagan 35, 103, 187, 199, 205, 243, 312
goddesses 43–44, 109–110, 122, 153, 188, 279, 283, 305, 362
gold 20, 65, 73–74, 77, 82–83, 108, 117, 120, 124–125, 153, 160, 180, 182, 186, 190, 220–222, 240–243, 252, 256, 269, 279, 283, 288–289, 297, 307, 315, 331, 342, 348
  armlet 37, 224
  ring 146, 282, 361
Gorislava 116, 128, 317

Gormsdottir (or Ozursdottir), Gunnhild *Konungamodir* ("Mother of Kings") 14, 36, 48, 52, 56, 90, 245, 265, 281, 312
Gormsson, King Harald *Blatonn* ("Bluetooth") 15, 52, 56, 68–69, 89–93, 97–98, 104, 108–110, 150–151, 161, 164, 171, 176–178, 184, 186, 207–208, 257, 276, 299–300, 317–318, 321–322
Gotland (Gotaland) 54, 65, 135, 163, 219, 282, 319, 328
Gotlanders 164, 171
Graenlendinga Saga, the 307, 368
Grammaticus, Saxo 25, 59, 109, 143, 178, 186, 190, 284, 324, 328, 371
grave robbers 39, 64
Great Heathen Army 19, 23, 181
Greece 76, 121–122, 129, 167, 364
Greek(s) 45, 77, 83, 85–86, 104, 111, 121, 124, 126–127, 129–130, 138, 196, 199, 202
  fire 60, 76
Greenland 8, 43, 66, 299, 307–309, 368
Greifswalder Oie 336–337, 364
grivny 87, 121
Gulf of Finland 107, 113, 319
Gulf of Riga 65, 114
Gunnhildssonnene 33, 67
gunwales 60, 177, 187, 190, 192, 206, 315, 343, 347, 349, 364

Haervejen (Army Road) 93
Hagia Sophia 7, 124–125, 172
Hakon, *Gamli* ("the Old") 49, 51–52, 54–55, 219
Hakonarson, Eirik 14, 110–111, 184, 186–188, 205, 245, 267, 275–276, 305, 319, 345–346, 354–356, 368
Hakonarson, Erlend 14, 184, 267–268
Hakonarson, Sigurd 34, 184, 356
Hakonarson, Svein 14, 184, 186–188, 245, 267, 275–276, 305, 319, 346, 355–356
Halogaland 67, 109, 189, 279, 292–294, 315, 356
Hamburg 152, 159, 164, 201, 366
Haraldsdottir, Thyri 15, 176, 180, 317–318, 320–322, 326, 329, 331–332, 343, 355
Haraldsson, Eirik "Bloodaxe" 14, 19, 22, 31, 33–36, 40, 42, 46, 173–174, 220, 228, 254, 312, 314, 322, 353
  sons of 33–36, 40, 42, 322
Haraldsson, Hakon "the Good" 14, 33–37, 41, 216, 254, 276, 287, 353–354, 356
Haraldsson, Olaf II 14, 356, 358, 361–362
Haraldsson, Svein "Forkbeard" 15, 98, 110–111, 151, 161, 171, 177–178, 180–181, 183, 242–245, 249–250

Havelberg 149, 157–158
Hebrides Islands, the 14, 174, 205–206, 258, 261, 308
Heimskringla ("Circle of the World") 24, 26, 32–36, 52–55, 58, 61, 66–67, 73, 92–93, 97, 120, 122, 128, 131, 140, 173, 177, 179, 182, 185–187, 191, 197, 216, 243, 298, 304, 319, 337, 368, 370–371
Helgason ("Einar of the Shieldmaiden"), Einar 69, 89, 91, 186
hell:
  Christian 122, 198
  torments of 198, 260
Helmold of Bosau 145, 155, 369
heralds 32, 37–38, 40
heritage 74, 111, 215
hillforts 65–66, 80, 84, 116, 118
Historia de Antiquitate Regum Norwagiensium ("History of the Antiquity of the Norwegian Kings") 24, 40, 372
Historia Norwegiae ("History of Norway") 24–25, 37, 40, 49, 63–64, 141, 171, 173, 193, 195–196, 329, 335, 342, 366, 369
Hjorungavag 187, 259
  Battle of 185, 192, 204, 231, 233, 242, 249, 257, 270, 283, 305, 317, 324, 345, 351, 354
Hlodvirsson, Sigurd "the Stout" 14, 136, 185–186, 205, 259, 305, 351
Holgabrud, Thorgerd "Holgi's Bride" 109–110, 187–189, 263, 268, 282–283, 305–307
holmgang ("island-going") 215–217, 261, 359
Holy Land, the 59, 361
Holy Roman Empire 94, 97, 100, 137, 156, 161, 165–166, 171, 372
Hordaland 91, 262
housecarls 32, 38, 41, 71, 73, 110, 220, 228, 233, 326, 343
Hyrning 277, 313–314, 326, 346–347, 350

Ice Age 101, 194
Iceland 8, 11–12, 18, 24–25, 27, 33–36, 43, 82, 100, 106–107, 120, 125, 135, 140–141, 155, 172, 197, 205, 209, 216, 224–225, 257, 259, 299–303, 307–309, 326–327, 340, 346, 354, 357, 359, 362, 367–371, 382
Icelanders, the 8, 215, 295, 300–303, 327, 346, 361, 368
idolatry 149, 271, 286
infantry 93–96
Ipswich 20–22, 227, 230, 250
Ireland 10, 32, 97, 108, 157, 173–175, 204, 207, 212–213, 219, 221–222, 224–226, 238–239, 241, 245–246, 249, 258, 262, 281, 356

INDEX

Irish, the 16, 174–175, 206–207, 212, 222–223, 225, 242, 257, 261
Irish Sea, the 174, 176, 204, 206, 208, 212, 221–222, 225, 242, 340
Islendingabok ("Book of Icelanders") 25, 299, 302, 357, 367, 369
Isle of Man, the 174–175, 206, 244
Israelites 122, 198
Italy 16, 150–151, 237

jarldom 48, 67, 109–110, 260–261
Jarnbardin (Iron-Plow) 187, 345–346, 348–349, 355
Jerusalem 202, 300, 357, 361
Jomsborg 15–16, 135, 137–141, 143, 148, 153, 155, 157, 160, 165, 168, 171, 175–179, 222, 250, 282, 332–333, 335, 342, 369
Jomsviking Saga, the 109, 179–180, 185–190, 368–369, 371
John the Baptist 201–202, 300
Jomsvikings, the 16, 179, 181, 185, 190–191, 205, 242, 257, 259, 317, 332, 348
Jutland 69, 93, 97

Kark, Skopti 188, 190, 267–270
Kattegat, the 282, 321, 324
Khazars 75–78, 101, 107, 111, 366
Kinnrifa, Eyvind 292, 294, 354
kinship 102, 106, 108, 114, 221
"Klakka", Thorir 14, 246, 262–263, 265
knarrs 57, 59, 61, 137, 163, 308, 315
Klerk 66–67
Klerkon 62, 66–67, 83–84, 87, 116
Knutsson, Harald "Gold-Harald" 15, 68–69
Kolbeinsson, Bjarni 181–183, 185, 189
kontsy (hilltop villages) 81
Kristni Saga ("Book of Christianity"), the 209–210, 369
Kung Tryggves Grav (King Tryggvi's Grave) 7, 39
kuny (marten pelts) 87, 121
Kyiv 10, 13, 15, 76–79, 103–105, 111, 114, 117–119, 121–123, 127, 129–130, 137, 250, 271, 370
  Novgorod–Kyiv route 114

Lade 10, 34, 46, 48, 53, 67, 246–247, 269–270, 275, 282, 286–287, 362
  jarl(s) of 14, 36, 245, 346, 356, 361
Lake Ilmen ("Weather Lake") 78–80, 82, 101, 113, 137
Lake Ladoga 58, 107, 113, 121, 319
langskips (longships) 57, 265, 284, 291, 294, 308, 314, 339
  Serpent 310

Leifsson, Gunnlaug 24, 368, 370–371, 382
lendermann ("landed man") 52, 219
Liber Eliensis ("Book of Ely") 22, 229, 234–235, 370
Limfjord 69, 97
Lindisfarne 21
  Abbey 64, 278
livestock 42, 171, 220, 224
Longfellow, Henry Wadsworth 18, 26–27, 29, 133, 273, 353
Long Serpent, the 315–316, 326, 329, 333, 337–339, 341–352, 354–355, 360, 363–364
Lundenburh (London) 10, 220, 243, 249–250

Malachy, High King 213, 221–222, 225, 241
Maldon 8, 21–22, 227, 230–232, 235–236, 249–250
  Battle of Maldon, the 8, 21–22, 227, 229–230, 233, 236–239, 243–244, 252, 261, 340, 367, 370
Malusha 85, 103, 194, 248, 271, 334
marauders 58, 111, 253
marketplaces 81, 83, 139, 143, 254
marriage 37, 54, 90, 140, 146, 151, 180, 194, 210, 211–213, 221, 230, 247, 257–258, 279–280, 283, 288, 292, 317, 322, 327, 362
  proposal 115, 279, 327
marshes 101, 114, 138, 233, 266
marshland 79, 84
Mediterranean, the 59, 83, 107, 123, 136, 201
mercenaries 47, 56, 76, 82–83, 114, 121, 165–166, 225, 258, 348, 369
Mercia 17, 142, 181, 210, 220, 235, 254
messenger(s) 32, 129, 152, 184, 195, 227–228, 271, 282, 317, 322
Middle Ages, the 217, 368
Mieszko I, Duke of Poland 15–16, 140, 150
Miklagard (the "Big City") 111, 121, 357
Mjolnir 7, 102, 199, 311
Monachus, Theodoricus ("Theodoric the Monk") 24–25, 34, 40, 56, 286, 366, 369, 372
monasteries 24, 26, 117, 149, 152, 158, 199, 219, 223, 225, 237–238, 300, 361–362, 364, 367, 370, 382
Mostr (Moster) 262, 301, 328, 334
Mstislav 16, 151, 159
Mstivoj 16, 151–152, 154, 159, 164
murder 31, 33, 38, 40–41, 43, 45–46, 53, 68, 83–84, 87, 90, 92, 103, 105, 111, 116–117, 130, 150, 157–158, 170, 174, 180, 188, 208, 216, 243, 251, 265, 283, 295, 304–306, 313, 316, 320, 357, 364

New Testament, the 122, 167
New World 8, 309
Nidaros ("mouth of the river Nid") 282, 290, 303, 305, 308, 324, 326, 366
Njord 136, 145, 304
nobleman/noblemen 22, 65, 102, 184, 194, 219, 235, 238, 247, 358
Nordmark, the 16, 150, 164
Normandy 10, 193, 237, 254, 283
Normans, the 215, 253–254
Norns, the 42, 45, 80, 99, 136, 180, 195, 197, 304
North Atlantic 43, 57, 307–309
Northern Europe 9, **10**, 25, 43, 366
   Northern Europeans 174
Northey Island 8, 21–22, 227
Northmen, the 21, 59, 128, 299, 316, 362, 372
North Sea 19, 21, 93, 164, 173–174, 228, 234, 242, 254, 259, 279, 308
Norseman/Norsemen 18–19, 143, 254
Norway 9, 12, 14–15, 19, 23–25, 31–37, 40, 42, 44–47, 51–54, 56, 60, 67–69, 72, 85, 89–90, 97–99, 108–111, 141, 155, 176, 182, 184–186, 189–190, 197, 204–205, 216, 219, 224, 244–249, 254–255, 257–262, 275–278, 280, 282–283, 289–290, 298–305, 307–309, 312–313, 316, 318–335, 338, 340, 342–343, 345–347, 350–351, 353–364, 366, 368–370, 372
Norwegians, the 14, 33–36, 46–47, 52, 91, 93, 95–96, 171, 173–174, 185–187, 190, 205, 215, 248, 265, 276, 284, 287, 290, 299, 329–330, 332, 336, 338, 341–345, 347, 352
Novgorod **10**, 15, 58, 71, 74–75, 77–81, 84–85, 88, 99, 101–102, 104–108, 111, 113–115, 117, 119, 123, 129, 137, 139, 168, 178, 212, 222
   Novgorod–Kyiv route 114
Novgorodians, the 87, 102, 129, 143

Obrestad 37, 46, 48
Oder channel/strait 143, 178, 336
Oder Lagoon 137, 165
Odin 35, 38, 90, 95, 98, 100, 102, 145, 199–200, 207, 288, 294, 297, 312, 341
Olafsdrapa Tryggvasonar ("Song of Olaf Tryggvason"), the 164, 173, 219, 370
Olafs saga Tryggvasonar en mesta ("The Greatest Saga of Olaf Tryggvason") 25, 367, 370–371
Olafsson, Magnus "the Good" 362–364
Olafsson, Styrbjorn "the Strong" 15, 176, 180, 243
Olafsson, Tryggvi 14, 17, 32, 36, 38–39, 69, 362

Olava, Princess/Queen 15, 84–87, 103, 105–106, 122, 127–131, 212
Old English 11–12, 21–23, 211, 213, 215, 219, 231–232, 367
Old Norse 11–12, 18, 22, 24, 46, 61, 66, 73, 75, 106, 145–146, 187, 190, 213, 215, 221, 224, 231, 287, 292, 296, 321, 336, 366–368, 371
Olga of Kyiv 15, 76–78, 85–86, 103–104, 111, 118
Opplond (the "upper land") 47, 53
Oprekstad 37, 72, 219
Orkneyinga Saga, the 25, 59, 206, 259, 261, 371
Orkney Islands, the 25, 49, 69, 90, 205, 244, 258–259, 261, 300, 305
Osel (Saaremaa) 63–65
Oslofjord 43, 47, 184, 289
Ottarsson, Hallfred "Troublesome Poet" 24, 163–165, 173, 175, 302–304, 326–327, 340, 359, 368, 370–371, 382
Otto I, "the Great" 151
Otto II, "the Red" 16, 91–92, 96, 104, 150–151, 164–165, 207, 319
Otto III 16, 164

paganism 25, 34, 178, 254, 276, 286, 294
palisades 20–21, 93–94, 96, 116, 118, 139, 144, 178
Palnatoki 15–16, 177–180, 182
Pechenegs, the 76–78, 101–103, 119
perfume 82, 124
Perun 77–78, 102, 114, 128, 144–145, 148, 170
Peryn 102–103
Petlandsfjord (Pentland Firth) 259, 308, 356
pirates 52, 58, 61, 93, 176, 362
   Eistland 59, 65, 83, 108, 136, 246, 281
   Estonian 58
   raids 42, 163, 330
   ships 61, 65, 246
plague 123, 169–170, 196, 288
Podol, the 117–118
Poland 16, 92, 128, 135, 137–138, 140, 369
Poles, the 15, 139–140
Polotsk **10**, 114–118, 121, 123, 128, 300, 317
Pomerania, Bay of 137, 140, 335
Porphyrogenita, Princess Anna 127, 358
posadnik 86–87, 102
prima signatio (prime-signing) 120, 126, 172, 187
Procopius of Caesarea 124–125
property 38, 47, 54, 104, 156, 163, 190, 193, 210, 218, 258, 290, 297, 302, 320–322, 325

INDEX

Ragnarok 35, 199
raid(s) 19–20, 32, 34, 41–42, 49, 75, 89, 92, 120, 136, 149, 163–164, 171, 173–177, 182, 185, 206, 223, 229, 234, 237, 243–244, 259, 278, 301, 305, 319
  Viking 21, 32, 52, 64, 165, 167, 173, 181, 204, 225, 246, 251, 319
ramparts 66, 89, 93–94, 116, 118, 139, 222
Randsfjord 44–46
Raud "the Strong" 294–297, 310, 314
Reas 67, 70–73
religion 26, 34–35, 102, 104, 107, 127, 130, 144, 151, 157, 171, 178, 199, 260, 262, 266, 283, 287, 304–307, 331, 354, 362
Rethra 153–154, 156
rivers:
  Danube 76–77, 188
  Daugava (Western Dvina) 114–115
  Eider 89–90, 93
  Elbe 90, 149, 157–159, 161–162
  Neva 113, 319
  Oder 137–138, 162, 333, 336
  Polota 114–115
  Schlei 92, 335
  Tollense 148, 152
  Volkhov 78, 80–82, 84, 101, 107, 113–115, 129–130, 178, 188, 319
rivets 60, 63
Rogneda (Ragnheld) 114–117
Rome 76, 94, 104, 123, 136, 149, 202, 237, 357, 361
runes 44, 127, 161, 198, 200
Rurik 75–76, 86, 106, 114, 319
Rurikovo Gorodische ("Rurik's Settlement") 80, 84–85, 102, 105, 113, 116
Rus, the 11, 15, 74, 76–78, 81–82, 85–87, 102, 105, 111, 113–114, 121, 123–124, 137, 144–145, 164, 170, 245, 252, 366
  Kyivan 15, 75–76, 115, 117, 121, 130, 171–172, 358
Russia 11, 13, 56–58, 72, 74, 113, 115, 118, 129–130, 135, 248, 340, 370
Russian Primary Chronicle (*The Tale of Bygone Years*), the 75, 113, 370
Rustah, Ahmad ibn 74–75, 78, 80–81, 84, 86

Sandwich 20, 227, 230, 238, 250
Saxons, the **10**, 16, 19, 21, 76, 90, 92, 96, 138–139, 145, 148–151, 154–157, 161–162, 165–167, 171, 178, 239, 252, 262, 301–302, 331, 369, 372
  Anglo-Saxons 8, 20–21, 23, 142, 166, 174, 210–213, 215, 220–221, 228–230, 236, 252–254, 366–367
Saxony 16, 90, 92, 98, 148, 150–151, 155, 158, 161, 164, 167, 171, 195, 209, 243, 300

Scandinavia 11, 23, 25, 31–33, 41, 44, 46, 59, 71, 83, 85, 92, 106, 108, 111, 114, 122, 131, 136–137, 141, 143, 161, 166, 178–179, 196, 199, 204–205, 210–211, 220,, 222, 226, 242, 257, 275, 280, 297, 299, 314, 325, 331, 357, 359, 361, 366
  Viking 42, 366
Scandinavians 55, 57, 65, 82, 87, 92, 121, 157, 166, 199, 206, 279
Schleswig (Hedeby) 65, 72, 89, 92–93, 97–98, 136, 161, 164–166, 176, 335, 372
scholars 25, 102, 124, 230, 307, 367–368, 370
  National Association of Scholars 391
Scilly Islands 7, **10**, 193, 204, 212
Scotland **10**, 32, 173–175, 206–207, 213
seidmenn (sorcerers) 290–293, 309, 354
servants 41–42, 44, 64, 75, 87, 144, 181, 195, 213, 225, 317
Shetlands 14, 82, 174, 205, 261, 299
shields 100, 167–168, 196, 209, 217–218, 224, 228, 234, 307, 339, 342, 350–352
shield wall 8, 95, 101, 233, 236, 343
Short Serpent, the 315, 326, 333, 338–339, 341, 346–347
Sigfusson, Saemund "the Wise" 24, 354, 367, 370, 382
Sigtryggsson, Olaf (Amlaib mac Sitric, "Cuaran") 16, 212–213, 221–222, 257
Sigtuna 106–108, 113, 325
Sigurdarson, Hakon "the Bad" 14, 45–46, 48–50, 52–56, 67–70, 90–93, 95–99, 108–111, 150, 176, 182–191, 205, 207–208, 244–249, 254, 257, 259, 261–265, 267–271, 275–276, 282–283, 286, 288, 299, 303–306, 313, 319, 322–323, 351, 354, 363
Sigurdarson, Harald "Hardrada" 11, 14, 283, 362, 364
silver 20, 65, 73, 82–83, 87, 108, 150, 153, 157, 160, 163, 166, 168, 186, 204, 209, 220, 222–223, 225, 239, 241–244, 252, 256, 280, 289, 297, 331, 348
Sitric mac Amlaib (Sigtrygg II Olafsson), "Silkbeard" 16, 222, 256–258, 280, 356–357
Sjareksson, Thord 361–362
Skagadottir, Thora 14, 69, 264
Skeggjason, Hjalti 302, 361–362
skjaldborg (overlapping shields) 95, 101
Skjalgsson, Erling 14, 278, 292, 327, 358, 361–362
slavery 61, 73, 82–83, 225, 246–247, 305
slaves 20–21, 42, 56, 61, 63–67, 70, 72, 74, 82, 87, 107, 109, 115, 128–129, 137, 170, 188, 209, 220–221, 225, 239, 246, 256, 264, 268–269

389

slave market/trade 25, 62, 82–83, 247, 256, 356
Slavic Revolt of 983: 148, 155, 162, 164–165, 331
Slavs, the 71, 75, 81–82, 86, 102, 129, 138–139, 141, 143, 145, 148–154, 157–158, 161–162, 169–170, 176, 243, 366
Snorrason, Odd 12, 24, 26, 31, 36, 40, 54, 106, 169, 275, 351, 367–368, 370–372, 382
Sokkason, Berg 25, 33, 36, 51, 100, 120, 163, 203, 209, 313, 367–368, 371, 382
sorcery 36, 49, 118, 265, 290–292, 294
Southampton 19, 251
spears 22, 32, 45, 59, 94–96, 100–101, 116, 125, 141, 153–155, 175, 185, 189, 200, 206, 228, 231–235, 250, 295, 316, 341, 343, 346–347, 349, 351, 357
  ballistae (spear launchers) 94, 156
  spear-duel 23
  spear-ford 70
  spearheads 63
  spear-storm 164, 185
spices 82, 331
Stargard 140, 332
stormann (a man of means) 37, 47, 49, 72, 219
Strut-Haraldsson, Sigvaldi 15–16, 179–186, 189–190, 192, 242–243, 257, 317–318, 322–325, 330, 332–333, 337–339, 341–342, 348, 357, 360, 364
Sturluson, Snorri 24, 26, 32, 34, 36, 215, 256, 326, 335, 368, 370–371, 382
surrender 105, 118–119, 156, 240, 263, 351
Svetovit "Holy Lord" 144–145, 148, 153, 170
Svolder 335–339, 341, 360, 364
  Battle of 8, 335–336, 340–341, 351–352, 355, 359, 362
svynfylking ("boar's snout") 95, 101, 234
Svyatoslav I (Prince of Kyiv) 15, 76–78, 85–86, 101, 103–104, 111, 114, 118
Sweden 7, **10**, 15, 24, 31, 43, 47–54, 56–58, 60–63, 65, 71, 85, 93, 98, 106–108, 111, 113, 135, 137, 140, 163, 176–177, 213, 217, 219, 243, 251, 276, 280, 282, 284, 288, 305, 319–321, 324–325, 327–331, 336, 338, 340, 343–347, 355–356, 368, 371
Swedes, the 15, 39, 51–53, 59, 64, 66, 107, 166, 188, 288, 324, 326, 330, 332, 338, 340, 343–346, 348

swords 29, 32, 38, 49, 59, 61–64, 71, 78, 94–95, 97, 100, 111, 118–119, 121, 125, 146, 149, 157, 164, 173, 175, 187, 190–191, 197, 206, 216–219, 226, 228, 231, 234–235, 250, 260–261, 267–268, 281, 285, 303–304, 340, 343, 345, 347, 350, 359, 362, 382

Thambarskelfir, Einar "Bowstring Shaker" 355, 362–364
Thangbrand of Saxony 167–168, 171, 195, 209, 224, 262, 301–302
"The Saga of King Olaf" 29, 133, 273, 353, 382
Thietmar of Merseburg, Prince-Bishop 91, 94, 98, 152–155, 157–159, 161, 164, 188, 209, 372
Thingeyrar (Thingeyraklaustur), the 24, 367–368, 370–371, 382
Thor 7, 29, 35, 102, 129, 133, 187, 199, 288–289, 294, 296–297, 311, 316, 345, 347–349
Thorgils 41, 47, 49, 58, 60–62, 65–67, 71–74
Thorgilsson, Ari "the Wise" 12, 24, 299, 367, 369, 371, 382
Thorgilsson, Stefnir 300, 357
Thorkell, Nefja ("Beaknose") 277, 326, 339, 350, 357
Thorkell, *Dyrdill* ("Short Tail" or "Hanger-On") 47, 73, 310, 339
Thorkell, "the Tall" 16, 180–182, 185, 189, 242, 251, 348–349, 357
Thorolf, *Lusarskegg* ("Lice-Beard") 41, 43–47, 49, 57–58, 60, 62, 83
thralls 42, 47, 56, 67, 188, 190, 246, 264, 267
Tinghaugen, "Assembly Hill" 34, 287
Tjotta 292–294
Torg, the 81–82, 84, 87, 105, 116
Tostisdottir, Sigrid "the Haughty" 15, 54, 140, 213, 276, 279–285, 291, 319–320, 322–325, 356
travelers 32, 58, 65, 74, 143, 291, 361–362, 372
treachery 37, 40, 46, 48, 55, 69, 118, 185, 196–197, 253, 265, 333
treasure 23, 120, 141, 157–158, 224, 228, 238, 327, 329
Trondheim 9, **10**, 29, 34, 36, 45, 52, 247, 262–264, 270, 282, 287, 289, 354–355, 363, 366, 372
Tryggvadottir, Astrid 37, 41, 49, 247, 277–280, 292, 327, 358, 361
Tryggvason, Gytha 17, 210–213, 219–223, 225, 230, 235, 249, 257–258, 280–281, 319–320, 327, 357

INDEX

Tryggvason, Olaf I 8–9, 12, 14–15, 17, 24–27, 29, 54, 64, 89, 97–98, 111, 145–146, 156, 160, 163, 168, 171, 173, 193, 195, 201, 204–205, 213, 230, 236, 248–249, 259–261, 269–271, 273, 275–276, 280–283, 287, 289–292, 296–298, 304–309, 313–314, 316–334, 336–344, 346–348, 350, 352–365, 367–371, 382
Tsargrad (the "City of Caesar") 121, 123
Tunsberg (Tonsberg) 43, 184, 289–290

Ukraine 13, 76–77, 103, 117
Uppland ("up the coast") 53, 280
Uppsala 53, 55, 58, 106–107, 177, 282, 288
Usedom Island 137–138, 157

Vaeringjar (Varangians) 71, 74–76, 78, 83–84, 87, 102, 117, 119, 121, 123–124, 126–127, 130, 188
Valhalla 35, 38, 64, 122, 198–199, 286, 341
vassal(s) 36, 38, 89–90, 183, 212, 259, 305–306, 323, 345, 355, 362
veche (popular assembly) 86, 102, 124, 140
Verkhny Zamok ("Upper Castle") 115–116
Vigi 224, 266, 295–296, 329, 355
Vik, the 31, 182, 184, 246, 262, 277–278, 305, 313–314, 355
Viken 14, 31–32, 34, 36–37, 40, 51
Viking Age, the 7–8, 47, 60, 107, 136, 199, 223, 256, 283, 328
  Second 166

Visetisson, Bui 16, 136, 179, 182, 184–186, 189–190, 192, 205, 305, 351
Visetisson, Sigurd 16, 136, 179, 182, 185, 189
Vladimir I (Prince of Novgorod), "the Great" 15, 71, 74, 85, 106, 111, 121, 340
Vruchiy (Ovruch) 103–104

Walcheren 165–166
Wales 19, 192–193, 204, 256
Warrior's Gate 93, 95–97
Wendland 137, 140–141, 145, 147, 152, 155, 163, 165, 168, 171, 175, 180, 193, 242, 246, 317–318, 320–325, 327, 329–332, 335, 340, 357–358, 360
Wends, the 10, 15, 92, 137, 140, 143–145, 148, 151, 156–157, 163, 169, 171, 176, 222, 322, 331, 347
Widukind of Corvey 76, 89–90, 149, 372
Winchester 20, 230, 251
witchcraft 290–292, 295
wizards 33, 265–266, 291, 309, 328
Wolin 137–138, 143–144, 178, 369
Wulfstan of Hedeby 65, 72, 136, 372

Yaqub, Ibrahim Ibn 137–140, 144, 152, 169, 369
Yaropolk I 15, 77, 103–106, 113–115, 117–119, 128, 358
Yggdrasil 148, 200, 279
Ynglinga Saga 53, 63

Zealand 34, 91, 93, 177, 181, 335, 357

ABOUT THE AUTHOR

Don Hollway is an historian, illustrator, historical re-enactor and classical rapier fencer. For over 30 years his writing on history, aviation and re-enacting has appeared in magazines ranging from *Aviation History, Excellence, History Magazine, Military Heritage, Military History, Wild West* and *World War II* to *Muzzleloader, Porsche Panorama, Renaissance Magazine* and *Scientific American*. Many of his articles are available free on his website, *donhollway.com*, where a number of them rank in the top two or three in global search results. He is a member of the Organization of American Historians, the National Association of Scholars and the Viking Society for Northern Research in the UK.

His first book, *The Last Viking: The True Story of King Harald Hardrada* (Osprey, 2021), a gripping history of the Norse king, is an Amazon bestseller in the US and UK, acclaimed by *The Times* of London and by Michael Dirda, Pulitzer Prize-winning critic for *The Washington Post*. His second book, *At the Gates of Rome: The Fall of the Eternal City, AD 410* (Osprey, 2022), was similarly well received. And his *Battle for the Island Kingdom* (Osprey, 2023), about the decades leading up to the pivotal Battle of Hastings in 1066, was shortlisted as one of *Military History Matters* magazine's best history books of 2024.